BLOOM

AMY M. KING

BLOOM

The Botanical Vernacular

in the English Novel

OXFORD

UNIVERSITY PRESS

2003

OXFORD
UNIVERSITY PRESS

Oxford   New York
Auckland   Bangkok   Buenos Aires   Cape Town   Chennai
Dar es Salaam   Delhi   Hong Kong   Istanbul   Karachi   Kolkata
Kuala Lumpur   Madrid   Melbourne   Mexico City   Mumbai   Nairobi
São Paulo   Shanghai   Taipei   Tokyo   Toronto

Published by Oxford University Press, Inc.
198 Madison Avenue, New York, New York 10016

www.oup.com

Oxford is a registered trademark of Oxford University Press

Library of Congress Cataloging-in-Publication Data
King, Amy M.
Bloom : the botanical vernacular in the English novel / Amy M. King.
  p. cm.
Includes bibliographical references and index.
ISBN 0-19-516151-3
1. English fiction—History and criticism. 2. Botany in literature. 3. Literature
and science—England. 4. Flowers in literature. 5. Plants in literature. I. Title.
PR830.B68K56 2003
823'.009'364—dc21   2002192564

9 8 7 6 5 4 3 2 1

Printed in the United States of America
on acid-free paper

For Nicholas

ACKNOWLEDGMENTS

Linnaean botany made the informed study of the natural world a practical possibility, as long as one was willing to get outside and pay close attention. Although more library dust than soil has dirtied my hands these past few years, I have been fortunate in having teachers, colleagues, and friends who also at times were willing to forego the pleasures of the outdoors and pay attention instead to the words that make up this book. I owe the greatest debt to Elaine Scarry, whose earnest hand kept me to paths both less trodden and more fertile; in her this project found an imaginative sympathy born of wonder for real blossoms, generously extended to my writing on bloom. To Philip Fisher, who taught me more than any other before him about the seriousness and dignity of ideas, I owe whatever intellectual rigor this book may possess. Lynn Wardley's guidance of this project's early formulations was a crucial resource, and the example she set as a researcher, reader, and friend helped form the scholar I have become.

The initial work on this project was enabled by a Mellon Dissertation Fellowship and various other financial supports provided by the Graduate School of Arts and Sciences at Harvard University. The California Institute of Technology has provided valuable support in the form of a generous research leave policy. I am grateful as well for the libraries in which I have worked, as well as their staffs and resources: Widener and Houghton Libraries, and the Library of the Gray Herbarium, Harvard University; the British Library, London; the Linnean and Kewensia collections at the Library and Archives of the Royal Botanic Gardens, Kew; the printed ephemera collection at the Museum of London; the New York Public Library; and the LuEsther T. Mertz Library of the New York Botanical Garden. A condensed, earlier version of chapter 1 and material from chapter 3 were published previously in *Eighteenth-Century Novel* 1 (2001) as "Linnaeus's Blooms: Botany and the Novel of Courtship." My thanks to the journal for permission to reprint material. At Oxford University Press, Elissa Morris and Jeremy Lewis provided the encouragement and further assistance that this project needed.

I am indebted to those who read and commented upon—often with an amazing attention to detail—some or all of the manuscript over the years, including three anonymous readers for Oxford University Press, a reading group at Haverford College, and my colleagues at Caltech, as well as Isobel Armstrong, Jonathan Freedman, Lisbet Koerner, Mary Ann O'Farrell, Jonah Siegel, Gabrielle Starr, and Alison Winter. Two people were particularly important at various stages of the conception and writing of this book, and I want to single them out for my particular gratitude. I thank Abby Wolf who listened and contributed to the earliest germs of the ideas, and read and edited the manuscript in its final stages, both of which have left palpable traces on the work. And second I thank Noah Heringman for his generosity and conversation when we began to explore common texts from eighteenth-century landscape aesthetics. Among the many people whose friendship and insight along the way made a difference, Tom Augst, Sharon Cantor, Amanda Claybaugh, Anna Farrow, Eva Kaye, Lev Kaye, Jeff King, Katie King, David Levine, Anna McCarthy, Judy Mintz, Martha Nadell, Martin Puchner, Maria Sanchez, Gus Stadler, and Eric Wilson deserve special mention.

I am blessed in my parents, Jeffrey and Linda King, who from the beginning nurtured my inner bookworm and interest in plants alike, and who provided me with the love and stability that made possible sustained immersion in thinking and writing. Of my vast extended family, my two grandmothers, Ethel Giering and the late Dorothy King, deserve my particular gratitude for the support and enthusiasm they lent to my education.

Some years ago now I built a makeshift desk in the corner of my apartment for Nicholas Dames, who then took it upon himself to become my most dedicated reader. That subsequently we have shared a desk in a way more profound than this moment would suggest is the result of his devotion, for he not only lived with and nurtured this project but he lived with and nurtured me across the years of its writing and revision. His intelligence and grace informs every page. This book is dedicated to you, Nico, with all my love.

CONTENTS

BLOOM

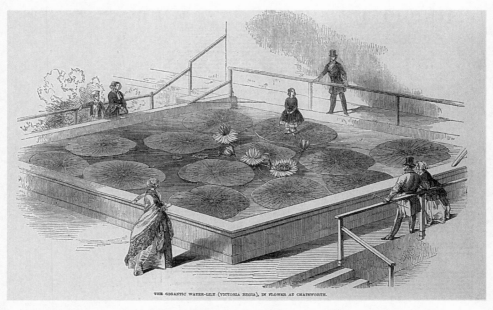

THE GIGANTIC WATER-LILY (VICTORIA REGIA), IN FLOWER AT CHATSWORTH.

FIGURE I   "The Gigantic Water-Lily (Victoria Regia), in Flower at Chatsworth."
Illustrated London News, November 17, 1849, p. 328. Courtesy of the General Research
Division, The New York Public Library, Astor, Lenox and Tilden Foundations.

INTRODUCTION

The Girl and the Water Lily

It is the chain of accessory ideas that makes me love botany.

—Jean-Jacques Rousseau, *Les Rêveries du promeneur solitaire*

A young girl stands with a mixture of pride and unconcerned obliviousness, poised on top of an enormous flower, a gigantic water lily, which holds her weight without difficulty: such is the image presented to us in the *Illustrated London News* of November 1849 (see fig. 1).[1]

The flower on which she stands, discovered in British New Guinea in 1801, was named *Victoria regia* in 1838 in honor of the newly crowned queen, and it was to her that Joseph Paxton brought its first pink and white blooms. Measuring fourteen feet in circumference, the lily pad drew crowds both at Chatsworth and later at the Crystal Palace, whose design Paxton borrowed from the water lily's ribbed leaves.[2] The mixture of social decorum and natural force, proper and youthful femininity and gorgeously displayed floral spectacle, that the line-drawing condenses is not only peculiar—not simply an arresting "natural wonder"—but deeply characteristic, tied to the notions of an entire culture. It is no coincidence that it is a young girl so poised, nor that her posture on the water lily should seem so much like *waiting*—how else to read this strange image than that this young girl is herself waiting to "bloom"?

If we turn from this single drawing to a consideration of the culture, and specifically the novelistic culture, out of which it arises, we find that just as the young girl is buttressed by the lily, so conceptions of girlhood, maturation, and the social dispositions of marriage are buttressed by a botanical language strong and pervasive enough to uphold them—a language coming out of a wholesale cultural interest in the floral that dates from the eighteenth-century taxonomies of Carl Linnaeus (1701–78). Largely because of the simplicity of Linnaeus's *methodus propria*, or "sexual system" of plant classification, botany became a widely practiced and vernacularized science from the 1770s through the early nineteenth century and beyond. This book provides a history and rhetorical study of Linnaean botany in England, demonstrating ways that Linnaeus's system made sexual courtship—what Linnaeus called the marriage of plants—a legitimate subject for representation.[3] This book furthermore suggests that the classical novel is able to represent the sexual component to courtship through a broad recourse to vernacularized botanical language and practice. Botany was not merely an end in itself; its "chain of accessory ideas," to which Rousseau alluded, form the center of this inquiry, and the most crucial of these accessory ideas is its enabling imprint on the fictional representation of female maturation and courtship.

At the center of this representational matrix is a single figure on which this book will concentrate: the girl "in bloom," or the female whose social and sexual maturation is expressed, rhetorically managed, and even forecast by the use of a word (bloom) whose genealogy can be traced back to the function of the bloom, or flower, in Linnaeus's botanical system. That the classical novel of the late eighteenth and nineteenth century habitually centers on the mechanics of courtship and female socialization is a familiar enough fact, but that the nexus between courtship's physical and social dimensions is managed by a largely scientific rhetorical system will be the burden of my investigation. In the chapters that follow, which will traverse the path from the eighteenth-century novel of seduction to the nineteenth-century lineage most profoundly linked to what I call the "bloom narrative"—Jane Austen, George Eliot, and Henry James—the focus will be primarily on the figure of the marriageable girl, be that figure Austen's Anne Elliot, Eliot's Hetty Sorrel, or James's Isabel Archer. These blooming heroines are defined by a presentation that conflates a putatively bodily fact—the fact of being "in bloom"—and a social position: the fact of the girl's imminent insertion into a marriage plot. That conflation is underwritten by the most significant fact about the Linnaean system: the way his classificatory method terms the sexual reproduction of a flower *marriage*, a terminology that makes a horticultural fact a human fact, and by extension a human act (marriage) a horticultural, "natural" act (blooming). In the nineteenth-century tradition of Austen, Eliot, and James, we see a depiction of female maturation that is, albeit with differing emphases, consistently bringing a botanical process into collision with a social arrangement. Tracing the consequences of that collision will take us far into the worlds of these novelists, and the world of nineteenth-century English culture. The productive consequences of the vernacularization and dissemination of a scientific method propel this study.

Bloom's Cultural Work

The following passage from Jane Austen's *Persuasion* (1818) furnishes us with an example of how bloom is used in the period's fiction:

A few years before, Anne Elliot had been a very pretty girl, but her bloom had vanished early; and as even in its height, her father had found little to admire in her, (so totally different were her delicate features and mild dark eyes from his own), there could be nothing in them now that she was faded and thin, to excite his esteem.[4]

"Her bloom had vanished early": we might today assume that bloom is simply a reference to complexion, health, or physical beauty—to the solely physical aspects of Anne's person with which Sir Walter is so patently concerned. That, however, would be to misunderstand the instance of the botanical vernacular Austen's text here reflects. What is condensed in this use of the strange noun "bloom" is surprising: it is not simply a corporeal or even sexualized fact (the heightened complexion of excitement, for example) but rather a fact of age or sequence—Anne, as we have been told, is no longer a young girl—as well as a fact pertaining to her position in a narrative genre. Simply put, the lack of bloom is a lack of a marriage plot. Anne's early loss of bloom was directly related to the early loss of her suitor, Captain Wentworth: her "attachment and regrets had, for a long time, clouded every enjoyment of youth; and an early loss of bloom and spirits had been their lasting effect."[5] When the suitor returns, so does the twenty-seven-year-old Anne's bloom, suggesting that bloom is not merely a physical fact, or a fact of youthful physiology, but a sign of a social process working according to form. Yet, crucially, bloom keeps its physical meanings as well; her reblooming is not only novelistic shorthand for a renewed marriage plot but a physical fact: Anne does regain her signs of bloom in physical proximity to Captain Wentworth, which in turn reexcites his interest in her as a marriageable girl. The euphemism "marriageable" here is apt, for it points to one of the central facts of what is being disguised when we come across a blooming girl in the English novel: the sexual attractiveness and readiness, and not only the marital eligibility, of the girl. Bloom is a lexicon that combines sex, social position, bodily facts, and affective life into one word, a word that leads us back to Linnaeus and the social-sexual fluidity of his taxonomic system.

The cultural work of bloom, as it comes from Linnaeus, consists of the productive conflation of social, physical, and affective factors. Yet this work is what we might call surreptitious; throughout its active history, the figure of bloom has remained a persistently opaque figure, one that is capable of expressing sexual maturation and availability while nonetheless fitting securely within the decorous contours of classical British narration. Both explicit (as it is in Linnaean systematics) and safely implicit, bloom is a mediating figure par excellence: a figure that can traverse the range from innocent to provocative, and that can bridge the accepted social appearances of courtship with the specifically physical manifestations of maturation and enticement. How exactly bloom managed neither to offend nor to fall into illegibility will be the focus of much that follows; that said, a few opening reflections on the manner in which bloom both expressed, yet occluded, nascent sexuality are in order.

Part of the reason for the productive opacity of bloom is its pre-Linnaean history. In the late eighteenth and into the nineteenth century the word *bloom* would be associated with the Linnaean system and a host of other horticultural and scientific significations, including the central fact about the flower after Linnaeus: its sexual function. However, bloom could also be associated with an earlier system of signification: the association of girls, sexual innocence, and flowers in literature as enduring as the figures of Shakespeare's Ophelia, or Milton's Eve. The pastoral tradition, which associated flowers with innocence and girls, made its usage blameless, even as the codification of modern botany necessarily brought new detail, meaning, and embodiment to that older linguistic trope. That is, bloom is not strictly a vocabulary emanating from Linnaeus, and a total account of the word's history would have to look into its long pre-Linnaean heritage. Rather, the claim of this book is that the very ordinariness of the word, its possession of a scope wider than the usual scientific term, enabled its thorough cultural dissemination and equipped it for a series of cultural tasks. If cultural meaning works associatively more than denotatively, then novelistic bloom evokes both competing systems of signification (the Linnaean and the prior literary-historical context). Thus a girl's bloom is a figure that invokes its Linnaean range of meaning—the sexual content of the blooming flower—as well as its prior, more acceptable literary-historical meanings.

The excavation of a vocabulary and system of reference from a specific historical age allows us to rediscover a way of reading, a conferral of implicit meaning, that we both seem to know yet have forgotten. By historicizing the novelistic vocabulary of bloom, we begin to return the text to its cultural moment: an act of recovery that does not seek a delimited scientific source for a figurative system of the novel but rather reopens the text to a historically specific, if diffused, cultural language—what I call the "botanical vernacular." The botanical vernacular was both a set of shared cultural assumptions about the meanings of botanical practice and a specific vocabulary that registers, in both the novel and popularized science of the later eighteenth century, that general understanding. This book seeks to excavate how the representational universes of the novel and science collude, and how the novel of courtship in the late eighteenth and early nineteenth centuries is indebted to a system of meaning we have now forgotten.

Bloom's meaning is associative; it is explicit yet denuded of illicitness. It is precisely this fact that made bloom so well suited to expressing the erotics of courtship in a genre unable to represent it directly. Its referent was both intelligible and obscure because it invoked both a scientific system centered on a sexualized understanding of flowers and blooms and the earlier, more acceptable lexicon. The eighteenth-century discovery that the flower was the sexual and reproductive part of the plant, and Linnaeus's dissemination of that scientific fact, empirically verified the association in literary texts, from *Song of Songs* and beyond, between sexuality and flowers. Linnaean botany made that prior association literal and scientific; moreover, it socialized it, for it placed that sexual association firmly within the rubric of marriage. That bloom could signify sexual maturation and availability in the novelistic plot yet not be construed as inappropriately candid is a result of the complex patterns of transmission that underpin bloom's meanings. Bloom, in a sense, names that which is known but not acknowledged: bloom's meaning *is* a meaning, if a culturally occluded one.

That lack of acknowledgment has significance for the way this book goes about its work. Bloom's occlusion has historically prevented the explicit notation of its sexual content in the available records we have of novel-reading in the age of the classical novel: reviews, diaries, letters, autobiographies, literary polemics of various kinds. While we do have vivid and unmistakable evidence, contained in responses to Linnaeus's system throughout the eighteenth century, that bloom's conflation of social and sexual narratives was noted (and often rejected on the basis of its salaciousness or impiety), similar evidence of bloom's workings for novel readers is absent, with the notable exception of Henry James's literary criticism. The traditional methods of the history of audiences—from the study of individual accounts of reading to analyses of publishing processes—are less adept at excavating a rhetorical and figural history that, while crucial for the novel, remained surreptitious; indeed, its very power depended on its ability to remain safely inexplicit.[6] Whereas bloom in its pre-Linnaean uses could reflect either an unstained innocence or an improper sexual frankness, the work of the Linnaean system for the novel was to conflate the two meanings into a passable, workable figure that could represent marital sexuality without transgressing the boundaries of decorum. Bloom offers us a window into a "reading formation" of considerable importance and longevity, but one that only the tools of a specifically literary analysis can uncover; its stealthy yet prevalent life within the novel is discoverable primarily *in* the novel, in an analysis of its use and development by a series of novelists acutely aware of its potential and its history.[7] Bloom's occlusion in and through its Linnaean use—the use that was crucial for the novel—requires specifically interpretive work to uncover.

It is an occlusion that has persisted to the present day. That today bloom is a cliché—an awareness of the erotic potential of a blooming girl is still a part of contemporary usage, even (or especially) in advertising that draws on adolescent images or themes—gestures to an earlier, unfixed association between bloom and youthful female sexuality, an association we seem to know yet whose origins we have forgotten. Part of the work of this book will be to restore to full consciousness the sexual content of the language of bloom, and by extension, the physicality of the courtship plots whose workings are at once veiled and revealed by the opacity of Linnaean language. The impulse behind this study might be summarized as arising from a suspicion that today's readers of the nineteenth-century courtship novel register a physicalized erotics whose exact workings have remained just beyond the reach of critical clarity, and that that fact is best explained by the functioning of bloom: a system of signification whose effectiveness has only been partially obscured by the gradual erosion of botany's cultural pervasiveness. Its cultural meaning, if difficult to revive in its full historical complexity, is not only traceable but also persist-ent. As this project hopes to demonstrate, an awareness of the multiple, unsys-tematic, and continually mutating forms of cultural signification can yield a fuller sense of how a trope lives, and how its life finds expression in myriad spaces and fields.

Plotting Bloom's Cognates

One of my primary concerns is to show how the formal meaning of bloom has to be historically revivified with reference not only to the word's basis in Linnaean taxonomy but also to the many signs of popular inter-est, during the late eighteenth and early nineteenth century, in the natural world. Therefore, the following chapters will not solely concentrate on one-to-one correspondences between botanical theory and novelistic practice, however foundational those correspondences might be. The story of bloom will involve broadening out its historical context to a range of cognate fields, including botany, natural history, and landscape aesthetics, all of which are part of this book's efforts to achieve a full, rigorously historical genealogy of bloom, one that charts the field of signification that bloom might have had in the late eighteenth- and nineteenth-century novel. Bloom is clearly not sim-ply a botanical term, although its origins derive from the organizing principle of modern botany; nor is it, as I will show, a strictly literary term, although by the end of the nineteenth century Linnaean bloom finds itself almost entirely confined to a novelistic register. Quite the reverse: spread out across a host of other disciplines and endeavors associated with horticultural practice and the-ory, bloom took no single path from its Linnaean formulation to its novelistic expression. Whether the female shape be analogized to the landscape, as I will show in Austen's novels, or whether, as in Eliot's natural histories, the girl is lo-cated in the midst of a fecund, sexualized, and ordered nature, bloom operates both directly (through the language of blooming, so familiar to the novel reader) and indirectly, through cognate fields, to map narratives of courtship and female maturation. The full force of what I call the botanical vernacular cannot, therefore, be measured without reference to these other fields.

Accordingly, the following chapters consider a variety of cognate topics: how scientific botany helped shape the debates about the natures and rights of women between Hannah More and Mary Wollstonecraft, as well as how botany informed the work of Erasmus Darwin, Charlotte Smith, and Maria Edgeworth; garden spaces, their various meanings, and how the design of urban and rural gardens lent force to narratives of sexual initiation such as Frances Burney's *Evelina*; theories of landscape aesthetics that went under the name *picturesque*, and how Austen's novels find in landscape an apt mediating figure for sexualized courtship. The reason these cognate topics are necessary to a history of novelistic bloom is a simple one, however complex its effects: these protoscientific, classificatory endeavors in the late eighteenth and nineteenth centuries take from Linnaean botany a key principle, the centrality of the female figure. The conflation of human and vegetable reproduction in Linnaeus's botanical theory, and the fact that reproduction became the key to botanical taxonomy, implied for Linnaean botany the paramount importance of a feminized figure (a flower, a bloom); those cognate fields that shared a tax-onomical impulse with Linnaean botany had a similar tendency to place the female at the center of their work. Not the least of these fields that privileged a rhetorical construction of the female was the novel. The representation of the heroine in Austen's novels depends on a taxonomic logic of generalization and individuation; even more crucially, like the corolla or bloom in Linnaeus's sexual system of classification, it is the girl's bloom around which the classical novel's courtship plot revolves.

If this book maintains a certain distance from tracing explicit references to Linnaean botany in various literary genres, it is still less a total history of nine-teenth-century botany and its influence on fictional narration. It also differs from, even as it intersects, recent accounts of the marriage plot that see courtship as a conservative process by which a novel's class and gender norms get instantiated and reproduced. Rather, this book provides an account of how sexual attraction also is represented in the classical novel's marriage plot through bloom and its cognates. Linnaeus shares with the classical novel a par-allel substitutive logic, one that represents sexual courtship—of flowers and humans alike—through the social institution and term of marriage. The clas-sical novel might seem to insist, as Linnaeus did, that it is narrating the plot of marriage, but that is not only a gesture toward hiding sexual content; on the contrary, courtship has sexual content because marriage traditionally realizes the promise of sex, a fact that Linnaeus, and, as I will show, the marriage plot both obscure only insofar as marriage is a social term.

This book traces the formal lineage of the bloom plot in the nineteenth century in its most salient practitioners, from Austen to Eliot to James. In chapter three I explore how the representation of the sexual content of "pub-lic" courtship is achieved in Jane Austen's novels. Chapter 4 traces the way George Eliot's novels extend the courtship plot to nonmarital sexuality, or what Linnaeus called "clandestine marriage." The lineage reflects the reinvigo-ration of the bloom plot by Eliot's realist mandate, because bloom, as evident in Charles Dickens's novels, had become so transparent by the mid–nineteenth century as to be able to be employed as novelistic cliché; chapter 4 deals in part with this subject. I also explore how nineteenth-century natural history and its classificatory energies are employed by Eliot to not only represent versions of courtship anticipated by Linnaeus (yet neglected by novelists) but also to achieve, more broadly, a new kind of realism in which the representation of the social world is achieved through organizing principles derived from natu-ral history. In chapter 5 I show how Henry James inserts himself into the Eng-lish novelistic tradition, forming the final stage of the nineteenth-century bloom lineage. James's novels about the marriageable girl are decadent texts that feed on the prior literary convention; the bloom plot becomes in these novels its formal subject, rather than that which the novels dramatize.

My goal is to account for how novelistic representation and scientific representation are mutually constitutive by employing a cultural history of science to better understand one of the formal developments of the novel. To this end, this book seeks a balance between a formal reading of Linnaean taxonomy and a consideration of its place in culture. Both approaches ultimately serve literary questions: what are the cultural strategies and tropological systems that inform the classical novel's (largely unacknowledged) representation of sexualized courtship? How do we account for the sense of the erotic that the classical novel, despite its manifest and myriad evasions, nonetheless provides?

And so we return to the young girl held up by that giant water lily, who we can imagine being at the center of a narrative of sexual and social maturation that her place on the lily pad implies. Supported by a blooming plant, the anonymous girl in the illustration is like the novel's blooming girl: the essential fact is that she is being held up, even displayed, not only by a vegetable wonder but by a botanical platform. The vernacularization of botany has its most crucial and sustained impact on the novel, where bloom enabled the traditional narrative of courtship to merge with the impetus of realism to represent courtship's more physical, even erotic, dimensions. The narrative, which the courtship novel spawned, remains with us today, for we unconsciously know that to say someone is blooming is to invoke an adolescent perfection and an innocent sexuality. If the idiom of bloom lingers, however, we have forgotten the botanical content behind bloom, and therefore the sexual content to the novel of courtship; we would do well to remember that the sexuality of flowers—how, in Linnaeus's terms, they court, have sex, and *marry*—was a commonplace when the novel entered its classical period. The young girl poised on the water lily beckons us forward, then, to the specifics of Linnaeus's taxonomical system, and the representational possibilities it generated in the nineteenth-century novel.

ONE

Linnaeus's Blooms
The Birth of the Botanical Vernacular

Oh! that we had a book of botany.

—Dorothy Wordsworth, *Grasmere Journal,* May 16, 1800

Examples are rife, in the late eighteenth- and early nineteenth-century novel, of girls "blooming" or "in bloom"—from Frances Burney's *Evelina,* whose blooming complexion attracts libertines and suitors alike, to John Cleland's Fanny Hill, whose bloom is explicitly tied to sexual initiation, to Jane Austen's Fanny Price, whose bloom corresponds with her belated début.[1] Austen's Anne Elliot, in fact, blooms twice in her story, and even George Eliot, looking back to the close of the eighteenth century in *Adam Bede,* produces Hetty Sorrel, whose cheek "like a rose-petal" is matched by "eyelids delicate as petals . . . lashes curled like the stamen of a flower."[2] The prevalence of this figurative language of "bloom" and the ease with which botanical facts are matched with female physiology invites a question: whence does it arise, and what gives it its sustaining power as a method for depicting nascent female sexuality in the marriage plots of the nineteenth-century novel? And what is the effect—if we relate a specific novelistic figure to a scientific classificatory system—of foregrounding a descriptive vocabulary when we study how a narrative works?

Tracing the answer to such a question will lead to the newly sexualized botany of Linnaeus and his mid-eighteenth-century exegetes, where aesthetic practice and scientific classification meet, and where the novel subsequently finds a significant register for discussing and disposing of female destinies. Buddings, blooms, and other flourishings permeate the late eighteenth-century novel of courtship. Blooms, specifically the corolla or flower of a plant, are also at the center of Linnaeus's sexual system of modern botany, a representational system, codified in the encyclopedic 1753 *Species Plantarum,* that was popularly practiced by lay individuals all over Europe, England, and America. Dominant in England from the 1770s, the Linnaean system articulated a plant morphology that was not unlike human anatomy and physiology, creating a system of representation that went a long way toward conflating the human and the vegetative, and breaking down the notion that the relationship between humans and plants was purely poetic.

Furthermore, this newly emphasized relation between the human and the floral reinforced the physicality of their shared activities, particularly their central endeavor, at least according to the Linnaean system: marital courtship and reproduction. This was, however, no unsocialized physicality; not the least of the surprising aspects of the Linnaean human/floral conflation is its mutually reinforced socialization, in which the sexuality of human and plant reproduction is always, inescapably, brought under the term "marriage." Plants marry because humans marry, but the representation of human marriage receives both its physicality, and its naturalized status, from the fact that plants marry: such is the logic of the botanical vernacular. The courtship novel does not socialize an originally "free," and therefore unrepresented, erotic instinct but instead relies on Linnaean descriptive language for the body that is already the sign of socialized sex (an eros both social *and* sexual). "Marriage"—the telos of the courtship plot—is therefore not an acculturation that occurs at the point of closure but is instead the rational conclusion to an already forecasted and managed erotics, forecast by a scientized language borrowed from botany.

The Linnaean language in the classical novel is indeed pervasive. For instance, when *Persuasion*'s Anne Elliot is spoken of as having the "bloom and freshness of youth restored," we can understand this not as the cliché it has become today (a cliché created by the courtship novel) but as a vocabulary of the novel that indexes the Linnaean system—a system that has the bloom, or blossom, at its center, and that embodies nascent sexuality.[3] Yet the descriptive systematics of bloom do not represent a simple exchange between imaginative and scientific literature, for Linnaean classification is organized around principles of marriage and gender roles that were recognizable, protonovelistic narratives. In fact, Linnaeus himself, in the first edition of the *Encyclopedia Britannica*, was accused of novel writing: "one would be tempted to think, that the author had more reasons than one for relishing this analogy so highly. In many parts of this treatise, there is such a degree of indelicacy in the expression as cannot be exceeded by the most obscene romance-writer."[4]

In the Linnaean botany flowers embody potential reproduction because their ephemeral appearance is the very sign of plant sexual reproduction *about to happen*. The novel finds in this scientific fact an apt analogue for its narration of courtship, for like the flower the "girl" in the novel is a nascent and ephemeral state: the novel of courtship takes as its subject this state, a period of time between the maturation of the girl and her marriage. Linnaean botany likewise is organized around the story of the courtships and marriages of plants, a taxonomical intertwining of natural and social worlds that conflates the workings of the plant's sexual parts with the term *marriage*. The science's ascription of human sexual characteristics and narratives to the blooms of plants came to confer botanical characteristics onto the blooms of girls. The "blooming girl"—the representation of a girl at her sexual and social peak—is a subjectivity in the late eighteenth-century novel that gets its meaning from a culture, saturated with botany, that would think of a bloom (or flower) when it read of a girl's "bloom" (her "blooming," her being "in bloom").

Linnaean classification disseminated the newly understood fact that the bloom or inflorescence of the plant was its sexual reproduction—it was not until 1694 that a German botanist, Rudolph Jakob Camerarius, had conclusively demonstrated that pollen is indispensable for the production of seeds that germinate.[5] Linnaeus's classification system employed that idea by making plant sexuality central to his classification—his "methodus propria," or "sexual system." The system becomes dominant in England by the 1770s, when the diffusion of his taxonomical system is reflected in the adoption of Linnaean binomials by such standard-bearers as *The Gardener's Dictionary* by Philip Miller.[6] It was Linnaeus's sexual system that vernacularized the late seventeenth-century scientific discovery that the flower is the sexual organ of the plant.[7]

The dissemination of this idea by Linnaeus's system made literal what had previously been only a metaphorical association among girls, flowers, and sexual innocence, for it articulated what literature had long suspected—that blooms, or flowers, are sex organs. Sex became spoken, in a sense, because flowers, always a suitable subject for representation, were revealed as sexual. The Linnaean system made bloom a safe lexicon for the novel, one that held in tension both the sexual reference of a bloom and its potential insertion into a proper plot of marriage; in other words, it was the Linnaean sexual system that brought that tension—between sex and marriage—into a prominent sphere of representation. Bloom in the novel is a scientific vocabulary, a metonymy for the sexualized flower, and it was through that metonymic vocabulary that the novel's representation of the erotics of courtship occurred.

The Rise of Botanical Culture

In the first of many illustrations of botanical sexuality in *New Illustration of the Sexual System of Linnaeus* (1799) by Robert John Thornton, Cupid stands among subtropical foliage and prepares to shoot his arrow at what appears to be a banana plant. "Cupid Inspiring Plants with Love" is a frontispiece to Thornton's lavish, folio-sized tome (see fig. 2).

The painting precedes what were hailed as "picturesque botanical plates," appearing among a number of typical introductory adornments to a popular scientific text: a dedication to Queen Charlotte, "patroness of botany and the fine arts," and a painting in which personifications of Flora, Cupid, Ceres, and Asclepius encircle and honor a bust of Linnaeus.[8] The painting of Cupid shooting his amatory arrows into a clump of plants—foliage of palm, rubber, banana, and tropical fern rendered with an attention to verisimilitude—serves

FIGURE 2 "Cupid Inspiring Plants with Love." Robert John Thornton, *New Illustration of the Sexual System of Linnaeus* (London, 1799–1810). Courtesy of the Print Collection, Miriam and Ira D. Wallach Division of Art, Prints and Photographs, The New York Public Library, Astor, Lenox and Tilden Foundations.

a double function. In one sense, it is a popularizing attempt, an example of the way a science whose formalization is still in process makes itself accessible to the general public. In another sense, the reader is constructed as an amateur by the very rhetorical structure of the text, and then invited by the realism of the illustration to be a botanist. In a representational universe where Cupid appears among real foliage and Linnaeus is invoked alongside the Greek goddess Flora, a complex relationship between literature and science is clearly visible.

The end of the eighteenth century was still the age of the scientific amateur, an age in which science and the pursuit of scientific knowledge were part of the culture in a way that seems unthinkable to our contemporary separation of professional science from amateur knowledge. Though temporally not far from the age when Newtonian physics was explained in the fashionable coffeehouses of London, this later age of the natural sciences was less indebted to that thirst for grand universal explanations and more suggestive of a culture's collective attempt to understand and narrate its place in what was soon to become known as the biological world.[9] The Linnaean system's recourse to human social-sexual narratives (marriage, in particular) became a way that sex, and sexual potentiality, could be not only legitimately invoked but narrated. It should not be surprising, therefore, that the descriptive climate that ensued as a result of the conflation of human and plant sexuality by Linnaeus's system produced a *plot*: the classical novel's narration of erotic marital courtship.

Linnaeus, or Carl von Linné, was of course neither the first nor the only botanist to put together a classification system for plants—over fifty natural botanic systems existed in the eighteenth century—but his artificial system, with its extraordinary utility, became extremely popular.[10] In England it was Linnaeus's system that made botany accessible to a broader array of enthusiasts, and Linnaeus's classification system that disseminated the idea that the flower is the sexual organ of the plant.[11] This process followed the translation of Linnaeus's early-century works in the 1760s; Linnaean botany entered the realm of popular knowledge, thus, in the latter half of the eighteenth century, even though Linnaeus was primarily writing and publishing in the first half of the century.[12] Benjamin Stillingfleet was the first in 1759 to introduce and validate Linnaean concepts to England by translating and publishing some of the dissertations done under Linnaeus. In 1760, James Lee, a well-known London nurseryman, published his groundbreaking and best-selling *Introduction to Botany*, which consisted of extracts from Linnaeus's writings translated into English. It was not until the 1770s that such things as botanical fieldtrips and teaching demonstrations were introduced in England. Other markers of the integration of Linnaean botany into England include the founding of the Linnaean Society in 1788, and the launching in 1787 by William Curtis of what would become the immensely popular *Botanical Magazine*; later renamed *Curtis's Botanical Magazine*, it was a gardening magazine for the general public that used and encouraged the use of Linnaean nomenclature.[13]

The practice of botany in England came out of the larger adoption in the late seventeenth and eighteenth centuries of a scientific worldview in which the order of the natural world could be understood through empirical observation.[14] Botany was part of a culture of natural history, which included the growth of the national botanical garden, the popular collection of natural objects, and the imperialistic collection of plants from around the world; Linnaeus's students, as well as interested followers, flung themselves to the far corners of the earth in order to find new species, new parts to classify within a fixed order of creation. The ever-growing desire for new specimens of plants was satisfied by plant-hunters, increasingly sponsored in the early part of the nineteenth century by a network of government organizations, private enterprises (including retail nurseries), and aristocratic patronage. By the time Darwin embarked on the HMS *Beagle* in 1836, there had been a long lineage of naturalist collectors, including, most famously, Sir Joseph Banks, who sent large collections of new species to the Chelsea Physic Garden from his post as resident botanist on James Cook's circumnavigation of the globe; Alexander von Humboldt and Aimé Bonpland's self-financed efforts in South America between 1799 and 1804 doubled the number of plants previously known to the Western world.[15] Many of the plants we now think of as indigenous to America and England were actually introduced during this botanical renaissance; for instance, the lilac—since Whitman seemingly such an American trope—was indigenous to Persia. This was also a time in which natural history books and narratives were best-sellers; according to G. S. Rousseau, Georges-Louis Leclerc de Buffon's opus *Historie naturelle* was one of the ten most popular books in England during the second half of the eighteenth century.[16]

Botany became increasingly a part of polite female culture in the late eighteenth and into the nineteenth century. The utility and inclusive rhetoric of the Linnaean system had made botany, as Lisbet Koerner has shown, a common practice in the second half of the eighteenth century among nonprofessionals, especially women.[17] Botany was considered both a science and an accomplishment, a popular pursuit that was considered a suitable and required body of knowledge for the educated girl; it became thought of as a science particularly suited to the feminine and recommended as an activity that was morally improving.[18] Linnaean classificatory botany for girls, as demonstrated in Rousseau's small pedagogical work on botany entitled *Lettres élémentaires sur la botanique* (1785), was complemented by what was called "elegant botany"—a term that covers many of the fads of Georgian England, including flower painting, flower pressing, the making of paper flowers, and ordered collections of natural objects.[19] Two friends of Queen Charlotte, the Duchess of Portland (who had one of the most substantial plant collections in England) and Mrs. Delaney, sponsored a salon for natural history conversation.[20] Daniel Solander, Linnaeus's student and one of Sir Joseph Banks's curators, was the salon's great attraction, and it was the blue stockings of Benjamin Stillingfleet, Linnaeus's translator, that made this natural history salon the origin of a famous term for female pedants. Flower painting especially became fashionable in late Georgian England and both Napoleonic and post-Napoleonic France, when Francis Bauer and Pierre Joseph Rédouté respectively taught and practiced their art. Likewise, private plant collecting became an indication of fashion and wealth in both England and France.[21]

Although Linnaeus was based in Uppsala, the Swedish university town, the systematic study of the natural sciences took some time to catch on at the university level, and the degree to which amateurish pursuit was the norm should not be discounted.[22] Botany was not being studied solely in the exclusive environments of universities or botanical gardens, and Linnaeus's system was not an arcane professional language but rather a widely accessible and disseminated practical tool. Even the examples of the most intense botanical ambition in the first half of the nineteenth century—Joseph Hooker's plant-collecting for Kew in the Himalayas, or the Duke of Devonshire's financing of the Great Conservatory at Chatsworth and the exploration to India to fill it with new plants—reflect more the enthusiasm of the age for all things botanical than a separate professional interest. These extreme examples of early nineteenth-century enthusiasm were mirrored, albeit on a much less grand scale, by the enthusiasms of countless amateur botanists in England, including women and working-class men, from the late eighteenth deep into the nineteenth century. As Anne Secord has shown in her studies about working-class participation in scientific pursuits from the late eighteenth and nineteenth centuries, participation in botanical study was not restricted by class.[23]

Female participation in the collection and classification of the botanical world was no historical accident. Lisbet Koerner has shown that Linnaeus explicitly included rather than excluded women from the study of botany; he extended botanical pursuits "even for Women themselves."[24] Linnaeus reached out to lay and learned audiences alike, encouraging translations of his works from the Latin to vernacular languages as well as adaptations of his work into short clear botanical handbooks and penny versions that were small enough to be portable. As Koerner has shown, Linnaeus's very reputation was based on the democratizing accessibility of his classification, in that the artificiality of his system was tolerated because of its utility: "in his guides and handbooks, and in the structure of his systems as such, Linnaeus lowered the educational and financial entrance fee to the study of nature."[25] The vernacularization of botany was due in no small part to the fact that Linnaeus himself welcomed a nonprofessional audience and provided the means—by not requiring special equipment or training, and by encouraging modern translations of his work—for a broader audience to pursue the study of nature. Not until the 1830s did a natural system of classification introduced by Antonie-Laurent de Jussieu begin to make inroads among professional botanists; it was not a uniform process, however, even among professional botanists, because Linnaean nomenclature was so accessible for amateur and professional life that even the great William Hooker continued to use the Linnaean system in new editions of his *British Flora* (1830) through the 1840s.[26]

Linnaeus's system in part inherited England's budding interest in the natural sciences. As G. S. Rousseau reminds us, in the second half of the eighteenth century a faddish interest in natural history emerged, taking the place of the early eighteenth-century fascination with astronomy, physics, and mathematics.[27] During the seventeenth century, John Ray (1627–1705) had created a natural taxonomy, setting in motion in England an interest in botany that was later superseded by Linnaeus's streamlined system. Linnaeus is most famous for having invented the system of binomial nomenclature, based on a Latinate conjunction of genera and species, that still has currency today. Binomial nomenclature and Linnaeus's *methodus propria* were presented in separate forums and should be distinguished. Linnaeus's sexual system of plant classification was presented to the international public in *Systema Naturae* (1735); the system of binomial nomenclature was introduced first in *Philosophia Botanica* (1751) and subsequently in *Species Plantarum* (1753). The dissemination of Linnaean science was international and widespread; for instance, between 1755 and 1824 *Philosophia Botanica* was reprinted ten times in Latin and translated into six modern languages. *Species Plantarum* is thought of as the starting point of modern descriptive botany, but the combined ideas of these two texts made the Linnaean system the standard of eighteenth- and early nineteenth-century botany. Under the Linnaean system the "phrase name" is transposed into a biverbal, reducing a plant's name from a polysyllabic mouthful into a simpler and more easily obtained two-word formula. For instance, the plant *Physalis annua ramosissima ramis angulosis glabris foliis dentato-serratis* becomes simply *Physalis angulata*. The popularization of botany can be traced in part to the appeal and utility of Linnaeus's simplified system, a practical, streamlined organizational schema with which one could identify the class and order of a species in the field without elaborate equipment or knowledge.

Nevertheless, when Linnaeus's sexual system of botany first was introduced in England, there were detractors who charged that Linnaeus and his botanical classification system were obscene. These detractors picked up on an early strain of objection to Linnaeus's work. Johann Siegesbeck, a St. Petersburg academic, referred in 1737 to Linnaeus's earliest articulation of his system as "loathsome harlotry," for he believed that God would not have permitted "several males" to one "female"—as much so in the vegetable as human kingdom—and that "so licentious a method" should then not be taught nor used.[28] Linnaeus, in what can only be termed an act of taxonomical revenge, proceeded to name a particularly noxious smelling weed *Siegesbeckia*. In the 1768–71 first edition of the *Encyclopedia Britannica* its editor (and sometime contributor) William Smellie took a disparaging stance toward the Linnaean system in his entry on botany; a member of the "anti-sexualist" school at Edinburgh, Smellie was particularly disapproving of Linnaeus's system and concepts. Smellie, "in deference to modesty," refused to translate portions of Linnaeus's system; concerned with what he termed the "metaphors or analogies" being traced between humans and plants, he called the Linnaean system a series of "disgusting strokes of obscenity" that have a "bad tendency upon morals."[29]

The objections of Edinburgh's antisexualist school did not prevail, however, for by the late eighteenth century evidence of the Linnaean system's acceptance can be found in countless works intended for a female audience. Reverend John Bennett, for instance, author of *Letters to a Young Lady* (1789), encouraged the study of Linnaean botany, for botany was in Bennett's opinion "particularly feminine" and "calculated to amuse the mind, improve the health and spirits, and to inspire at once cheerfulness and devotion."[30] Bennett's conduct book reasoned that botany was inherently modest, even if he felt that Linnaeus's texts were too technical for the female reader. One of the most popular redactions of the Linnaean method was *An Introduction to Botany* by Priscilla Wakefield; it reached its sixth edition by 1811, and far from seeing botany as obscene, it suggests that botany acts to counter "pernicious habits" and is an "antidote to levity and idleness."[31] Several arguments coalesced ultimately to win out over the anxiety about the system's explicit foregrounding of the flower's sexuality. Most important, the study of nature was perceived as an act of devotion, an act of marveling at God's creation and, ideally, contributing through new classification to a wider understanding of what had been created. Other factors, such as the symbolic innocence of the flower and the potential health benefits of the practice of field botany, contributed to the sense that botany was an ideal pursuit.

This sketch of the cultural impact of Linnaean botany is, however, only a start.[32] My investigation continues an established effort to map a cultural history of late eighteenth- and nineteenth-century botany, but my particular interest is in the rhetorical and representational, or more specifically literary, aspects of Linnaean botany more than its status as an episode in a cultural history.[33] The figurative explicitness of the flower bears significantly on the representational project of the novel, where girls and bloomings are central subjects and where late eighteenth-century polemical battles over gender, sexual politics, and botany had a crucial, if less explicit, impact. The shaping force that botany exerted over the novel would outlive the public fixation over Linnaean systematics and its frankness and would influence the classical novel's plotting of nascent female sexuality deep into the nineteenth century. But it was the broad popularization of Linnaeus's system that led to widespread legibility about the sexuality of flowers—a world in which the practice of counting a flower's sex parts was the route to classification, and thus the revelation of God's creation. We should speak of Linnaeus's impact on the English novel as one of diffusion—an indirect influence, rather than a direct source, in which his dissemination of the scientific concept of the sexuality of the flower gave fresh viability and force to the representation of legible sexuality in the novel.

The Mechanics of the Botanical Vernacular

> *Chamædaphne of Buxbaum* (*Andromeda polifolia*) was at the time in its highest beauty. . . . The flowers are quite blood-red before they expand, but when full-grown the corolla is of a flesh colour. Scarcely any painter's art can so happily imitate the beauty of a fine female

complexion; still less could any artificial colour upon the face itself bear a comparison with this lovely blossom. As I contemplated it I could not help thinking of Andromeda as described by the poets; and the more I meditated upon their description, the more applicable they seemed to the little plant before me, so that if these writers had had it in view, they could scarcely have contrived a more apposite fable. Andromeda is represented by them as a virgin of most exquisite and unrivaled charms; but these charms remain in perfection only so long as she retains her virgin purity, which is also applicable to the plant, now preparing to celebrate its nuptials. . . . As the distressed virgin cast down her blushing face through excessive affliction, so does the rosy-coloured flower hang its head, growing paler and paler till it withers away. Hence, as this plant forms a new genus, I have chosen for it the name of *Andromeda*.[34]

The ruminations of Linnaeus in his journal, while taking a tour of Lapland in his native Sweden, are both botanical and literary. *Lachesis lapponica; or a Tour in Lapland*, is a journal that combines anthropological observations with botanical findings; crude sketches of tools, clothing, and reindeer harnesses sit among descriptions of coming upon a new plant in bloom; the breastfeeding habits and fish diets of the native peoples are as much sources of fascination as are the plants he comes to collect. The opportunity to observe the plant *Andromeda polifolia* in bloom is a particularly significant moment, however, because its discovery leads to the formation of a new genus. Linnaeus imbues this taxonomical moment with a rhetorical flourish, turning to the descriptive evocativeness of the female complexion—a girl's bloom—to adequately express his admiration for the plant he calls *Andromeda*. The plant, like the girl of the Andromeda myth, is only perfectly beautiful while it retains its "virgin purity." In fact the plant, whose aesthetic claims consist of coloring that is like flesh, specifically that of "a fine female complexion," is most beautiful when it is, to use Linnaeus's euphemism, "preparing to celebrate its nuptials" (see fig. 3).[35]

Linnaeus's moment of exuberance may have prompted a particularly colorful name for this flower, but the equation of plant and human sexuality ran much deeper than a single episode. The very practice of identifying and classifying a plant by class and order depended on the study of the sexual parts (stamens and pistils) intrinsic to the reproductive act. In effect, his methodology asked its practitioners to pay attention to that which existed prior to the climactic moment of reproduction: the plant's sexual organs, gendered feminine and masculine by scientific representation. Botanical classification depended on counting and studying those parts of the plant intrinsic to the reproductive act; the stamen was gendered "male" and the pistil "female." Linnaeus wrote in *Philosophia Botanica*: "the flower is nothing else but the generative act of plants" (*PB*, 150). The flower represented sex or the potential sex of plants largely because of the diffusion of the scientific fact of the flower's sexual content by Linnaeus's popular system.[36]

FIGURE 3   "Andromeda," an erotic drawing and plant description in Linnaeus's hand from his Lapland diary, in E. Ährling, ed., *Carl von Linnés Ungdomsskrifter* (Stockholm, 1888), 68. Courtesy of the Library of the Gray Herbarium, Harvard University, Cambridge, MA.

What is crucial for my purposes is the following: the gendering of essential sex characteristics in Linnaean botanical writing suggests that the science relied on a prior assumption about human courtship and sexuality to construct its account of plant sexuality. This understanding arguably stems from both social life and literature alike—in Linnaeus's classification system plants "court" and "marry," which is language that both borrows from everyday accounts of heterosexual coupling and literalizes previous metaphorical associations between girls, flowers, and sexual romance. Under the general category of "Marriages of Plants," Linnaeus breaks down those relations into "Public Marriages" and "Clandestine Marriages." There were twenty-four classes in Linnaeus's system, ranging from "Monandria" to "Cryptogamia." Monandria, the first class, describes a plant with one stamen in a hermaphrodite flower, or—as Linnaeus's 1758 description had it—"maritus unicus in matrimonio [one husband in marriage]" (*SN*, 29). Cryptogamia, the twenty-fourth class, is a category that includes all plants in which the flower is concealed in some irregular manner; the class was popularly known as "Clandestine Marriage," for as Linnaeus wrote, "nuptiae clam celebrantur [nuptials are celebrated privately]" (*SN*, 22). Linnaeus's sexual system of classification was not only imbued with social-sexual language but also constructed by an explicit social-sexual system of analogy between humans and plants (see fig. 4).

Thus the new Linnaean systematics based on stamens and pistils made the corolla—what we colloquially call the bloom, blossom, or flower—the focus

CLAVIS SYSTEMATIS SEXVALIS.

NVPTIAE PLANTARVM.
Actus generationis incolarum regni vegetabilis.
Florescentia.

[*PVBLICAE.*
Nuptiae, omnibus manifestae, aperte celebrantur.
Flores vnicuique visibiles.

[MONOCLINIA.
Mariti et vxores vno eodemque thalamo gaudent.
Flores omnes hermaphroditi: stamina cum pistillis in eodem flore.

[DIFFINITAS.
Mariti inter se non cognati.
Stamina nulla sua parte connata inter se sunt.

[INDIFFERENTISMVS.
Mariti absque subordinatione.
Stamina longitudine indeterminata.

1. MONANDRIA	7. HEPTANDRIA.
2. DIANDRIA.	8. OCTANDRIA.
3. TRIANDRIA.	9. ENNEANDRIA.
4. TETRANDRIA	10. DECANDRIA.
5. PENTANDRIA.	11. DODECANDRIA.
6. HEXANDRIA.	12. ICOSANDRIA.
	13. POLYANDRIA.

[SVBORDINATIO.
Mariti certi reliquis praeferuntur.
Stamina duo semper reliquis breuiora sunt.

14. DIDYNAMIA.	15. TETRADYNAMIA.

[AFFINITAS.
Mariti propinqui et cognati sunt.
Stamina cohaerent vel inter se, vel cum pistillo.

16. MONADELPHIA.	19. SYNGENESIA.
17. DIADELPHIA.	20. GYNANDRIA.
18. POLYADELPHIA.	

[DICLINIA (a δις bis et κλίνη thalamus) duplex thalamus.
Mariti et Feminae distinctis thalamis gaudent.
Flores masculi et feminei in eadem specie.

21. MONOECIA.	23. POLYGAMIA.
22. DIOECIA.	

[CLANDESTINAE.
Nuptiae clam instituuntur.
Flores oculis nostris nudis vix conspiciuntur.

24. CRYPTOGAMIA.

CLAS-

FIGURE 4   "Clavis Systematis Sexualis" (*above*) and "Key of the Sexual System" (*right*). Table and its English translation of Linnaeus's sexual system. Latin from Carl von Linné, *Systema Vegetabilium* (Gottingen, 1797), 20. Courtesy of The LuEsther T. Mertz Library of the New York Botanical Garden, Bronx, New York. English from Carl von Linné, *A System of Vegetables* (Litchfield, 1782–83), vol. 1, 22. Courtesy of the Arents Collection, The New York Public Library, Astor, Lenox and Tilden Foundations.

KEY OF THE SEXUAL SYSTEM.

MARRIAGES OF PLANTS.

Florescence.

(PUBLIC *MARRIAGES.*

Flowers visible to every one,

 (IN ONE BED.

 Husband and wife have the same bed.

 All the flowers hermaphrodite : stamens and pistils in the same flower.

  (WITHOUT AFFINITY.

  Husbands not related to each other.

  Stamens not joined together in any part.

   (WITH EQUALITY.

   All the males of equal rank.

   Stamens have no determinate proportion of length.

1. ONE MALE.	7. SEVEN MALES
2. TWO MALES.	8. EIGHT MALES.
3. THREE MALES.	9. NINE MALES.
4. FOUR MALES.	10. TEN MALES.
5. FIVE MALES	11. TWELVE MALES.
6. SIX MALES.	12. TWENTY MALES.
	13. MANY MALES.

   (WITH SUBORDINATION

   Some males above others.

   Two stamens are always lower than the others.

    14. TWO POWERS | 15. FOUR POWERS.

  (WITH AFFINITY

  Husbands related to each other.

  Stamens cohere with each other, or with the pistil.

16. ONE BROTHERHOOD.	19. CONFEDE-
17. TWO BROTHERHOODS.	RATE MALES.
18. MANY BROTHERHOODS.	20. FEMININE
	MALES.

(IN TWO BEDS.

Husband and wife have separate beds.

Male flowers and female flowers in the same species.

21. ONE HOUSE.	23. POLYGAMIES.
21. TWO HOUSES.	

(CLANDESTINE MARRIAGES.

Flowers scarce visible to the naked eye.

  24. CLANDESTINE MARRIAGES.

CHA-

of study and representation. The blossom-centered system depended on the scientific practice of visual observation (as opposed, for example, to dissection), making the aesthetics of sight (color, shape, and form) primary. Linnaeus's choice to build on Camerarius's discovery that plants, as well as animals, have an egg and a fertilizing agent was one that proved fortuitous.[37] In choosing, for instance, to let root or leaf structure fall out of his classification system, Linnaeus privileged the utility of his system over the issue of its status as an artificial system. Would it be easy to use? Would it prove satisfactory as an organizational device when the vast number of species yet to be "revealed" were found? That Linnaeus's system was based on deductive rather than inductive logic is less important for my purposes than the literary act that he performs: he calls the potential sexual reproduction of the flower "matrimonio" or "marriage." By drawing on a human social state to further elucidate his system and constructing, in a sense, a broad method for remembering the various botanical classes, Linnaeus certainly makes his classification system more functional. But it perhaps also made his artificial system *seem* more natural, for it relied on a social understanding of marriage as the normative way to describe sexuality. Linnaeus's decision to employ the suffixes *-andria* (from the Greek *aner,* "husband") and *-gynia* (from the Greek *gyne,* "wife") for his botanical classes—Monandria, for example—made the system even more recognizable and seemingly natural. The ease of binomial nomenclature cannot be overemphasized, but even more important, the classification system functions like a mnemonic on a grand scale by likening plant reproduction to a dominant form of human social experience—gender difference, reproductive sexuality, and marriage.

The result of this sheer comprehensibility of Linnaean botany, as well as its widespread dissemination and usage, was its rapid vernacularization. Although certainly not everyone became an amateur botanist, the diffusion of the analogical relation between plants and humans in the classification system was so broad, and the comparison so comprehensible, as to ensure its becoming widely understood. A cultural consensus was achieved: the scientific identification of sex with flowers was launched and became a shared cultural knowledge. The fact that the flower was understood to be the sexual organ of the plant, as well as the site of a plant's marriage, created what I term a "botanical vernacular": a language that reflects the popularized knowledge of botany generally shared in that historical moment. Bloom is the terminological trace in the classical novel of the botanical vernacular, the language that reflects that culture's general understanding of the sexual dimension to the flower.

The character in the classical novel that blooms is, almost without exception, the marriageable girl. That bloom, which invokes the sexual content of the flower, is combined so consistently with the representation of the marriageable girl suggests that the word *bloom* invokes the sexual content of "marriageability." A bloom, in the Linnaean register, is a highly charged analogue of human sexual courtship, and it is this analogue the novel draws on in its representation of courtship. That is, the cultural meaning inherent in the novelistic vocabulary comes from a popular scientific description of an actual phenomenon: that the flower equals potential sexual reproduction. And yet Linnaeus's system is more complex than simply offering a transparent elucidation of the sexual purpose of flowers—in a sense, it turns that fact into a *narrative* by calling potential sexual reproduction by the name of its human social counterpart: marriage. Linnaeus's classification system describes actual configurations of plant sex and gives them a social valence, for botanical class is determined by the kind of sexual reproduction ("matrimonio" or "marriage") that is each flower's destiny. In modern Linnaean botany, plants reproduce, but they also court, as we can see in Linnaeus's sketch of plant pollination in *Sponsalia Plantarum* (1746), entitled "Amor Unit Plantas" (see fig. 5).

The idea that bloom is both a sexual fact and a social category is a point best made by going directly to Linnaeus's texts. Linnaeus endows the plant with sentient features generally associated with the human; he provides scientific accounts of plant irritability, pleasure, movement, and sensitivity. In describing the flower—the designation for the grouping of the corolla, calyx, filaments, antherae, pollen, stigma, style, german, pericarpium, and seeds—Linnaeus in *Philosophia Botanica* (1751) suggests the following: "The Calyx then is the marriage bed, the corolla the curtains, the filaments the spermatic vessels, the antherae the testicles, the dust [pollen] the male sperm, the stigma the labia or the extremity of the female organ, the style the vagina, the german the ovary, the pericarpium the ovary impregnated, the seeds the ovula or eggs" (*PB*, 151). Linnaeus's analogy is both physiological and social, for in his elucidation of plant reproduction he brings together the physical dimensions of the plant in relation to the human—a plant's "stigma" is like a woman's labia, "antherae" like a man's testicles—as well as the social context in which he supposes sex to take place: the "marriage bed," its privacy guaranteed by bed "curtains."

Although the likening of the flower's sexual parts to the human reproductive parts is meant partially as an explanatory figure, it is less of a metaphor and more like a constitutive analogy germane to the science. In the section "Of the Sexes of Plants" in *Philosophia Botanica*, Linnaeus writes: "fructification consists in the genitals of plants; so that their flowering is analogous to generation, and the ripe fruit to the compleat foetus" (*PB*, 149–50). In his classification system Linnaeus appears to conflate human and vegetable sexuality, but here, in *Philosophia Botanica*, Linnaeus's conflation approaches a homology: the fruit and the formed human fetus are shown to share a similar structure, and there is an oblique if unsubstantiated claim of a shared anterior origin. In this register, the representational relationship between humans and flowers, more than poetic, is a scientific analogue. In light of this analogue, the valences of the flower would be both sexual and poetic, to a more rigorous and explicit extent than our historical moment, when botany has faded from our own scientific vernaculars.

The use of human analogues and narratives in Linnaeus's taxonomy is, perhaps, characteristic of sciences that have yet to be "formalized."[38]

25

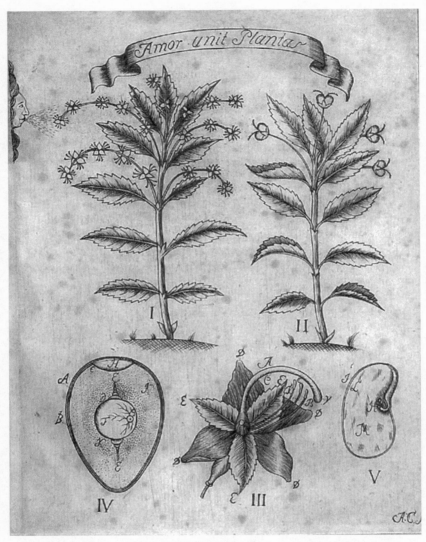

FIGURE 5   "Amor unit Plantas." Drawing illustrating plant pollination, fancifully captioned "Love Unites the Plants." Carl von Linné, *Sponsalia Plantarum* (Stockholm, 1746). Courtesy of The LuEsther T. Mertz Library of The New York Botanical Garden, Bronx, New York.

Philosophia Botanica had condemned the use of figurative language and instead advocated a plain style for botany, but that rhetorical principle is violated repeatedly in the writings and the classification system itself.[39] Linnaeus's first principle, for example, in *Philosophia Botanica* is that nature mimics the biblical account of creation: "in the first place we shall shew that there was only one pair of every living thing, whether animal or vegetable species, created at the beginning" (*PB*, 148). That these analogues occur in the original writings of Linnaeus is significant, for it is the taxonomy itself that employs the kind of analogical language that one might have expected from interpreters or disseminators of the science.[40] These analogies are neither the work of popularizers nor secondary metaphors for purposes of dissemination to laypersons; not only do the analogies originate with Linnaeus, they are in place at the primary level of his taxonomy. In the first volume of *Systema Naturae*, Linnaeus describes the seed as "pregnant with a new plant" and otherwise endows the plant with every aspect of sentience except consciousness: "vegetables . . . imbibe nourishment through bibulous roots, breathe by quivering leaves, celebrate their nuptials in a genial metamorphosis, and continue their kind by the dispersion of seed within prescribed limits." In describing the structure of the stamen, the basis of the class, he writes of "the stamen, an external organ, constituting the Male; consisting of a slender filament supporting the anthera big with prolific pollen or dust" (*SN*, 2–3). The pistil, which constitutes the botanical order, is the female genital: "an interior organ, constituting the Female; consisting of a germ or rudiment of the fruit and seated beneath, a style placed in the middle and supporting the moist pubescent stigma" (*SN*, 4). The fact that both the stamen and the pistil are visible external parts of the flower, and that Linnaeus elsewhere writes that "in a flower we find all the internal parts of a plant unfolded," strongly suggests that the interiorizing of the female pistil is an act of gendering according to observed human anatomy (*PB*, 152). Linnaeus's structuring analogy is not, therefore, as transparent as it might seem but rather alters, or at least infiltrates, the supposed empirical facts.

Linnaeus's account of plant reproduction is but one way, however, that modern botany is constructed along human sexual and social lines. The Linnaean system of classification for plants, specifically the way classes and orders were demarcated, drew on human gender hierarchies and social arrangements. Courtship, generation, the feminine, the masculine, the hermaphroditic, androgyny, polygamy: all of these are botanical descriptions within Linnaeus's principal taxonomical category of "marriage." For example, variations of Cryptogamia include: "Equal Polygamy—many marriages with promiscuous intercourse"; "Superfluous Polygamy—when the married females are fertile, and thence the concubines superfluous"; "Frustraneous Polygamy—when the married females are fertile, and the concubines are barren"; "Necessary Polygamy—when the married females are barren, and the concubines fertile"; "Separate Polygamy—when many beds are so united that they constitute one common bed" (*SN*, 32–4). Other classes are constructed around the number of "husbands" in the "same marriage," the height of the "husbands," how some are united "like brothers," how some seem to have "two mothers." The twentieth Linnaean class, Gynandria, imposes a social judgment about gender relations on a botanical structure, for Gynandria—or "Feminine Males"—is a class of plants in which there are "husbands or wives growing together" (*SN*, 29–32). Linnaeus's representational system makes social what he is earnestly describing as actual scientific phenomena; in reading through these extraordinary categories, it is sometimes hard to remember that he is classifying plants and not peoples.[41]

These various botanical classes offer an intriguing number of unorthodox social and sexual possibilities. Linnaeus's system describes traditional groupings—relationships between "brothers," or a single "husband" and "wife"—as well as illicit, secret, and marginalized practices: concubinage, polygamy, sex without fertility. The broadest criterion of distinction is between "public" and "clandestine" marriages, which is the distinction between plants that manifest flowers versus plants whose flowers cannot be seen by the naked eye; another level of distinction is based on whether husbands and wives live in the "same bed" (exist in the same flower) or whether they "have separate beds" (exist in separate flowers). Ideas of power are also prominently represented, for the defining distinction among the first fifteen classes is determined by whether the males exhibit "equality" (referring to length) or if some are "subordinate" to the others. One of the most intriguing anthropomorphisms of how Linnaeus's botanical classes are determined centers on relationships among men, specifically if they are related to each other or not related to each other—what Linnaeus calls with or without "affinity." Whether or not stamens are joined together in the corolla, for instance, and hence are related or not related, is not only a botanical description but also a rich narrative about how to describe certain relations among men.

What is never represented, perhaps predictably, is any sexual configuration that we might identify as homosexual, for Linnaeus's classification system is structured around (potential) reproduction. However, the social groupings of certain botanical classes are far from normative, as in the case of the second through the thirteenth botanical classes; in these botanical classes, there are anywhere from two through twenty to "many" males (stamens) in proportion to the female pistil. The various social configurations that Linnaeus's system makes visible also stray from a model of monogamy and would seem to defy the logic of the marriage analogue he employs. The twenty-second botanical class, Dioecia, suggests the possibility of "husbands" and "wives" living in "two houses"—that is, being married but living separately. Although Linnaeus's system never strays far from the ultimate purpose of the flower itself—the sexual reproduction of the plant—it does offer an intriguing set of social and sexual possibilities within a heterosexual frame.

Many representational possibilities intrinsic to Linnaeus's system are not, of course, realized in the classical novel—that is, until Eliot's *Adam Bede*, when the bloom narrative as represented by the public marriages of Austen's novels turns to a full-scale clandestine bloom narrative centered on Hetty and Donnithorne. Eliot takes her realist idiom to its logical place by representing what Linnaeus's classification system had determined to be the first-level distinction between types of florescence, or flowering: whether it was public (visible to the eye) or clandestine (not visible to the naked eye). Clandestine marriages, in the plant kingdom, included the (scarcely visible) flowerings of such plants as mosses, ferns, and fungi. As I will show in chapter 4, the flowering that occurs between Hetty and Donnithorne also cannot be seen, as their clandestine sexual encounters take place in the wood, outside the structures of the social world that made a public marriage impossible or undesirable. The text assumes a botanical vernacular that perhaps cannot be counted on today, for the mosses and ferns that literally provide the background, and perhaps the bed, for this clandestine courtship are the very plants that define the botanical class "Cryptogamia" or the class of Clandestine Marriage. Although Linnaeus's science, like the novel, may be part of a regime of knowledge that ignores several substantiations of human sexuality, it is, like Eliot's novel, nonetheless committed to a realistic (if partial) representation of some illicit possibilities.

Why, one might ask, are all these various types of plant sexuality under the umbrella term "marriages of plants?" Certainly, Linnaeus's botanical system relies on a social understanding of marriage as the natural, normative way to describe sexuality; one might then ask what is the effect, besides the pervasive way that science has regularly contributed to the construction of sexual normativity, of marriage being the blanket term for these various types of plant sexual configurations? What the classificatory system does is conflate the sexual or reproductive act—whatever its configuration, among just two or multiple stamens and pistils—with marriage, effectively turning marriage into a shorthand for sex. Although on the one hand Linnaeus's system is part of a repressive regime, one that takes a diversity of potential sexual pairings and social configurations and turns them all into husbands and wives, one can also see that Linnaeus's system opens up the possibility of heterosexual marriage defined primarily by sexuality and not by its status as a social institution. As I will show, in the classical novel the potential variations on marriage in Linnaeus's system are diversely realized. Although the marriage plot, like Linnaeus's classificatory system, may repress or normalize polymorphous sexual possibilities and social configurations, it also tenaciously represents the sexual potential, and not just the social fact, of marriage. In sexual potential the novel gets as close as it can to the actual representation of sexuality, ascribing to bloom not only a predictive function for that which exists beyond the narrative (sexual consummation) but also the ability to sign the look of sex itself: a girl's bloom is a physically notable sign of the quickening of erotic attraction between the denizens of the courtship plot.

Botanical Mimetics and the Novel

Linnaeus believed in the idea that, confronted with the same plant and using the same classification system, every botanist could give exactly the same description. He predicted that someday those descriptions would become so precise that the words of the description would reproduce the form of the plant. Like a pattern-poem, these botanical "calligrammes" would take on the cast of plants, their very materiality dictated by the structure of the natural object being described.[42]

Linnaeus's botanical calligrammes may not have been realized in print, but his faith that a realistic mimesis of a natural object could be achieved through visual observation and descriptive language points us in the direction of the realist novel. A convergence occurred in the late eighteenth and early nineteenth centuries between the growing dominance of the classical novel's realist forms and the wide dissemination of natural history's classificatory endeavors. That the novel is a genre centrally preoccupied with the mimetic representation of both social and natural realities is by now a truism.[43] Linnaeus, in a system that has much in common with that novelistic impulse, tried to express the totality, in form and content, of the world he is trying to describe; the novel tries to represent fictionally a social world that is intelligible and knowable. The articulated connections between classification and the novel are few, limited for the most part to an early eighteenth-century criticism that Linnaeus's system borrowed too heavily from the novel's salacious tendencies. The residues of the connection between the two, however, are traceable, their connections made more readily obvious, by an examination of their common representational strategies. There are mimetic connections that the two representational systems share, for the novel's narrative energies are not opposed to scientific classification, and indeed the novel's representational strategies may even sometimes borrow from eighteenth-century science.

Both enterprises, both systems of representation, share an epistemological bias, for both privilege visual sight as the mode for conveying description and characterization; this bias gives sight, as Foucault has written, an "almost exclusive privilege" in natural history classification and makes it the dominant mode of representation in the novel form.[44] Both the novel and the classification system depend on a description of visual detail and a process whereby visual facts are turned into corresponding language. The object of both representational fields is what we might call a full description: the attempt to achieve a fuller and more accurate mimesis through physical description. In this apparently simple connection rests the theoretical connection, as distinct from the historical confluence, between botany and the novel. The late eighteenth-century impetus to know nature through classification conditioned, perhaps even informed, the novel, with its increasing commitment to realism. But influence, in a sense, is not the essential point; my interest here is that both genres, both systems of representation, are *mimetic*. This is ultimately a literary point: the botanical system, like the novel, tries to capture a reality through a physicalized mimesis.

In classificatory botany, the process of describing visual detail—what is known as establishing *character*—is perhaps less familiar than the techniques with which readers of realist narrative are usually acquainted: it is achieved by noting each of the "identities" (or facts), and each of the differences, of a plant—in short, everything that it is, and everything that it is not. Linnaeus, among other eighteenth-century systematists, thought it was more practical to limit what could be described—even limit the formation of a "botanical character"—to a single structure or part of the plant. Unlike either Buffon or Jussieu, Linnaeus thought it was necessary to not extend the basis of the classification to all aspects of the plant (known as a total comparison), for, as everyone knew, to extend it made it considerably more difficult to achieve the description. Rather than making a total comparison, Linnaeus's classification system is organized around a structural limitation: that being, of course, the reproductive system (or flower) of the plant. Therefore, his descriptions would list the identities and differences of various plants' reproductive systems and would systematically ignore anything else that was not part of that structure (such as leaves or roots, for example).[45]

What kind of mimesis is then achieved? In Linnaean botany, anything not related to the sexual parts of the plant would necessarily be ignored in the service of "establishing the character"—the plant's description, place in the natural continuum, and, most important, name. The comparison between botanical classification and the novel, as tempting as it may be, does not rest on the odd coincidence of the language of characters; if both understood their projects, in part, as a process of establishing "character," botanists and novelists did so within their own hermeneutic domains, and most likely without reference to each other. What is useful, however, about the linguistic confluence is the way it invites us to compare the descriptive tactics of botany with those of the realist novel, asking specifically whether the novel's mimetics depend, as did Linnaeus's, on a deliberately conceived structural limitation.

The marriage plot is a kind of structural limitation that is immediately apparent to any historian of the novel, especially those who wonder at and even bemoan the degree to which female experience in the classical British novel is adjudicated through that structure. The form limits its interest to characters whose age makes them candidates for the plot of marriage; children famously have no place in Austen's fiction. And unlike the multiplot narratives that would become ascendant in the mid–nineteenth century, the marriage plot focuses almost exclusively on a single person, or if you will, a single natural object. This node of narrative interest is routinely female, and routinely the age of the "marriageable girl." That she blooms, we know; the question one quickly gets to is the one that botanical classification has taught us: whether that structural limitation, the deliberate decision to eliminate everything except the terms of the description, achieves a full description, and what that description looks like.

The marriage plot, like Linnaeus's artificially contracted morphology, is equally committed to the elimination of elements that are peripheral to the main description. We can see this in the aforementioned absence of children, but more pointedly, in its persistent interest in the state *prior* to marriage, courtship, and not the long-term state of marriage itself.[46] For the most part, the marriages we see represented in any detail in Austen's novels are versions of failure—Mr. and Mrs. Bennet, Charlotte and Mr. Collins, the Bertrams—while in general Austen is more apt to create social configurations of marital absence (she is fond of parents who are widows and widowers). Not only does the marriage plot foreground the blooming girl and courtship but it also creates narrative conditions that make the representation of an established marriage less likely. We can see in the representational strategies of the marriage plot the structural limitations that Linnaeus placed on his classification scheme; in both, blooms are central.

Even when the reader of the marriage plot could reasonably expect an exception to its ways—in *Persuasion*, for instance, Anne Elliot seems beyond the blooming age at twenty-seven—the classificatory rigors of the marriage plot hold sway. Like Linnaeus's classification system, built to focus on the plant's sexual potential, the marriage plot focuses on the sexual potential of the marriageable girl. Anne is but a different, if related, species from the others; her "identities" can be noted as among the same grouping as the other blooming girls in Austen's body of work, but the differences are notable in that she is considerably older, and has bloomed already. That she blooms again makes her distinctive as a marriageable girl, and a distinctive (but not in the least anomalous or unreal) kind of natural entity.

Persuasion's place among Austen's novels as the most elaborately interested in the conditions of its heroine's blooming reminds us of the extent to which the mimesis of the "blooming girl" is almost naturalized out of our sights in other fiction; that is, we forget the degree to which that plot has radically delimited its object of description in order to achieve its mimetic aims. The blooming girl—whether Evelina, Elizabeth Bennet, or Hetty Sorrel—is almost always a specific plant in her own right: she is almost always around a certain very specific age, an age that with amazing regularity tends to be seventeen or nineteen years old. It is as if the novel's commitment to representing the girl's bloom is articulated by avoiding the clichéd peak age of eighteen, instead creating a sense of it being the general time, or season, of bloom. The marriage plot's representational goals are as deliberately delimited as Linnaeus's classification system; by focusing on a specific entity—the blooming girl, the flower—both are able to achieve their mimetic aims, aims that are, perhaps surprisingly, compellingly alike. If one makes a classification, while the other produces a narrative, both produce a vision of reality based on structures of sexual potential: the flower and the bloom.

Behind the dual representational projects of taxonomical botany and the novel is the desire to capture a world and to articulate it in what might be called recognizable categorizations of type, value, and purpose. The standard botanical handbook in England during the peak of Linnaean influence, *A Botanical Arrangement of all the Vegetables Naturally Growing in Great Britain* (1776), by William Withering, demonstrates how Linnaeus's system can be seen as organizing the natural and social worlds, and the demonstration is carried out in remarkably English ways. All the plants of Great Britain are "divisible . . . into twenty-four classes," Withering writes, and the vegetable kingdom is analogous to the kingdom of England in the following way:

Classes ——— to the Counties ———	Vegetables resemble Inhabitants
Orders ——— to the Hundreds ———	Classes resemble Nations
Genera ——— to the Parishes ———	Orders resemble Tribes
Species ——— to the Villages ———	Genera resemble Families
Varieties ——— to the Houses ———	Species resemble Individuals[47]

Withering's influential popularization of Linnaean botany purports to capture a broad reality (the entire indigenous flora of England) that relies on human social categories; the county, village, parish, and house are recognizable structures through which social reality is articulated. Here we might be reminded of Austen's fictions, and the degree to which the representational worlds of her fictions depend on the same classificatory hierarchy—individuals, or species, are represented within a broader scheme, that includes reference not only to the house one inhabits but also the village one lives in or near, the parish to which one belongs, and the county from which one came. (Characters whose references are vague, such as Wickham in *Pride and Prejudice* or Willoughby in *Sense and Sensibility*, are belatedly recognized as dangerous because of those imprecise facts.) The analogues on which Withering's botanical handbook depends suggest a way the late eighteenth-century classification of the natural world shares with the novel a joint impulse to capture a world and articulate it in recognizable ways.

Austen's novels share with botanical science a taxonomic logic. From this, necessarily abstract, vantage point one might say that the historical convergence of Austen's growth into a novelist, and the wide-scale dissemination of a new and scientific language for the natural world, is a telling confluence. Linnaeus's system contributed in no small part to the process of simplifying a description of the natural world and making it more precise. This was achieved primarily, as I have suggested, through the introduction of binomial nomenclature, which replaced long phrase descriptions with shortened biverbals—what this practically meant was that remembering the name of a plant was possible, for it was a vastly simplified name. The taxonomic shift that Linnaeus introduced through binomials reflected a twin desire—a desire that was both representational and scientific—to represent something as simultaneously within a broad inclusive system and individuated.[48] This method of description and representation was shared by the growing energies toward realism in the late eighteenth-century novel. Austen's blooming girls are represented through this taxonomic logic, as simultaneously part of a group or type of social person and an individual. A social entity going through an agreed-on set of normative actions appropriate to her grouping, and a private entity experiencing things as an individual, the blooming girl is, in a sense, a taxonomic construction. Thus Elizabeth Bennet, whose characterization on the most primary level is defined by this logic; she is of the age of bloom, and a "reputed beauty"—a grouping, or type, that coalesces around the fact that she is one of five sisters in the same position—but she is also uniquely individuated, rendered absolutely as one of her kind, so much so that the fact that she belongs within the broader grouping of the marriage-able girl is almost forgotten.

The blooming girl is the most profoundly taxonomic element of the novel because it is most directly borrowed from taxonomic science. The blooming girl is at the center of this study because she is the type in the novel whose representation is most dictated by taxonomic logic, for the blooming girl embodies the representational center of Linnaeus's classification system in being the character type most profoundly engaged in and defined by marriage. Put another way, one of my central postulates is that, as the most vivid instance of the novel's Linnaean energies, the blooming girl is most like the flower at the center of the Linnaean classification system—both represent potential sexual reproduction within the parameters of what Linnaeus and novelists alike call marriage. Blooms are at the center of Linnaean botany, and blooming in the marriage plot is integral to the way the sexual potential of marriage is foretold. The full articulation of both genres, in a sense, depends on the central principle of a bloom.

The Eighteenth Century: Occluded Blooms

If in Linnaeus's system the linkage between marriage and sexuality is patent, we might ask why that linkage has seemed more obscure to readers of the novel, why the potential sexual content of marriage has been emptied in our accounts of the courtship plot. Descriptions of that plot have too soon foreclosed on the obvious—that marriage in the late eighteenth and into the nineteenth century would mean the opportunity for licit sex and reproduction—in order to achieve a political or cultural understanding of marriage as an institution. In reopening these novels to the discursive context of Linnaeus, we are reminded that Linnaeus used the assumption that marriage and sexuality were synonymous as an explanatory device (and not, for instance, as a point of radical departure, such as Darwin's continuity between humans and apes). The broad diffusion and acceptance of his system give us a window into his age's naturalization of marriage and sex, and how clearly felt the association was between marriage and licit sexual potential.

Flowers in Linnaean botany are marriages; the classification system is the result of trying to describe various manifestations of marriage. That is, the narrative of marriage is *embedded within description*, since marriage is the general principle behind the many descriptions of various kinds of flowers. In the novel, likewise, marriage might be said to be the general principle behind the description of a specific kind of "flowering"—the blooming or flowering of the young girl in the grip of the courtship plot. Although we can imagine other kinds of flowerings, or growth, in the novel—most notably the (primarily male) *Bildungsroman*—the novelistic language of bloom is generally not used in the service of any character other than the blooming girl.[49] Neither David Copperfield nor Pip, to take two prominent nineteenth-century examples of *Bildung*, is said to bloom. Instead we see bloom used in a more strict Linnaean register, as a way primarily of describing that which occurs prior to marriage for young women and not as a general moniker for growth. Girls bloom because they are going to marry; it is the way the marriage plot earmarks them as the center of its narrative interest but, even more important, as the means through which the sexual dimension to courtship is narrated.

Like Linnaeus, so confident that his students of botany would understand the analogy of sexual potential in the terminological conflation of flowers and marriage that he based the coherence of his classification system on it, the novel assumes we understand the sexual potential behind bloom and the marriage that follows close on it. In the age of the botanical vernacular, flowers and marriages and blooms and blooming would have had a sexual content that is hard for us, living in an age when sexual potential and marriage are not consequentially linked, to recover. Linnaeus was able, in some respects, to equate plant sexuality and human sexuality in his classification because of a preexisting literary tradition that normalized the comparison, and literary representation in the wake of Linnaeus saw the effects of the botanical vernacular in its ability to connote (both more specifically and more licitly) sexual promise. Linnaeus's system teaches us the historically specific assumption of his age: a flower is to marriage as potential sex is to both.

The bloom of a girl, like the bloom of a plant, is a description of a potential and ephemeral sexual reproduction; it is both a description and a narrative, the state of flowering and the story of courtship. Bloom is, in other words, a vocabulary of the novel with the force of a narrative. Moreover, the girl "in bloom" is the novelistic figure that locates a *narratological* and a *poetic* concern. The narratological concern is the novel's marriage plot—*when* the girl blooms, or the sequence that occurs when blooming and marriageability coalesces, is the novel's strongest indicator of plot. That is, a girl's blooming suggests the quickening of the marriage plot as well as the particularities of that resolution (whom she will marry portended by whose presence she is said to bloom in). The poetic concern gets worked out upon the blooming girl, for *how* a girl blooms is a concern of description. The bloom figure, thus, not only refers to appearance but also indicates the specifics of the novel's resolution in marriage. For a heroine to bloom is for her to enter the trajectory of the marriage plot, since the look of sexual response and beauty that bloom describes is our best narrative indication that she is in the state leading to (the sexual potential of) marriage. Her bloom, like Linnaeus's blooms, is synonymous with marriage, which is a fact that is borne out in Austen's oeuvre, for only the heroines in the throes of the marriage plot are actually said to bloom.

Marriage and, perhaps most famously, the representation of attempted sexual exploits prior to marriage was of course an established topic in the classical novel by the mid–eighteenth century. But the difference is this: the diffusion of the flower's sexual content via Linnaean botany brings to the novel an acceptable (perhaps even scientific) vocabulary for representing the sexual dimension to licit courtships. In its pervasive, vernacularized abstraction from its morphological base (the corolla, or flower), bloom manages a legible substitution for sex. Within its previous plane of representation, the novel had been unable to narrate the sexual dimension to licit courtship, severing, as in Samuel Richardson's *Pamela*, erotic actions from the courtship leading to marriage. The bloom or flower, as a metonymy for sexual potential, is nonetheless able to be associated with a virginal girl. One could say that both have cultural meanings that benefit from the obscuring logic of substitution. Girls in novels can be said to bloom, and flowers can remain innocent figures, because the logic that exists at multiple levels of Linnaeus's classification system substitutes a more acceptable idea (a flower, a bloom) for the thing meant: potential sexual reproduction.[50]

The simultaneous legibility and obscurity of the sexual meaning of the flower in the Linnaean botanical vernacular can be seen explicitly in popular redactions of his botany. The aforementioned *Botanical Arrangement of all the Vegetables Naturally Growing in Great Britain*, by William Withering, eliminates references to botanical sex characteristics. In deference to the "Ladies," Withering thought it was "proper to drop the sexual distinctions in the titles to the Classes and Orders, and to adhere only to those of Number, Situation, &c."[51] His address to the "Ladies" suggests that women are expected to be among his readership, even though he is discussing sexual content. What is remarkable is the degree to which botanical terms are deemed potentially prurient; his solution is to substitute alternative words for the botanical, seemingly improper, ones, so that in his guide the word "chives" substitutes for the male "stamen" and "pointals" for the female "pistil." Withering's logic suggests that the botanical names of the flower's parts might be seen as improper, but not the parts themselves or the act of counting them for classificatory purposes. Withering's example helps us see that the flower did not have an ambiguous meaning, but rather a doubled one; like the pistil, which for propriety's sake had to be called a "pointal," the corolla needed to be censored in order to make it into a proper flower. The seeming inexplicability of the substitution is itself telling, for it reveals how removed we are from the age of the botanical vernacular.

As the Withering example suggests, flowers and their parts could literally signify sex in an age that was so aware of the sexual content of botany that it needed to censor its language for its most delicate practitioners.[52] And yet, as the example highlights, rather than retreating from the sexual content of the flower, the broad taking-up of Linnaean botany reproduced and disseminated the idea via its peculiar brand of metonymic substitution; that is, flowers substituted acceptably for sex. In the realm of the novel, the novelistic vocabulary of bloom is an instance of this substitution. In an age that worried that botanical vocabulary (stamens and pistils) would make a lady blush, yet offered that content to her in a different linguistic guise, the slippage among flowers, blooms, and "blooming" was characteristic. Furthermore, in an age that contained a popular impulse to attenuate the impropriety of stamens and pistils, the flower clearly had a new set of sexual significations. The flower had become an acceptable representation of sexuality, and novelistic bloom an acceptable allusion to both the sexual potential of flowers and the sexual content of human courtship.

Prior to the age of the botanical vernacular in England, bloom appeared in the eighteenth century novel to very different purpose, and without the occluding force of its subsequent Linnaean meanings. A striking part of Samuel Richardson's *Clarissa: or the History of a Young Lady* (1747–48) is the description of Clarissa's coffin, ordered by herself in advance of her death. Inscribed on the coffin are several emblems, including a crowned serpent, a winged hourglass, an urn, and a white lily. The specificity of the description of the white lily sets up its allegorical significance:

> Over this text is a white lily snapped short off, and just falling from the stalk; and this inscription over that, between the principal plate and the lily: *The days of man are but as grass. For he flourisheth as a flower of the field: for, as soon as the wind goeth over it, it is gone; and the place thereof shall know it no more.* Ps. Ciii, 15, 16.[53]

The broken white lily, like the other emblems and biblical texts on the coffin, is a pointed reference to Clarissa's narrative, its significance drawn from the convergence of their emblematic meanings and the specifics of her life. The white lily, snapped in half and falling from its stem, is understood as an allegory of Christ and Christ's sacrifice—an emblem meant to illuminate the nature of Clarissa's suffering at the hands of Lovelace. Exhorting John Belford to not "let the wonderful creature leave us, " Lovelace, in the letter that follows, linguistically refutes the possibility of the death Clarissa is preparing for: "But *nineteen*, Belford!—*nineteen* cannot so soon die of grief, if the doctor deserve that name; and so blooming and so fine a constitution as she had but three or four months ago!"[54] We see in these two examples, located in such close conjunction to each other, earlier and competing systems of signification around flowers and blooms; in the space of several short pages in this vast novel we see Clarissa employing the allegorical meaning of a lily and Lovelace employing a literal physical description of her person: a blooming and fine constitution. Just as Clarissa is asserting her impending spiritual state, Lovelace wants to assert in return her continuing physical state—just as she, in willing her death, wants to assert the ultimate importance of what has happened to her, and he, refuting her, asserts that it is "a *jest* . . . a mere jest to die for."[55]

In an example from early in the novel, Belford praises Clarissa but is strict about distinguishing between the intellectual and physical: "there is not of her age a finer woman in the world, as to her understanding. As for her person, she is at the age of bloom, and an admirable creature; a perfect beauty: but this *poorer* praise, a man, who has been honoured with her conversation, can hardly descend to give."[56] The praise of her physical person includes the dual claims that she is a perfect beauty and that she is of the "age of bloom," the latter suggesting that she is of the age (she is nineteen) to be beautiful if she is going to be. That her bloom is considered "poorer praise" than praise of her mental capacity and intelligence suggests that bloom references a purely physical attribute. The mid-eighteenth-century novel employs bloom as a physical description (both to denote health and physical attractiveness), but not until the vernacularization of Linnaean botany does the sexual implications of bloom become at once fully realized and fully licit in the novel.

Bloom does appear in the early eighteenth-century novel—the later dissemination of Linnaeus does not prompt the introduction of the word *bloom* into the novel, for bloom as novelistic language prior preexists Linnaeus, as do a set of longstanding floral metaphors. Rather, as we see with this example from *Clarissa*, bloom has a meaning in the early novel that is associated with pure physical description and even illicit sexuality. The early eighteenth-century novel inherits a literary history that associates the floral with innocent sexuality. There is obviously a long literary tradition, both religious and secular, that draws on this figurative relation, including—in a sweeping effort to survey one of the most general of literary tropes—the *Song of Songs*, the poetry of Ovid and Milton, Chaucer's allegorical *Romance of the Rose*, and many of Shakespeare's plays.[57] It was this acceptable representational state that Camerarius's 1694 discovery of the sexual function of the flower encountered. In some sense, the analogy Linnaeus draws between the flower's sexual reproduction and human sexual reproduction is acceptable because of that prior referential range; girls can botanize, despite the explicitness of Linnaeus's sexual system, because flowers are suitable figures. If Western literature had been prophetic about the sexuality of flowers, it took the scientific discovery of that fact and its broad dissemination through Linnaeus's system to turn bloom into a reference of (licit) sexual potential, and not just physicality.

To turn closer to home, in Henry Fielding's *Tom Jones* (1749) Sophia's beauty is described through that established referential range—the proverbial literary trope of the lily and the rose: "Her Complexion had rather more of the Lily than of the Rose; but when Exercise, or Modesty, encreased her natural Colour, no Vermillion could equal it."[58] *Joseph Andrews* (1742) employs a similar register in relation to Joseph as well as his bride Fanny; in its satirizing of the plot of threatened female virtue, Joseph is described in feminine terms: at twenty-one, he has "wanton ringlets down his back," lips that are "full, red, and soft," and "cheeks, in which the blood glowed."[59] In the novel's final pages, when Joseph's long-threatened virtue is finally rewarded in marriage, the register switches to Fanny, "his blooming bride," who when undressed for the wedding night is described in terms almost exactly like those used for Sophia in *Tom Jones*: "the bloom of roses and lilies might a little illustrate her complexion, or their smell her sweetness: but to comprehend her entirely, conceive youth, health, bloom, beauty, neatness, and innocence." Fanny's floral complexion is a sexual promise that is quickly satisfied in the novel's final turn: "Joseph no sooner heard she was in bed, than he fled with the utmost eagerness to her."[60] Here, the proverbial roses and lilies combine with an emergent novelistic bloom that is able, under the umbrella of satire, to imagine marriage as the site of sexual excitement.

By the age of the botanical vernacular the novelistic vocabulary of bloom was thoroughly revised by the Linnaean association of flowers and licit sexuality or marriage. As the example of *Clarissa* shows, the early and mid-eighteenth-century novel, prior to the age of the botanical vernacular in England, bloom appeared in novels as a sign of physicality, and more particularly a kind of illicit sexuality denuded of marital reference. In fact, its earliest formations—in Samuel Richardson's *Pamela, or Virtue Rewarded* (1740) and John Cleland's *Memoirs of a Woman of Pleasure* (1748–49)—manifest the association between sexuality and bloom more profoundly than later novels in which bloom's blatant sexual connotations have been acceptably occluded. The novels of Samuel Richardson, where one might think to turn when considering the subject of a sexualized courtship and marriage, do not represent bloom as a socialized erotics. Richardson's use of the word is descriptive rather than narratological; the bloom of a face is a sign of physical beauty, not an indication, as it will become in Austen, that the heroine has entered the marriage plot's resolution. In *Pamela* bloom is such a marker of illicit sexuality that it is used in the context of a slur; appearing but once, Pamela's bloom is referred to in a late moment in Mr. B— 's seduction:

> You have been told, I suppose, that you are *most* beautiful in your tears!—Did you ever, said he, to *her* (who all this while was standing in one corner of the parlor,) see a more charming creature than this? Is it to be wondered at, that I demean myself thus to take notice of her?—See, said he, and took the glass with one hand, and turned me round with the other, what a shape! what a neck! what a hand! and what a bloom on that lovely face!—.[61]

The context of his utterance is one of many physical assaults; angry and jealous on discovering she has been corresponding with a parson, he grabs her, directly comments on her body, calls her a "hussy" and "intriguing little slut," and then tries to force himself on her: he kisses her and "would have put his hand into [her] bosom." The invocation of bloom in *Pamela* occurs in a litany of physical comments on her body—shape, neck, hand, bloom, face—that suggests bloom here refers to a purely physical, even sexual, quality. Mr. B— 's verbal and physical assault occurs just prior to his written offer to make her his mistress; that offer is a direct reference to a nonmarital sexual relationship, for in addition to his threat that she "is already in my power," he offers an advance of money, a life annuity, family patronage, and a clothing allowance. The blatancy with which his illicit sexual attraction is brought to light by this scene brings the meaning of bloom close to the pornographic.

The meaning of bloom in *Pamela* resonates with the context in which bloom is employed in the contemporaneous underground best-seller, Cleland's *Memoirs of a Woman of Pleasure*. In this book the descriptive language of bloom is employed by the heroine herself as she remembers her youthful physicality, sexual attractiveness, and virginity: "I sat pensive by the fire, with my

eyes brimming with tears, my neck still bare, and my cap fall'n off in the struggle, so that my hair was in the disorder you may guess, the villain's lust began, I
suppose to be again in flow, at the sight of all that bloom of youth which presented itself to his view, a bloom yet unenjoy'd."[62] The scene, in which her
virginity is being offered up for sale, takes place when she is fifteen; the "bloom
of youth" is a description of her physical body (she is naked in the scene),
specifically her virginity, for she has fought off the man who has bought her
for the evening, leaving her virginity intact. Fanny Hill's willingness, of
course, increases exponentially as she describes her life of pleasure; by the time
we get to the second volume, she is just about to turn eighteen, the age at
which we learn she has fully bloomed. Happily employed in an upscale
brothel, Fanny describes herself as she supposes herself to be seen by the men
and women watching her, as the group is cooperatively engaged in watching
each pair of lovers have sex: "I could not appear a very disagreeable figure, if
you please to recollect what I have before said of my person, which time, that
at certain periods of life, robs us every instant of our charms, had, at that of
mine, then greatly improv'd into full and open bloom, for I wanted some
months of eighteen."[63] The reader is positioned to look at her, just as the
group is doing in the room as she displays herself for view; what her bloom
consists of is detailed after a colon, as if all the physical description is an elaboration, as well as an enumeration, of "full and open bloom":

> Then greatly improv'd into full and open bloom, for I wanted some
> months of eighteen: my breasts which in the state of nudity are ever
> capital points, now in no more than grateful plenitude, maintained a
> firmness and steady independence of any stay or support . . . Then I
> was as tall, as slim-shaped as could be consistent with all that juicy
> plumpness of flesh, ever the most grateful to the senses of sight and
> touch, which I owed to the health and youth of my constitution.[64]

Her full bloom, like her breasts or her flesh, is a description of a sexual quality;
once "inflammatory liberties" ensue, Fanny's bloom turns into the action that
the word implies— sexual response, or a "glow" that builds to "desire":

> My friend . . . humoured their curiosity, and perhaps his own, so far
> that he placed me in all the variety of postures and lights imaginable,
> pointing out every beauty under every aspect of it, not without such
> parentheses of kisses, such inflammatory liberties of his roving hands,
> as made all shame fly before them, and a blushing glow give place to a
> warmer one of desire, which led me even to find some relish in the
> present scene.[65]

Bloom refers pointedly in *Memoirs* to the potential of sexual pleasure; like the
"virgin-flower" that Fanny lost earlier to her lover Charles, and then loses
repeatedly in performances as a virgin-prostitute, bloom draws on a preexisting typology that had long popularly called virginity a flower "yet uncrop'd"

and thought of flowering or bloom as the height of youthful sexual attractiveness.[66]

The prurient realism that the genre of erotica encourages links bloom with the quality of complexion proper to both the perfection of her age and the peak of her sexual excitement. In contrast, in *Pamela* for Mr. B— to speak of Pamela's bloom is to pronounce an insult, for in the context of a text about the trials of female innocence, a reference to a sexual beauty is an impropriety. Unlike *Pamela*, and the sentimental tradition more generally, the literary impulse in Cleland's novel is to celebrate sexuality rather than invoke it in order to cancel it. If in *Pamela* bloom is an insult uttered by the yet-to-be-reformed rake, and in *Memoirs* bloom is a compliment of an approving narrative, both uses of bloom refer to the sexual appearance of the heroine's complexion.

What Cleland's novel, like Richardson's two novels, demonstrates is that bloom was a novelistic vocabulary prior to the age of Linnaeus and that this usage was not necessarily original, for the meaning of bloom in these novels depends on preexisting popular typologies of flowers, girls, and sexual attractiveness. The systems of signification that inform the novelistic language of bloom are thus both literary and nonliterary and in some sense defy the attempt to find an original precedent. In these midcentury novels, though, we can detect a profound difference in the way bloom is used from that of the late eighteenth-century novels. In the midcentury novel bloom is characteristically a physical reference, or even an explicitly sexual reference, with blooming functioning, at best, as a lexicon for physical attractiveness, and in its extreme manifestations as a slur or a pornographic reference.

As late as Frances Burney's 1778 novel *Evelina*, for a character to speak about a woman's bloom is to hazard offending a delicate sensibility. We see in this the remaining traces of the preexisting vocabulary of bloom; for instance, at a ball at which Evelina unwittingly insults a man by refusing to dance with him, she gets insulted in turn: "'how conscious you must be, all beautiful that you are, that those charming airs serve only to heighten the bloom of your complexion!' 'Your freedom, Sir, where you are more acquainted, may perhaps be less disagreeable; but to me—.'"[67] Later, Sir Clement reads sexual availability from the color of her complexion: "my dearest life," cried he, "is it possible that you can be so cruel? Can your nature and your countenance be so totally opposite? Can the sweet bloom upon those charming cheeks, which appears as much the result of good-humor as beauty—."[68] Sir Clement's reference to her "sweet bloom" implies a conflation of subjectivity and coloring that becomes contained in the word *bloom*; his assumption is that her coloring implies a disposition that will welcome his erotic advances.[69] In another instance, Lovel intentionally insults Evelina by implying that her innocence is adopted, her blush really rouge: "oh, my Lord, if health were the only cause of a lady's bloom, my eye, I grant, had been infallible from the first glance, but—."[70] That it is an insult is manifest from the reaction of Lord Orville, the novel's paragon of gentlemanliness and Evelina's eventual suitor, who threatens a duel over Lovel's imputation. And yet the insult, unlike in *Pamela*, seems less dependent on bloom's being a slur and more on the suggestion that Evelina has used cosmetics to achieve the appearance of bloom. Clearly, like the use in the mid-eighteenth-century novel, bloom here is about physical description, but it is not so clearly a salacious remark.

The difference in *Evelina* is that bloom is being contextualized within a plot of marriage, for the bloom on Evelina's cheeks that the other men comment on is the same bloom that Orville responds to in his courtship of her, even to the extent of offering to defend her honor when the reality of her bloom (hence her innocence) is questioned. In *Pamela*, references to Pamela's physical person drop out of the narrative once Mr. B— decides to marry her, while in *Evelina*, the blushing, blooming body of Evelina remains present throughout the text. The system of signification around bloom has changed: Evelina's bloom, to Orville and the reader, signs both innocent marriageability and implied sexual potential. What had changed in the interval between Richardson and Burney to set in motion the socialization of the bloom figure? What had transpired were the broad vernacularization of Linnaean botany in England, and its taxonomical intertwining of "natural" and "social" worlds. The midcentury novel's use of bloom as pure physical and even erotic description gives way in the late eighteenth century to a novelistic vocabulary that has denuded bloom of its illicit connotations. *Evelina*, in a sense, embodies the transition that the classical novel is undergoing; if bloom is, in several instances, employed as an inappropriate physical comment, it also inspires, in the proper context of the courtship plot, Evelina's suitor to her defense (and eventually to the altar).

The occlusion of the preexisting meanings of bloom in the midcentury novel was due to the naturalizing effect that Linnaean botany had on the sexual content of the inherited typologies of flowers, blooms, and related flowerings. What the science does is socialize the sexual content of the flower into an acceptable taxonomy of marriage, which normalizes, even sanitizes, the illicit sexual content—a process that does not take the sex out of flowers but oddly makes that fact more legible and general. The late eighteenth-century novel undergoes a concurrent change; informed by competing systems of signification, the novelistic vocabulary of bloom is nevertheless perceptibly altered by the broad acceptance of Linnaean representation. The Linnaean system made bloom a safe lexicon for the novel, one that held in tension both the sexual reference of a bloom and its potential insertion into a "proper" plot of marriage, for it was the Linnaean sexual system that brought this tension (between sex and marriage) into a prominent sphere of representation. In an odd twist of literary poetics and scientific practice, the rendering-visible of sexual content by the science was more acceptable to what was becoming increasingly recognizable as the realist novel than the implied sexuality of the earlier referential range. In this way the taxonomies of Linnaeus begat the representational possibilities of the later eighteenth-century novel. Thus the purely physical or even erotic blooms of Richardson and Cleland metamorphose into the sexually licit bloom of the classical novel's courtship plot.

Toward the Nineteenth Century: The Bloom Narrative

From the welter of late eighteenth-century manifestations and uses of Linnaean botany, the systematics of bloom takes up specific residence and finds space for development within the English novel of the nineteenth century. At this point bloom develops its own formal properties, its own generic contours, and its own laws that operate independently of the nineteenth century's developments in botanical and biological sciences. This is most evident in the literary criticism of Henry James, whose reflections on the Anglo-American novel establishes a critical tradition about the blooming girl that in turn becomes part of the narrative's history. James's backward-turned critical lens provides an illuminating end to bloom's literary development in the nineteenth century and thus is a useful introduction to the arc of this book's overall argument.

James's literary criticism is famous for its self-consciousness about the history of the novel in its varied incarnations, so it is perhaps not surprising that this great reader of the English novel noticed and wrote about the novelistic type of the blooming girl—a type that he calls the girl going through the "blooming season."[71] In his embrace of Eliot's example, and his distancing of his own portraits from the supposedly insufficiently differentiated girls of Trollope, James finds one of his own most compelling subjects. For James, she is the inexhaustible and inevitable subject for the novel, inevitable because the history of the novel with which he is concerned takes her as its *donnée*: "the girl hovers, inextinguishable, as a charming creature, and the job will be to translate her into the highest terms of that formula, and as nearly as possible moreover into *all* of them" (*FW/P,* 1079–80).

This sleight-of-hand manifesto is from the preface to the New York Edition of *The Portrait of a Lady,* in which he asserts his belief in "the value recognized in the mere young thing" (*FW/P,* 1078). James sees the "mere young thing" as a compelling subject deriving from Eliot and the novelistic tradition: "it is an example exactly of the deep difficulty braved—the difficulty of making George Eliot's 'frail vessel,' if not the all-in-all for our attention, at least the clearest of the call" (*FW/P,* 1078–9). But James will conceive of his mission as an alteration of this tradition, specifically in *Portrait of a Lady,* by bypassing the traditional narrative mode of placing weight on the surrounding (male) characters' relation to the girl and instead placing the "center of the subject in the young woman's consciousness . . . her relation to herself" (*FW/P,* 1079). James is aware that the young woman or girl is not an altogether new subject but rather an alteration of an established subject, in the novel. He explores the possibilities of reviving this trope, through an intensified consciousness that can best be termed a *self-consciousness* about the effect of prior novelistic representations of the blooming girl on the very reality his novels otherwise seek to reimagine.

Although it is the legacy of George Eliot's bravery in writing of her "Hettys and Maggies and Rosamonds and Gwendolens" that James cites as a model for his own artistic labor, he seems to identity the stereotype of bloom most clearly in Trollope (*FW/P*, 1078). His tone toward Trollope is generally one of condescension; James writes that Trollope is "trustworthy" if not "eloquent," a writer whose novels will long be available for "readers with an eye to that sort of entertainment" (*EW,* 1353). In this piece, written for *Century* magazine in 1883, James makes his awareness of the blooming type evident; he writes of Trollope's proclivity for writing of a "simple maiden in her flower," for the "British maiden under innumerable names," for "Trollope's girls," who—with the exception of Eleanor Bold, who "is not in her flower"—have a "strong family likeness" (*EW,* 1350). In contrast to these girls, Trollope's spinsters are characterized as not blooming: "but the young women I have mentioned had ceased to belong to the blooming season; they had entered the bristling, or else the limp, period" (*EW,* 1350). The blooming season is reserved for his "girls," characters who are distinguished by their very uniformity and whose simplicity of character is mimicked in James's unusually paratactic prose:

> She is always definite and natural. She plays her part most properly. She has always health in her cheek and gratitude in her eye. She has not a touch of the morbid, and is delightfully tender, modest and fresh. Trollope's heroines have a strong family likeness, but it is a wonder how finely he discriminates between them. One feels, as one reads him, like a man with "sets" of female cousins. Such a person is inclined at first to lump each group together; but presently he finds that even in the groups there are subtle differences. (*EW*, 1350)

The condescension is not total here. In a list structure, James checks off the elements of the now-familiar trope—her "natural" qualities, the "health in her cheek," the "gratitude in her eye," her "tender," "modest," and "fresh" contours—but he is willing to allow that even typologizing allows for some "subtle differences" (*EW*, 1350). However James might commend Trollope for his subtlety though, his mock-reverent tone here undercuts his praise and contributes to the mood of general condescension. James's characterization of the whole of Trollope's oeuvre after *Barchester Towers* revolves around his claim that there is little that is erotic in Trollope's girls: "Trollope settled down steadily to the English girl; he took possession of her, and turned her inside out . . . he bestowed on her the most serious, the most patient, the most tender, the most copious consideration. He is evidently more or less in love with her" (*EW*, 1349–50). According to James, Trollope is a "paternal lover" to each of his girls, all of whom he makes "affectionate," both of which are rather subtle ways of indicating the lack of eroticism James detected in reading about these girls of the blooming season. For James, Trollope's characterizations of girls are so repetitive as to become a typology: girls who belong to the blooming season but who are generally so undifferentiated that they cease to be individually attractive.

The service James provides us here, and the reason for my attention to James's treatment of a noted rival, is his unwitting explanation of why Trollope is not a significant heir to what I have been calling the bloom narrative. Trollope's girls of the blooming season seem to have all the physical and mental attributes of the blooming girls in Austen, but by the time Trollope has taken his turn at them, the trope has ossified into a typology—one that does not get reworked, as I will show, until George Eliot revisits it through the altering lens of the clandestine bloom plot. Trollope's novels are thus not bloom narratives, since the blooming girl has been reduced to a typology, and bloom lacks a narratological function in relation to the marriage plot; Trollope evolved a different kind of courtship novel that has little to with the eroticized courtship plots of Austen, Eliot, and James. What James's criticism registers is the degree to which bloom had become a literary convention by midcentury, a shorthand for a certain character type, and not, as it had been in Austen's or even in Eliot's revivified (clandestine) bloom plots, a way of indicating the sexual potential of marriage. This is an idea I will explore in depth in chapter 4. If James seems to point to Trollope as a paradigmatic practitioner of blooming girls, he does so from the perspective of an author who, when describing how he approached the writing of *Portrait of a Lady* and the depiction of a young woman, thought "what better field could there be for a due ingenuity?" (*FW/P,* 1079). This study will not take up Trollope's courtship novels, but one could adduce Lily Dale from *The Small House at Allington,* Mary Lowther from *The Vicar of Bullhampton,* or even such relevant Dickensian examples as *Oliver Twist*'s Rose Maylie, *David Copperfield*'s Dora Copperfield, *Bleak House*'s Ada Clare, or the parodic example of *Little Dorrit*'s Flora Finching. This list, with its characteristic sprinkling of botanical first names, provides an excellent glimpse of the standardization of the blooming heroine that James will read, and reactivate, with his critical understanding of them as cultural clichés. That the marriageable girl had become a type seems the very reason James takes up the challenge of representing her. In this sense, *Portrait of a Lady* is a formal response to his feeling "almost as a pang the beautiful incentive" to write about the "mere young thing" (*FW/P,* 1079).

James finds a significant precedent for the blooming heroine in Eliot, not Trollope. In writing about *Middlemarch,* James's praise for the characterization of Dorothea intuits the narrative of bloom: "her heroines have always been of an exquisite quality, and Dorothea is only that perfect flower of conception of which her predecessors were the less unfolded blossoms" (*EW,* 959). James's praise for Rosamond Vincy further emphasizes his language characterizing Dorothea's bloom, for Rosamond is contrasted to Dorothea using a botanical analogy: "the author's rare psychological penetration is lavished upon this veritably mulish domestic flower" (*EW,* 963). Dorothea is the perfect bloom, while Rosamond is a domestic flower, a sterile hybrid—a mule. That James seems to understand, if not name, the bloom narrative, and zeroes in on Eliot's novels in doing so, points to an important fact about the nineteenth-century literary history of bloom. The lineage of Eliot to James is one that James himself claims when describing *Portrait*, in effect creating a genealogy that recognizes that certain novelists abjured the subject of the marriageable girl: for "many an expert painter, as for instance Dickens and Walter Scott . . . [or] R. L. Stevenson, has preferred to leave the task unattempted" (*FW/P*, 1077). James is right: neither Scott nor Dickens performed precise taxonomic descriptions of the single heroine in the throes of the marriage plot, which speaks to why several more important practitioners of the novel in the nineteenth century are not represented in this study.

Furthermore, although the bloom narrative is specific to the marriage plot, even then its history is not static, except in the sense that the force of repetition changes the fields of signification that bloom had in the late eighteenth and into the nineteenth century. A sustained attention to the development of this narrative in three paradigmatic examples—Austen, Eliot, James—will best demonstrate the importance of bloom to the classical British novel, although a corresponding analysis of the cultural force of the botanical vernacular is a necessary precondition to a study of this lineage. In Austen's novels bloom is the primary way in which the sexual potential of marriage is narrated within the parameters of licit courtship—in Linnaean terms, the "public" marriages, or visible flowerings, of girls in the throes of the marriage plot. Eliot's novels—*Adam Bede* and *Middlemarch*, especially—reinvigorate the bloom narrative by situating sexual courtship outside the probable parameters of marriage. In both *Adam Bede* and *Middlemarch*, Eliot is formally innovative in exploring "second blooms," thereby making the associations of bloom with virginity or youth less hard. Both novels successfully broaden their subject matter beyond the confines of the traditional marriage plot, but *Middlemarch* returns the topic of the sexual potential of marriage first through a marriage's failure and then through renewed courtship. Eliot inaugurates the formal innovation of the bloom narrative that James would continue, albeit in a much more self-conscious manner; the increasing self-consciousness about the representational history of the girl is part of the increasing decadence of the trope. In his oeuvre given over to the marriageable girl—most prominently *Portrait of a Lady*, *Wings of the Dove*, and *The Awkward Age*—James writes about courtship and female maturation as social processes defined by literary (even, more specifically, novelistic) history. In James's novels girls do not simply bloom; the dominant narrative question becomes how a girl should *be*—or, more specifically in *Portrait of a Lady*, "what will she *do*?"—in the face of her representational history. James's formal innovations away from the inherited typology do not suggest a wholesale rejection of the plot but rather an innovation in which the narrative is most interested in the cultural effect of the (nineteenth-century) novel's representation of female type.

The literary history that will be traced here is one that outlines the following above all: how a field of signification becomes a literary narrative. In foregrounding a single word in trying to analyze the evolving mechanics of the courtship plot across the nineteenth century, this project tries to account for how sexual attraction, an aspect of courtship not literally alluded to within the parameters of the classical novel but the presence of which has been sensed by many readers, gets represented. In tracing the history of the bloom narrative we begin in botanical science and we move to a vocabulary of the novel in order to better understand a mimetic property and formal development of the novel. Switching radically between two scales of representation—the single word, and an entire narrative—the meanings of bloom are revealed.

TWO

Imaginative Literature and the Politics of Botany

For me, content to decipher in your wake some words in the pages

of the vegetable realm, I read you, I study you, I meditate upon you,

I honor you, and I love you with all my heart.

—J. J. Rousseau to Linnaeus, September 21, 1771

Having retreated to the Island of Saint-Pierre in 1765 after being stoned at Môtiers, Jean-Jacques Rousseau, while in "the first flush of enthusiasm for botany," sets himself the task of composing a flora for the entire island.[1] As Rousseau recollects in his *Rêveries du promeneur solitaire* (1778), "every morning after breakfast . . . I would set out with a magnifying glass in my hand and my *Systema Naturae* under my arm." Rousseau begins a course of study that is explicitly scientific, yet this botanizing creates in him an unusually heightened emotional response: "nothing could be more extraordinary than the raptures and ecstasies I felt at every discovery I made about the structure and organization of the plants and the operation of the sexual parts in the process of reproduction."[2] Rousseau's unique conflation of botanical practice and literary feeling seems to be inspired, oddly enough, by an encyclopedic index—Linnaeus's *Systema Naturae* being the cherished accoutrement of his solitary walks. The strangeness of the implied comparison invites the question: how can nature, at least for Rousseau, bear so effortlessly the observational eye of the scientist and the emotional reaction of the Romantic philosopher? If it seems strange to us today that the structure and organization of plants could elicit rapture, it perhaps tells us how far removed we are from the ecstasy of watching a plant's "sexual parts in the process of reproduction." The late eighteenth century's botanical vernacular could bear, in other words, a range of feeling wider than one might immediately suspect.

Rousseau's botanical ecstasies were not unique in the late eighteenth century, but his heightened expression and assertion of botany's palliative effect do make his voice unmistakable:

It is the chain of accessory ideas that make me love botany. It brings together and recalls to my imagination all the images which most charm it: meadows, waters, woods, solitude and above all the peace and tranquility which one can find in these places—all of this it instantly conjures up before my memory. It makes me forget the persecutions of men, their hate, their scorn, their insult and all the evil deeds with which they have repaid my sincere and loving attachment to them . . . and very often it makes me happy even now, amidst the most miserable fate ever endured by mortal man.[3]

The systematic study of botany brings Rousseau closer to nature and enables the process of memory, and thought, that inspires the *Rêveries*, his final literary work. What seems particularly significant is that Rousseau, roaming "nonchalantly from plant to plant and flower to flower," is caught up in a reverie that is also a scientific project, comparing "characteristics," "similarities and differences," and "studying the organization" of plants:

Bright flowers, adornment of the meadows, cool shades, streams, woods and green glades, come and purify my imagination of these hideous images . . . only sensation is left me, and it alone can now bring me pleasure or pain in this world. Attracted by the charming objects that surround me, I look at them, observe them carefully, compare them, and eventually learn to classify them, and lo and behold, I am as much of a botanist as anyone needs to be who only wants to study nature in order to discover ever new reasons for loving her.[4]

The separation we habitually create between empirical science and psychological inwardness is not reflected by Rousseau's writing; in fact, the process of classification is a panacea, first as a substitution for academic work and then as an agent of purification for his imagination.

The connection that Rousseau's work makes between the process of botanizing and the experience of emotion is part of a broader extrapolation from botany played out on other late eighteenth-century stages. Most notably, the question of whether botany induced feelings of modesty or immodesty was a topic that went to the heart of many late-century concerns about female life. Rousseau's botanical ecstasy, as he represented it for himself, was unproblematic, but the young girl's pleasure in the botanical examination of a flower would become a fulcrum around which debates about female education were waged. When faced with the question of whether the sexual knowledge imparted by botany was appropriate for young girls, Rousseau took a more careful position. In *Lettres élémentaires sur la botanique*—an elementary text about botany, it went into eight editions after having been translated into English in 1785 by Thomas Martyn, the holder of the chair in botany at Cambridge—Rousseau suggests that his addressee (his cousin, Madeleine-Catherine Delessert) reveal the intimate "mysteries" of nature to her young daughter only at her discretion. When describing the naked sexual organs of the lily, he advises her that "you will not start by telling all this to your daughter, and still less subsequently when you will be initiated into the mysteries of vegetation; but you will develop in her by degrees only what can suit her age and sex in guiding her to find things by herself rather than by teaching them to her."[5] He believed that botany was more appropriate for women than zoology because, as he wrote, of the "great advantage that plants do not bleed."[6] *Lettres* is a serious introduction to the study of botany but one that is marked by a more conventional rhetoric about the continuity between plants and femininity: "I picture to myself a charming scene with my beautiful cousin busy with her glass, taking apart heaps of flowers a hundred times less flourishing, less fresh, and less agreeable than herself."[7] Indeed, despite his seriousness of purpose in *Lettres*, Rousseau is also resolute that women not undertake the more theoretical and abstract aspects of botany, just as he was adamant that women did not have the capacity for the "exact sciences."[8]

The kind of ecstasy that Rousseau describes having experienced in the field perhaps lay behind much of the concern of conservative writers about Linnaean botany. The botanical vernacular would assimilate this and other discussions about botany, modesty, and sexuality and would in turn reflect those connotations back onto botany and its cognate fields. The increasing sense that botany was gendered female solidified the semantic connections among botany, blooms, and girls, even as it eventually drove apart professional and amateur interests in botany and contributed to the professional demise of the Linnaean system by the 1830s. In the late eighteenth century, though, the set of meanings about botany and botanical practice were forming, and it is to those processes, both literary and polemic, that we should turn to understand the botanical vernacular in its emergent stages.

Botany's Gendered Controversies

The botanical vernacular that came into being in the late eighteenth century perhaps can be best sensed in the polemical debates of the 1790s about the nature and rights of women. Rousseau was not alone in discussing the relation between botany and proper female behavior; in England a number of intellectuals invoked botany in relation to issues of female education and the charged topic of modesty. The age's notable controversialists, including Mary Wollstonecraft and Hannah More, discussed botany in their writings; the subject became a way that contestations about the role of women in a time of political upheaval could be adjudicated. Richard Polwhele, a virulent anti-Jacobin polemicist, used botany as a means of attacking Wollstonecraft personally and revolutionary sentiments more generally, while Erasmus Darwin made botany part of his progressive efforts for female education.[9] Although these thinkers represent the spectrum of political positions, each engages botany as both topic and anecdote, as a subject in itself and as the means to discuss a broader subject; their invocations imply a commonly understood cultural debate, or a shared consciousness, surrounding the botanical.

Since Linnaean botany had become a prevalent, and even popular, pastime in England from the 1770s, what is then notable about these invocations of the science in the 1790s is that they suggest the extent to which botany had become a cultural touchstone. Political writers assumed botany was a topic of general understanding and significance, and the currency of botany, in combination with the sexual language that formed its classification system, made botany a topic through which questions of social and sexual import could be discussed. By invoking a science that centered around the sexual characteristics of plants, writers concerned with the social issue of human sexuality could state their views with the impunity granted to the rational pursuit of science.

Common to the many kinds of discourses that explicitly or implicitly invoke botany in the late eighteenth century is the invocation of crises in meaning around gender roles and sexuality; the flower's very semantic volubility attracted opposing cultural and political positions. Botany's status as a rational and healthy pursuit shielded it from absorbing any one political connotation. For instance, a number of British naturalists in the eighteenth century were Quakers, for botany was considered a useful and therefore permissible recreation for them.[10] And yet botany could be employed in the service of radical agendas, as in the case of Erasmus Darwin's narrative poem *Loves of Plants* (1789), which shows how various sexual arrangements, such as monogamy, are arbitrary rather than natural social states.[11]

The specific concerns of various writers invoking botany in the late eighteenth century were wide ranging, and their political positions were equally diverse: both radical and conservative writers took up botany for their cause. In fact, opposing sides on issues as complicated as female education, female citizenship, and democratic revolution invoked botany as a good. If the Linnaean system had at first alarmed the sensibilities of such figures as William Smellie and Johann Siegesbeck, by 1790 thinkers as conservative as Hannah More and as radical as Mary Wollstonecraft recruited botany in the service of their respective political agendas. Indeed the morality of the act of botanizing became part of a broader debate about morality: was botany a modest or immodest inquiry? Did botany enable the reverent study of nature or a radical social agenda? Around the issue of female education the debate was particularly clear, for conservatives maintained that the reverent study of plants was conducive to traditional female sensibility, while more radical writers suggested botany could help challenge antiquated notions of female propriety. For conservatives botany could signify a kind of modesty associated with a traditional position for women, while for radicals it could express a kind of sexual legibility associated with an emergent, liberated position for women. For botany to represent such opposing images around the issue of modesty is a sign of how the flower did not have an ambiguous meaning but rather a doubled one, in the age of the botanical vernacular—and perhaps how bloom became such a compelling figure for the classical novel.

That this was a contest over the rhetorical domain of such a popular science became clear in arguments between revolutionary sympathizers and anti-Jacobin thinkers. As Claudia Johnson has argued, the discourse around revolutionary politics in the 1790s was often rhetorically linked to "proper sentiments of sex."[12] Johnson notes that one way the anti-Jacobin rhetoric worked was to assail the modesty of women supporting the progressive cause by mocking their attitude toward botany. In Richard Polwhele's poem *Unsex'd Females* (1798), he attacks Wollstonecraft's idea that botany was a way to eradicate the false delicacy of girls by referring to her method as mere "Instructions in Priapism." Polwhele's virulent response to Wollstonecraft's proposal that botany could teach sexuality is telling in that it does not condemn the Linnaean system but rather Wollstonecraft's interpretation of Linnaean botany; in Polwhele's formulation, Wollstonecraft's desire to use the Linnaean system to instruct girls in sexuality is a perversion of the inherent modesty implicit in botany. Polwhele's *Unsex'd Females* avoids condemning botany and the study of nature by locating shamelessness in immodest female perception: "with bliss botanic as their bosoms heave / still pluck the forbidden fruit with mother Eve / For puberty in sighing florets pant / Or paint to the prostitution of a plant / Dissect its organ of unhallow'd lust / And fondly gaze at the titillating dust."[13] It is "puberty" that "pants" through the flower, the gaze of the heaving bosoms that makes the "dust" (a term for pollen, the plant's male emission) "titillating." Botanic here becomes a synonym for sexual, and it is that—the knowledge of sexual bliss—which Polwhele sees as incompatible with female modesty. Polwhele furthermore attacks those who would "paint," that is, *perceive* plants as sexual by suggesting that those who see them that way are oversexed ("with bliss botanic"). Thus, from the logic of Polwhele's poem—the logic of *Honi soit qui mal y pense*, which is, of course, a charge that can rebound against its user—it is no wonder that these oversexed girls see "puberty" in flowers, prostitution in a plant, and "unhallow'd lust" in the scientific dissection of a flower. Polwhele's poetry seeks to deflect attention from the sexuality implicit in the system on to the perception of radical women, for, as Wollstonecraft had deftly reasoned, to condemn the science would be to acknowledge that social notions of modesty were not grounded in enlightened religious thinking.

What Polwhele saw as Wollstonecraft's "impropriety" was the fact already implicit in the science of botany itself, which had initially elicited concern, even censure, from earlier conservative religious thinkers: that the prevailing Linnaean botany was a sexual system, a system that when practiced required the practitioner to pay close attention to the sexual parts of plants. Wollstonecraft made an explicit case out of what was implicitly known, but not stated, in the age of the botanical vernacular: for a young lady to practice Linnaean botany is for her to pay intimate attention to plant reproduction. The only suggestion of discomfort around this fact seems to have been restricted to the occasional decision by a redactor to substitute new, more "modest" language for the botanical terms *stamen* and *pistil*. Flowers came to represent a legible yet licit sexual content, and by the 1790s botany was part of the female curriculum and was considered a morally elevating activity. The virulence of Polwhele's attack on Wollstonecraft bespeaks the degree to which the sexuality of the Linnaean system was both implicitly understood (even by cultural conservatives) and explicitly unarticulated. Botany's status as an acceptable, even moral, activity depended on this very conflation.

The obfuscation of what it meant to study botany seems to have only increased the polemical rhetoric around it. Wollstonecraft, for instance, suggests that through botany the false modesty of women might be overcome and proposes that botany be part of a curriculum for the coeducational instruction of children without regard to social class. Wollstonecraft proposes "an elementary day school, where boys and girls, the rich and poor, should meet together (and study) botany, mechanics, and astronomy; reading, writing, arithmetic, natural history and some simple experiments in natural philosophy."[14] Botany is but one part of the ideal curriculum for egalitarian education that Wollstonecraft proposes in *A Vindication of the Rights of Woman* (1792), but it assumes a more particular status when she takes up the subject of female modesty (to Wollstonecraft, the central impediment to the equal status of women). Wollstonecraft attempts to revise the accepted definition of modesty by showing botany to be both a socially sanctioned but nevertheless sexualized activity. She suggests that botany is not consistent with "female delicacy" by way of arguing that delicacy is at odds with true modesty and knowledge of God:

> What a gross idea of modesty had the writer of the following remark!—the lady who asked the question whether women may be instructed in the modern system of botany consistently with female delicacy? was accused of ridiculous prudery; nevertheless, if she had proposed the question to me, I should certainly have answered— "they cannot." Thus is the fair book of knowledge to be shut with an everlasting seal! On reading similar passages I have reverently lifted up my eyes and heart to Him . . . and said "O, my Father, hast Thou, by the very constitution of her nature forbid Thy child to seek Thee in the fair forms of truth? And can her soul be sullied by the knowledge that awfully calls her to Thee?" I have then philosophically pursued these reflections till I inferred that those women who have most improved their reason must have the most modesty.[15]

Wollstonecraft suggests that modesty is the product of a cultivated, not an ignorant, mind. Her ideas are threatening precisely because she reappropriates from cultural conservatives the Enlightenment idea that study of the natural world brings one closer to the knowledge of God's perfection; she employs that idea to show how the social construction of modesty is at odds with a religious discourse about knowledge.

For Hannah More, the popular evangelical and conservative writer who in *Strictures on the Modern System of Female Education* (1799) had maintained that

53

Buffon's *Natural History* was too immodest to be admitted to a young lady's library, the revelation of God that came from the study of nature was an ideal compromised by gender. More struggles with the contradiction implicit in the making profane of what, according to enlightened Christianity, was the handiwork of God: how can the sexual not be profane? Why should girls not study flowers, even if they are sexual, if they reveal the perfection of God?[16] Linnaeus's dissemination of the fact that the flower was the sexual organ of the plant was a flashpoint in a debate that pitted the religious elevation of the study of nature against the social construction of female modesty. That the flower was now recognized as the sexual organ of the plant was confusing, for the logic of Linnaean botany required that sexuality be considered innocent and the providence of the Divine Author. The prevailing social ideology that made knowledge of sex for women profane was at odds with the prevailing idea of the sacredness of that revealed by the study of nature. More manages this difficult rhetorical point by constructing a hierarchy between the "natural" process of ripening and the "artificial" process of "forcing" (as in a greenhouse) that enables her to differentiate between good and bad knowledge: "a talent for conversation should be the result of instruction, not its precursor; it is a golden fruit when suffered to ripen gradually on the tree of knowledge; but if forced in the hot-bed of a circulating library, it will turn out worthless and vapid in proportion as it was artificial and premature."[17]

More, in a rhetorical move similar in intent if not tone to Polwhele's, attacks the characters of certain practitioners of botany rather than botany itself.[18] More's *ad hominem* rhetoric is reserved particularly for those who would use botany as an arena for flirtation rather than for the religious contemplation for which it was originally intended:

> On all the rational enjoyments of society, on all the healthful and temperate exercise, on the delights of friendship, arts and letters, on the exquisite pleasures resulting from the enjoyment of rural scenery, and the beauties of nature; on the innocent participation of these we may ask the divine favor—for the sober enjoyment of these we may ask the divine beneficence: but do we feel equally disposed to invoke blessings or return praises for gratifications found (to say no worse) in levity, in vanity, and waste of time?[19]

More believes that the education of girls should encourage moral excellence in order that the domestic sphere be improved. That More approves of botany in the abstract, if not in some of its actual incarnations, suggests that she thinks of botany as inherently moral. More worries about botany in practice, evoking Polwhele's distinction between the inherent good of botany and its prurient application; her warnings suggest that botany might easily become a sexualized activity, even though, as More claims, it is supposed to be "the most valuable and sober part of the reigning female acquisition."[20] The apparent contradiction reveals a rhetorical struggle, an effort to suppress the titillation of botany in order to maintain its status as an elevating female accomplishment:

Would not those delightful pursuits, botany and drawing, for instance seem likely to court the fields, the woods, and gardens of the paternal seat, as more congenial to their nature, and more appropriate to their exercise, than barren watering places, destitute of a tree, or an herb, or a flower, and not affording an hour's interval from successive pleasures, to profit by the scene even if it abounded with the whole vegetable world from the "Cedar of Lebanon" to the "Hyssop on the wall?"[21]

More, like Polwhele, believes that it is in the false interpretation and practice of an inherently modest subject that immodesty occurs. The rhetorical contortions that both Polwhele and More go through, however, suggest their investment in not revealing the contradiction between female modesty (and its suppression of sexual knowledge) and the religiously sanctioned pursuit of the revelation of the natural world.

The occlusion of that contradiction was not of course the exclusive province of More, or any one polemicist, for botany was a complex rhetorical site that absorbed ideas as varying as traditional religious conceits deriving from a vulgar pantheism ("God is in a wildflower") to disgust at the sexual base of the science. A constant, however, is that the direct attacks on Linnaeus's character and the indelicacy of his system that one sees in the 1771 edition of the *Encyclopedia Britannica* do not repeat themselves. By the late eighteenth century botany was a common subject of education for male and female children, as Priscilla Wakefield's widely disseminated textbooks *Mental Improvement; Or, the Beauties and Wonders of Nature and Art* (1794–97) and *An Introduction to Botany, in a series of Familiar Letters* (1796) suggest; the first teaches Linnaean botany via an exchange of letters between two sisters, and the second, via Platonic dialogues between parents and children, teaches the moral elevation that comes with the study of nature.[22] *An Introduction to Botany* was the first botanical handbook written by a woman to introduce the Linnaean system; it was very popular, inspiring eleven editions between 1796 and 1811, and, even more than Rousseau's comparatively austere *Lettres élémentaires sur la botanique,* was committed to teaching the moral as well as the practical dimensions of botany. The botanical practices of arranging and ordering plants imparted a model of moral and social order that pedagogical texts of varying stripes found exemplary.

The prominence of botany in lay circles was firmly established by the late eighteenth century and continued through much of the nineteenth century, for botanizing increasingly was thought of as a social activity that promoted health and morality. Ann Shteir has argued that botany contributed to "the social construction of femininity," and that the teaching of botany became a part of what was considered "good mothering."[23] Girls and women were encouraged to pursue botanical studies as a means of exercising their minds and improving their looks, for the time spent in the fields was considered healthy for body and mind; botany, alongside chemistry, became the science that was considered most suitable for study by literate women and girls in Britain and America. The presence of popularizing texts such as Wakefield's, situated as they were within a domestic and familial sphere, shepherded in a gradual shift in Linnaean botany's place in culture from a popular high science to one that might be more accurately called a popularized science. Almira Hart Lincoln Phelps's *Familiar Lectures on Botany*, written for the education of girls, sold 375,000 copies. Her *Botany for Beginners* sold some three hundred thousand copies in America alone.[24] By 1850, in a particularly colorful example of the sustained popularity of botany, a botanical fad was diagnosed as a disease: "Pteridomania," as it was called, medicalized the desire for fern gathering and collecting that was to send so many Victorian women to the woods, to their microscopes, and to their drawing rooms, where live plants were displayed in glass terrariums known as Wardian cases.[25]

The feminine connotations that increasingly became associated with the scientific study of plants contributed to the impulse for the professionalization of natural history, a movement that divided the generalist mode into the specific academic disciplines of zoology, botany, and geology; botany, with its commitment to visual observation and classification, seemed increasingly split off from the rest of natural history.[26] The work of distinguishing academic botany for so-called amateur effort was achieved in part by the turn away from Linnaean nomenclature by many members of the English professional community during the 1830s and the embrace of the more difficult Continental "natural systems" of Jussieu and Candolle. In differentiating themselves from amateurs, especially women, the new institutionally affiliated botanists employed a gendered rhetoric, one that emphasized the new rigor of the natural system in contrast to botany as "merely an amusing accomplishment."[27] By feminizing the Linnaean system, university botanists established more exclusive grounds of practice on which to build a professional identity and in doing so sought to reinscribe botany with a masculine identity.

At the turn of the century botany was associated positively with moral education and negatively with nonanalytical classification. Samuel Taylor Coleridge's impatience with botany's classificatory focus suggests a more general condescension about the intellectual profundity of the subject:

> What is botany at this present hour? Little more than an enormous nomenclature; a huge catalogue, well arranged, and yearly and monthly augmented, each with its own scheme of technical memory and its own conveniences of reference. . . . The terms system, method, science, are mere improprieties of courtesy, when applied to a mass enlarging by endless appositions, but without a nerve that oscillates, or a pulse that throbs, in sign of growth of inward sympathy. The innocent amusement, the healthful occupation, the ornamental accomplishments of amateurs . . . it has yet to expect the devotion and energies of the philosopher.[28]

Coleridge's reference to botany as an "accomplishment"—innocent, amusing, healthy, and ornamental—is an implicit criticism of botany's association with female life; the amateurism he invokes with derision is constructed as his (the philosopher's) opposite. Coleridge's voice was just one among an emergent professionalization process that sought to deemphasize amateur contributions to the science. By 1832 John Lindley, in *An Introduction to Botany*, was so defensive of botany's reputation as the "science of the idle philosopher" and an "accomplishment"—like Coleridge's reference, an imputation of frivolous femininity—that he overcompensates by likening "the modern science of botany" to religious transcendence: "it is the science that converts the useless or noxious weed into the nutritious vegetable; which changes a bare volcanic rock, like the Ascension, into a green and fertile island."[29] Lindley, a premier figure in the Royal Horticultural Society and professor of botany at the University of London from 1829 to 1860, was a leading proponent of making botany more "scientific"; his was an opinion shared by others in the increasingly professional scientific community, leading to what Shteir has characterized as an "increasing stratification" between popular and professional positions in botany.[30] Even Robert Thornton, who defends the sexualist system in his introduction to *New Illustration of the Sexual System of Linnaeus*, inadvertently reveals botany's fraught reputation as unmanly and nonanalytical: "by this analytical mode of studying Botany we rise far superior to the Contempt which is commonly cast on this lovely Science, by those who are ignorant of our Procedure . . . it must be allowed on every side to be a manly sort of Puzzle, as amusing as it is instructive."[31]

Botany's associations as amateur and feminine were further developed by the pervasive claims that it was a science that increased moral virtue; chemistry also was thought to be suitable, but it was botany that was identified as the primary science for women.[32] Botany specifically geared toward amateurs, and especially botany for women, was wedded to the Linnaean system; it was not until 1842, when Jane Loudon published *Botany for Ladies; or a Popular Introduction to the Natural System of Plants*, that a popular botany book for women encouraged the "natural system" that had displaced Linnaeus in professional botanical circles; Loudon's introductory text was written as a response to John Lindley's *Ladies' Botany* (1834), a text whose intention to introduce the "natural system" to women is mitigated through a gendered rhetoric so condescending as to discourage its adaptation. Classificatory botany based on the Linnaean system maintained its hold in amateur circles for reasons that can be intuited from the ease and pervasiveness of the known Linnaean system in contrast to the difficulty of the new natural system, as well as from the rhetoric of the professionalizers who benefited from the divide.

The botanical vernacular to which I have alluded was the effect of the broad dissemination and popularization of the Linnaean system—the result of its relative simplicity as a taxonomical system in combination with the vividness of the sexual reproduction of plants analogized to the human model. This vernacular did not alter in accordance with professional shifts away from Linnaean botany in the 1830s, for that would assume that the general public turned to the Jussieuean system as readily as its professional proponents and found in that system a similar compelling narrative and logic. Even as the line between professional and amateur natural history hardened in the first half of the nineteenth century, Linnaeus's system retained its currency alongside the natural system. The eclipse of Linnaean botany that occurred was not general but predominately professional.

Even more important, the botanical vernacular did not undergo an imaginative shift as Linnaean classification began to be eclipsed. One of the most important reasons that this book does not trace the impact of botany, in its specific and changing manifestations across the nineteenth century, on the novel is that the botanical vernacular was tied specifically to the diffusion of botanical knowledge that Linnaeus's system enabled. The literary genre of the bloom narrative that would evolve in the midst of the popularization of botanical science would rely on a vernacular understanding of Linnaean botany but would eventually develop and assume its own internal logic and history. The bloom narrative was born out of the Linnaean context and then developed as a literary narrative; bloom does not shift in accordance with the botanical changes of the 1830s and beyond but rather with the literary tides out of which that narrative grew.

Botanical Modesty: Edgeworth's *Belinda*

In *Letters for Literary Ladies* (1795), Maria Edgeworth cites Erasmus Darwin's famous line in order to criticize the present state of botany:

> Science has of late "been enlisted under the banners of imagination," by the irresistible charms of genius. . . . Botany has become fashionable; in time it may become useful, if it be not so already. Chemistry will follow botany. Chemistry is a science well suited to the talents and situation of women; it is not a science of parade; it affords occupation and infinite variety; it demands no bodily strength; it can be pursued in retirement; it applies immediately to useful and domestic purposes: and whilst the ingenuity of the most inventive mind may in this science be exercised, there is no danger of inflaming the imagination.[33]

Edgeworth's fictional letter-writer—a gentleman responding to a letter written to him on the birth of a daughter—speaks of chemistry as a subject for female education, but botany is the implicit subject, for all that chemistry "is not" in this quotation is what botany was perceived to be at the close of the eighteenth century. "A science of parade" and fashion, botany could not be pursued in retirement, nor was it undemanding of physical strength; and, perhaps most important, botany did present a danger—by evoking Erasmus Darwin, Edgeworth's epistolary persona implies how botany might inflame the sexual imagination. The letter is in favor of female education, its author pledging to give his daughter "the love of knowledge, and the power of reasoning," yet at the same time expresses the worry that any daughter would become "merely a botanist."[34] Botany is sacrificed, one could say, in the service of the larger goals of a general and rational female education; the letter-writer does not want his daughter to be "merely" a musician, painter, poet, or mathematician either but to have the habits and power with which she might take up "any pursuit."

The controversy over whether education, and botany in particular, engendered modesty or immodesty in girls was, as I have shown, contemporary to this epistolary exchange. *Letters for Literary Ladies*, Edgeworth's first foray into fiction, was published just three years after Wollstonecraft's *Vindication* and can be seen as responding to its discussion of female education. Edgeworth is famously known to have been educated unconventionally by a father who prohibited novels but encouraged her to read political and philosophical thinkers (including Edmund Burke, Adam Smith, and Jeremy Bentham). In *Letters* Edgeworth tactfully disparages botany, although not from a conservative position but from the perspective of someone who believes its practice should be disassociated from the rhetoric of female modesty; in professing an ambivalence toward one kind of learning, Edgeworth affirms her support of a system of education that would not necessarily exclude botany but would be suspicious of its primary associations with female education.

All the more interesting, thus, that *Belinda* (1801), Edgeworth's second novel, has at its moral center a family who botanizes. *Belinda* is a courtship novel that marks a departure from *Castle Rackrent* (1800), the novel that Edgeworth wrote secretly and published under a pseudonym. The complication of how to read and represent modesty is *Belinda*'s primary subject, the scrutiny of its eponymous heroine's innocence its major mode of inquiry.[35] As I have shown, the polemical discussion around botany was a version of the debate about female modesty and who was to define it, and *Belinda* is a novel that should be understood within that context. In *Belinda*, the issues of proper female behavior, especially as it relates to the sexual modes of innocence and coquetry, and female education are taken up as its primary concerns. Botany in *Belinda* is a sign of reason and the kind of modesty Wollstonecraft had defined in her writings, while horticultural fashion is a sign of depravity and false modesty. The opposition of botany with botanical fashion illuminates the novel's complex discussion of feminine modesty.

Modesty, as critics of the novel have illuminatingly shown, was not only the locus for debates about female morality and education but also a complex system of signage in the late eighteenth- and nineteenth-century novel.[36] In *Belinda*, the eponymous heroine is nothing if not modest, consumed by blushes and willing to lose her social standing rather than suffer any imputations to her modesty. Female modesty, as Ruth Yeazell has argued, is understood as a sexual virtue, for modesty plays a "privileged role in the sequence of events . . . called courtship." Yeazell suggests that the blush can arouse speculation about its relationship to sexual desire, even as it signs an appropriate innocence: "long before nineteenth-century science speculated openly about the physiological resemblance of a blush to other forms of sexual flushing and excitement, lovers of the modest woman read an erotic promise in her blushes—all the more so, no doubt, because so little other than her cheek was conventionally available for contemplation."[37] Belinda's sexual innocence is questioned by the as yet unreformed Lady Delacour precisely because of her blushes, the very sign of which, depending on who is reading that sign, simultaneously confirms and impugns her innocence. Modesty is a larger umbrella topic for the narrative of sexual potential that bloom signs; certainly the botanical vernacular enables the licit representation of sexual potential in the novel, but, as the debates in the 1790s about female modesty suggest, botany was but a part of a much larger cultural transformation around sexual morality and its representational status. And yet, as the merging of the debate about modesty and botany suggests, modesty is not a monadic concept but one that contains multiple resonances. That is, a girl in bloom may perform a kind of modesty, but the specific meanings connoted by the narrative arc of her "blooming" owe their resonance more to the botanical vernacular than to the novelistic exigencies of female embodiment and subjectivity. What Yeazell considers a "conventional trope for female virtue"—the "sensitive plant" or "familiar guise of the sensitive plant"— might be profitably resituated within the late eighteenth-century botanical vernacular.[38] When Edgeworth writes *Belinda*, she does so at the close of a decade suffused with discussions of modesty and botany's relation to that subject, and so it is not surprising that her courtship novel prominently connects the two subjects.

The eponymous heroine of *Belinda* is, conventionally, motherless and under the care of an aunt with a reputation for mercenary matchmaking; it is her relation to Mrs. Stanhope that first makes Clarence Hervey doubt Belinda's innocence, for her very lack of overt coquetry invokes the possibility that she is a self-designed innocent, a proficient in what the novel calls "scientific coquetry."[39] Belinda is actually artless and unaffected but, in a telling distinction, not modestly ignorant. Like Wollstonecraft, who decries in *Vindication* a virtue based on ignorance, Edgeworth endows her heroine with a sense that is not at odds with modesty. So, for example, Belinda does not feign a lack of understanding when met with the following accusation by Lady Delacour that she has designs on Lord Delacour: "your protestations of innocence are wasted on me—I am not so blind as you imagine—dupe as you think me, I have seen much in silence. The whole world, you find, suspects you now" (*B*, 200). Belinda shows that she understands that the rumor is an accusation of sexual impropriety by leaving the Delacours, for the implication of sexual impropriety stemmed from living with the couple. In retreating to the Percivals' house, Belinda proves what is understood in the fashionable world as a lack of modesty: her understanding.

The alternative to the fashionable culture that had read Belinda's real innocence as coquetry is a family, the Percivals of Oakly-park, whose interests
include science as well as literature; the marriage of the Percivals represents the
rational ideal of marriage that Wollstonecraft had urged:

> Between Mr. Percival and Lady Anne there was a union of interests,
> occupations, taste, and affection. . . . In conversation, every person ex-
> pressed without constraint their wishes and opinions; and wherever
> these differed, reason and the general good were the standards to
> which they appealed. . . . Lady Anne Percival had, without any
> pedantry or ostentation, much accurate knowledge, and a taste for lit-
> erature, which made her the chosen companion of her husband's un-
> derstanding, as well as of his heart . . . the partner of his warmest affec-
> tions was also the partner of his most serious occupations. (B, 196–7)

Edgeworth's representation of domestic happiness and rational family life is
also a defense of the right kind of modesty, for here Belinda's knowledge is
not at odds with the culture of improvement that pervades the family: "Mr.
Percival was a man of science and literature, and his daily pursuits and general
conversation were in the happiest manner instructive and interesting to his
family. . . . From the merest trifles he could lead to some scientific fact, some
happy literary allusion, or philosophical investigation" (B, 196). Belinda re-
gains her reputation through a seemingly inconsequential act of botanizing in
a family whose interests include botany, chemistry, gardening, music, and
painting.

The fulcrum of *Belinda*'s two primary plots and concerns—the reformation of the aristocratic family and the correction of the idea of female modesty—centers on an action surrounding a plant. The gift of an aquatic plant
sets in motion Lady Delacour's reformation, a reformation that returns Belinda, who remains under her protection, to a morally upright social position:

> Marriott brought in the gold fishes; some green leaves floating on the
> top of the water in this glass globe. "See, my lady," she said, "what
> Miss Portman has been so good as to bring from Oakly-park for my
> poor gold fishes, who, I am sure, ought to be much obliged to her, as
> well as myself." Marriott set the globe beside her lady, and retired.
> "From Oakly-park! and by what name impossible to pronounce
> must I call these green leaves, to please botanic ears?" said Lady Dela-
> cour. "This," replied Belinda, "is what *th' unlearned, duckweed—
> learned, lemma, call*; and it is to be found in any ditch or standing pool."
> (B, 260)

The plant in the fishbowl is identified by Belinda first by the vernacular name
(duckweed), and then by its formal botanical name (lemma). Lady Delacour
ridicules botany's difficult nomenclature, even as she asks how she might
"please botanic ears." The passage then provides the telling context for the
botanical detail:

"And what possessed you, my dear, for the sake of Marriott and her gold fishes, to trouble yourself to bring such stuff a hundred and seventy miles?" "To oblige little Charles Percival," said Miss Portman, "He was anxious to keep his promise of sending it to your Helena. She found out in some book that she was reading with him last summer, that gold fishes are fond of this plant; and I wish," added Belinda, in a timid voice, "that she were here at this instant to see them eat it." Lady Delacour was silent for some minutes, and kept her eye steadily upon the gold fishes. At length she said, "I never shall forget how well the poor little creature behaved about those gold fishes. I grew amazingly fond of her whilst she was with me." (*B*, 260–1)

"Your Helena" is Lady Delacour's child, who is kept exclusively at boarding schools in order not to disturb the dissipated lives of the Delacours. The duckweed, carried close to two hundred miles to oblige a child, serves to inspire in Lady Delacour a maternal feeling for her own forgotten child—a child so isolated from family that Lady Delacour remembers the child with nostalgia ("I grew amazingly fond of her whilst she was with me"). The reconciliation that Belinda then proposes between mother, child, and father has been prepared by the emotion the duckweed inspired. Lady Delacour's redemption is tentative, for she only proposes that Helena stay with her for "few days," but the botanical inspiration is the certain beginning of a return to moral and physical health with which the novel will close. The reader is meant to understand that botany symbolizes all that is reasonable and natural in family life, for here a plant effectively reunites a child with an unloving mother, creating the kind of home in which Belinda's modesty is not mistaken for sexual guile. This botanical moment, in fact, is key to the secondary plot of courtship, for after the botanical reconciliation of mother and daughter Belinda is able to remain in the house whose delinquency had lent doubt to her own sexual innocence. *Belinda*, in other words, fixes on a botanical moment to represent a crisis in meaning around innocent femininity, invoking botany not as a sensational language but as a body of knowledge that is productive of a knowing virtue.[40]

The confluence of modesty and botany climaxes in the novel's conclusion, a long subplot about Clarence Hervey, who has educated a girl according to the principles that Rousseau sets out in *Émile*. *Belinda* expresses Edgeworth's antipathy, following on Wollstonecraft's critique, for Rousseau's ideas about the education of girls: "he read the works of Rousseau: this eloquent writer's senses made its full impression upon Clarence's understanding . . . he formed the romantic project of educating a wife for himself " (*B*, 329). Not only does the project not conclude with the perfect wife that Rousseau imagined, but Hervey, who comes to dread the marriage to his protégé, sees Virginia St. Pierre's "bloom fading daily" as she contemplates it (*B*, 356).[41] The bloom plot is righted through the exchange of Belinda for Virginia St. Pierre, a conclusion that marks a turn away from an ideal of female modesty based in ignorance.

Botanical Poetry: Charlotte Smith and Erasmus Darwin

In poetry, where one might expect nature to maintain its pastoral signification most tenaciously, we find in the work of Charlotte Smith and Erasmus
Darwin flowers evoked within a deliberately scientific register. This is not to
suggest that flowers cease generally to be objects of poetic meditation in the
late eighteenth century; the emblematic and pastoral meanings associated with
the floral remained, even as the sexualist system brought additional detail to
the flower as figure.[42] It is not surprising that it is in poetry that these earlier associations maintain a firmer hold, for the Linnaean system was constructed
around a narrative of marriage and sexual reproduction that was more conducive to the prose narrative than lyric poetry. Smith's poetry is distinctive,
however, in intentionally invoking a botanical referent; she glosses her long
poem *Beachy Head* with footnotes about natural history, which results in floral
images that invoke their botanical context and not only their emblematic,
metaphorical, or aesthetic associations. Erasmus Darwin (1731–1802), grand-
father of the more famous Darwin, was an important popularizer of Linnaeus's system whose botanical poetry pushes to the foreground the erotic aspects of the Linnaean system. His *The Loves of the Plants* (1789), part of his
larger work *The Botanic Garden*, amplifies and vivifies certain botanical concepts through poetic expression and an elaborate scientific gloss. In combining
science with poetry, Erasmus Darwin explicitly performs what I have previously suggested was implicitly occurring in the classical novel: the importation
of scientific meaning into imaginative literature. Moreover, Darwin's poem
unambiguously conflates narratives of human courtship with the marriages of
flowers that Linnaeus describes in his botanical work.

Charlotte Smith (1749–1807) has most often been understood as a precursor to the canonical male Romantic poets, especially Wordsworth, who admired and cited her poetry as an influence; Smith also wrote ten novels between 1788 and 1798, developing the genre of the sentimental-gothic that Ann
Radcliffe was subsequently to refine. Yet Smith's poetry, specifically her
posthumously published volume of verse *Beachy Head and Other Poems* and her
earlier *Conversations Introducing Poetry, chiefly on Subjects of Natural History for the
Use of Children and Young Persons* (1804), was also part of a popular scientific
writing that included, most prominently, the natural history writings of Oliver
Goldsmith and Gilbert White, as well as the children's natural history writing
of Jane Marcet, Anna Barbauld, and Priscilla Wakefield. Smith provides us
with a self-consciously literary instance of the leakage of a scientific register
into poetic, or imaginative, discourse.

Nature for Smith is not a transcendent category but a material reality observed with a scientific, as well as poetic, eye. In her poem "To the Firefly of
Jamaica, seen in a Collection," Smith takes as her subject an entomological
specimen; although dead, the insect pinned into the board nevertheless receives a poetic treatment similar to the living flowers that are often her (more
understandable) subject. The primary titles of her poems often seem typical of

British romantic poetry—one example is "A Walk in the Shrubbery"—but their subtitles reveal a more demonstrably scientific investment: for "A Walk in the Shrubbery," "To the Cisus or rock rose, a beautiful plant, whose flowers expand and fall off twice in twenty-four hours." The particularity of Smith's references to botany, ornithology, and geology suggests a poet who was engaged by the scientific beauty of nature, and a poetry that did otherwise than transmit older literary connotations of flowers. Flowers in Smith's poetry have the status of absolute objects—the poetry does not push them to transcend their material reality and become images for an alternative preoccupation. The scientific flower is Smith's preoccupation, so much so that when she employs the vernacular names of flowers she assiduously glosses them with their Latin binomial, in effect bringing to each floral reference a material singularity not susceptible to any figural elaboration. As Stuart Curran has suggested, Smith's poetry "testifies to an alternative Romanticism that seeks not to transcend or to absorb nature but to contemplate and honor its irreducible alterity."[43]

The botanical context of the flowers, rather than their emblematic meanings, seems central in *Beachy Head*. At a particularly telling moment in the poem, Smith invokes cuckoo-flowers—"the banks with cuckoo-flowers are strewn"—seemingly only so that she can correct Shakespeare's insufficiently precise use of the flower: "Cuckoo-flowers. *Lychnis dioica*. Shakespeare describes the Cuckoo buds as being yellow (in *Love's Labour's Lost*, V.ii.894). He probably meant the numerous Ranunculi, or March marigolds (*Caltha palustris*) which so gild the meadows in Spring; but poets have never been botanists. The Cuckoo flower is the *Lychnis flosuculi*."[44] The tongue-in-cheek reference to poets as bad botanists is only the most obvious manifestation of a general trend, in which Smith writes against a set of received pastoral meanings about her poem; her poetry as a whole might be understand as almost an aggressive correction of received meanings. Individual lines seem to require specific knowledge of botany, or at least the desire to be complicit with her pedagogical aims. The poetry's general subject matter is itself a compelling fact, for it is poetry that assumes a world in which botanical science and natural history are to some degree vernacularized.

Smith particularizes pastoral language through a scientific vocabulary that is imported almost directly into her poetry. In *Beachy Head*, a poem that begins at the top of the land mass that is the first spot one sees when crossing the Channel, the references to the objects *within* the landscape (where her poem quickly goes) are glossed with scientific notes. *Beachy Head* refers repeatedly to particular elements within the landscape:

An early worshipper at Nature's shrine
I loved her rudest scenes—warrens, and heaths,
And yellow commons, and birch-shaded hollows
And hedge rows, bordering unfrequented lanes
Bowered with wild roses, and the clasping woodbine
Where purple tassels of the tangling vetch

With bittersweet, and bryony inweave,
And the dew fills the silver bindweed's cups—
I loved to trace the brooks whose humid banks
Nourish the harebell, and the freckled pagil. (231)

"Vetch" is glossed by Smith as *Vicia sylvatica*; "bittersweet" as the species *Solanum dulcamara*; "bryony" as *Bryonia alba*; "bindweed" as *Convolvulus sepium*; "harebell" as *Hyacinthus non scriptus*; the flower "pagil" as *Primula veris*. And yet despite this literal deployment of the botanical, Smith also wrote a popular book entitled *Elegaic Sonnets* that was indebted to more traditional Petrarchan themes. A classically inflected poet, Smith is also a studied natural historian; natural history literally permeates the lines of the poetry with an insistence that is rare in Romantic verse. *Beachy Head* uses a familiar poetic style, even as its content hews to a natural history model in which references can be found to the area's geology, fossil record, botany, and insect and bird life.

In other points of the poem, Smith employs experts to enrich her peda-gogic aims; in evoking mountain thyme—"the mountain thyme / Purples the hassock of the heaving mole, / And the short turf is gay with tormentil, / And bird's foot trefoil, and the lesser tribes / Of hawkweed; spangling it with fringed stars" (236)—she footnotes *The Gardener's and Botanist's Dictionary* (1797) by Thomas Martyn. Shortly thereafter Smith quotes an essay by Dr. Aiken, "On the Application of Natural History to the Purposes of Poetry," which situates her reference to "fern-flies" within a poetic tradition of the Dor Beetle—the hum of this beetle, she suggests, has been evoked in Shakespeare's *Macbeth*, Milton's *Lycidas*, and Gray's *Elegy Written in a Country Church-Yard*. As is evident from Smith's paratextual support, any felt distinction between poetic texts and scientific texts for specialists is not honored.

The titles that make up Smith's poetry collection for children, *Conversations Introducing Poetry, chiefly on Subjects of Natural History for the use of Children and Young Persons*, reveal Smith's preoccupation with natural history: "The moth," "The heath," "Violets," "To the snow drop," "Ode to the missel thrush," "To the mulberry tree," "Invitation to the bee," "The wheat-ear." The focus on the object in nature, rather than abstract moral or intellectual con-cepts, suggests that Smith's first concern is nature itself; any didactic purpose instead seems epiphenomenal, far less central than the poetry's commitment to exhaustive particularity. In the poem "Wild flowers," for example, it is not until the final line of the poem that God is invoked as the creator of nature. In-stead its gloss, like that of *Beachy Head*, gives the Latin binomial, while the poem focuses on the objects of nature and, in the word "calyx," invokes a botanical terminology: "Then thickly strewn in woodland bowers / Anemonies their stars unfold; / There spring the Sorrel's veined flowers, / And rich in vegetable gold / From calyx pale, the freckled Cowslip born, / Re-ceives in amber cups the fragrant dews of morn" (190).

If literature had long created associations between flowers and sexuality, the literary intuition that flowers are sex organs became a fact of both science and representation in the later eighteenth century. It was that fact that cleared the way for Erasmus Darwin, a writer whose scientific interests and ideological passions would make Linnaean botany the centerpiece of his poetic and scientific practice. His poem *The Loves of the Plants* is both an imaginative and pedagogic tribute to Linnaeus's system and the medium for his vision of a more inclusive sexual morality. The footnotes in *The Loves of the Plants* appear on the same page as the poem and in the same typeface, often taking up more than half and sometimes as much as three-quarters of the page; *The Loves of the Plants* is both prose and poem.

Darwin's understanding of plant morphology, following Linnaeus, was analogically based on humans; what may seem to us like broad metaphorizations of science reflect that system of analogy. For example, in the section entitled "Vegetable Placentation" Darwin calls the bud a "foetus," while the sap travels in the "umbilical cords of buds." On the basis of an experiment he performs on October 20, 1781, Darwin argues that "the leaf is the parent of the bud."[45] To explain the purpose of plant sap, the poem reads: "Swell the green cup, and tint the flower with gold; / While in bright veins the silvery sap ascends, / And refluent blood in milky eddies bends" (45–6). In the footnote, the "silvery sap" is described as part of the scientific process of "vegetable placentation," in which the bud (being the offspring of the plant) needs to be nourished through a "placental vessel."[46] In the prose section entitled "Vegetable Impregnation," in which he cites no fewer than six scientific articles or authorities, the analogy borrows from Linnaeus's analogy between seeds and eggs: "seeds exist in the ovarium many days before fecundation" (122). Likewise the honey or the nectar of a flower is "designed to lubricate the vegetable uterus" (123). What is striking about Darwin's poetic simplifications is that they are like the science itself, in that both Linnaeus and Darwin refuse to grant the status of a simile to their observations about plants.

The rhetorical aim of Darwin's poem is to teach the science of Linnaeus in a poetic medium, to "inlist Imagination under the banner of Science." This, Darwin's advertisement for his book, argues that the fiction the poetry constructs is real, that "imagination" is governed by science, and that his poetical metaphors, unlike those that "dress out the imagery of poetry," are strict and the result of exact reason. The claim being put forth is that his poetry imaginatively represents scientific reality without drawing on false analogies.[47] In the very first footnote to canto 1 of *The Loves of the Plants*, Darwin glosses his poetic expression "vegetable loves" as follows: "Linnaeus, the celebrated Swedish naturalist, has demonstrated, that all flowers contain families of males and females, or both; and on their marriages has constructed his invaluable system of Botany" (137). That is, Darwin insists that the lyrical term ("vegetable love") is implicit in the Linnaean system's preexisting socialization of sexual acts. For Darwin the social aspect of the sexuality of plants is not metaphorical but a scientifically verifiable fact of Linnaeus's system of classification.

In reflecting contemporary botany's analogues, and certainly exploiting their lyrical qualities by making them the subject of his poem, Darwin literalizes the poetic tradition he inherited, exhausting the possibility of metaphor and replacing it with a new, scientific language of flowers. The frontispiece from the 1799 edition of *The Botanic Garden,* entitled "Flora at Play with Cupid," implies through a literary reference the newly scientific sexualizing of the flower (see fig. 6).

And yet it would be misleading to suggest that Darwin, taking his cue from Linnaeus, maps a system of metaphor onto a science originally free of metaphor or analogy. Londa Schiebinger has argued that in Linnaeus's system there is "an explicit use of human sexual metaphors to introduce notions of plant reproduction into botanical literature."[48] Schiebinger's attribution of metaphor to Linnaeus's system separates metaphor from science, suggesting that there was a rhetorical act that "introduces" metaphors into a science that could have otherwise been free of metaphor. Linnaeus's science often depends on a serious analogy between plant and human anatomy and physiology; that is, not everything in Linnaeus's taxonomy can be traced to the importation of metaphor. For example, Linnaeus's schema grants sentience to the genital parts of flowers, a descriptive act that reflects contemporary theoretical notions of plant sentience within late eighteenth-century botany. Linnaean botany, reflected in Darwin's work, grants a human quality to the plant as an empirical description, not as an act of translation through metaphor.[49] The links that Darwin draws between humans and plants are scientifically defendable in the 1790s.

That said, *The Loves of the Plants* employs poetic figures that go beyond that which Linnaean botany explicitly articulates, an effect of translating between two very different genres. The generic qualities of Linnaeus's work are closer to a list than a poem, so Darwin's poem would necessarily vivify some of the terms Linnaeus uses. For instance, Linnaeus refers to plant reproduction as "nuptials," a term that suggests a human counterpart but is made more vivid when Darwin portrays the flower as a bride and groom. At times Darwin embroiders on Linnaeus's primary analogy of marriage; he refers to the place of the "house" and the characters of "suitors." Other language, such as the familial titles of "brother" and "husbands," is meant to invoke Linnaean class directly. For instance, the seventeenth class is "Diadelphia," or "Two Brotherhoods," which describes a flower in which "stamens are united by their filaments into two bodies"; the Linnaean analogue is translated as "Husbands arise from two bases, as if from two mothers" (l. 31). In *The Loves of the Plants* Darwin represents a plant (Genista, or Dyer's Broom) from that class: "sweet blooms Genista in the myrtle shade/ And *ten* fond brothers woo the haughty maid./ *Two* knights before thy fragrant altar bend" (ll. 57–9). If the science was not entirely clear from the poetry, Darwin glosses his own lines in the footnote: "ten males and one female inhabit this flower. The males are generally united at the bottom in two sets, whence Linnaeus has named the class 'two brotherhoods'"

London:Published June 1ˢᵗ 1799 by J. Johnson S.Pauls Church Yard.

FIGURE 6   "Flora at Play with Cupid." Frontispiece to Erasmus Darwin, *The Botanic Garden,* vol. 2, containing "The Loves of the Plants" (London, 1799). Courtesy of the General Research Division, The New York Public Library, Astor, Lenox and Tilden Foundations.

(138). As these examples begin to suggest, Darwin's poem does not for the most part metaphorize an objective science but rather exploits what is already present in Linnaean rhetoric.

The poem has lyrical ways of describing physical facts, as in his evocation of the Amaryllis flower's six stamens: "Fair Amaryllis flies the incumbent storm, / Seeks with unsteady step the shelter'd vale, / And turns her blushing beauties from the gale. / Six rival youths, with soft concern impress'd, / Calm all her fears, and charm her cares to rest" (ll.152–6). The sexual meanings are layered over traditional pastoral structures; the apostrophe "fair Amaryllis" makes the botanical name seem like the flower's given name, while her "unsteady step" and movement from the storm makes the flower into a distressed damsel. The personification of the flower Amaryllis takes on significantly different meaning in light of the scientific footnote that glosses the lines; the footnote reads (in part):

> *Amaryllis*. l. 152. Fomosissima. Most beautiful amaryllis. Six males, one female. Some of the bell-flowers close their apertures at night, in rainy or cold weather . . . and thus protect their included stamens and pistils. Other bell-flowers hang their apertures downwards, as many of the lilies; in those the pistil, when at maturity, is longer than the stamens; and by this pendant attitude of the bell, when the anthers burst, their dust falls on the stigma; and these are at the same time sheltered as with an umbrella from rain and dews. (141)

Here the flower is imagined to be a girl named "Amaryllis." The association of a human narrative about courtship with a botanical narrative about fertilization imparts meaning in both directions: a social analogy onto the botanical description, and a botanical meaning onto the social person. That "blushing" girl surrounded by six rival youths who want to calm her fears takes on a sensational meaning, for the footnote helps us understand that the "soft concerns" of the six males are pollen—Amaryllis is about to be fertilized by six stamens, or "rival youths," in turn. The importation of the botanical-sexual system into poetry makes real the erotic in courtship; that blushing girl, surrounded by six rival youths, is about to be impregnated.

Darwin's ideological agenda seems apparent in his interest in representing the multiple sexual arrangements present in the botanical world; he was a practitioner of free love after his wife's death, as well as an atheist and advocate of the principles of the French Revolution.[50] His description of Osmunda, a plant belonging to the Clandestine class, is revealing: "The fair Osmunda seeks the silent dell / The ivy canopy, and dripping cell; / There hid in shades *clandestine* rites approves, / Till the green progeny betrays her loves" (ll. 97–100). Here *clandestine* describes both a kind of moss that grows on moist rocks in the shade and the kind of social interaction that is sexual and secret—a clandestine affair. (We might note that in 1753, the same year that *Systema Naturae* is published, the Clandestine Marriage Act outlawed marriage without the consent of parents, inaugurating the practice of clandestine marriage in Scotland.)

One cannot *see* the flowers on a plant of the Cryptogamia class—mosses and ferns are the most prominent examples—so the language choice is scientific rather than strictly figurative. As one can see, Darwin's poetry makes use of the image present in Linnaeus, but the vividness of the subject comes as much from the language of the sexualist system as it does from Darwin's imagination.

The use of botany to comment on or characterize social-sexual arrangements is pervasive in Darwin's poem. The first flower that is evoked is canna, the Indian reed, which displays a traditional kind of heterosexual monogamy. The sexual organs (one male, one female in the same flower) seem to dictate their social relation: "first the tall Canna lifts his curled brow / Erect to heaven, and plights his nuptial vow; / The virtuous pair, in milder regions born, / Dread the rude blast of autumn's icy morn; / round the chill fair he folds his crimson vest, / And clasps the timorous beauty to his breast" (ll. 39–44). If the pair is traditionally "virtuous," they are also traditionally gendered, for the tumescence of the male is matched by the frigidity of the female. Darwin, however, generally favors less traditional sexual-social arrangements. For example, the Iris is a plant in which one female is served by "three unjealous husbands" (l. 71). Another social alternative is embodied in the cypress, a kind of plant that has male and female parts in separate blossoms but on the same plant. Darwin is reminded in that arrangement of a twin-bed sexual arrangement: "Cupressus dark disdains his dusky bride, / *One* dome contains them, but *two* beds divide" (ll.73–4). With the plant Osyris, the males and females are on different plants, a state that in Darwin's imagination looks like the arrangement of a wealthy and estranged couple: "the proud Osyris flies his angry fair, / *Two* houses hold the fashionable pair" (ll. 75–6). Yet, alternatively, lychnis has male and female flowers on different plants "often at a great distance from each other." Darwin's footnote describes the delayed sexual maturity of the male stamens, and the female pistils' elongation just prior to fecundation is imaginatively described as "rising about the petals as if looking abroad for their distant husbands" (140). The poetry imagines the pistils' movement away from the stamens just prior to fecundation as a willful refusal.

Darwin's poem makes more visible the degree to which Linnaeus's system blanketed a variety of sexual arrangements with the term *marriage*; he evokes a number of alternative sexual practices and attitudes, as well as social arrangements, present with the Linnaean system. Voyeurism is implied by the representation of the turmeric flower, a flower that has one male, one female, and four "imperfect" males (filaments without anthers, making an incomplete stamen) that Linnaeus called "eunuchs": "woo'd with long care, Circuma, cold and shy/ Meets her fond husband with averted eye: / Four beardless youths the obdurate beauty move / With soft attentions of Platonic love" (ll. 65–8). The sexuality of the older woman is represented through the flower gloriosa, in which the female has sex with two sets of stamens that mature in succession; the first set are charmed by her virginity, the second set of "three other youths" are "the flatter'd victims of her wily age" (ll.111–24). Female modesty has its botanical analogy as well; the botanical quality of "sensitivity"—a plant's tendency to close due to being touched or a change in weather—is represented as the modest behavior of the girl: "weak with nice sense the chaste Mimosa stands / From each rude touch withdraws her timid hands" (ll. 229–30).

In general, sex in *The Loves of the Plants* is oriented toward reproduction. The exception is the category of "vegetable mules," or plants that are called by botanists "monsters" for their inability to propagate by seed. The first human-designed hybrid, a cross between a carnation and sweet william, was achieved in 1717. Hybrids produced a great deal of cultural anxiety in the eighteenth and nineteenth centuries, for their inability to reproduce themselves by seed seemed a great deformation of nature. In 1788, James Lee in *Introduction to Botany* referred to hybrids as "bastards" and "monstrous."[51] Rousseau in *Lettres élémentaires sur la botanique* refers to double-flowers, a great technical innovation of the florists, as "deformed monsters." The strong moralistic strain seems to stem from the infertility of the hybridized double-flower, as if its infertility was a punishment for the vanity of pursuing beauty without regard for reproduction. Rousseau contributes to this discourse of normative sexuality by urging botanists to "waste no time in examining them" because they are "deformed" and the disastrous product of "our whim."[52] The elder Darwin has a similar approach to the hybrid. The poem's evocation of one such plant, dianthus (the species colloquially known as pinks), describes that kind of vegetable sex as "illicit loves" and calls the product "monster-offspring" (ll. 306–7). That both Darwin's and Rousseau's texts, in varying degrees, privilege species that are not made by human intervention but reproduce through what is understood as "natural" means suggests a certain cultural investment in enforcing normative ideas about sexuality, plant or human.

Nevertheless, Darwin's unique redaction of Linnaean theory into imaginative literature is one that, on the whole, advocates a radical socio-sexual agenda. In general the poem seems to favor less traditional monogamous arrangements, as in the orgy of "vegetable love" that concludes the poem:

> A hundred virgins join a hundred swains,
> And fond Adonis leads the sprightly trains
> Pair after pair, along his sacred groves
> To Hymen's fane the bright procession moves. . . .
> As round his shrine the gaudy circles bow,
> And seal with muttering lips the faithless vow
> Licentious Hymen joins their mingled hands
> and loosely twines the meretricious bands,—
> Thus where pleased Benus, in the southern main,
> Sheds all her smiles on Otaheite's plain,
> Wide o'er the isle her silken net she draws,
> And the loves laugh at all but Nature's laws. (ll. 489–508)

The poem's movement from monogamy to this description of polygamy as natural mirrors what we know about Darwin's distaste for the social state of marriage and his endorsement of free love.[53] That both Linnaeus's botanical taxonomy and Darwin's botanical poetry conflate sex and marriage is not, as we might be tempted to think, an indication that they are both social conservatives. The radical difference between the provincial Linnaeus and the free-thinking Darwin should make that plain; Linnaeus tried to marry off his uneducated daughters to his students, while the elder Darwin considered marriage at odds with nature and hence a dishonest vow.[54] Between the monogamous flower in the poem's opening lines and the radically promiscuous tree in the poem's final lines, many kinds of sexualities and living situations are evoked and perhaps, by example, urged on the reader. Perhaps these sexual examples were, as Schiebinger has suggested, made "palatable to young minds" by the blanket term of *marriage,* and hence coexisted peacefully within the European moral tradition of "lawful marriages."[55] Nevertheless, if Linnaeus conveniently calls male and female reproductive parts "husbands" and "wives," it is not because these are the only models of social or sexual arrangements explicit within his system; Darwin's poem simply amplifies the libertine qualities already present in Linnaeus's system, a system that outlines the many other sexual alternatives to monogamy in the plant kingdom.

Darwin's openness to the wide range of social-sexual options that were otherwise preserved only under the cover of the term "marriage" is evident in his commitment to representing those options. The options he represents are far more broad, of course, than those that would be deployed in the novel form. Darwin's poem made explicit that which the botanical vernacular had comfortably occluded: the potential libertinism of Linnaeus's system and the degree to which his schema made that fact possible by employing the general term of "marriage" (or "nuptials") for the sexual act.[56] The vernacularization of botany made the representation of sexual potential possible, both in the sense that the botanical meaning of a bloom obtained, and in the sense that the sexual system of Linnaeus had passed into an acceptable realm of knowledge. Although Darwin's poetry is unlike the classical novel in flaunting its representation of sexuality, it shares with the classical novel a debt to Linnaeus for making possible a representation in imaginative literature that would otherwise have been far outside its representational parameters.

Smith and Darwin alike conflated imaginative literature with the popular genre of natural history writing. Their poetry demonstrates a series of important cultural facts, including the vivid leakage of a scientific vocabulary into literary and popular discourse. As I have shown, the way botany functioned as a locus in controversies about gender in particular points to the confluence of narratives of female destiny and botany. As I will show, the pervasive gendered controversies and "loves of plants" of the last decades of the eighteenth century give way in Jane Austen's novels to the Regency era, where bloom becomes a tacit, if nevertheless still charged, expression of the sexual potential of marriage.

THREE

Austen's Physicalized Mimesis
Garden, Landscape, Marriageable Girl

Gustavus-Vasa, & Charles 12th, & Christina,

& Linneus—do their Ghosts rise up before you?

—Jane Austen to Francis Austen, July 3, 1813

T he age of Austen overlapped with the age of Linnaeus, a time distinctive for the zealousness with which the taxonomical and observational sciences sought to find and then represent natural entities.[1] That expression of an individual natural entity—for instance, the newly introduced, named, and zealously embraced flowers *Paeonia suffruticosa*, or tree peony, and *Lilium tigrinum*, or tiger lily, brought from China in 1787 and 1804, respectively—entered the English lexicon through the Linnaean taxonomy. It was Carl Linnaeus's system that enabled the ordering of the (known) natural world, a world in which Jane Austen was conterminously living and writing. Her letters, memorable for their miniaturism and colloquial energies, suggest the degree to which a scientific lexicon had entered the fabric of everyday speech; in one of many like it, written to her sister, Austen's letter of February 9, 1807, describes the plants she has ordered for her new garden: "at my own particular desire, he procures us some Syringas. I could not do without a Syringa, for the sake of Cowper's line."[2] *Syringa vulgaris* is the botanical name that Linnaeus himself assigned to the lilac. Austen's employment of it in planning her garden illustrates the incorporation of the Linnaean botanical lexicon into poetry and everyday speech alike—the vernacularization of the contemporary interest in the scientific and natural.

Linnaean taxonomy described and ordered the natural world, a world that was becoming larger every day, as differences among plants were accounted for and new species from abroad were brought back to England. Linnaean taxonomy was a tool and a system of naming the observed world, but more figuratively, it was a way to linguistically represent and provide a mimetic account of the natural world and its organic objects. It structured the emergence of a new language, of new words that were only now becoming generally known or were even just coming onto the horizon in English. Linnaean taxonomy simultaneously accommodated and vernacularized the new influx of language; for instance, chrysanthemums, cultivated in China since 500 BCE, reached Europe for the first time in 1789; the binomial *Chrysanthemum vestitum* was vernacularized to form the name in common usage. The incorporation of new language for plants, of course, did not originate in the eighteenth century, for there had been previous influxes of new plants from abroad, such as those introduced at the end of the sixteenth century (including the evening primrose, black-eyed Susan, marigold, and Chinese peony). It is not entirely clear, for instance, if Austen, in a letter of May 1811, is referring to the famous and new tree peony or one that had been relatively long established in England: the "young Piony [*sic*] at the foot of the Fir tree has just blown & looks very handsome."[3] What is more certain is that the Linnaean taxonomy structured the emergence of, and made more comprehensible, an ever-broadening natural world, assimilating a new influx of diverse and previously unknown species— including the dahlia, bluebell, Easter lily, cosmos, yarrow, gladiolus, strawflower, Japanese iris, zinnia, morning glory, tiger lily, kousa dogwood, and poinsettia—within the three decades around the turn of the century.

The broad cultural interest in plants, botanizing, and plant collection contributed to an increased commercial stake in nature. Between 1750 and 1850, approximately five thousand foreign species of plants were introduced into England, some of them by botanists sponsored by institutions such as Kew Gardens and others by botanists employed by the large and prosperous private nurseries of the day.[4] The Vineyard Nursery was granted the only exception to the blockade during the Napoleonic Wars in order to supply new varieties of roses to the Empress Josephine, who had gone 2 million francs into debt in the service of her garden.[5] The increased interest in the natural world was not only met but also fueled by commercial enterprises, especially those nurseries that opened and flourished in London during the eighteenth and nineteenth centuries; as the example of James Lee, the nurseryman who first introduced Linnaean concepts to England in 1760, suggests, commercial enterprise contributed to the vernacularization of taxonomic knowledge and growing interest in the natural world.[6]

What is the importance of this cultural phenomenon? More specifically, what is its importance for students of the classical novel, a genre whose own trajectory of growth toward realism parallels the emergence of that botanical culture? We can better understand its cultural role, and its impact on the representational practices of the novel, if we remember that this "nature," so elaborately studied, taxonomized, and celebrated in the late eighteenth century, was throughout a sexualized nature. As I have shown, the effect of Linnaeus's sexual system on the circumambient culture was to see the natural world through an organizing principle of sex; most prominently, the flower began to be broadly understood as the sexual part of the plant, a collection of stamens and pistils engaged, in Linnaeus's terms, in courtship and "marriage." Other realms of the "natural"—including landscape and garden aesthetics—shared a similar taxonomical impulse and epistemology: the effort to classify landscapes, flora, and persons that are engaged in such oddly human activities as flirtation, courtship, and reproduction.

In constructing and defining the category of the marriageable girl, Austen's novels reflect preexisting eighteenth-century registers—including botany, natural history, and landscape aesthetics—that had in them a taxonomical impulse and epistemology. The eighteenth-century scientific paradigm of classification, standing on an Aristotelian platform, was one of both generalization and individuation; Linnaeus's binomial nomenclature, for instance, synthesized plants into groups and analyzed plants into individual kinds. In Austen's novels the blooming girl follows the same representational model of generalization and individuation: a social entity going through an agreed-on set of actions appropriate to her group, and a private entity going through a set of experiences particular to her as an individual. The taxonomic logic behind the blooming girl is present also in natural history and picturesque landscape aesthetics, for the observational methodology of natural history and the aesthetic grounds of picturesque landscape theory depend on the logic of generalization and individuation, as well as an a priori model. That is, an "ideal" is figured in every observation, and the individual (an object in nature, a picturesque view) is then understood as the particular instantiation of that ideal. This representational model, of course, extends beyond landscape aesthetics and natural history, but the additional fact of their presence within Austen's novels might suggest their importance to Austen's blooming girl. The representation of the blooming girl—like the plant's binomial, or a picturesque view, or the recording of a natural phenomenon—is one that locates her within a general category even as it insists on her unique status.

I am proposing that Austen's anatomization of Regency courtships and social arrangements was underpinned by, and informed through, the taxonomical urges of eighteenth-century sciences and related studies of nature, and that these sciences can be detected through an investigation within the texts of three *sites*: the garden, the picturesque landscape, and the marriageable girl. Each of these sites, or topoi, reveals a shared understanding that to speak of a garden, a flower, or even the arrangement of a landscape in Austen's time is to invoke an implicit sexual narrative. Just as Linnaean botany brought new meaning to the image of the flower yet was still "covered" by an earlier lexicon or referential range, the image of the garden, especially in its contemporary picturesque idiom, had a similar structure: the sexual discourse of picturesque aesthetics was covered by a prior, acceptable referential range. Because gardens and landscapes implied a sexual content, the garden in which the blooming is often found confers similar implications on her. The garden in Austen's novels is not a meaningless space or one that can be accounted for simply by the claims of realism but a space that invokes a sexualized nature. By locating productive courtship almost exclusively in the outdoors, Austen's narratives rely on the representation of a sexualized landscape to help delineate the category of the more or less "natural" and marriageable girl and to tell that which cannot be explicitly represented: the sexual content of courtship. What I will term Austen's *physicalized mimesis* borrows from the taxonomies of sexualized sciences and the representational possibilities of the picturesque garden.

This physicalized mimesis, and the logic that animated it, found its ideal representational subject in the marriageable girl. The method of description employed by the Linnaean system rendered a plant more readily and precisely nameable; moreover, this method of taxonomization made it possible to identify its place within a larger category and as an individuated entity. This, put simply, is a method of description and representation that is common to the growing energies toward realism in the novel of the late eighteenth century. The marriage plot is a deliberately conceived structural limitation in precisely the same way that the descriptive tactics of Linnaean botany are a structural limitation; the marriage plot's focus on the marriageable or blooming girl is like Linnaean botany's focus on the flower's bloom. Each limitation yields description; each focus on a single natural object; each focus on a bloom. In the novel, these cruxes of narrative interest are routinely female, specifically females of the age that make them likely candidates for marriage. In Austen the center of narrative interest is the marriageable girl, and the girl who "blooms," just as the center of descriptive interest in Linnaeus is the bloom of the plant. The representational roots of novelistic bloom are in Linnaeus and, more generally, in the physicalized mimesis of the natural sciences, to which realism's fidelity to the local and the observational is, at least in part, indebted.

At the center of this study is the blooming girl, because not only does Austen make her central but, by the logic of his analogical system, so does Linnaeus: both make potential sexual reproduction within the parameters of marriage central to their mimetic projects. Put another way, one of my central postulates is that the blooming girl is the most vivid instance of the novel's Linnaean energies, the most like the flower at the center of the Linnaean classification system, for both represent potential sexual reproduction within the parameters of what Linnaeus and novelists alike call marriage. Blooms are at the center of Linnaean botany, and blooming in the marriage plot is integral to the way the sexual potential of marriage is implied—the full articulation of both genres, in a sense, depends on the central principle of a bloom.

This, then, is the key fact: the blooming girl is a taxonomic construction. The novel of courtship universalizes the experience of blooming, even as that novel insists on treating each blooming girl as an individual narrative. We can see this most readily through Austen's characterization of Elizabeth Bennet. She is of the age typically thought of as the age of bloom—a grouping, or type, that is a broad social category, a point made emphatic by her being one of "five out at once"—but she is also made unique and is rendered so much an individual that the fact that she belongs within the balder grouping of the marriageable girl is almost forgotten.[7] Each of Austen's bloom narratives, including *Pride and Prejudice*, *Mansfield Park*, *Emma*, and *Persuasion*, takes as its starting point this taxonomical logic, balancing the claims of the blooming girl's more general categorization with her individual claims of person and situation. Emma Woodhouse's resistance to marriage, Anne Elliot's age, and Fanny Price's uncertain social status are potential variations on the blooming girl (personified by Elizabeth Bennet) that Austen exploits. If each of these Austen heroines belongs to the broad classificatory schema of the "marriageable girl," the unique claims of each of their "bloomings" marks them as individual species. Austen does not repeat her narratives but explores certain specific variations on bloom—including age, resistance to marriage, social position— to form taxonomically distinct courtship plots.

My investigation of this taxonomic logic, and three ways that human social and sexual concerns are adjudicated in Austen's novels—the garden, the picturesque landscape, the blooming girl—will begin with the late eighteenth-century urban history of the garden, its origins as a place of "pleasure" both licit and illicit. By turning to Frances Burney, one of Austen's immediate novelistic predecessors and influences, I explore how the libertinism of the urban public garden—specifically, the walks of Vauxhall and Marylebone rendered in *Evelina*—illuminates the meanings implicit in Austen's rural gardens. In *Evelina* sexualized courtship (and literal sexual proposition) occurs in the city's pleasure gardens, rather than in the built environment, which suggests the sexual connotations of garden space—a connotation not unique to the city's gardens, for courtship, of the licit and the illicit kind, follows Evelina to private gardens in the country.

The second section turns to the picturesque landscape and how it conditions the representation of the marriageable girl in Austen's courtship plots. The language of picturesque landscape theory itself contains a metaphorical dimension that is indebted to a common social narrative: the "improvement" of the marriageable girl approaching a matured perfection. The landscape and the girl depend on a shared aesthetic vocabulary and shared values of "naturalness" and "improvement." Both contemporary landscape aesthetics (as well as the aesthetics of Hogarth and Burke) and Austen's marriageable girl are grounded in these principles; both value naturalness while distrusting the cultivated or formal image, a focus that owes much to the value placed in the eighteenth century on representing the natural world through systems that were mimetic of what already existed in nature. The value placed on improvement is linked to the value of naturalness, for the aesthetic theory behind both picturesque landscape theory and the representation of the marriageable girl is that, despite intense cultivation or "improvement," finally both the girl and the landscape must appear originally to be natural. The girl and the picturesque landscape labor under the same burden of naturalness that eventually condemned Linnaeus's system.

What I have sketched out so far are two figural systems, the garden and the picturesque landscape, that are present very much as topics themselves within Austen's novels. In the final section of the chapter I return to a more buried figural system in Austen's classical novel—the concept of bloom—that is less the object of representation in Austen than a governing principle of representation. In other words, bloom underpins the marriage plot and, unlike the picturesque landscape or the garden, is not an overt subject within the narrative, except for the occasional reference to blooming complexions. Rather—a point crucial to what follows—bloom is a narrative indicator of sequence and action leading to the novel's closure in marriage. Through detailed readings of four Austen bloom plots (*Pride and Prejudice*, *Mansfield Park*, *Emma*, and *Persuasion*) I will show how these texts represent the sexual dimension to courtship. In doing so, the argument about bloom suggests an alternative account of readerly pleasure in closure, one that emphasizes the sexual potential with which the novel closes: marriage as the initiation into an already forecast erotics.

Lovers Walk: Burney's *Evelina* and Austen's *Pride and Prejudice*

Lovers do walk, and in London they walked in "Lovers Walk," one of the infamous dark paths of Vauxhall, a fashionable and popular pleasure garden of the eighteenth century. The name of the path at Vauxhall is an acknowledgment, enabled by its anonymity, that lovers do, indeed, walk—to be unobserved, to have an erotic encounter, whether that be in the garden of one's home or the pleasure gardens of London. The idea that lovers take walks together is a cultural cliché for us, the conceit behind such things as popular songs, greeting cards, and personal ads. But the fact that in *Evelina* "lovers walk" is both a place and an action is key to understanding how sexualized courtship is narrated in the later eighteenth-century novel.

In *Evelina, or the History of a Young Lady's Entrance Into the World* (1778), Frances Burney places the eponymous heroine several times within a metropolitan space that has long since vanished from London's cityscape. The pleasure gardens were part urban green spaces, part amusement parks; in the mid-to late eighteenth century the pleasure gardens tolerated both genteel and prurient behavior and functioned as a public space for bourgeois and aristocratic classes alike. As *Evelina* bears out, the urban pleasure garden created a space in which the implicit sexual behavior of some of its denizens did not detract from the explicit purpose of visiting the garden. The private rural garden shares with the urban garden an enabling explicit narrative, for to walk in a garden, urban or rural, is to seemingly perform a tasteful and innocent act, even if that very act enabled a privacy that challenged innocence.

The change from the country to the city precipitates the courtship plot in *Evelina*, for Evelina at seventeen years old temporarily leaves her retired home with a country parson for a London season, and returns to it (after a number of plot contrivances) only after she is married. Even though this is a textual structure that conflates the city with marital opportunity, the most heightened scenes of courtship do not occur within the city's public or private interiors but within its natural landscapes. Thus the country is imported into the city, in the sense that the pleasure garden is both natural, like the "country," and, like the "city," achieved. The contrast between country and city, as Raymond Williams has shown, was a classical formation, and the images and associations attached to the contrast persisted despite or perhaps because of historical change.[8] The mutual constitution of the urban pleasure garden and the private rural garden is explicit in the novel's parallel evocations of these two spaces of courtship, while in Austen's work that interconnection is not only less explicit but intended to be understood as a contrast. *Evelina*, in its movement between the country and the city, implies what Austen's more hermetic environments almost repress: that the private rural garden is not as far from urban manners as its seclusion would seem to indicate, that the country is not merely represented in miniature in the city but that the city is present in the country's gardens as well; in short, that as Williams has suggested, the urban–rural pairing is mutually informing rather than firmly opposed. The implicit linkage between rural and urban spaces is denied, of course, in Burney's novel, as in Reverend Villars's anxious hope that "this one short fortnight spent in town has not undone the work of seventeen years spent in the country."[9]

The places in which Evelina encounters the potentially toxic influences of the town are not just the theaters or public balls but, more pointedly, public outdoor spaces called pleasure gardens; Vauxhall, Ranelagh, and Marylebone are the three named in the novel.[10] J. Trusler's *London Adviser and Guide* (1790) indicates that in its heyday Vauxhall offered myriad amusements in addition to the walks, hedges, and trees of the gardens themselves—both Trusler's guide and Warwick's nineteenth-century history of the pleasure gardens say that the entrance from a dark passageway into the garden, fully lit at midcentury by up to fifteen hundred lamps, was thought to be the most impressive aspect of the experience. Other amusements included juggling, pantomimes, fireworks, theater, music, supper rooms, an 800-foot rotunda, tableaux, cascades, temples, colonnades, tightrope acts, a Chinese pagoda, the Italian Walks, and "illuminations"—these being pictures, in lights, some spanning up to 40 feet, of such things as butterflies and other animals.[11] Although these pleasure gardens may seem more precursors to the modern day amusement park than natural gardens, they were also green spaces—Vauxhall, closely planted with trees, was about 12 acres in area, taking its aesthetic cues from the formal layout of the French garden (see fig. 7). Even if going to Vauxhall meant leaving the exact environs of the City (it was located in the region of greater London now known as Pimlico), Vauxhall was firmly a pastime of urban life.

Although the pleasure gardens were as much evening entertainment as any other urban destination, they were like rural gardens in being seasonal and dependent on the vicissitudes of weather; each of Evelina's trips is threatened by rain. Unlike a private estate, pleasure gardens functioned as sites for the promiscuous mingling of the classes and the sexes. An early nineteenth-century pamphlet entitled *The Pleasure Gardens of London* advertises that the gardens brought together people from varying social classes. Accounts suggest that in 1732, men outnumbered women at Vauxhall by ten to one, and many of the visitants were in masque; by 1750, however, by most accounts Vauxhall seems to have shed

A General Prospect of Vaux Hall Gardens
Showing at one View the disposition of the whole Gardens.

Vue Detaillee des Jardins de Vaux Hall

GENERAL PROSPECT OF VAUXHALL GARDENS, 1751.

[To face p. 301.

FIGURE 7   "Prospect of Vauxhall Gardens, 1751." Warwick W. Wroth, *The London Pleasure Gardens of the Eighteenth Century* (London, 1896), 300. Courtesy of the General Research Division, The New York Public Library, Astor, Lenox and Tilden Foundations.

some of its initial connotations.[12] In *Evelina*, only certain parts of the gardens are notorious, while the overall experience of attending a pleasure garden is acceptable, as if the contending meanings of the pleasure garden have become geographically distributed. Wroth's history tells of numerous complaints in 1759 of the disorderly characters who walked in the dark walks; in 1763, in response to similar complaints, the walks were actually cordoned off, but they did not remain closed—the following year a riot of fifty young men tore down the railings so that the dark walks could reopen. What is clear is that despite the somewhat notorious connotations of certain of the garden's parts, connotations that certainly would have waxed and waned over the course of the century, the pleasure gardens remain an acceptable place to frequent.

The widespread patronage of these urban green spaces within and just outside of London in some ways suggests a growing need to retreat from what was a fast-growing metropolis, but they seem also to owe their success in part to the late eighteenth-century fascination with the horticultural, a phenomenon contemporary to the explosive growth of London during this period. In this way, we should understand the urban pleasure garden as only part of the larger cultural fascination with the natural world, of which botany's popularity from the 1770s was also a part. The public's interest was inspired in part by widely circulated accounts of exploration, especially Joseph Banks's descriptions of Botany Bay, which he reached with Captain Cook in 1770,[13] while the gentry's interest in horticultural topics "expressed a positive enthusiasm for botany that would be hard to rival."[14] George III, Queen Charlotte, and Princess Augusta were avid gardeners and botanists whose horticultural efforts became the foundation for the Royal Botanic Gardens of Kew, located just outside of London in Richmond.

Even the social world with which the epistolary novel is primarily concerned illustrates the currency of the natural world, for the garden is not only an important setting in *Evelina* but also a primary analogue of Evelina's innocence. Raised exclusively in the country, Evelina personifies guileless innocence, a quality we are meant to understand as reflecting a nonurban set of values. And yet the novel persistently dissolves the conceptual boundary between country and city. The novel is structured around an epistolary exchange between Rev. Villars in the country and Evelina in the city, a correspondence that encourages Evelina and the reader to think that the country and the city are morally dissimilar, even opposing, places; the reader soon understands that the respective values associated with those spaces are so far from being opposed that they are often confused with each other. Most notably, Evelina's actual guilelessness is mistaken for a knowing conniving, and her real innocence is perceived as a self-conscious imitation of modesty; urban manners, which imply a search for the authentic and natural, unwittingly confuse the country and the city, and therefore end up embodying a constructed notion of the country in lieu of any authentic markings. The urban dandy Lovel, for example, questions Evelina's sexual innocence because it does not manifest itself in a legible way: "if health were the only cause of a lady's bloom, my eye, I grant had been infallible from the first glance; but—" (*EV,* 79). Evelina's provincial manners epitomize the very category of female innocence on which London's metropolitan code of erotic courtship is based, but because she is not tutored in urban manners her innocence is persistently questioned.

Not only do Evelina's very manners disrupt the neat dichotomy between country and city but also her judgments and beliefs often bring the concerns of the country to the city. Evelina's appraisal of Vauxhall transports a vocabulary most often used on rural estates to a city landscape: "the Garden is very pretty," Evelina writes, "but too formal; I should have been better pleased had it consisted less of strait walks" (*EV,* 193). Evelina brings to her analysis of this public metropolitan garden the vocabulary of the private country estate, a vocabulary indebted to the aesthetic revolution of picturesque improvement that Capability Brown and Humphrey Repton practiced—in essence transplanting the expectations of what it meant to walk in the country garden to this metropolitan one, as well as the manners and values associated with it. The confusion between country beliefs and city beliefs is the background out of which the intermingling of country and city sexual manners emerges.

Evelina's preference for "less . . . strait walks" articulates a preference for the English private estate, the place in which we, as readers of the novel of manners from Richardson to Austen, have become habituated to thinking courtship occurs. Key scenes of courtship in Austen's novels, for instance, take place largely outside, either in the gardens of private estates or on long walks in the vicinity of one's home.[15] In *Pride and Prejudice* successful courtship begins in the picturesque perfection of Pemberley and not (as was the case in Darcy's failed marriage proposal) within the confines of the drawing room. In *Mansfield Park*, the scene most suggestive of a sexualized courtship occurs at Sotherton, the estate soon to be improved, when Edmund, Mary Crawford, and Fanny walk in the estate's wilds. In *Emma*, the most charged moments of courtship between Frank Churchill and Jane Fairfax occur in the summer heat of Donwell Abbey and Box Hill, while Mr. Knightley's marriage proposal to Emma is made in the gardens of Hartfield, away from the parlor where Mr. Woodhouse sits oblivious of the suitor's arrival. We understand that these are heightened scenes of courtship for reasons other than what is said; the context of these scenes, the situatedness of these unavowed lovers walking in a garden space, contributes to the sense of heightened courtship. The garden provides an enabling privacy, which suggests erotic potential within the reassuring context of the garden's innocent symbolics. The reader understands a courtship is climaxing before the dialogue or even sometimes the interior monologue registers that fact, precisely because of the situation of the characters in the garden.

The regularity with which Burney sets scenes of courtship in garden spaces is itself telling. When Sir Clement Willoughby, the suitor with illicit intentions, escorts Evelina down another dark walk near Lovers Walk, he is doing so, as he will admit to her, because it is a walk "where we shall be least observed" (*EV,* 197). The affront Evelina experiences is not based, however, on his desire to be unobserved but on his misleading her, for the practice of walking unobserved is so common in the novel of manners as to be a structuring principle of the courtship plot. Sir Clement asks, evidently confused by the incongruity of person and place, what Evelina means by disgustedly refusing his sexual advances: "you distract me, why, tell me,—why do I see you here?—is this a place for Miss Anville?—these dark walks!—no party!—no companion!—by all that's good, I can scarce believe my senses!" (*EV,* 197). Sir Clement's misreading of Evelina's intentions depends on the reputation of Vauxhall's dark walks and the fact that Evelina is somehow away from "that part of the garden whence I perceived the lights and company." That Evelina is "away" from the company, however, is not a deviation from but a conformation to the function of the garden—a garden is where one goes to be unobserved or seek intimacy. Evelina's error is in her unintentional participation in Sir Clement's literalization of the sexual text of the garden: bringing city manners and their attending promiscuity to a courtship whose sexual implications are safe only if confined to the highly scripted garden of the rural estate.

By *Evelina* sexualized courtship is no longer strictly antithetical, as it was in Richardson's *Pamela*, to licit courtship (that is, courtship productive of marriage). In *Pamela*, sexual attention is a deviation from the proper code of conduct that impedes the marriage plot, while in *Evelina* the eponymous heroine is constantly placed in situations where titillating sexual innuendo provokes not only the concern but the interest of Lord Orville, the man whom she will eventually marry. Rather than drawing a sharp distinction, as *Pamela* did, between illicit courtship (courtship with erotic attraction and intentions at its center) and marital courtship (courtship with morality, and not erotic attraction, as its animating principle), *Evelina* blurs the distinction between the two. The animating principle behind Orwell's courtship of Evelina is beauty enhanced by sexual threat, for each of their encounters is structured around a set of ambiguous mishaps that make Evelina blush and require Orwell's intervention. The ambiguity of Evelina's position as an innocent in a series of compromising moments drives the courtship between Evelina and Orwell, a courtship that is both erotic and marital in its local manifestations and telos.

Despite the strong innuendo structuring the novel's marriage plot, *Evelina* does not explicitly represent erotic moments but rather substitutes scenes of walking as a figure for sexual engagement. These walks take place in the pleasure gardens, with their enabling figurative connotations; Evelina's narration of her cousin's experience in the dark walks of Vauxhall focuses on how the cousin had been *walked*: "she proceeded to tell us how ill she had been used, and that two young men had been making her walk up and down the dark walks by absolute force, and as fast as ever they could tear her along; and many other particulars, which I will not tire you by relating" (*EV*, 204). That the men "had been making her walk" in the dark paths "by absolute force" stands in for what cannot be said (the "other particulars, which I will not tire you by relating"). The intensity of sexual experience is here being signaled by the speed at which one is walked and the level of coercion used. The novel of manners turns to the vocabulary of walking for the same reason that Evelina will not "tire" her guardian with relating the "particulars" of her cousin's story: these details are not acts representable to the polite reader. Here, the preterition employed invites the reader to speculate about the particulars of the cousin's walk, particulars that are clearly enough implied, even though Evelina cannot enunciate them.

Walking binds the anonymous courtships of Vauxhall with the socially scripted, highly individualized courtships that occur on the rural estate. The pleasure garden and the rural garden are places repeatedly returned to in the novel; by treating as paradigmatic two such scenes I will show how the anonymous sexual encounters in public gardens inform what on the surface seem to be the unsexual courtships of private gardens. What will become increasingly clear are the following points: first, that the real suitor will never mistake the radically sexualized garden space for a lapsed innocence, and second, that the courtships of the public gardens are productive of *Evelina's* nominally private courtship plot.

The pleasure gardens of Vauxhall and Marylebone are the site of what is essentially the same scene repeated. At Vauxhall Evelina, against her better judgment, enters the dark walks with her female cousins who "would first have a little pleasure" before returning to the duller pursuits of their father's and brother's company:

> Quite by compulsion, I followed them down a long alley, in which there was hardly any light. By the time we came near the end, a large party of gentlemen, apparently very riotous, and who were hallowing, leaning on one another, and laughing immoderately, seemed to rush suddenly from behind some trees, and, meeting us face to face, put their arms at their sides, and formed a kind of circle, that first stopped our proceeding, and then our retreating, for we were presently entirely enclosed. (*EV*, 195–6)

Evelina escapes only to "run into the arms" of another man; soon, in this company, "both my hands, by different persons, were caught hold of; and one of them, in a most familiar manner, desired to accompany me in a *race*" (*EV*, 196, emphasis mine). Evelina's body is forcibly being held by several men, so when one man proceeds in "a most familiar manner" we expect a further physical attack; instead, that implied physicality turns into speech and, strangely, the request (uttered "in a most familiar manner") to "accompany me in a race." Walking—walking fast—is the enunciated proposition, and like her cousin's experience of being "walked" fast, a desire that in this plane of representation seems to stand in for sexual encounter. Into this scene enters Sir Clement, who putatively rescues her, only to take her down yet another dark walk and then venture, in the language of the text, "freedoms." These freedoms consist of verbal declarations of love, esteem, passion, and fervent hand-holding, but what is clear is that his proposed walk is just another version of the proposed "race," for Evelina responds with an astonishment not equal to the literal proposition that they walk on: "astonished, I stopped short, and declared I would go no further" (*EV*, 197). Evelina's refusal to walk any further with Sir Clement seems not to be incited by the freedoms themselves, for the narrative distinguishes her individual encounter with Sir Clement from the violence of the crowd of men by her emotional reaction (her response changes from fear at the crowd of men to anger at Sir Clement). Rather, Evelina's astonishment and anger has to do with his misrepresentation of their location within the garden (that he has taken her down yet another "dark walk") and the insult implied by that act in light of their prior acquaintance. Walking is condemned as an inexcusable freedom because Sir Clement acts on the implicit sexuality of the garden, effectively unveiling the contradiction of the garden space. Far from being exceptional, Clement's manners only enact that which is possible within a garden so public, and so anonymous, as to trouble the traditional scripting of courtship.

Lord Orville, whom Evelina will ultimately marry, meets her in an even more radically sexualized garden space than Vauxhall; she is separated from her party and in the company of prostitutes at Marylebone Gardens:

I walked, in disordered haste, from place to place, without knowing which way to turn, or whither I went. Every other moment, I was spoken to, by some bold and unfeeling man. . . . At last, a young officer, marching fiercely up to me, said, "You are a sweet pretty creature, and I enlist you in my service;" and then, with great violence, he seized my hand. I screamed aloud with fear, and forcibly snatching it away, I ran hastily up to two ladies, and cried, "For Heaven's sake, dear ladies, afford me some protection!" They heard me with a loud laugh, but very readily said, "Ay, let her walk between us." (EV, 233)

The prostitutes who want her to "walk between" them try to direct her movements just as surely as the officer from whom they rescue her. Their conversation, not related to the polite reader, convinces Evelina that she is being used as a lure for their trade: "I will not dwell upon a conversation which soon, to my inexpressible horror, convinced me" (EV, 233). The baldness of the sexual content that Evelina chooses not to relate to her guardian is implied, however, through this odd figure of walking. The details of walks in the garden—whose arm one holds, where the walk occurs, at what speed—stand in for unutterable details of sexualized activity.

This scene at Marylebone mirrors the previous scene at Vauxhall by way of illuminating the difference between two suitors. Unlike Sir Clement, Lord Orville presumes that the sexual innuendo implied by Evelina's physical situation in the garden is a mistake and not an invitation for license; rather than taking her to a "dark walk," as Clement had done, he escorts her back to her party. For Orville, the garden is a site of marital courtship even when it seems to imply a more obvious sexual meaning, a distinction that marks him as the successful suitor in the marriage plot. Unsurprising, then, that their meeting at Marylebone is actually thought of by Evelina later as propitious, even productive of courtship:

Generous, noble Lord Orville! how disinterested his conduct! how delicate his whole behavior! willing to advise, yet afraid to wound me!—Can I ever, in future, regret the adventure I met with at Marylebone, since it has been productive of a visit so flattering? Had my mortifications been still more humiliating, my terrors still more alarming, such a mark of esteem—may I not call it so?—from Lord Orville, would have made me ample amends. (EV, 241)

Evelina had just spoken of the evening as "the most painful of my life"; only when Orville visits her the next day does pain and mortification turn to pleasure, making her unable to "regret the adventure" (EV, 235, 241). In Evelina's terms, the mortification of the garden encounter, flanked by prostitutes, is "productive" in that it prompts this "mark of esteem"; it is a visit that not only suggests his attraction but promotes its fruition. This visit is their first tête-à-tête, an occasion that leads to his kissing her hand—the courtship plot's first explicit sexual gesture. The narrative suggests that sexual mortification in the presence of a man of sensibility, and one with marital intentions, promotes licit and sexualized courtship and is perhaps desirable when mortification produces the particularized sexual attention of the courtship plot. Indeed, her sexual mortification, the recollection of which causes Evelina's attractive blush, enabled Lord Orville's calling on her the following day. Evelina blushes "violently," the only reference to such an extreme in coloring in a novel saturated with references to the blush, as if the violence of the scene at Marylebone gardens has now entered the drawing room. The possible pleasures of the garden scene seem to be productive of this scene's eroticism.

Two scenes in rural gardens share with the city's pleasure gardens a structure of secluded walking that produces erotic courtship; these encounters take place in the garden of Lady Beaumont's rural estate near Bristol. Both occur in the same secluded arbor, with the difference being the kind of consummation proposed by Sir Clement and Lord Orville, respectively. In the first scene, Evelina has been walking in the garden, a place where she might appropriately secrete herself: "I quitted her, to saunter in the garden . . . here I believe I spent an hour by myself; when, hearing the garden-gate open, I went into an arbor at the end of a long walk" (*EV*, 342). This long garden walk invokes the long, if not the dark, walks she had abhorred in the urban pleasure garden. Sir Clement's behavior in this garden is represented in the same vocabulary of implied sexuality previously employed in the Vauxhall scene; following her to a place in which they will not be observed—the garden's most secluded space, an arbor—he detains her by force, holding her hand violently while uttering passionate phrases of devotion. Evelina's response matches her response in the public garden: "Sir Clement, release me, let go my hand!" She continues to protest, calling out for aid to a passerby, just as she did in the urban garden; here, in the private rural garden, that passerby is Lord Orville, to whom she cries, "pray, pray, my Lord, don't go—Sir Clement, I insist upon your releasing me!" (*EV*, 344). A later arbor scene with Orville mirrors the arbor scene with Clement; it follows quickly on an abbreviated indoor marriage proposal, for the outdoor space enables solitude and intimacy. In this case, the sexual promise of the garden space is suspended until Evelina admits her uncertain parentage; in the arbor, secreted away from possible observers, Evelina and Orville cement their intimacy and the courtship climaxes: "my heart is yours, and I swear to you an attachment eternal" (*EV*, 369). As Mrs. Selwyn, passing by their retired spot, so wryly and knowingly exclaims, "what, still courting the rural shades!—I thought ere now you would have been satiated with this retired seat" (*EV*, 368). Here the solitude and intimacy of the outdoor space is not threatening but productive.

The arbor at the end of a long walk invokes the contradictions of the urban pleasure garden, for like the urban garden space it harbors both licit and illicit erotic courtship.[16] Even though Sir Clement in the arbor is no stranger, she invokes the "dark walks" by crying out for aid and twice asking that he physically let her go. The anonymous and illicit sexual encounters of Vauxhall get mapped onto Sir Clement in the arbor because his intentions are sexual but not marital. Sir Clement's desire is narrated through the anonymous promiscuity of the urban pleasure garden because his desires can be read no other way—only the particularized sexual attention of the courtship plot leading to marriage can be sustained, for as the marriage plot works toward its conclusion any version of sexual devotion or practice other than marriage must be eliminated. Even if his courtship can be deprecated as a particularly urban kind of courtship (sexual intentions outside of marriage), its physical situation within the generically significant site of a garden alludes nonetheless to licit courtship. If Lovers Walk at Vauxhall bears any relation to the walks in the gardens of a private estate, it is because in each place there is both a potential action and an explicit enabling narrative. The relationship between a privately owned garden space and the anonymous spaces of public pleasure gardens is reciprocal: the events that occur in each inform the other.

The walk in the garden in Austen's novels, like the walks taken in Burney's urban and rural gardens, is an action that figuratively stands in for the erotic aspects of the event of the walk. Walks are an intricate part of courtship and are one way that erotic courtship is narrated within the representational parameters of the marriage plot; the details of walks often reveal the nuances of romantic attachments. In *Persuasion*, for instance, the detail of whose arm a woman is supported by during a country walk goes a long way toward establishing the particular attachments of the persons involved: Mary Musgrove's arm is dropped only when her husband Charles can no longer stand Mary's peevishness (an apt figure for the state of their declining marriage), while the specific state of Wentworth's feelings for Anne (that he had feelings for her but could not forgive her) are made palpable when he remedies her fatigue not by giving her his arm but by placing her in his sister's carriage. A number of intimate scenes in Austen's novels occur on walks.[17] It is possible to trace a more sustained analysis of the walk figure by looking in *Pride and Prejudice* at the scene when Darcy and Elizabeth accidentally meet at Pemberley; the walk they take enlivens her dawning change in sentiment and enacts the renewal of sexual courtship.

The walk at Pemberley is marked by a change in feeling from embarrassment to pleasure, an affective change that is enacted by the walking itself. They part on first meeting in embarrassment; Elizabeth turns from him and unthinkingly enters "a beautiful walk by the side of the water," a walk whose "every step was bringing forward a nobler fall of ground, or a finer reach of the woods." The landscape had previously inspired delight, but now walking with the Gardiners and Darcy's gardener she cannot see it in her distraction. Soon, however, Darcy reappears in a walk near them:

> The walk being here less sheltered than on the other side, allowed them to see him before they met. Elizabeth, however astonished, was at least more prepared for an interview than before. . . . For a few moments, indeed, she felt that he would probably strike into some other path.

This idea lasted while a turning in the walk concealed him from their view; the turning past, he was immediately before them. (*PP*, 254)

The locational aspects of the garden's walks are emphasized; the scene's tension emanates from the details of the walks whose paths offer a variety of potential affective possibilities, including one that Elizabeth can hardly believe possible: "that he intended to meet them," that he would not "strike into some other path." Elizabeth, who immediately recognizes it as a gesture of civility, intuits the importance of their sharing a path; however, when he invites them to return to his property, to these very walks, in order to fish, she recognizes it as a verbal declaration of a changed manner. His kindness to her uncle suggests a devotion to her that she thinks is impossible: "'it cannot be for *me*. . . . It is impossible that he should still love me'" (*PP*, 255). The significance of the walks is figurative, for their literal characteristics—being beside a stream full of fish—are important only insofar as they suggest Darcy's devotion to their friendship, to the very "*me*" and "for *my* sake" of Elizabeth's incredulous thoughts.

The scene changes when Austen begins to explore the active sense of "walk" rather than its previously locational character; a physical place becomes an action, and "a walk" turns to walking, with the unlikely addition of a moment of botanical absorption:

> After walking some time in this way, the two ladies in front, the two gentlemen behind, on resuming their places, after descending to the brink of the river for the better inspection of some curious water-plant, there chanced to be a little alteration. It originated in Mrs. Gardiner, who, fatigued by the exercise of the morning, found Elizabeth's arm inadequate to her support, and consequently preferred her husband's. Mr. Darcy took her place by her niece, and they walked on together. (*PP*, 255–6)

The moment of botanical absorption creates new physical alliances; as Elizabeth and Darcy are paired in a "tête-à-tête," the walking takes on a manifestly more physical character as they continue at an increasingly faster pace: "they soon outstripped the others, and when they had reached the carriage, Mr. and Mrs. Gardiner were half a quarter of a mile behind" (*PP*, 257). In their silent rapid walking they leave the others behind, a detail, which reminds us of their mutual physical vigor (as opposed to Elizabeth's aunt, who walks slowly and is "fatigued by the exercise of the morning"), their charged emotions—and, perhaps, the sexual content behind their just-renewed courtship. Their pace, although not exactly a race in the style of Evelina's experience at Vauxhall, does give them the kind of enabling privacy that Evelina's "suitors" were so eager to achieve.

The scene is expressive in a way beyond the explicit topics of representation because of the accumulation of telling detail: that Darcy seeks Elizabeth on Pemberley's most picturesque and natural walks; the speed of their walking (leaving the others behind); the exchange of partners over a "curious water-

plant" and with a man (all too aptly) named Gardiner. The brief botanical interlude gives way to a more sustained walk, which aptly captures the way
Austen's fictions employ a combination of bloom's expressive cognates; here
the scene's erotic tension, implicit yet aptly felt and articulated to the reader
through Elizabeth's interior monologue, engages three of bloom's topoi, including the garden walk, the picturesque landscape, and the marriageable girl.
Elizabeth's pleasure in Darcy is enunciated when she admits aloud that "she
had never seen him so pleasant as this morning," but the reader has already understood that the physical activity of walking has figuratively signed their sexualized (if still socially incipient) interest in each other.

Austen's slight but studied reference to the "curious water-plant" should remind us that the sexuality of the figure of walking borrows much of its power
from the space in which the walking occurs: the natural world, which not only
includes the licit space of the garden but also botany's sexual connotations. In
both *Pride and Prejudice* and *Emma* the climaxing of courtship occurs in the enabling privacy of the outdoors, on a walk and in a garden, respectively; in *Persuasion*, the acknowledgement of Anne and Wentworth's renewed attachment,
with a reduction of the natural world appropriate to their diminished freshness,
occurs not in a garden but in the setting of outdoor walking—first on a sidewalk
on "Union-Street" in Bath, then on a "retired gravel walk," where they "slowly
paced the gradual ascent, heedless of every group around them" (*P,* 240–1).
Austen's rural gardens prefigure the erotic initiation of the marriage with which
the novel concludes, even though there is no sustained presence of the city and
its pleasure gardens to literalize the sexual text of the rural garden. The implied
eroticism of the walk at Pemberley may seem a world far from the walks taken in
Evelina and a site far from the provocations of Vauxhall and Ranelagh, but what
binds the two scenes is the use of the figure of walking amid a nature implicitly
understood in the later eighteenth century as sexual. Austen and Burney have
been seen traditionally as continuous with one another, with Burney as the
most striking anatomist of the London marriage market in the epistolary form
and Austen the premier realist of the rural gentry's marital arrangements; these
distinctions are brought together by their shared dependence on the figure of
the garden and the walk, which illuminates the sexual content of the otherwise
mannered courtships of both writers. That "lovers walk" in Austen is a fact
whose representational impact derives from the dark walks of Burney's London
lovers—and from the garden spaces that sheltered them.

Improving Grounds, Improving Complexions

Driving into Pemberley Woods, Elizabeth's eye is "instantly caught" by the
sight of Darcy's house "situated on the opposite side of a valley, into
which the road with some abruptness wound." The lines of the picturesque
landscape that Elizabeth has entered afford her a number of pleasing sights that
come in and out of view, precisely because of the winding line that organizes

her perspective; by the time she reaches the house, her pleasure in the landscape is strong: "Elizabeth was delighted" (*PP*, 245). Her delight is repeated when she exchanges this position for one inside the house:

> Elizabeth, after slightly surveying it, went to a window to enjoy its prospect. The hill, crowned with wood, from which they had descended, receiving increased abruptness from the distance, was a beautiful object. Every disposition of the ground was good; and she looked on the whole scene, the river, the trees scattered on its banks, and the winding of the valley, as far as she could trace it, with delight.
> (*PP*, 246)

Elizabeth's eye follows the landscape's serpentine line, a line that for the second time has produced for her the strongly affective emotion of delight; the approbation of others is limited to the more expected "admiration." Tracing the curving line, Elizabeth's delight transports her to the delights of marriage: "at that moment she felt, that to be mistress of Pemberley might be something!" (*PP*, 245). The delights of Pemberley, far from simply inspiring a mercenary gaze, emanate from the landscape's lines: the winding lines that her body in the carriage and then her eyes follow, part of a nature, a "natural beauty," that she registers as unprecedented in its attractiveness.

The winding line on which so much of Elizabeth's change of sentiment rests is a line that picturesque landscape theory had adopted and recognized for the pleasure, and even sensuousness, it visually elicited. The sensual delight that Elizabeth experiences—"delight" that inspires thoughts of marriage—is not an idiosyncratic reaction but one that theorists of the picturesque discuss as a formal property of the line. William Hogarth in his 1753 *Analysis of Beauty* attempted an explanation of the sensual, visual pleasure produced by this line, a line that picturesque theorists and practitioners, including Capability Brown and Humphrey Repton, prominently employed in their designs. Hogarth suggests that since the human body has the most serpentine lines of any object in nature, it is the most beautiful object—its beauty, he writes, "proceeds from those lines."[18]

Hogarth considers the question of why a certain waving line is more pleasing than another by examining a series of drawings of stays, or whalebone corsets for the female body (fig. 8). Hogarth refers us to the fourth stay specifically:

> Number four is composed of precise waving-lines, and is therefore the best-shaped stay. Every whalebone of a good stay must be made to bend in this manner: for the whole stay, when put close together behind, is truly a shell of well-varied contents, and its surface of course a fine form; so that if a line, or the lace were to be drawn, or brought from the top of the lacing of the stay behind, round the body, and down to the bottom peak of the stomacher; it would form such a perfect, precise, serpentine-line as has been shown. (*A*, 49)

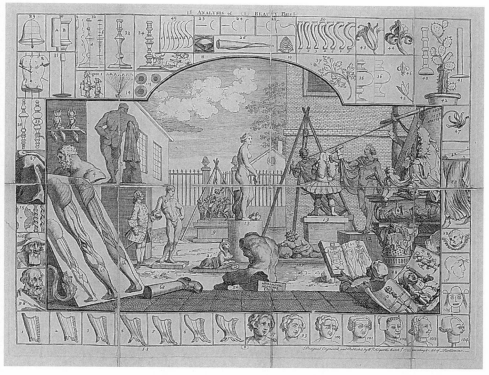

FIGURE 8   Plate 1 from William Hogarth, *The Analysis of Beauty* (London, 1810).
Courtesy of the General Research Division, The New York Public Library, Astor,
Lenox and Tilden Foundations.

The human body, which the whalebone stay conforms and shapes, as Hogarth
notes, has "scarce a straight bone"; the corset of "precise waving-lines" merely
shapes the formal property of the body to form a "perfect, precise, serpentine-
line" (*A*, 55, 49). The quality of not possessing a straight edge but being made
up of curving or winding lines is this aesthetic's key component of beauty.
Hogarth finds this line repeated throughout nature, as in the shapes of "plants,
flowers, leaves, the paintings of butterfly wings, shells," but most notably in
the human form and in landscape. The line has "little other intended use,"
Hogarth writes, "than that of entertaining the eye with the pleasure of variety" (*A*, 16). That Hogarth finds this pleasing line most often in the human
form, and most perfectly in the female form and the accessories meant to
shape it, suggests the reason behind Elizabeth's "delight" in Pemberley: the
pleasure that its sight lines provide stands in for and expresses a sensual pleasure,
or "delight," that owes as much to the implied presence of the human body as
it does to the landscape itself.

Hogarth turns to a variety of natural objects in order to determine why
the serpentine line—the essential difference between the new picturesque aes-

thetics and the formality of the French garden—is most pleasing.[19] In so doing, he turns the objects of natural history (the flower, the shell) into the templates for the lines of the picturesque, making landscape aesthetics and scientific exploration of the natural world overlapping concerns. An object that is particularly pleasing to Hogarth's eye is a human bone enwrapped by plant foliage, a strange version of a body part in bloom: "such shell-like winding forms, mix't with foliage, twisting about them, are made use of in all ornaments" (A, 55). That image satisfies what Hogarth will call our "desire for intricacy," a formal term in picturesque theory for lines that are varied and asymmetrical. Linking the desire for intricacy to instinct, Hogarth suggests that the pleasure the eye receives in following a curvy line is a "love of pursuit" and a physical drive (A, 24).[20] The intricate line, Hogarth writes, especially the serpentine line of a winding walk in a garden or a river, "leads the eye a wanton kind of chase" (A, 25). Those curvy lines in the landscape form the basis of the picturesque garden aesthetic of the picturesque, lines that are pleasurable to look at because they are, in fact, enacting a flirtation.

This "love of pursuit" encourages the eye to act, in Hogarth's language, wantonly. The landscape, in effect, flirts with the viewer and inspires pleasure—or "delight," as Austen twice characterizes Elizabeth's feelings in visually encountering Pemberley. The landscapes of Austen's novels flirt with the reader, leading the eye, across the narrated lines of the landscape, to see wantonly. Because the lines of the landscape embody sexual content, the formal lines being represented imply erotic courtship; for Elizabeth to respond with delight at the sight lines of Pemberley is to imply the beginning of a newly pleasurable courtship with Darcy. What must be stressed here is that the figure in the garden (here, Darcy, implied by his ownership of it) is involved in a sexualizing discourse because flirtation is essential to the pleasure found in the picturesque landscape: it is a central formal quality.

More often than not the marriageable girl is not examining the landscape (as Elizabeth is here) but is found within the landscape. Courtship takes place largely outdoors in a context widely understood, through this aesthetic, as flirtatious; thereby in situating its characters within it, the flirtatious, even sexualized, dimensions to the courtships are implied, even doubled. Within the representational parameters of the genre, of course, the landscape could "flirt" in ways that a suitor could not. The picturesque landscape's particular dedication to the curving lines of the female form means that the picturesque landscape more readily invoked the female form. Thus the female character within the garden implies the same capacity to be seen—she asks us to see her lines, or her figure, in the compositional terms of winding walks and serpentine rivers, and thus to have our eyes follow her, walking in that landscape, in a "pleasurable" and "wanton kind of chase." Therefore, that the flirtatious and erotic aspects of courtship in the novel takes place within the garden makes sense not only for reasons of plot—it affords privacy, for example—but because the work of representation that the novel performs is to connect the formal aesthetic principles of the landscape with the narrative of courtship. By the vividness of its description, the landscape invites us to see its lines, its "body," in a way that is more direct than Austen's usual subtlety with regard to bodily description. Hence, via the visual pleasures of the picturesque, a sexual content is implied to the reader, who, in the figural terms of the text, is the viewer of the prospect.

It is important to remember that Austen's novels followed quickly in the wake of an aesthetic tradition that commonly equated landscape with the young female form. Edmund Burke's book *A Philosophical Enquiry into the Origin of our Ideas of the Sublime and Beautiful* (1756) established the female form as the exemplary category of the beautiful: "observe that part of a beautiful woman where she is perhaps the most beautiful, about the neck and breasts; the smoothness; the softness; the easy and insensible swell; the variety of the surface, which is never for the smallest space the same; the deceitful maze, through which the unsteady eye slides giddily, without knowing where to fix, or whither it is carried."[21] Beauty, a general principle applicable to the landscape as well as the female, depends on the properties of smoothness, color, delicacy, and, most important, "gradual variation"; a principle opposed to the sublime, variation is pleasurable in being neither too symmetrical nor too astonishing. Theorists of the picturesque, such as Uvedale Price, may have rejected the general categories of the sublime and the beautiful for the picturesque, but landscape continued to be discussed, as Burke and Hogarth situated it, through the female form.[22] Richard Payne Knight in *An Analytical Inquiry into the Principles of Taste* (1805) employs a sustained analogical argument between the picturesque landscape and the female body, a discussion that Alan Liu has aptly characterized as fetishistic. [23] Knight's description of the picturesque landscape does indeed employ a frank erotic analogue: "the fairest nymph of St. James's, who, while she treads the mazes of the dance, displays her light and slender form through transparent fold of muslin."[24] The attraction of the picturesque landscape, as Price would suggest in *An Essay on the Picturesque* (1794), was felt as an attraction to a woman, whose "unguarded disorder which sometimes escapes the care of modesty . . . coquetry imitates." Indeed, Price suggests that the very line of the picturesque is constructed around female coquetry: "it is the coquetry of nature; it makes beauty more amusing, more varied, more playful, but also, 'less winning soft, less amiably mild.' Again, by its variety, its intricacy, its partial concealments, it excites the active curiosity which gives play to the mind."[25]

Hogarth explicitly distinguishes the female form, rather than the human form in general, as expressive of the most number of these serpentine lines.[26] The female body's lines are most beautiful because of what Hogarth describes as the plump "shell-like" skin of the female and the curving lines of her hair:

> The most amiable in itself is the flowing curl; and the many waving and contrasted turns of naturally intermingling locks ravish the eye with the pleasure of the pursuit, especially when they are put in motion by a gentle breeze. The poet knows it, as well as the painter, and has described the wanton ringlets waving in the wind. (*A*, 28)

The "flowing curl" and "waving and contrasted turns of naturally intermingling locks" are formal descriptions of lines that produce pleasure, for ringlets (especially those set in motion by wind) "ravish the eye with the pleasure of pursuit." Put simply, a line that invites a pleasurable pursuit overwhelms the eye; the waving lock flirts with, even ravishes, the viewer. Hogarth suggests that the formal principle behind the pleasure of the eye's pursuit of the female body—whether it is the stays that shape it, or the curls that adorn the head—is the same formal quality behind the line in the landscape. We might, with Ronald Paulson's analysis in mind, call this Hogarth's epistemology of pursuit.[27]

As is commonly known, Austen's novels routinely represent picturesque landscapes, as well as conversations about the theory and practice of picturesque aesthetics. Within *Mansfield Park*, for instance, we can find an extended discussion about landscape improvement, a trip to visit a soon-to-be-improved estate, several references to landscape improvers, and exuberant monologues about landscape by Fanny Price; yet although certain characters are satirized through their attitudes toward landscape, there is no definitive abstract grid through which a reader might reduce a character by knowing his or her sensibility toward landscape. Fanny, for example, likes the old-fashioned avenue of trees at Sotherton and despairs of the improvement in the name of the new picturesque that would tear them down, yet elsewhere speaks in praise of the Parsonage's grounds using high picturesque language. Maria Bertram, meanwhile, speaks knowledgeably of the picturesque—of "woods," "the situation of the house," and an "ill-looking . . . approach"—while Mary Crawford, the other model of femininity being deprecated in the novel, is not only insensible to the beauty in landscape but makes clear her lack of interest in it: "I have no eye or ingenuity for such matters . . . had I a place of my own in the country, I should be most thankful to any Mr. Repton who would undertake it, and give me as much beauty as he could for my money; and I should never look at it, till it was complete . . . it must all be done without my care" (*MP*, 81–2, 57).[28]

What is less commonly discussed about the picturesque, however, is the way its aesthetics provides a set of terms for the marriageable girl, above and beyond the way the picturesque is literally discussed by the novel; in *Mansfield Park* Fanny is described by the amateur improver Henry Crawford as "indescribably improved," having undergone what he calls a "wonderful improvement" in the space of six weeks (*MP*, 229–30). Henry Crawford's analysis of Fanny's beauty directly follows Hogarth's analysis of the beauty of female hair. His new appreciation for her revolves partially around his new perception of the lines of her hairstyle; he describes her heightened beauty in terms familiar to us as terms of the picturesque (Uvedale Price's second principle of "intricacy" and Hogarth's discussion of the serpentine line). Crawford speaks of her color being "beautifully heightened" and turns to "her hair arranged as neatly as it always is, and one little curl falling forward as she wrote" (*MP*, 296–7). Crawford's fetishistic attention to the single curl that escapes and drapes over her face invokes the intricacy of the serpentine line; Hogarth, beyond the local discussion of the female curl, which Crawford's analysis parallels, uses the same analogy in his analysis of the landscape, specifically the eye's pleasure in looking at or pursuing the serpentine line of a winding walk, of a driveway or river, or of a garden's edge; his long description of the kind of "judicious improvement" that Edmund might undertake at Thornton Lacey engages these characteristics of landscape (*MP*, 244). Picturesque terms—specifically, intricacy in form and variety in coloring—are key to understanding how Fanny Price can be narratively transformed from an unattractive girl at the beginning of the novel to a blooming beauty worthy of Henry Crawford's attention by the novel's midpoint. *Mansfield Park* depicts the gradual process of the application of picturesque theory to a female body, a body that is "improved" in the course of the narrative.

Picturesque landscape aesthetics is but one of several classificatory endeavors in the late eighteenth and nineteenth centuries that had the tendency to find the figure of the female at the center of their efforts. In this way, picturesque aesthetics and Linnaean botany are cognate endeavors, for in both the natural world is in some measure sexualized—in picturesque aesthetics, the female shape is analogized to the landscape, while in Linnaean botany sexual reproduction is the organizing principle. Landscapes and flowers are represented in parallel ways, for both are engaged in the oddly human activities of flirtation, courtship, and reproduction. In the representational parallelism of landscapes, flora, and persons we can begin to see how bloom's cognates play an important role in this story: the full force of the botanical vernacular, and the understanding of the natural world as simultaneously licit and sexual, cannot be adequately felt without examining the specific ways that a more inclusive notion of the natural world reflected this expressive connection. Thus Richard Payne Knight in *An Analytical Inquiry into the Principles of Taste*: "we do not, indeed, so often speak of beautiful smells, or flavours, as of beautiful forms, colours, and sounds . . . we apply the epithet . . . as correctly as to a rose, a landscape, or a woman."[29] A rose, a landscape, a woman: three sites that reveal a shared if implicit understanding of the sexuality of the natural world, all of which contribute to Austen's representation of courtship.

The picturesque landscape garden was a garden aesthetic, among other things, with a renewed interest in naturalness and plants, and not just formal lines. Accounts and genealogies of the picturesque have been well traced by scholars, many of whom construct complex paths of how rural scenery becomes a landscape, and how landscape begins to take on a pictorial quality and becomes a visual phenomenon unto itself; many emphasize how the picturesque was both a specific kind of landscape and a lived touristic experience.[30] Yet, perhaps because of the dominant interest in landscape's formal design history, the horticultural dimension to the garden has been underemphasized, even though the concurrent interest in botany and landscape improvement were not unrelated cultural phenomena.[31] As Janet Browne has suggested, the landowning classes who employed landscape improvers were also the people who owned the glass houses that housed the horticultural collections of the latest exotic plants: "plants were evidently an important element in the cultural context of a particular segment of late eighteenth-century British society, literally surrounding the gentry as they took their leisure in garden, conservatory, or library."[32] The interest in the plants within the English landscape was strongly related to the general surge in interest in plant material, an interest enabled by the new diversity of such material and attributable in part to the popularization of botany.[33]

Not surprisingly, Austen's critics have registered the importance of the picturesque to her work, but generally as a topic within her novels rather than an aesthetic principle that conditions representation.[34] Critical thinking about Austen traditionally has not considered the picturesque as a property of the body, but rather as a literal description of place; moreover, the subjectivities of Austen's characters have discouraged claims that would position them within descriptive categories used for insentient landscapes. Austen criticism has been more likely to demonstrate how a character's response to the picturesque landscape is revelatory of that character's ethical tendencies.[35] The question whether Austen ironizes picturesque excess and criticizes radical improvement, or whether she approves of those landscapes, has excited the imaginations of Austen's most dedicated readers.[36] Certain studies extrapolate from landscape analysis the politics that the texts, and Austen herself, are seemingly endorsing. The picturesque has also been considered as an explicit historical topic and an example of Austen's engagement of the social and political debates of her time.[37]

My premise is different: that the natural world of Austen's picturesque landscapes structures, rather than merely reflecting, the interests and social dispositions of her characters, particularly her marriageable girls. First, the valences of "improvement" in Austen travel back and forth between the adolescent female and the improved landscape, an "improvement" in both cases that, implying an intervention from outside, is not maturation, even if metaphors of maturation were occasionally used to naturalize the gardener's intervention. Second, aesthetics of the maturing female body as a metaphor in the writing of picturesque theorists—symmetry, variety, and visual pleasure—informed the representation of the girl in Austen. Last, the sexualized "nature" of these improved landscapes offer us avenues of insight into the structure of courtship in Austen. In the end, what I am proposing is a series of near-conflations: between the landscape and the female body, between alterations physical, social, and natural, and between the putatively natural and the artificial.

It may seem surprising that the female body shares with the picturesque a common set of aesthetic terms; too often the picturesque has been reduced to a set of qualities including roughness, wildness, and even decay, seemingly the very opposite of the girl in the courtship plot. But the presence of the picturesque in the novels also suggests a model of seeing, a way the girl can be politely apprehended. The picturesque provides a vocabulary and a model for that apprehension; namely, the picturesque always relies on a preexisting ideal.[38] The female protagonist in Austen is understood in a way that is similar to the apprehension of a picturesque landscape—that is, through the preexisting ideal and the individual instance. Austen's heroines, however individuated they seem, are, like a picturesque landscape, meant to be understood as a particular instance of the ideal of the marriageable girl. The picturesque is a vocabulary through which the novelist can plot the process of a representative girl becoming the particular object of its narration, and a means through which the polite apprehension of her body is suggested.

In *Pride and Prejudice*, a perspectival vocabulary is used to describe Darcy's resistance to and growing attraction for Elizabeth. At first Elizabeth's beauty is not even admitted—Miss Bingley, in a fit of jealous but accurate rage, remembers "how amazed we all were to find she was a reputed beauty"; the scene to which she is referring has Darcy, "turning around," and looking at her—he "catches her eye," he judges her as "tolerable; but not handsome enough to tempt me" (*PP*, 271, 12). The use of a picturesque frame of reference—including most generally the picturesque emphasis on perspective but also the distinctly picturesque aversion for symmetry—is central to Darcy's reappraisal of Elizabeth:

> Mr. Darcy had at first scarcely allowed her to be pretty; he had looked at her without admiration at the ball; and when they next met, he looked at her only to criticize. But no sooner had he made it clear to himself and his friends that she had hardly a good feature in her face, then he began to find it was rendered uncommonly intelligent by the beautiful expression of her dark eyes. . . . Though he had detected with a critical eye more than one failure of perfect symmetry in her form, he was forced to acknowledge her figure to be light and pleasing. (*PP*, 23)

The change in Darcy's initial appraisal of Elizabeth is more a change in perspective than a moral reassessment; it would be premature to understand Darcy's change through the novel's larger warnings against "first impressions," for his reappraisal happens long before his more sweeping reconsideration of past misjudgments. This is an aesthetic reevaluation that owes a great deal to a change in perspective; as the narrative is at pains to emphasize, he "had looked at her" and "he looked at her only to criticize," but those perspectives had been inadequate, for they had failed to show him the best "feature," and the defining aspect of her attraction for him: the "beautiful expression of her dark eyes." Darcy's aesthetic reevaluation of Elizabeth emphasizes a changed physical perspective; in his second meeting with her, he expects to criticize her again—"when they next met, he looked at her only to criticize"—only to find himself forced to acknowledge that a new perspective on her features made them newly attractive. This is not quite a vocabulary of sight lines but rather a subtle evocation of the importance of perspective that gains momentum in the details of his reevaluation: he sees in her figure's "failure of perfect symmetry" an attractiveness ("light and pleasing") that he had not counted. Asymmetry is, of course, an essential formal element of the picturesque, for symmetry is devalued in a picturesque landscape. The preference for the asymmetrical is a convention of landscape that Austen so completely understands that she has Elizabeth speak it facetiously in a later scene: "'no, no; stay where you are. You are charmingly group'd, and appear to uncommon advantage. The picturesque would be spoiled by admitting a fourth'" (*PP*, 53). Austen is clearly at ease with the vocabulary and principles of the picturesque, a fact that is registered, if least explicitly, in the way a picturesque frame of reference enables the polite apprehension of Elizabeth's physical attractiveness.

Landscape improvement, the practical application of picturesque landscape theory, also corresponds with the representation of Austen's marriageable girls. A general rhetorical feature of picturesque landscape improvement was an insistence on rendering the landscape improved in a way that was undetectable; to improve a landscape often meant to make it look less as if the hand of man had touched it. Thus the beauty found in an improved landscape was felt to be in direct proportion to the degree to which, to paraphrase Humphrey Repton, the "deception" remained undiscovered. As I have shown, picturesque theorists saw a figurative connection between the landscape and the female form, and even more particularly the picturesque landscape and the maturing female; both Price and Knight conceive of the picturesque line in terms of the coquettishness of the adolescent female, with Knight going so far as to connect it to the débuting girl dancing at St. James.[39] There is a similar preoccupation in Austen's novels around the naturalness of the marriageable girl. In *Mansfield Park*, Mary Crawford's appearance, endowed with fresh beauty, health, and elegance on horses and with harps alike, suggests an untarnished nature. But on closer acquaintance, Mary Crawford's consciousness of that self-representation becomes evident to Fanny and then Edward, who ends his courtship of her on the basis of (what he perceives to be) her practiced deception.

Not only is the metaphor of female adolescence used by these theorists, but the more general way that the land is figured as unformed—in need of a guiding hand to bring out its innate beauties and improve its defects—suggests, at least, a conception of the land as immature and even adolescent.[40] Moreover, the emphasis in picturesque theory on the appearance of "naturalness" is like the principle of "naturalness" essential to the representation of the marriageable girl. Above all else, a girl must seem natural and unmodified, even though one of the primary subjects of Austen's novels is the "improvement" of the marriageable girl: the social narrative of the adolescent girl approaching a matured perfection. The apparent contradiction within picturesque landscape theory—that the landscape needs to be improved to achieve its most natural beauty—exists similarly in the figure of the marriageable girl, who improves herself (through accomplishments) in order to achieve a natural perfection.

In *Persuasion* the characters engaged in improvement are marriageable girls, Henrietta and Louisa Musgrove, nineteen and twenty years old, respectively. The piano-forté, harp, and flower-stands that adorn the parlor testify to what the narrative rather contemptuously refers to as the "usual stock of accomplishments" that was "brought from a school at Exeter." The narrative characterizes the entire Musgrove family as "improved" or "altered," but the focus on the girls' accomplishments, manners, and looks suggests that a family's improvement is achieved through the female line: "the Musgroves, like their houses, were in a state of alteration, perhaps of improvement. The father and mother were in the old English style, and the young people in the new" (*P*, 40). Although these accomplishments contribute to the spirit of the Musgrove household that Anne so admires and to the "unembarrassed and pleasant" manners of the Musgrove girls, Anne "would not have given up her own more elegant and cultivated mind for all their enjoyments" (*P*, 41). These achievements, "brought from a school at Exeter," seem to trouble Austen, whose novels persistently question the value of accomplishments over more abstract qualities.[41] When one thinks of Austen's oeuvre as a whole, one is struck by the number of her heroines who are intelligent and not uninstructed yet are self-proclaimedly unaccomplished—most notably Emma, Elizabeth, and Fanny. Although Jane Fairfax is a prominent exception, the most accomplished girls in Austen's fictions are the source of either her moral invective or gentle satire: the Bertram sisters, Mary Crawford, Miss Bingley, Mary Bennet, Henrietta and Louisa Musgrove. Austen's novels evidence a sustained disagreement with a system of improvement that puts so much stock in visible accomplishments.

The subject of accomplishments versus innate, or natural, moral worth pervades Austen and has the clearest relationship to the questions emanating out of natural landscaping.[42] Should artifice be hidden? Can the natural be trusted if it is in fact constructed? In *Mansfield Park*, Fanny's uncertainty about the value of picturesque improvement does not only reveal her conservative feelings about aristocratic avenues of trees; her unhappiness with the suggested improvement at Sotherton also suggests her uneasiness with the improver's self-conscious imitation of the virtues of the picturesque. The imitation of real virtues is, of course, the very fault embodied by Henry Crawford, not surprisingly the character who most thoroughly embraces the work of "improvement" at Sotherton. This potential fault, the tendency toward imitation of the natural, was something that picturesque theorists were conscious of and in fact warned against; for instance, Whately rejected artificial ruins and Arcadian hermitages thus: "all are representations . . . the defect is not in the resemblance, but the consciousness of the imitation."[43]

The first principle of the courtship novel is that the marriageable girl has undergone a change in form that we call adolescence and that, importantly, precedes each of the novels; in the case of *Mansfield Park*, Fanny's figure changes conterminously with the narration of social adolescence, the début.[44] Henry Crawford, after having ignored Fanny, claims "none of you seemed sensible of the wonderful improvement that has taken place in her looks within the last six weeks" (*MP*, 229). The use of the word "sensible" in a discussion of Fanny's physical "improvement" is telling, for the sensibility of improvement is so common a register of the landscape as to be almost metonymic of the picturesque. Henry, who is known as an enthusiast of estate improvement, applies that same knowledge and eye to Fanny. He particularly notes the variation in shades that Fanny's cheek undergoes, and her bodily changes are articulated in terms that merge formal analysis with fetishistic attention to detail:

> You see her every day, and therefore do not notice it, but I assure you she is quite a different creature from what she was in the autumn. She was then merely a quiet, modest, not plain looking girl, but now she is absolutely pretty. I used to think she had neither complexion nor countenance; but in that soft skin of hers, so frequently tinged with a blush as it was yesterday, there is decided beauty; and from what I observed of her eyes and mouth, I do not despair of their being capable of expression enough when she has anything to express. And then— her air, her manner, her *tout ensemble* is so indescribably improved! She must be grown two inches, at least, since October! (*MP*, 229–30)

Henry Crawford's description follows a telos of maturation, from the lack of complexion and countenance to the attainment of blush and expression, and circles around the frankness that telos might imply by using French (her *tout ensemble*) eventually to get to the acceptable idiom of improvement and the socially allowable comment on figure, or height. The attention to her improved lines makes Crawford's appraisal of her potential "expression" or expressiveness all the more indicative of a picturesque frame of reference for the body. Fanny's *spring* is here implied—a state that seems seasonal since it is emphatically set up in opposition to what "she was in autumn . . . October." This is not a direct reference to bloom but one that relies on its expressive cognate, the picturesque; she has undergone a change, and is not only "different" but also "indescribably improved," a use of aposiopesis common to picturesque discourse. Austen's rendering of Crawford's sudden change in perspective toward Fanny's person seems to emulate a famous distinction of Uvedale Price: that the picturesque renders beauty "more captivating." Crawford, for one, is captured by it. The oft-noted oddness of *Mansfield Park* is related to the fact that Crawford's appreciation for Fanny's physical attractiveness (the appreciation of an "improver") is ultimately rejected in favor of a marriage not grounded in sexualized courtship.[45]

The language of picturesque theory does not merely determine the smaller units of description in Austen, however; it can help illuminate the structure, and the absences, of Austen's plots. In *Mansfield Park*, most notably, we have a productive conflation of picturesque and natural language, one that combines a literal examination of landscape improvement with its metonymic possibilities as a representation of the novel's key narrative fact, courtship. At Sotherton, the novel's most sustained episode of interaction with the natural world, the meticulousness with which the landscape is described is a constant reminder that the characters are being represented within a deeply physicalized and carefully mapped space; we are moved through the house and outdoors with an almost obsessive minuteness that leaves nothing unnoted, even that which Austen, more typically, could safely have assumed the reader would intuit. For instance, when the party moves from the house to the outdoors we know it because a door opens: "the young people, meeting with an outward door, temptingly open on a flight of steps that led immediately to turf and shrubs, and all the sweets of pleasuregrounds, as by one impulse, one wish for air and liberty, all walked out." There they admire "plants and pheasants" but soon move onto the part of the landscape that needs to be improved, a "bowling green" and "a long terrace walk balked by iron palisades" (*MP*, 90). The physical setting is so detailed that the reader could easily draw a map from the prose; the details of gates, the height of a flight of steps, the exact size of the woods ("two acres"), the species of trees ("larch, laurel, and beech"), and the way the trees are laid out are all made present to the reader (*MP*, 91). The narrative employs the eye of the improver by referring to the faults of the bowling green and the regularity of the forest plantings, and the virtues of the native trees. The erotic attachments among the two love triangles—Edmund, Mary Crawford, and Fanny, and, secondly, Henry Crawford, Maria, and Mr. Rushworth—are narrated through the details of the landscape.

The narrative sustains the context of physical space by contrivances, such as several locked gates, and by continuing to refer to the characters moving through their physical environment: "they should endeavor to determine the dimensions of the wood by walking a little more about it. They would go to one end of it, in the line they were then in (for there was a straight green walk along the bottom by the side of the ha-ha) . . . Edmund urged her remaining where she was . . . she watched them till they had turned the corner" (*MP*, 96). The erotic attachments of the characters are clear; Mary and Edmund leave a fatigued Fanny alone in the woods while they set off "across the ha-ha"; their crossing of the ha-ha, a ditch that improvers frequently used to keep livestock from the cultivated areas around the house, is a way the landscape signs how far their affection now extends.[46] The intention is to stay "in the line they were then in," a "straight green walk"—but as Fanny will find out, the farther park "had tempted them very soon after their leaving her" (*MP*, 96, 103). The fact that Fanny is left behind, and essentially forgotten, is clear enough from the events of the narrative; what the details of the landscape, so carefully given, contribute to the emotional account is the implied erotic attachment between Edmund and Mary. Having been "tempted" away from their intention not to stray far from their friend, from their "line," to only venture to a nearby "straight walk," they venture to the natural lines of the park, where the serpentine lines of nature stand in stark contrast to the straight lines of the wood where Fanny is left; she hears them return before she sees them, because their return from the wilderness requires a "few more windings" on their path (*MP*, 103). Plainly put, they leave Fanny among straight lines for the curving lines of the park. There, the formal properties of the serpentine line *enact a flirtation,* one that the narrative can only imply through the expressive system of landscape. Where the two lovers end up is far beyond—by which we are meant to understand an affective relation as well as a physical space—where Fanny goes that day.

The two lovers enter the park that forms the prospect the house enjoys; Fanny, "with great regret she was not stronger," cannot follow them into the less regulated lines of the park (*MP*, 96). Mary, who finds resting fatiguing, enters with her intended lover the far prospect, the space more apt to be characterized by what Hogarth would have known as the serpentine lines of nature. It is Mary's person, actively moving through the landscape to the farther reaches of the park, which is engaged in active courtship; the lines of the landscape confer on Mary, and not Fanny, its erotic implications. It is not surprising that the two lovers' walk in the outer reaches of the gardens also provides an enabling privacy, the events of which remain unexpressed, save for a short account of the landscape they had lost track of themselves in:

> They were just returned into the wilderness from the park, to which
> a side gate, not fastened, had tempted them very soon after their leav-
> ing her, and they had been across a portion of the park into the very
> avenue which Fanny had been hoping the whole morning to reach at
> last; and had been sitting down under one of the trees. This was their
> history. It was evident that they had been spending their time pleas-
> antly, and were not aware of the length of their absence. (*MP*, 103)

The privacy that the two achieve, in conjunction with the scene's sustained reference to the physical realities of the landscape, invokes the erotics of the landscape that contains them. By walking across the ha-ha and the park—a space that would have been characterized by its lack of formality, of being un-mown and accessible to the livestock that Rushworth kept—Edmund and Mary had reached an "avenue" of trees, the place that Fanny had most wanted to see. An avenue of trees is a formal line of trees, hence perhaps one of the features of the landscape that Rushworth was contemplating cutting down in the name of "improvement"; here the detail of the avenue explicitly (and climactically) evokes a picturesque thematic, in an episode already marked by its detailed attention to landscape. The affective implications of the picturesque thematic are clear enough: Fanny's inability to walk across the natural lines of the park, and her desire to be in the "very avenue" of trees that Edmund and Mary had been in alone together, marks through landscape what we might call a positional jealousy. Fanny would like to put herself, both literally and figuratively, in Mary's place: in that "very" avenue of trees (the spatial relation), "under one of the trees" (the "natural" relation), and in "their history" (the narrative relation).

The way this scene creates a positional or perspectival jealousy in its landscape is the way the novel as a whole creates what I would term *negative courtships*. That is, love relationships in *Mansfield Park* proceed through absences and failures: there is the absence of courtship between Edmund and

Fanny, the failed courtship of Edmund and Mary, and Henry's failure at court-ing Fanny. After Mary and Henry Crawford cease to be potential spouses for Edmund and Mary, there is a deficit of courtship in the novel. That is, there is no compensatory courtship between Fanny and Edmund narrated in the pres-ent action of the novel; instead, their story is narrated as a back-formation: Edmund is said to have begun to think that "a very different kind of woman might do just as well—or a great deal better; whether Fanny herself were not growing as dear, as important to him in all her smiles, and all her ways, as Mary Crawford had been" (*MP*, 470). Their courtship is absent, present only insofar as Fanny's desire to be in Mary's position in the landscape creates a negative courtship out of a perspectival jealousy.

The negative courtships of *Mansfield Park*, so thoroughly signaled by the heavily charged walks around the sexualized landscape of Sotherton, suggest something further: that just as an absence of explicit courtship in the novel is compensated for by an erotics narrated through the "natural" (Sotherton's soon-to-be improved avenues, Fanny's improved looks), the absence of any sort of sexual explicitness in Austen is similarly managed through the interven-tion of a language of nature. Behind the silences of Austen's texts on erotic matters are the expressive cognates of bloom, including gardens, landscape aesthetics, as well as botanical knowledge—and so to bloom we return.

Bloom: *Pride and Prejudice, Mansfield Park, Emma, Persuasion*

When Hogarth shifts the terms of his analysis from serpentine lines to the female face, the twinned issues of bloom and age enter the analysis of beauty:

> In the age from twenty to thirty, barring accidents, there appears but little change, either in the colors or lines of the face; for though the bloom tints may go off a little, yet on the other hand the make of the features often attain a sort of settled firmness in them, aided by an air of acquired sensibility; which makes ample amends for that loss, and keeps beauty till thirty pretty much upon a par. (*A*, 134)

The "bloom tints," distinct from the colors or lines of the face, are for Hog-arth the distinguishing feature between beauty at twenty and the beauty of thirty. Thus, *Mansfield Park*'s Fanny Price and *Persuasion*'s Anne Elliot delin-eate the outer boundaries of the blooming girl's possible age. Fanny, at nine-teen, is in the first bloom of youth and experience, while Anne Elliot, the twenty-seven-year-old whose courtship had gone awry, has suffered what Hogarth might have called an "accident." The unhappiness and sustained re-gret that she experiences over the course of seven years inflict an early "fad-ing," with a resulting loss of beauty and *joie de vivre*: "her attachment and re-grets had, for a long time, clouded every enjoyment of youth; and an early loss of bloom and spirits had been their lasting effect"(*P*, 28). In a letter to

Cassandra, dated April 25, 1811, Austen writes of her beloved niece Anna Austen in terms that also suggest a temporal narrative of youthful beauty: "she is quite an Anna with variations—but she cannot have reached her last, for that is always the most flourishing and shewy—she is at about her 3rd or 4th which are generally simple and pretty."[47] Like Austen's novels, whose sequence of marriageability and blooming is the strongest narrative indicator of plot, Austen's letter about her niece predicts a last stage that unites a youthful perfection with an end point. What else, we might ask, could Austen mean except the sequence of bloom and marriage?

The "last stage," then, as distinct from the "3rd or 4th": Anna's bloom, in her aunt's mind, is distinct from mere youthful prettiness; it is something more "flourishing and shewy," something unnamed for which Austen nevertheless is waiting: "it came upon us without much preparation;—at the same time, there was *that* about her which kept us in a constant preparation for something."[48] Austen's reference to Anna's precipitous engagement to Ben Lefroy is countered with her acknowledgment that they were not caught absolutely unaware but had been "in a constant preparation for something"—a state of readiness induced by *that*, the unnamed prior sign, which Austen allows had made them aware that "something" would later occur. That this intrigue about Anna revolves predictably around marriage suggests the degree to which Austen's "that" might be soundly understood as bloom, as that ineffable quality distinct from color that signals a flourishing readiness for marriage. As I will show, in *Pride and Prejudice* (1813), *Mansfield Park* (1814), *Emma* (1816), and *Persuasion* (1818) the heroine's bloom unites a poetic and narrative fact, one that functions both as description and portent of the novel's specific marital resolutions.

Austen's blooms emanate out of the botanical vernacular, their novelistic function and meaning as central to the courtship novel as the corolla (a plant's bloom) is central to Linnaeus's taxonomical system. That the flower is conceptually a Linnaean flower is palpable in Austen's narratives, for if bloom was solely a remnant of an older, allegorical association between girls and flowers, one would expect it to have disappeared by the early nineteenth century: one would expect it to dissolve in the face of the new impetus of realism. Instead, what we find as the nineteenth century dawns is the proliferation of this narrative, its pervasiveness in fictions of realism—as the novel itself becomes more realistic, the metonymy of bloom becomes more visible and legible. Thus in Austen's novels we find a bloom that resonates with the Linnaean conflation of description, sexual reproduction, and marriage in the bloom or corolla of a plant.

Only one of the two broad Linnaean taxonomical categories is explored by Austen's novels: what is known in Linnaeus as the narrative of "public" marriage. In Linnaeus, a public marriage is a kind of flowering, or inflorescence, that is visible, unlike the category of "clandestine" marriage, where one cannot see the flower (as in the case of ferns, mosses, algae, and fungi). The first-level distinction in Linnaean classification is around whether a plant has a public marriage or a clandestine marriage—in Austen, that distinction finds its *exact parallel*, for whether courtship and marriage is public or whether it is clandestine is the distinction on which Austen bases her principle of representation. Elizabeth's and Darcy's courtship, and not Lydia's and Wickham's courtship, is represented because, for Austen, clandestine courtship is beyond the limits of suitable representation. It is so far from being representable that when Lydia follows the regiment to Brighton and elopes with Mr. Wickham, Austen departs from the present action of the text and conveys the events of their clandestine courtship through the indirect narrative of letters. Clandestine marriage is implied by Jane's first alarm that Lydia "was gone off to Scotland with one of the officers," since Scotland was the common place to which one elopes; this alarm gives way to "fear they are not gone to Scotland," or, as Elizabeth tragically surmises, that with "no money, no connections, nothing that can tempt him to—she is lost for ever" (*PP*, 273, 277). Lydia, of course, never blooms; she is saved from disrepute by Darcy's intervention, but in Austen's world her marriage, having taken place outside the traditional sphere of family and publicity, is hardly a marriage at all, and certainly not one where the erotic implications of marital happiness could be safely hinted at. In point of fact, the Linnaean category of clandestine marriage may have derived from its terminological counterpart in mid-eighteenth-century marital law; the Bennet family's anticipation that Lydia will go with Wickham to Scotland follows from their general understanding of the banning, fifty years prior, of clandestine marriages in England in favor of the public display of marriage-banns.[49]

The blooming of a girl engaged in a "clandestine marriage"—the euphemism in Linnaeus, as it is for Eliot's novel, for an invisible sexual relation—does not enter the realist novel's sphere of representation until George Eliot in *Adam Bede* makes it her subject. For Austen, then, the blooming that leads to "public marriage" is her subject; the variations on that narrative are not as diverse as the sexual possibilities afforded by the vegetable kingdom—nevertheless, within a conventional frame of heterosexuality Austen manages to suggest alternative ways of narrating courtship, different versions on which to base the projected sexual promise of marriage. For a heroine to bloom in Austen is for her to enter the trajectory of the public marriage plot, for the look of sexual response and beauty that bloom describes indicates that she is in the state leading to marriage, with its correlative sexual potential. In Austen, bloom is synonymous with licit marriage, for in all of Austen's oeuvre, only the heroines in the throes of the marriage plot are actually described as blooming. The correlation between bloom and a licit sexuality is so firm in Austen that it might be termed a rule, and one so absolute that it shapes description to the point of incredulity: in *Pride and Prejudice*, Lydia is so willing to engage the erotic world that she elopes without promise of marriage, and yet she is never described as blooming, while in *Persuasion* Anne Elliot, represented as beyond the period of youthful beauty and marital aspiration, blooms for a second time in the presence of Captain Wentworth's returned physical regard.

Thus *Persuasion*'s Anne Elliot, whose age would seem to put her far beyond the (novelistic) pinnacle of blooming good looks, reblooms at twenty-seven in response to the reinvigoration of her marriage plot. Anne, "blessed with a second spring of youth and beauty," is a variation on the bloom narrative, and not unlike those perennial flowers known in garden circles as "repeat-bloomers" (*P*, 124). As suggested, the blooming girl in Austen seems both to be a unique and individual version and to belong to a broad classificatory schema.[50] The individuation of Elizabeth Bennet, Fanny Price, or Anne Elliot is so complete that the reader is apt to forget that they also belong to the larger category of the marriageable girl. The novels take as their starting point this taxonomic logic, balancing the more general category's claims with individual claims of person and situation; in *Persuasion*, for instance, the fact of Anne's being older than the typical age of courtship is the specific variation on which her broader identity as a marriageable girl is built. Fanny Price's uncertain social status is the equivalent of Anne Eliot's age, for both function as variations on the bloom narrative as personified by Elizabeth Bennet's bloom. The taxonomic construction of Austen's heroines does not diminish the uniqueness of their narrative destiny; Austen does not repeat her bloom narratives but uses the variations of age, social class, and resistance to marriage to form unique variations on the courtship plot.

Bloom, then, is the indication that the heroine has entered the narrative sequence that will end in marriage. Only the central female protagonist in the throes of the marriage plot is actually said to bloom, despite there being other females of that age and social position in the novel. Even though these heroines all belong to the broad classificatory schema of the marriageable girl and exist within a generic structure whose conclusion is foregone, the unique claims of their bloomings tell their individual stories; like the flower examined by the avid botanist, the blooming girl is the single entity on which we fix our contemplation, despite the rich variety of the world around her.

Pride and Prejudice

The ascription of bloom to Elizabeth in *Pride and Prejudice* signals the beginning of Elizabeth and Darcy's courtship; Elizabeth's bloom is a narrative indication, a figure that is the novel's strongest sign of incipient closure, as well as a poetic concern that describes sexual attractiveness. In this way bloom not only refers to appearance but also indicates the specifics of the novel's resolution in marriage. That Elizabeth blooms early in the novel is perhaps surprising, considering her seeming aversion to Darcy, but if the narrative's ascription of bloom to Elizabeth foreshadows their mutual attraction, it also seems initiated by Darcy's early physical attraction to Elizabeth. Her bloom metonymically suggests the sexual dimension to interactions between them; it also distinguishes her as the center of the marriage plot, and the narrative's central preoccupation, in a novel with several girls of marriageable age and (most particularly) a sister whose claims of age and beauty correspond with a courtship introduced in the novel's first sentence. Before Elizabeth will admit to herself an attraction to Darcy, the narrative has given the reader every indication that she has entered the trajectory of the marriage plot; the look of sexual response and beauty that bloom stands in for is a strong indication that she is in the state leading to marriage, with its corresponding sexual potential indicated by the state leading to it.

The absence of initial attraction does not impede the bloom narrative, but it does condition the possible contours of the plot; that is, since Elizabeth and Darcy's acquaintance begins with his indifference, followed quickly by her dislike, the possibility of an unimpeded courtship once his indifference is overcome is practically impossible. His first appraisal of her is physical—"she is tolerable; but not handsome enough to tempt *me*"—while he is affected in his second appraisal by her spirited refusal to dance with him (*PP*, 12). Darcy's reappraisal persists in its attention to physical beauty and the pleasure of attraction: "I have been meditating on the very great pleasure which a pair of fine eyes in the face of a pretty woman can bestow" (*PP*, 27). Resistance matched with a physical beauty deemed at first only "tolerable" translates into a burgeoning attraction defined by "admiration" and "pleasure"—an indolent, nonparticularized attraction that is inspired as rapidly as Miss Bingley's imagination.

The somewhat comic posture of this scene is followed by an episode in which Darcy's admiring, but nevertheless uncommitted, meditation on "fine eyes" and a "pretty woman" changes to a more acute and specific attraction to Elizabeth. This occurs when Elizabeth has walked three miles, "crossing field over field," arriving at Netherfield Park with a muddied petticoat, in order to see her ailing sister (*PP*, 32). Elizabeth is literally covered by nature; her skirts are encased in mud, and her cheeks speak a palpable sentience:

> Elizabeth continued her walk alone, crossing field after field at a quick pace, jumping over stiles and springing over puddles with impatient activity, and finding herself at last within view of the house, with weary ankles, dirty stockings, and a face glowing with the warmth of exercise. She was shown into the breakfast-parlour, where all but Jane were assembled, and where her appearance created a great deal of surprise. . . . Mr. Darcy said very little, and Mr. Hurst nothing at all. The former was divided between admiration of the brilliancy which exercise had given to her complexion, and doubt as to the occasion's justifying her coming so far alone. (*PP*, 32–3)

Elizabeth is literally immersed in the natural world, in that her skirts and stockings bear the traces of the mud and soil through which she has traveled; the landscape is written on her skirts, a landscape that the Bennet sisters often walk through and that Elizabeth demonstrably understands in terms of its picturesqueness. The physicality implied by her robust walking though the expressive space of the landscape suggests a generalized sexual flirtation—the gentlemen, including Darcy, respond to the "brilliancy" of her complexion and what Uvedale Price, writing about picturesque landscape in terms of a woman's looks, called the "unguarded disorder which sometimes escapes the care of modesty . . . and which coquetry imitates."[51] Bingley voices admiration while Darcy is all silent admiration; his only comments are elicited by the jealous Miss Bingley, whose interests are threatened by Elizabeth and hence subtly imply Darcy's admiration. The fact twice mentioned is her complexion—"a face glowing with the warmth of exercise," "brilliancy which exercise had given to her complexion"—and its attribution to exercise, a repetition that insists on the correlation between the girl and the natural world. That is, Darcy's implied admiration for her "glowing face," the "brilliancy" of her complexion, and perhaps even the "warmth" emanating from a body being exercised, is directly related to the fact of her movement through the natural world.

The context out of which Elizabeth emerges is the natural world—fields, puddles, mud, and landscape—with its connotations emanating from the elaborate attention paid it in the late eighteenth century. Taxonomy in particular, and the cognate interests in landscape and garden theory and practice, produced a sexualized nature, and here Elizabeth emerges from that expressive context. The physical marks of nature that make her unfit for the social world of the breakfast-parlor situate her within the natural world, with all its corresponding sexual connotations. The breakfast-parlor where she arrives after her long walk functions as the contrast to the outdoor natural world; there her appearance is shocking, for the women in the room find her appearance so incongruous that they liken her to an animal: "I shall never forget her appearance this morning. She really looked almost wild" (*PP*, 35). The disapprobation of the women is overwhelming, fixated as it is especially on the mark of nature on her clothing: "Yes, and her petticoat; I hope you saw her petticoat, six inches deep in the mud, I am absolutely certain; and the gown that had been let down to hide it, not doing its office . . . to walk three miles, or four miles, or five miles, or whatever it is, above her ankles in dirt, and alone, quite alone!" (*PP*, 35). It is the mud in particular, rather than her "untidy" hair, that inspires the two women's disapproval; although the dirt, as Mrs. Bennet had predicted, makes her not "fit to be seen," the disapprobation of the women is out of proportion to the social miscue (*PP*, 36, 32). Their reading of her appearance as wild, combined with their shock at her walking alone, is not only a criticism of her social decorum but a subtle imputation against her sexual propriety as well. The men defend Elizabeth by asserting her physical attractiveness and morality; Bingley says "I thought Miss Elizabeth Bennet looked remarkably well when she came into the room this morning. Her dirty petticoat quite escaped my notice . . . it shews an affection for her sister that is most pleasing" (*PP*, 36). Darcy's "doubt" as to whether Jane was ill enough to induce Elizabeth's display of strong feeling does not produce the censure that Miss Bingley invites; although he agrees with Miss Bingley's assertion "that you would not wish to see *your sister* make such an exhibition," it is not entirely clear what he would not have his sister do. That is, his response to Elizabeth is so admiring of her physical charms (her "fine eyes" were "brightened by the exercise," he says) that his deprecation of a like "exhibition" on the part of his sister seems to refer to his preference of not thinking of his sister in the terms he reserves for an erotic attraction (*PP*, 36).

The gendered reaction to Elizabeth's appearance is important insofar as it reveals that the disagreement among the men and women is organized around their different erotic reactions to a glowing complexion and muddied skirts. Masculine apprehension here is organized around physical admiration and even physical attraction; feminine apprehension is organized around alarm at muddied skirts, untidy hair, and the flouting of social convention, an alarm that seems to be composed both of envy (for the desire the breakfasting women have presumably failed to elicit) and sexual anxiety (at the sudden apparition of a woman deemed "almost wild"). Apprehension structures the scene, not unlike the way that apprehension is central to the picturesque, invoked here implicitly and persistently by the fact of mud on Elizabeth's petticoats. In *Principles of Taste*, Richard Payne Knight suggests that apprehension of the landscape had to be understood within the context of desire; he deprecated the application of abstract principles as "utterly void of all the warmth of sexual desire," pointing out that coloring is different from that which prompts "the choice of men," or, more directly, "their sexual predilections." Knight, in the spirit of the picturesque aesthetic he espoused, grounded beauty in male apprehension, in men's "experience and observation"; he essentially claims a gendered visual apprehension, one that distinguishes between simple coloring and bloom: "the redness of any morbid inflammation may display a gradation of tint, which, in a pink or a rose, we should think as beautiful as the purple light of love and bloom of young desire."[52] Knight sees desire through the visual terms of flowers and their coloring—the "gradation of tint" that evokes the "purple light of love" and "bloom of young desire."

The bloom that Knight sees in the tints of a carnation or rose is the bloom apprehended on Elizabeth's face, the glowing complexion caused by her physical movement through the natural world; the tints of the flower, evoking the "bloom of young desire," are apprehended in Elizabeth's face as well. The masculine apprehension of Elizabeth's glowing complexion suggests bloom, for Darcy's and Bingley's apprehension of her flourishing readiness for marriage indicates what I have been terming "marriageability." The fact that her physical attractiveness is asserted despite her unconventional, even "wild" appearance suggests not only that the attraction is operating apart from the social world but that it is operating in relation to the natural world out of which she has not coincidentally emerged. Darcy's attraction begins in earnest here, over the breakfast table, where Elizabeth's bloom foretells the ultimate resolution of the marriage plot.

Gendered apprehension is a topic that is repeated in *Pride and Prejudice*, a topic that is connected with the state of courtship as it emanates from that first scene of bloom. Jane, for instance, in discussing the affective reasons behind Bingley's sudden decampment from Netherfield, refuses to think him intentionally to blame and attributes his leaving, however mistakenly, to her miscomprehension of admiration: "women fancy admiration means more than it does" (*PP*, 136). Here, like Darcy's admiration for "a pair of fine eyes in the face of a pretty woman," admiration is understood as a physical attraction that is not particularized; Jane asserts, "we must not be so ready to fancy ourselves intentionally injured" (*PP*, 136). Darcy's criticism of the weight put on admiration—"a lady's imagination is very rapid; it jumps from admiration to love, from love to matrimony in a moment"—is parallel to Jane's claim that "women fancy admiration means more than it does." The fact that the novel's primary marriage plot initially goes awry in part because of Elizabeth's refusal to accept Jane and Darcy's precept on admiration is all the more interesting; Elizabeth, despite Jane's assertion that her fancy had made too much of Bingley's admiration, privileges its importance when rejecting Darcy: "do you think that any consideration would tempt me to accept the man, who has been the means of ruining, perhaps for ever, the happiness of a most beloved sister? . . . of exposing one to the censure of the world for caprice and instability, the other to its derision for disappointed hopes, and involving them both in misery of the acutest kind" (*PP*, 190–1). For Elizabeth, the retreat from admiration signals a capricious, even unstable, personality and "misery of the acutest kind." Darcy's response to Elizabeth's rejection of his marriage proposal—that "toward *him* I have been kinder than toward myself"—underscores his intellectual resistance to the importance of physical attraction in courtship, for he acknowledges that he had interrupted the sequence of courtship (of admiration to love to matrimony) for Bingley but had been unable to be so "kind" toward himself.

That Darcy initially acknowledges the lure, if not the importance, of sexual attraction is evident from an earlier scene at Netherfield, when Miss Bingley had asked Elizabeth to "take a turn about the room" with her; a desperate bid to attract Darcy, Miss Bingley's plan is undermined by Darcy's comic unveiling of its purpose:

> he could imagine but two motives for their chusing to walk up and down the room together . . . "you either chuse this method of passing the evening because you are in each other's confidence and have secret affairs to discuss, or because you are conscious that your figures appear to the greatest advantage in walking—if the first, I should be completely in your way; —and if the second, I can admire you much better as I sit by the fire." (*PP*, 56)

Like this scene, much of the early portion of the novel is given over to Darcy's ironic, and sometimes comic, deprecation of his burgeoning attraction for Elizabeth. That he is overwhelmed by his attraction—once referring to it as a "danger"—and eventually proposes to Elizabeth, as she says, "against your will, against your reason, and even against your character," is underscored by the manner of his first proposal (*PP*, 190). This much is apparent: for their courtship to proceed successfully, admiration must become a positive principle in the novel, and women's "fancy" (Jane's term) and "imagination" (Darcy's term) must become the principle on which the narrative of courtship is based.[53] Indeed, the sequence of "admiration to love to matrimony" that Darcy had comically denied is the sequence that Elizabeth's refusal teaches him to take seriously. "Pride," as we know, is the character flaw Darcy must learn to overcome, but it is "admiration," less commonly cited, that he must learn to value. Thus the renewed and successful courtship between Elizabeth and Darcy is not one based entirely in moral improvement but one that also has a new respect for the importance of sexual attraction.

The scene at Pemberley, as I have shown, is an extended meditation on the role of physical attraction in courtship as it is articulated through specific cognates of bloom. Elizabeth's approbation for Darcy's portrait within the house, and her growing admiration for his behavior, as a brother and landlord, are explicit ways the text signals her changing regard. However, as my earlier reading of the Pemberley scene suggests, her growing physical attraction to Darcy is articulated implicitly through the expressive terms of the picturesque landscape, and the walk they take in his gardens. After Elizabeth's visit to Pemberley, Darcy is given the opportunity to continue his sophisticated comic stance on "admiration," but he refuses to do so. In fact, Miss Bingley's teasing requires him to revisit his earlier position ("I particularly recollect your saying one night, after they had been dining at Netherfield, '*She* a beauty!—I should as soon call her mother a wit'"), which he then disowns: "but that was only when I first knew her, for it is many months since I have considered her as one of the handsomest women of my acquaintance" (*PP*, 271). The value in physical attraction that Darcy now willingly asserts to his most ironical of friends marks his embrace of the narrative's high valuation of physical attraction in courtship.

The sequence from admiration to love to matrimony, although not quickly achieved by Elizabeth and Darcy, nevertheless follows soon on their separate apprehension of their mutual attraction. For Elizabeth, this occurs when she discovers his role in Lydia's marriage, for "her heart did whisper, that he had done it for her" (*PP*, 326). For Darcy, his apprehension of her attraction to him comes from yet another scene in the garden, although this scene takes place between Elizabeth and Lady Catherine de Bourgh (who indignantly relays the scene to him). Lady Catherine is explicit about her desire to walk alone with Elizabeth: "Miss Bennet, there seemed to be a pretty-ish kind of a little wilderness on one side of your lawn. I should be glad to take a turn in it, if you will favour me with your company" (*PP*, 352). This walk, unlike the walk that Elizabeth and Darcy take at Pemberley, means to obstruct courtship, for Lady Catherine invites Elizabeth outside in order to demand, in terms and in a tone impermissible in the more polite realms of indoor spaces, that she not engage herself to Darcy. Elizabeth's refusal to agree to Lady Catherine's demands makes Darcy aware of her possible reciprocation of feeling, but the expressive system of the garden more forcefully signals the basis of Elizabeth's refusal. As much as the reader is privy to the change in Elizabeth's feelings, the figure of the garden is left to articulate the sexual subtext of the courtship plot, for the "wilderness" in which they walk is an explicit reference to a feature of the picturesque garden—a garden that signals an alternative courtship based on the implied erotics of the landscape and not the familial allegiance proposed by Lady Catherine. As a result of his aunt's unwitting report, Darcy returns with Bingley to Longbourne, from which they immediately take a walk; it is on this final walk where the unavowed lovers make their confessions and marital pledges, thereby completing the sequence of courtship begun in "bloom," among the breakfasters at Netherfield.

Pride and Prejudice closes with a certainty about marital happiness, a happiness based in the physical attraction with which the courtship has been consumed. The physicality of the courtship plot extends itself in the novel's closure, for marriage is the initiation into what had long been projected in the novel, and most appreciably in the climactic moment of the marriage proposal: Darcy is described as a man "violently in love," with "heartfelt delight, diffused over his face" (PP, 366). Darcy's delight reminds us of Elizabeth's "delight" with Pemberley, and by implication delight with Darcy, which stands in for the explicit articulation of love and attraction that Austen always withholds from her readers in the climactic scene. Since their marital happiness will surely not be based in their respective family ties (Lady Catherine de Bourgh and Mrs. Bennet ensure that), the happiness asserted at the novel's close depends primarily on the sexual attraction suggested by the courtship. The "liberties" that the married Elizabeth teaches Georgiana "a woman may take . . . with her husband, which a brother will not always allow" certainly refer to her spirited mode of conversation, but also in part to the carnal privileges of a wife; we are reminded of Elizabeth's "exhibition" at Netherfield, when her brilliant complexion, glowing from exercise, incites Darcy's attraction as well as his assertion that he would not want his *sister* to "make such an exhibition" (PP, 388, 36). The sexual potential of Elizabeth's bloom, projecting the telos of the marriage plot, is realized in marriage and the "liberties" we understand a woman may take with her husband. It is thus not surprising that the novel closes with reference to the episode that best foretold the sexual component of their marriage, and with a pun on the cultivation of the natural world—a turning back to the significantly named Gardiners, Elizabeth's aunt and uncle, "who, by bringing her into Derbyshire, had been the means of uniting them" (PP, 388).

Mansfield Park

Mansfield Park has no explicit courtship between its principal characters, even though their marriage concludes the novel—in fact, there is a deficit of courtship in the novel once Mary and Henry Crawford are irretrievably revealed as unsuitable partners for Edmund and Fanny. Despite Austen's authorial claim in the final chapter that she is "impatient to restore every body, not greatly in fault themselves, to tolerable comfort," that restoration hardly takes the form of a recognizable courtship, unless it is one whose force is felt in the overturning of what had taken three volumes to establish (*MP*, 461). The narrative retreats to a courtship defined by an unreciprocated attraction and an absence of details: "I purposefully abstain from dates on this occasion. . . . I only intreat every body to believe that exactly at the time when it was quite natural that it should be so, and not a week earlier, Edmund did cease to care about Miss Crawford, and became as anxious to marry Fanny, as Fanny herself could desire" (*MP*, 470). As I have shown, the courtship between Edmund and Fanny is present only insofar as Fanny's desire to be in Mary's position, metaphorically as well as literally in the landscape at Sotherton, creates a negative courtship out of a perspectival jealousy. In the place of an explicit courtship narrative is Fanny's bloom, a bloom that functions as a description of her physical flourishing and an anticipation of the novel's marital resolution. Fanny's bloom introduces her into a marriage plot whose trajectory is so awry that it seems impossible to right.

Throughout the novel, Fanny intends herself for Edmund; in his admiring presence she blooms. That his admiration is that of a cousin and not a lover is beside the point, because the perfection of Fanny's modesty is such that she will marry no one besides the man she loves (Edmund), even if that means a life in which she is banished from her adopted family and made to accept the relative poverty into which she was born. Unlike Austen's other novels, where the improvement of the female's character is one of the novel's primary energies, *Mansfield Park's* heroine does not need this kind of improvement; her "improvement" is the physical improvement of her blooming, while her character, as Edmund realizes, wants "no reliance on future improvement" (*MP*, 471). In *Mansfield Park* the man of the marriage plot (Edmund), not the marriageable girl, has to learn to disvalue his original choice and improve his marital aspirations.

Fanny blooms in a sequence that suggests her uncertain social status and not just her conforming to a temporally correct time of physical improvement. The fact that only Fanny is described as blooming, and not Mary or the Bertram sisters, indicates (as it did in *Pride and Prejudice*) that blooming is a narrative ascription rather than strictly a physical description. She blooms when she has her social début, an event that occurs belatedly, long after a sense of confusion about whether she was "out" has set in. Mary's incredulity that Edmund is not certain about Fanny's social status suggests the degree to which Fanny's bloom reflects not a physical norm but a social fact; she deviates from the common position of the eighteen-year-old marriageable girl in that she does not legibly sign whether she is available for marriage. As Mary points out, her behavior of dining out indicates that she is "out," while her quiet manner signals the manners of a "girl not out." Fanny's social début does not correspond to her physical age or maturation, for it is not arranged until Sir Thomas returns from Antigua. This delay directly reflects Fanny's uncertain social status in the Bertram household, for she has some of the privileges of a daughter but the social position of a companion.[54]

Sir Thomas returns from Antigua not only to find his house in a state of moral and physical disruption but to a niece who is a physically different creature. The difference that the uncle notes is one translated by Edmund to Fanny:

> Your uncle thinks you very pretty, dear Fanny—and that is the long and short of the matter. Anybody but myself would have made something more of it, and anyone but you would resent that you had not been thought very pretty before; but the truth is, that your uncle never did admire you till now—and now he does. Your complexion is so improved!—and you have gained so much countenance—and your figure—Nay, Fanny, do not turn away about it—it is but an uncle. If you cannot bear an uncle's admiration what is to become of you? You must really begin to the idea of being worth looking at.—You must try not to mind growing up into a pretty woman. (*MP*, 197–8)

Here the discourse of improvement is explicitly linked to bloom; Edmund is clear that his uncle's admiration is physical, for he notes that his father's compliments are "chiefly on your person" ("in time," he hopes, his father will see "as much beauty of mind"). The order of Sir Thomas's catalogue of Fanny, from "complexion" to "countenance" to "figure," matches the aspects of physical maturation in ascending importance. In lieu of a typical courtship plot, Edmund ventriloquizes Sir Thomas's frank and fatherly admiration, effectively producing a scene of sexualized courtship (for Fanny) without the subjectivity to match it. The appraisal of Fanny's changed physical person and beauty is realized in an episode of negative, rather than actual, courtship.

The idea of "improvement" (of landscape and persons) pervades *Mansfield Park*, and attitudes toward landscape improvement are signposts of a more elaborately developed notion that character, although it can be improved, cannot be changed. The scene at Sotherton, as I have outlined it, represents courtship through the expressive terms of the landscape, especially as it is understood as a landscape-to-be-improved. That negative courtship, in which Fanny's eventual marriage with Edmund is signed only insofar as a perspectival jealousy is set up through the terms of their relative positions in the landscape, sets the terms for the remainder of the novel. Like Elizabeth's and Darcy's instant dislike of each other, Edmund's and Fanny's relative positions in the landscape at Sotherton condition the possible contours of the novel's marriage plot: Fanny is left behind as Mary and Edmund walk to the very avenue of trees to which Fanny wanted to go. Fanny's relative position in the landscape reflects her position in the courtship, which is at best triangulated.[55] The scene functions as a declaration of Edmund's preference, a preference that must be overcome in order to achieve the eventual marriage to Fanny that her feelings, and her central position in the novel, would suggest. Thus what stands in for their "courtship," in light of his clear different preference for Mary, is a complicated twist on a traditional marriage plot; first Fanny's negatively conditioned position in the courtship, and second Fanny's blooming, despite Edmund's seeming lack of reciprocity.

Fanny's negative position in the novel's primary courtship between Edmund and Mary may be best understood through the scene at Sotherton, but it is no less evident when Fanny suffers a headache because of (what else?) picking roses. Fanny overextends herself picking roses at her aunt's behest while Edmund has been entertaining Mary Crawford; her subsequent headache, which she nurses without telling anyone of her pain, is discovered by Edmund returning from his visit; his subsequent tenderness is experienced as compensation for what she had experienced as his neglect and her envy. That she occupies a negative position in the courtship is evident because of Edmund's reaction, but the roses themselves also suggest it. Embodying the peculiarly implicit, neglected courtship of Fanny and Edmund, the headache-producing roses represent the state of their courtship, which at this moment is one of neglect followed by an enabling guilt. Indeed, Fanny is picking roses in the heat because Edmund has left the house to be with Mary and hence is not there to protect her from the importunity of Mrs. Norris and, here expressed, the thoughtlessness of Lady Bertram: "I was out above an hour. I sat three quarters of an hour in the flower garden, while Fanny cut the roses, and very pleasant it was I assure you, but very hot. It was shady enough in the alcove. . . I am afraid they will be the last this year" (*MP*, 72). Lady Bertram's empathy extends so far as to call Fanny a "poor thing" and to acknowledge the afternoon's heat but not so far as to recognize the claim of her niece's health at the expense of full-blown roses: "she found it hot enough, but they were so full blown, that one could not wait"(*MP*, 72). In an inversion of the marriage plot's usual poetics, the "full blown" roses that Fanny is compelled to pick by her aunts represent the neglect of her blooming person in favor of the other woman in the triangle. The episode functions as a scene of courtship, and a foreshadowing of her bloom, only insofar as both are negatively produced.

Lionel Trilling argued that Fanny becomes prettier only as a way of indicating and compensating for her earlier moral and physical weakness.[56] Seen from Trilling's position, Fanny's physical improvement is more a symbol of moral improvement than the fulcrum on which I would suggest the plot pivots. Before her physical improvement, Fanny's role in the narrative is consistently marginal; time after time, Fanny is on the sidelines, whether that be the sidelines of the play *Lover's Vows*, left behind in the woods at Sotherton, or being sidelined by Mary's desire to ride her pony. When Sir Thomas returns, noting her physical improvement and arranging for her social début, Fanny blooms; she does so not because a courtship between her and Edmund has quickened but because her social status is clarified by her uncle's return. He arranges for her début, a ball, by way of indicating that he is bringing her "out" under his familial protection rather than letting her remain in the uncertain social state of companion to Lady Bertram. Not "brought up to the trade of *coming out*," Fanny is nevertheless transformed by the experience—and so is the narrative (*MP*, 267). Once Sir Bertram returns, the somewhat sickly, easily fatigued Fanny is transformed into an attractive blooming girl; he specifically admires her improved complexion and matured figure. Sir Thomas's admiration for her improved complexion is echoed, with the appreciation of a connoisseur, by Henry Crawford: there is "decided beauty" in her complexion, "frequently tinged" by a blush color; despite his frank appraisal, including a reference to her having grown "two inches, at least, since October," in deference to modesty he does not directly allude to her figure but rather to the improvement in her "*tout ensemble*" (*MP*, 229–30). The third quality in Sir Thomas's catalogue of complexion, countenance, and figure is not available to Crawford because commentary on the female body is beyond the parameters of acceptable manners; what stands in for the erotic claims of her improved figure in Crawford's similar catalogue is the quality of skin that he all but names—her bloom.

When the ball is announced as the occasion of Fanny's début, the social narrative of marriageability corresponds neatly with the physical improvement in bloom. Nevertheless, the fact that Fanny continues in a triangulated courtship with Mary and Edmund remains, as is made evident by his desire for Fanny to wear the Crawfords' necklace over his own proffered gold chain: "'I would not have the shadow of a coolness arise,' he repeated, his voice sinking a little, 'between the two dearest objects I have on earth'"(*MP*, 264). That Fanny reads this as a mark of hope to match her own desires, as well as an affirmation of the increased impossibility of their ever being fulfilled, confirms the degree to which courtship is achieved in *Mansfield Park* through a series of negative, triangulated scenes: "she was one of his two dearest—that must support her. But the other!—the first! She had never heard him speak so openly before, and though it told her no more than what she had long perceived, it was a stab" (*MP*, 264). The ball continues that trajectory of negative courtship, but it also completes her blooming, that other indication of the novel's eventual conclusion.

The ball begins with a pun on engagement, for Fanny thinks he has engaged himself to Miss Crawford, when he has only engaged himself for the first two dances of the ball. It falls to the début itself, where she becomes the central object to be apprehended, to complete her bloom; that her courtship still exists in a negative capacity (she is the confidante, not the lover, of Edmund, and possessor of any two dances "except the first," which he reserves for Mary) is at odds with what her blooming person portends. Sir Thomas "spoke of her beauty with very decided praise," which Lady Bertram echoes in her own laconic way: "she looks very well. I sent Chapman to her." That she realizes that she was "approved" by Sir Thomas increases her beauty, for "the consciousness of looking well, made her look still better" (*MP*, 272). That her looks are newly heightened in a way that is difficult to quantify or describe is articulated by Lady Bertram after the ball; she says: "she could not recollect what it was . . . that Lady Prescott had noticed in Fanny" (*MP*, 283). Fanny's beauty is heightened beauty that evening; Mary compliments Lady Bertram "on Miss Price's looks," which prompts the normally laconic Lady Bertram to repeat her praise of Fanny's person. That she has bloomed is suggested by the use of a horticultural term as she begins the first dance at the ball; Sir Thomas contemplates her "transplantation" to Mansfield, as well as his gift of "education and manners" as he "watches her progress down the dance" (*MP*, 276). "Transplantation" evokes a horticultural meaning, one that, although subtle, is so precisely aligned with the exact formal moment in which Fanny comes out that it suggests bloom.

The uncertainty of Fanny's social position had made her bloom so late in time; if Sir Thomas's return had suggested her newly secure position, it is the public enactment of that fact at the ball that enables her bloom to truly unfold. The clarification of her social position, in alignment with her physical person, makes the début a success: "she was attractive, she was modest, she was Sir Thomas's niece, and she was soon said to be admired by Mr. Crawford. It was enough to give her general favor" (*MP*, 276). Fanny's bloom the night of the ball, however, foretells an engagement long in the future and not the impending courtship of the next few days that Sir Thomas had intuited in watching Henry Crawford. Although Henry produces a series of blushes, Edmund's deferred two dances are the source of Fanny's pleasure: "she was happy in knowing herself admired, she was happy in having the two dances still to look forward to . . . her indefinite engagement with *him* was in continual perspective" (*MP*, 278).

The instability of Fanny's bloom corresponds with her social instability; when Sir Bertram realizes that she is going to refuse Henry Crawford's very good offer of marriage, he returns her to the uncertain social state that had kept the narrative of bloom in abeyance until his clarifying return from Antigua. Seeing Fanny's refusal as evidence of her "understanding" being "diseased," Sir Thomas sends Fanny back to her parents as a "medicinal project"; in essence, he prescribes a dose of reality (*MP*, 369). His medical perspective on what was a moral and affective choice is of course a gross misunderstanding, but nevertheless Fanny's health and bloom are affected by his decision. Although he means to frighten her by taking away the physical luxuries of Mansfield, he promotes a return to a more ill state. The fact that it is Henry Crawford who, in visiting her at Portsmouth, returns her to health complicates an already burdened marriage plot; accustomed to staying in the close and dirty house at Portsmouth, Fanny was "beginning to feel the effect of being debarred her usual, regular exercise; she had lost ground as to health since her being in Portsmouth, and but for Mr. Crawford and the beauty of the weather, would soon have been knocked up now" (*MP*, 409). Crawford notes that even though Fanny is as "bewitching as ever," her "present residence" was not "salutary" for her. The effect of this is a lessening of bloom: "her face was less blooming than it ought to be" (*MP*, 409–10). Crawford tells Susan that he is concerned for her sister's health, that she "requires constant air and exercise . . . that she ought never to be banished from the free air, and liberty of the country" (*MP*, 410–1). He promises to return her to Mansfield if she grows unwell, but it is a promise that Fanny understands is linked with his marriage proposal. Crawford understands the threat to Fanny's bloom as deriving from a deficit of the healthy influence of the natural world—an understanding that works as a narrative red herring, given that his offer to return her to Mansfield's more salubrious environment implies nonetheless a reinsertion into a courtship plot that she has resolutely refused.

For Sir Thomas to banish Fanny from the landscape and natural world is to attempt to force what is, ultimately, meant to be understood as a natural response: bloom as the expression of the sexual courtship between two persons. Fanny's intentions, clear from the novel's very beginnings, established a preference that continues in her negative courtship with Edmund. Sir Thomas's efforts are an attempt, in a sense, to break the portended marriage plot; Crawford's worry that she is "less blooming" is a worry that colludes with Sir Thomas's coercion, in that previously her bloom had foretold a marriage plot antithetical to his own desires. A more serious challenge to the marriage plot forecast by Fanny's bloom is her change in feeling toward Crawford's character when he visits her at Portsmouth: he is not only "improved," she realizes, but "decidedly improved" (*MP*, 406). The fact that the preternaturally rigid Fanny is moved by Crawford's kindness suggests the degree to which her bloom was under threat not by the air of Portsmouth but by Crawford's persistent courtship in light of Edmund's continued absence.

The suggestion that Fanny might suddenly bloom for Crawford instead of Edmund is quickly silenced, however, when Crawford's improvement is proved false by a sudden act of adultery. This capricious act conveniently, if violently, rights a marriage plot set adrift by two forces: the uncertainty of how convincing Crawford is (both to the reader and to Fanny) as an improved person, and the impending engagement of Edmund with Mary. The effect of the adultery is immediately clarifying; the plot is contrived to vindicate Fanny, affirm her modesty, and set back in proper motion her negative courtship with Edmund. In the end, we are required to believe that the loss of Fanny's bloom is as much the effect of being banished from Edmund as the result of the insalubrious air of Portsmouth and the slatternly nature of her parents' household. Crawford's kindness at Portsmouth and moral improvement give way abruptly to adultery, which in turn neatly clarifies the marital impasse in which Edmund and Mary had found themselves. Fanny's bloom is not, as the scenes at Portsmouth might suggest, an indication of health but rather the narrative predictor of the improbable marriage between Fanny and Edmund.

No attempt is made to narrate how Edmund's familial feelings for Fanny are transformed into a marital courtship; the narrative, as if exhausted, gives way under the pressure of "unchanging attachments" and "unconquerable passions," leaving the readers to imagine the exact dates and circumstances of the subsequent new courtship. A marriage between Edmund and Fanny occurs, but it is only on Dr. Grant's death some years later, with Edmund's subsequent ascension to the living at Mansfield, that Fanny loses the "painful sensation of restraint or alarm" that she had felt while Mary Crawford's relatives remained (*MP*, 457). That is, the novel ends not with an affirmative comment on marriage but with a final remembrance of their negative courtship—on a note of the abeyance of pain rather than the onset of pleasure. If in *Pride and Prejudice* the reader is assured that the marital happiness of Elizabeth and Darcy is grounded in the sexual pleasures of marriage, in *Mansfield Park* Fanny's negatively inspired bloom and the history of her negative courtship makes us less secure in, and even casts doubt on, that proposition. Fanny's bloom seems less insistent in its invocation of the sexual meanings of Linnaeus's blooms; whatever the erotic investments the two cousins find, Fanny's bloom suggests marriage more than it definitively predicts the sexual potential of marriage—a fact not surprising when one considers that the majority of the novel is given over to courtships that flounder and a negative courtship that persists.

The conclusion of *Mansfield Park* has dissatisfied readers and critics alike, for both projects of improvement—Edmund's hope that Mary's character will improve on knowing Fanny, and Henry Crawford's attempts at reformation to prove himself capable of real and abiding change—do fail, and the two first cousins are left to marry each other, despite the seeming lack of any viable courtship plot. The suggestiveness of Fanny's bloom bears much of the weight of making the conclusion seem as plausible as it does, for it foretells the conclusion of marriage despite the complicating presences of Mary and Henry Crawford. The explicit courtships of the novel are ones that are not admirable—ones that either fail (Edmund and Mary) or succeed in the teeth of convention and ethics (Maria and Henry)—and the novel's truly successful courtship is only implicitly carried on via the figural network of bloom, until it can be explicitly realized at its conclusion.

Emma

In Jane Austen's *Emma* (1816), for Emma to be "blooming" is for her to succumb finally to the pull of a romantic-sexual alliance. The narratological indicators of bloom in *Emma* are appropriately more complex than they are in *Pride and Prejudice*, for the novel begins with Emma's declaration that she will never marry but will rather devote herself to her father and (less explicitly) the making of matches among her friends. Prior to her late realization that "Mr. Knightley must marry no one but herself," Emma does not bloom: she absents herself from the possibility of marriage, a choice that the text registers by having Harriet—Emma's chosen substitute—bloom rather than Emma (*E*, 408).

The novel's first description of Harriet, the poor dupe of Emma's matchmaking—and the victim the novel almost sacrifices to Emma's refusal to accept her central role as marriageable girl—invokes the girl's bloom:

> Miss Smith was a girl of seventeen whom Emma knew very well by
> sight and had long felt an interest in, on account of her beauty. . . .
> She was a very pretty girl, and her beauty happened to be of a sort

> which Emma particularly admired. She was short, plump and fair,
> with a fine bloom, blue eyes, light hair, regular features, and a look of
> great sweetness. (*E*, 23)

Here, Harriet's bloom seems to be a description of her complexion, which is
fair with a "fine bloom," that is part of a more general account of her physical
person: we learn that she is pretty, plump, rather short, with light-colored hair,
symmetrical features, and a sweet expression. Harriet's bloom metonymically
invokes the plant's bloom, or flower, that is the sexual dimension of the plant;
the bloom of complexion invokes a Linnaean register. That is, Harriet's "fine
bloom" calls to mind potential sexuality, which is perhaps Harriet's defining
feature. Harriet's bloom would seem to indicate that Harriet was to be at the
center of the novel's marriage plot, for it is a significant fact, and one worth re-
peating, that in each of Austen's other novels only the central female protagonist in the throes of the marriage plot is actually said to bloom, despite there
being other girls of that age and social position in the narrative. In *Pride and
Prejudice* only Elizabeth, and not Jane or Lydia, bloom; in *Persuasion*, Anne Elliot, and not Henrietta or Louisa Musgrove, blooms, even though Anne is
twenty-seven and had bloomed seven years previously; and in *Mansfield Park*, it
is Fanny, and neither the Bertram sisters nor Mary Crawford, who receives
that appellation.

Considering this textual history, it is particularly noteworthy that Harriet
is characterized as having a fine bloom; the reference to Harriet's bloom is not
only descriptive but narratological; it functions in the narrative as a sign of the
marriage plot that Emma herself is authoring. The free indirect discursive
mode that renders *Emma* so distinctive explains why Harriet, and not Emma,
is called blooming: Emma's perspective controls the narrative voice. "*She*
would notice her; she would improve her; she would detach her from her bad
acquaintance" (*E*, 23). That same free indirect discursive style informs the earlier description of Harriet as blooming; at this point in the novel, Emma wants
to marry off Harriet, so the narrative reflects that fact in noting Harriet's
bloom, as if she will be at the center of the novel's marriage plot just as Emma
desires. Emma's perspective conditions the narrative to such a degree that she
divorces herself from the bloom narrative and forwards Harriet as the most el-
igible young woman of Highbury. Harriet's lot is to act as a sort of narrative
place-marker until Emma decides that she wants to marry—only then does
Emma bloom, near the novel's close.

Much of the novel is given over to the marriage plot(s) that Emma wants
to orchestrate, of course, so Harriet remains at the center of the narrative, despite several matchmaking failures by Emma and repeated warnings that she is
making a mistake in keeping Harriet from Robert Martin. Readers are never
meant to believe, though, that Harriet is the novel's central interest; we are
meant to believe that she is Emma's central interest. Even when Emma has
ruled out marriage for herself, the reader has not and neither have other interested parties in her life. That Emma will one day bloom, that this narrative in-

dicator will appear to sign her being in the throes of a marriage plot of her own (a marriage that represents sexual potential), is foreshadowed in a conversation between Mrs. Weston and Mr. Knightley. Mrs. Weston is a surrogate mother to Emma, and her interest in Emma's eventual marriage, if considerably less vulgar in its manifestation, is as quick as Mrs. Bennet's in *Pride and Prejudice*:

> "Such an eye!—the true hazle eye—and so brilliant! regular features, open countenance, with a complexion! oh! what a bloom of full health, and such a pretty height and size; such a firm and upright figure. There is health, not merely in her bloom, but in her air, her head, her glance. One hears sometimes of a child being 'the picture of health'; now Emma always gives me the idea of being the complete picture of grown-up health. She is loveliness itself. Mr. Knightley, is not she?" (*E*, 39)

The breathlessness of Mrs. Weston's approbation for her old charge marks her particular interest in seeing Emma married; here she praises Emma to Mr. Knightley, while elsewhere we learn that Mrs. Weston has thought of her marrying Frank Churchill. Even when Emma has absented herself from the marriage plot, persons with an interest in her fate continue to plot for that eventual outcome. Mrs. Weston's admiration for Emma's person is a kind of recommendation to Mr. Knightley; that Emma's bloom is the point twice emphasized in this rhapsodic evocation of her person is significant, for her bloom seems to be the key to the recommendation. What exactly is being recommended? Although the claim in the sentence is that bloom is about health, Mrs. Weston's extravagant litany suggests that health does not quite capture the entirety of her meaning. Paired with bloom in the description are facts about age and physical attractiveness: Emma is not a child, she says, but a "picture of grown-up health" in her figure, size, and beauty; she is "loveliness itself." Mrs. Weston is recommending Emma to Mr. Knightley, the man Emma will eventually marry, as grown up, lovely, and, not without its sexual suggestions, having bloom.

Unlike that local plea for Emma's fineness by her former governess, Harriet's bloom is a narrative principle; it signals her immediate immersion in (what will be) a series of marriage plots: Robert Martin, Mr. Elton, Frank Churchill, Mr. Knightley, and Robert Martin again. Harriet's person seems always ready for marriage, while Emma does not bloom until she acknowledges to herself her love for Mr. Knightley. Prior to that late (and sudden) realization, Emma may be on the road to courtship's resolution, but it is not one she is capable of acknowledging until she is in the midst of his marriage proposal. The fact that we continue to apprehend events through Emma's point of view even late in the novel makes it impossible for the text to register her bloom: she does not see her courtship quickening, so the indirect discourse does not record it through her blooming. This is distinctly different from

Pride and Prejudice, where the somewhat more straightforward omniscient narrator records Elizabeth's blooming in the presence of Darcy far before either is an acknowledged lover. In *Emma* the reader witnesses the quickening of an unacknowledged courtship between Knightley and Emma, but she does not bloom; instead the sexual tension between the two is evident through what Mary Ann O'Farrell has memorably called the blush's "somatic act of confession": "Emma's colour was heightened by this unjust praise; and with a smile, and a shake of her head which spoke much, she looked at Mr. Knightley.—It seemed as if there were an instantaneous impression in her favour, as if his eyes received the truth from hers, and all that had passed of good in her feelings were at once caught and honored.—He looked at her with a glow of regard. She was warmly gratified" (*E*, 385).[57] This moment has been often read as Emma's acceptance of the lessons in shame and humility that Knightley has been teaching, for he is responding to her self-correction in the wake of her regret over treating Miss Bates poorly. Yet his glow seems to match hers, and, still more to the point, the moment also marks their first moment of sexual courtship: "He took her hand;—whether she had not herself made the first motion, she could not say—she might, perhaps, have offered it—but he took her hand, pressed it, and certainly was on the point of carrying it to his lips—when, from some fancy or other, he suddenly let it go" (*E*, 386). What is captured here is the ambiguity of a first touch—the question of who first reaches for the other—more than the pleasure of mortification.[58] Here, the blush enacts her body's conscious awakening to her love for Knightley, and marks the marriage plot's quickening, even though she still does not bloom.

Emma's self-awareness comes not only through her extended realization of her moral culpability in regard to Harriet but also through the discovery of her sexual feelings for Knightley. Just after this scene of acknowledged forgiveness and the blush of strong feeling, Emma is given the incentive to examine her feelings more pointedly: Harriet announces her love for Knightley. In interrogating her feelings—one of the first moments in which Emma evidences a thoughtful self-awareness—Emma's mind catches up with what her blushing body had previously made legible to the reader. Emma thinks: "why was it so much worse that Harriet should be in love with Mr. Knightley, than with Frank Churchill? Why was the evil so dreadfully increased by Harriet's having some hope of a return?" (*E*, 408). Emma's realization that she depends on being "first" with Mr. Knightley is the climactic moment of self-awareness, one that quickly follows on and is linked with her awareness of her moral failure in relation to Miss Bates and even Harriet. In *Emma*, Austen links self-assessment with blooming by making the first a condition of the second: unlike in *Pride and Prejudice*, where the mutual improvement that paves the way to Elizabeth and Darcy's marriage seems almost inevitable, the marriage plot in *Emma* feels always under a state of threat from Emma's obtuseness and personal failings. Emma considers marriage only after she undergoes a self-assessment and embarks on a set of personal improvements.

This self-assessment does not mean that Emma must abdicate control over her destiny, giving up her power in order to be swept up in what some have been tempted to see, and reasonably deprecate, as Austen's writing Emma into a more "naturally" feminine position. Emma continues to function as the text's authoritative narrator, resubstituting herself into the marriage plot where Harriet had once been: "it darted through her, with the speed of an arrow, that Mr. Knightley must marry no one but herself!" (*E*, 408). The declarative sentence here wins out, as does Emma's wish not to leave her father's house even though she marries. That is, Emma does not capitulate to the discipline of Mr. Knightley but rather willfully places herself back into the novel's marriage plot just as she had willfully removed herself from it. Harriet, narrative placemarker that she was, returns to the position she should have claimed in the novel's first pages: entering into a marriage of affection, and the novel's sense of her appropriate class position, with Robert Martin. Bloom does not happen to Emma; she blooms because she is ready, just pages after we can acknowledge her being in courtship's throes, and the text records that fact by locating the climax of her courtship in a garden. She is waiting for Knightley's return when the inclement weather clears; "it was summer again," and Emma "resolved to be out of doors as soon as possible. Never had the exquisite sight, smell, sensation of nature, tranquil, warm, and brilliant after a storm, been more attractive to her" (*E*, 424). The garden, which here provides the setting for the quickening of their courtship, is a space that the botanical vernacular figures as sexual. Although it might seem as if Emma's will threatens to be subsumed by the larger natural world that she figuratively becomes part of in this scene, even here her will is emphasized: Emma "resolved to be out of doors as soon as possible." From the exceptional quality of the natural world that surrounds Knightley and Emma as they become engaged one gleans the suggestion of her physical blooming, although characteristically what the text emphasizes is not the appearance of Emma's body but her thought processes: "while he spoke, Emma's mind was most busy" (*E*, 430).

The long conclusion to the novel is given over to sorting out the various complexities brought on by Emma's initial abdication of the role of blooming (or "marriageable") girl: the marital subplots of Jane Fairfax and Frank Churchill, as well as Harriet Smith. The wedding cannot be imagined until the novel's final page, when the robbery of Mrs. Weston's poultry-house induces Mr. Woodhouse to accept Mr. Knightley moving to Hartfield. That the marriage is predicated on the ridiculousness of Mr. Woodhouse's sensibility promotes the novel's comic dimension, which might seem to privilege the social dimension of marriage over its projected sexual meaning. But if we remember Mrs. Weston, whose own marriage opens the novel and who by the end of the novel has a baby girl on her lap, we are reminded that Emma's courtship has projected "the perfect happiness of the union"—among the novel's final words—in sexual as well as social terms. Mrs. Weston's rhapsodic, and in some sense prescient, recommendation of Emma's "loveliness" and "bloom" to Mr. Knightley marked the beginning of their courtship; his reply, coupled with Mrs. Weston's testament to Emma's bloom, marks the start of the bloom narrative: "I have not a fault to find with her person . . . I think her all you describe. I love to look at her"(*E*, 484, 39). The courtship is temporarily stalled by the need for Emma to assess and improve herself, but the bloom narrative, with its prediction not only of marriage but marriage's sexual potential, is nevertheless squarely begun here: in physical attraction, in bloom.

Persuasion

The novel in Austen's oeuvre that might initially seem to conform least to the bloom narrative is *Persuasion* (1818), in which the central character is not at the typical age of bloom but rather is a twenty-seven-year-old girl who had suffered "an early loss of bloom"—a loss, that is, of a probable marital future (*P*, 28). And yet if *Persuasion* does not seem a likely candidate for the bloom narrative, it is because our critical tradition privileges the sociological fact of marriage at the expense of its inferred sexual content. *Persuasion* repeatedly represents scenes of physical intimacy and implied sexual attraction, asking us to remember that courtship—even or perhaps especially those courtships temporarily stalled by resentment, as are Captain Wentworth's and Elizabeth Bennet's in *Persuasion* and *Pride and Prejudice*, respectively—has its physical component. These more negative versions of courtship invite us to see the marriage plot in terms other than as the conduit of legal and social sanction, primarily because the seeming difficulty of the plots' resolution suggests that something in addition to social consolidation is being represented. In *Persuasion*, the initial absence of a blooming heroine and a series of moments of physical intimacy outside avowed courtship work against an affirmative marriage plot; instead, physical intimacy and sexual attraction—always implied but more often obscured by the narration of events leading to closure in marriage—are at the center of what is being represented. Like the flowers known by gardeners as "repeat-bloomers," Anne Elliot goes through two seasons of bloom.[59]

The erotic component of marriage is articulated in the courtship plot of *Persuasion* with an increased explicitness in its recourse to bloom and its expressive cognates. That Austen locates the novel's climax—Anne's reblooming at Lyme, followed quickly by Louisa's fall from the Cobb—in a setting renowned for its scientific connotations is but one example of *Persuasion*'s more self-conscious iteration of courtship structured with reference to the botanical vernacular. The structure of the marriage plot is deliberately tied to bloom, for just as Anne "reblooms" in the face of Wentworth's reawakened attraction for her, Louisa falls and suffers a traumatic brain injury—bloom righting the marriage plot, returning it to a trajectory from which it had gotten perilously far away. Austen's final novel opens up for inspection the otherwise occluded corporeality of the story of bloom.

The social interaction with which the novel is primarily concerned is the renewed interaction between Anne and Wentworth, once engaged and now, seven years later, reunited by accident in a shared and intimate social setting.

The difference in Anne's age between the past and present action of the novel is more than seven years, for Anne had been nineteen when Captain Wentworth proposed marriage and now is twenty-seven: "Anne, at seven and twenty, thought very differently from what she had been made to think at nineteen" (P, 29). The change Anne experiences is one of consciousness, a change in opinion the text describes as the result of an "unnatural" fiction: "she had been forced into prudence in her youth, she learned romance as she grew older—the natural sequel to an unnatural beginning" (P, 30). Anne's re-blooming is the sequel of a story that ended wrong—that is, the interruption of her marriage plot.

Anne had gone through a loss of bloom that we might believe is the natural result of aging: "twelve years had changed Anne from the blooming, silent unformed girl of fifteen, to the elegant little woman of seven and twenty, with every beauty excepting bloom" (P, 153). The text, however, explicitly attributes the loss of bloom to the loss of a suitor and not the natural effect of getting older, or what Hogarth had described as the minimal changes that occur between twenty and thirty. The loss of bloom is a physical fact that signifies both an emotional and a narrative loss: "a few months had seen the beginning and end of their acquaintance; but, not with a few months ended Anne's share of suffering from it. Her attachment and regrets had, for a long time, clouded every enjoyment of youth; and an early loss of bloom and spirits had been their lasting effect" (P, 28). The passage emphasizes a causal link between the loss of her "attachment," her subsequent "regrets," and "their lasting effect"; absent is any reference to the fact she is no longer nineteen but twenty-seven. The narrative elsewhere emphasizes age, but it is an ironic preoccupation and one that tonally mimics Lady Russell's prejudices: "Anne Elliot, with all her claims of birth, beauty, and mind, to throw herself away at nineteen; involve herself at nineteen in an engagement with a young man. . . . Anne Elliot, so young; known to so few" (P, 27). The implicit mock horror in the repetition of "at nineteen," combined with Lady Russell's crude reappraisal of Anne's marital value when twenty-two—"however Lady Russell might have asked yet for something more, while Anne was nineteen, she would have rejoiced to see her at twenty-two, so respectably removed"—enjoins the reader to reject a prejudice that characteristically conflates age with marriageability and physical attractiveness (P, 29).

The bloom narrative in *Persuasion* begins on a note of uncertainty, for bloom, the novel's strongest indicator of plot, is first invoked in reference to Elizabeth Elliot: "in one of their spring excursions to London, when Elizabeth was in her first bloom, Mr. Elliot had been forced into the introduction" (P, 8). Like *Emma*, which Austen had written and published just prior to *Persuasion*, the novel invokes bloom in order to set up two competing claims for narration. Unlike Harriet, whom Emma in a sense substitutes for herself, Elizabeth is Anne's social equal and could well have been at the novel's center, just as Elizabeth Bennet's story could well have been Jane Bennet's; Elizabeth Elliot is at twenty-nine "quite as handsome as ever" and, like Jane Bennet, the elder sis-

ter (P, 7). Yet in Austen's novels, as I have shown, only the central female protagonist blooms, even though there are other marriageable girls in the novel;
indeed, blooming separates her from the other similarly situated girls within
the novel, functioning as a narrative indicator of the marriage plot's resolution
and her central status. The narrative competition set up by *Persuasion* suggests
that there is a moral as well as physical dimension to bloom; Elizabeth Elliot's
lack of sisterly regard and disdain for anything but "baronet-blood" distinguishes Anne as a more worthy object of narration: a discrimination Austen
produces by invoking Elizabeth's bloom only to cancel it (P, 7).

Austen's tendentious satire of Sir Walter Elliot likewise depends on a mis-
application of bloom. Sir Elliot, who in choosing to leave a landed seat rather
than economize represents the moral failure of his class, thinks of himself as
blooming: "Sir Walter might be excused . . . for thinking himself and Elizabeth
as blooming as ever, amidst the wreck of the good looks of every body else; for
he could plainly see how old all the rest of his family and acquaintance were
growing" (P, 6). This self-designation is meant to be understood as a ridicu-
lous vanity; that Sir Elliot, a complete buffoon, believes this of himself suggests
that bloom cannot be a self-generated category, and indeed throughout
Austen it requires the presence of mediators and object-choices, as well as a
narrator to record the blossoming. And yet the comedic value of Sir Elliot's
self-designation is overwhelmed by the moral critique, for his self-ascription is
a misplaced act of hubris that threatens to feminize him and hence implies the
larger class crisis that his rental of Kellynch Hall suggests. His moral failure is
obvious enough in itself but is also made more expressive by his personal
foibles, vanity being the paramount one. In light of the use Austen puts bloom
to in her satirical sketch of Sir Elliot, it is perhaps not surprising that complexion is his particular hobby-horse; he initially rejects Admiral Croft as a tenant
out of a prejudice against a sailor's complexion: they are "not fit to be seen," Sir
Elliot asserts, for the "sea-faring life" makes a "face the colour of mahogany,
rough and rugged to the last degree" (P, 20).

Taking into account the novel's insistence that bloom is a denomination
for a deserving as well as a beautiful woman, the narrative claims of bloom
seem all the more significant. When Captain Wentworth, on seeing Anne
again, remarks that she was "so altered that he should not have known her
again," we are meant to understand that this disparagement represents a failure
in Wentworth; he needs to learn a richer conception of bloom, not only because his slight of her represents his lack of forgiveness but because the evaluation is, in the manner of Sir Walter, so literal as to be shallow (P, 60).[60] The
poetics of the blooming body in *Persuasion* ultimately give way to a narrative
concern: the means by which an altered physical countenance becomes an altered destiny.

The narrative repeats three times Anne's loss of bloom; as the novel opens,
we learn that Anne "had been a very pretty girl" whose "bloom had vanished
early," while some twenty pages later we are reminded that she had suffered an
"early loss of bloom." Austen uncharacteristically repeats the description when

comparing Wentworth and Anne: "the years which had destroyed [Anne's] youth and bloom had only given him a more glowing, manly, open look, in no respect lessening his personal advantages" (*P*, 6, 28, 61). The insistence in the narrative about Anne's absent bloom signals that bloom is no mere description, for Austen's writing is known for its careful economy of description. That bloom refers primarily to the marriageable girl, and not the male suitor, is in the last example evident; Captain Wentworth improves physically while Anne Elliot declines, a difference the novel employs to assert the relative importance of courtship to female destiny. In this light, Anne's whispered speech to Captain Harville about female constancy suggests a socially gendered rationale for why the marriageable girl, and not her suitor, blooms in reference to the vicissitudes of courtship and why the bloom plot, at least until the late nineteenth century, revolves exclusively around the marriageable girl: when men suffer a loss they have "a profession, pursuits, business" to take them "back into the world immediately," while women live "at home, quiet, confined, and our feelings prey upon us" (*P*, 232). Anne's claim for women in her long disquisition on the "nature" of male and female love is one that claims an essential difference between men's and women's ability to project a narrative:

> I believe you equal to every important exertion, and to every domestic forbearance, so long as—if I may be allowed the expression, so long as you have an object. I mean, while the woman you love lives, and lives for you. All the privilege I claim for my own sex (it is not a very enviable one, you need not covet it) is that of loving longest, when existence or when hope is gone. (*P*, 235)

Anne's loss of bloom, and Wentworth's physical thriving, mirror this claim about women's ability to remain faithful to an impossible narrative and a lost object: Anne's loss of bloom exists as an embodiment of lost courtship, performing in a sense the very philosophy of gender difference she here articulates.

A large proportion of *Persuasion* is given over to a negative courtship plot between Wentworth and Anne; barely speaking, they nevertheless form a part of an intimate party that throws them repeatedly together. This improbable second intimacy leads to a series of physical encounters between the two, none of which could be said to form part of a recognizable dance of courtship but each of which registers Anne's, and eventually even Wentworth's, ongoing physical awareness of and attraction for the other. These physical encounters dominate this portion of the novel in a way that would be impossible in an acknowledged courtship, where physical intimacy and sexual attraction tends to be necessarily obscured. The encounters between Wentworth and Anne are nothing, however, if not charged. In a scene in the Musgrove's drawing room they exchange pointed, although polite, words over the fact that Wentworth was occupying her piano bench; their resistance to occupying the same chair at different intervals is not simply an expression of his resentment but rather an indication of their awareness of the other's physical person and a resistance to that felt physical intimacy (*P*, 72). Another scene finds the two occupying the same sofa, a physical intimacy that is mediated by Mrs. Musgrove, which, we are told, was "no insignificant barrier indeed." The moment is reserved but palpably physical, for "the agitations of Anne's slender form" are screened from Wentworth but caused by the fact that "they were actually on the same sofa." The sheer mass of the older woman is a barrier, but an enabling one, a screen so complete that Anne can sit on the same sofa not out of indifference but because her agitation is literally screened from view (P, 68).

Physical interchanges, the natural consequence of occupying the same drawing room, grow in significance and mutuality as the narrative progresses. There are two key physical exchanges between Anne and Wentworth prior to Lyme that I treat here as paradigmatic of the text's representation of physical intimacy, and implied sexual attraction, between the two. The first entails a moment when Wentworth removes a child from Anne's back, and the second a scene in which Wentworth places Anne in a carriage. Like the episode on the sofa with Mrs. Musgrove, the implied physical intimacy in this second scene is achieved through a mediating body, in this case a young child. Anne kneels at the sofa attending to a Mary's sick child, while Wentworth stands at a window:

> The younger boy, a remarkable stout, forward child, of two years old . . . made his determined appearance among them . . . As his aunt would not let him tease his sick brother, he began to fasten himself upon her, as she knelt in such a way that, busy as she was about Charles, she could not shake him off. . . . Once she did contrive to push him away, but the boy had the greater pleasure in getting upon her back again directly. . . . In another moment, however, she found herself in the state of being released from him; some one was taking him from her, though he had bent down her head so much, that his little sturdy hands were unfastened from around her neck, and he was resolutely borne away, before she knew that Captain Wentworth had done it. (P, 79–80)

The increased sense of their physical awareness of each other is achieved through the solidity of the child between them, and the implied touch that Anne experiences through the mediating body of the child. The physical details of her encounter with her nephew's person are palpable; we are made aware of his stoutness, the sturdiness of his hands, his firm clasp on her neck, the feeling of his being on her back, the pressure he exerts on her neck, and her inability to shake him off herself. Wentworth does not touch her and even stands on the opposite side of the room until he removes the child; neverthe-less, the feelings elicited by this interaction are so physical—it is called a "sen-sation"—that it is no mere social interaction. They touch through the body of the child whose intense solidity functions as a conduit of their physicality. Al-though we only have access to the effect on Anne's person—the relief of a body removed from hers, hands "unfastened," a neck freed from the pain of being "bent down"—Wentworth's physical person is implied by his silent act, and by his manner on entering the room: "finding himself almost alone with

Anne Elliot deprived his manners of their usual composure: he started" (*P*, 79–80). The child's misbehavior punctures their otherwise reticent sociability, necessitating a series of discrete actions (a bending of a head, the unfastening of hands) that produce the sensation of contact between the two. Anne's subsequent "disordered feelings" and "painful agitation, as she could not recover from" are the result of her "feeling" Wentworth's touch.[61]

The physical intimacy that functions in lieu of an affirmative courtship climaxes in a scene in which Anne's bodily discomposure is again at issue. The return portion of a long walk that the party takes to the Hayters' farm finds Anne "tired enough to be very glad of Charles's other arm" (*P*, 90). Soon, however, Charles's annoyance with Mary induces him to "drop the arms of both," and Anne, as the narrative is at pains to establish, is left with no physical support. Apprehending her fatigue, Wentworth jumps a hedge to procure a seat for Anne in the passing carriage of Mrs. Croft. The text is deliberately vague as to whether Wentworth makes physical contact with Anne, but as in the previous episode, she experiences it as physical contact:

> [T]hey would not be refused; they compressed themselves into the smallest possible space to leave her a corner, and Captain Wentworth, without saying a word, turned to her, and quietly obliged her to be assisted into the carriage. Yes,—he had done it. She was in the carriage, and felt that he had placed her there, that his will and his hands had done it, that she owed it to his perception of her fatigue, and his resolution to give her rest. (*P*, 91)

The use of the passive voice gives way to her sudden physical awareness of his agency; whether he actually touches her or not is left deliberately vague, for even though she believes "that his will and his hands had done it," it is not clear whether it was his will or his hands that make her *feel* placed in the carriage: "she . . . felt that he had placed her there." The physical ambiguity of the episode is the climax of their negative courtship: "this little circumstance seemed the completion of all that had gone before. She understood him. He could not forgive her,—but he could not be unfeeling" (*P*, 91). The sensations behind their implied or slight physical contact gesture to their ongoing feelings, sensations that for her are so heightened as to suggest their erotic origin.

The trip to Lyme produces two noteworthy moments: Louisa Musgrove's fall from the Lower Cobb, and Anne's reblooming in a triangulated scene between Anne, her cousin, and Wentworth. Lyme, the scene of Louisa's fall and Anne's reblooming, was a seaside resort renowned for its stores of fossils of interest to natural historians and its opportunities for naturalizing at the sea and sea-bathing.[62] Lyme was known as well in the late eighteenth century as a center of a kind of turn-of-the-century ecotourism, where the novel pleasures of sea-bathing and fossil-hunting were jointly available.[63] This much is apparent: out of this expressive context—a town virtually metonymic of natural history in the early nineteenth century—Anne reblooms. Her good looks, specifically her complexion, return at Lyme, while Wentworth's attraction to her is reinvigorated by another's desire:

> They ascended and passed him; and as they passed, Anne's face caught his eye, and he looked at her with a degree of earnest admiration, which she could not be insensible of. She was looking remarkably well; her very regular, very pretty features, having the bloom and freshness of youth restored by the fine wind which had been blowing on her complexion, and by the animation of eye which it had also produced. It was evident that the gentleman (completely a gentleman in manner) admired her exceedingly. Captain Wentworth looked round at her instantly in a way which shewed his noticing of it. (*P*, 104)

Two narratives combine: first, a social narrative of competition when Captain Wentworth observes Anne being admired by Mr. Elliot; and second, a physical narrative of sexual attractiveness. The triangulation produces the social narrative of marriage, while Anne's renewed bloom indicates a renewal of their courtship; for the first time since Wentworth left, Anne's bloom is "restored," indicating not only her flourishing readiness for marriage but the return, in intention as well as presence, of her lost suitor. This triangulated scene occurs several hours before Louisa's famous fall from the Cobb, an action whose narrative function is to right the marriage plot with a violence redolent of melodrama; the visual composition of the scene in which Anne and Wentworth stand over the unconscious body of Louisa produces an image, though a heavyhanded one, of a righted marriage plot.

There is, however, an external cause assigned by the narrative to Anne's "reblooming": a "fine wind blowing on her complexion" (*P*, 104). This is like the external cause (exercise) of Elizabeth Bennet's blooming complexion when she arrives at Netherfield. That Austen assigns an ostensible cause for the bloom that corresponds with a social narrative is striking, and even more striking when one realizes that in both cases their blooms emanate directly from encounters with the natural world. The sea—its "sands," its "flowing of the tide," its "south-easterly breeze," the "grandeur . . . of so flat a shore"—is the physical impetus behind Anne's physical transformation from being a faded twenty-seven-year-old to having her "bloom and freshness of youth restored" (*P*, 102, 104). Linnaeus is never so close as he is in this climactic scene, for the natural world is not only the background of Anne's reblooming and her renewed courtship plot but also the ostensible cause of it. Nor is Anne's reblooming simply an ephemeral reanimation from the sea wind, for those good looks are sustained when she travels to Bath; Lady Russell first notices that "Anne was improved in plumpness and looks," while Sir Walter certifies Anne's physical improvement by deigning to notice her complexion: "he began to compliment her on her improved looks; he thought her 'less thin in her person, in her cheeks; her skin, her complexion, greatly improved—

clearer, fresher. Had she been using any thing in particular?' 'No, nothing.' 'Merely Gowland,' he supposed. 'No, nothing at all'" (*P*, 124, 145–6). These, the physical attentions of parents, do not name her renewed attractiveness as blooming; only in the lover's presence does the narrative note the bloom of the heroine.

Bloom is not only a poetics of description, then, but also a narrative agent—one that projects a sequence that will end in marriage. The presence of the correct suitor is essential to bloom; Anne loses her bloom when Wentworth goes away, and it returns when he, or more precisely his admiring subjectivity, returns. The fact that Anne "reblooms" when Mr. Elliot and Wentworth both are looking at her is noteworthy, for it creates an uncertainty on which the suspense of the novel's second volume is based; bloom can be, therefore, more than simply a closural device. It functions, more precisely, as a narrative agent in the service of the delays and indecisions of desire. We can see, therefore, that as we come to the end of Austen's career with *Persuasion* her physicalized mimesis through the marriageable girl has become more and more self-conscious. Austen signals the passing of an eighteenth-century awareness of the sexuality of the flower into a nineteenth-century narrative genre that would still rely on—albeit with more and more self-consciousness—the botanical mimetics of Linnaeus's time.

FOUR

Eliot's Vernaculars
Natural Objects and Revisionary Blooms

I protest against all our interest, all our effort at understanding being

given to the young skins that look blooming in spite of trouble; for

these too will get faded, and will know the older and more eating

griefs which we are helping to neglect.

—George Eliot, *Middlemarch*

I protest": George Eliot's impatience with narrative's fascination with girls in bloom turns to a speech act, for the protest is a rejection that her fiction labors to live up to.[1] In extending the range of her fictions beyond the public marriage plot, Eliot seeks to displace the blooming girl from her central role and in doing so to offer alternative realities both for the women in her fictions as well as previously underconsidered subjects. These alternative realities include the possibility, new to the classical novel, of the representation of a "clandestine marriage" in the Linnaean sense: one where the flower, like the flowers of mosses, ferns, or fungi, is not visible to the naked eye. The clandestine marriage, both in the plant kingdom and the world of the novel, is unlike a public marriage in that the flower's bloom cannot be seen and scrutinized— the clandestine bloom is hidden, furtive, and less *celebrated* than those blooms that are acknowledged. These hidden blooms suggest alternative ways of narrating courtship, a different version of the same erotic possibility of marriage found in its public counterpart.

In Austen's novels bloom is the primary way that the sexual potential of marriage is narrated within the parameters of licit courtship—in Linnaean terms, the "public marriages," or visible flowerings, of girls in the throes of the marriage plot. The correlation between bloom and licit sexuality is consistent in Austen, for only heroines within the confines of the marriage plot are described as blooming, despite the presence in the narrative of other girls seemingly of the blooming age. In Eliot's novels, and in *Adam Bede* (1859) and *Mid-*

dlemarch (1872) in particular, we see the bloom narrative revised by its extension to the previously unrepresented kind of Linnaean bloom—to the world of illicit, clandestine marriage, to the kinds of stories where legal marriage and sexuality are not synonymous, where the sexual implications of courtship are actually realized. In *Adam Bede* "clandestine marriage" newly enters the realist novel's sphere of representation, while in *Middlemarch* Eliot returns to the topic of the sexual potential of marriage first through a marriage's failure and then through renewed courtship. The formal innovation of the bloom plot in Austen's *Persuasion* points forward to Eliot at midcentury, where the exploration of "second-blooms" and second loves pick up on the possibilities offered in Austen's late fiction. Anne Elliot blooms because her marital possibilities return; in her late twenties, her reblooming is no inherent natural fact but a crucial fact in an alternative arc of courtship: that is, a formal exploration of how to represent the sexual as well as romantic possibilities of a late-in-time courtship.

If Eliot is impatient with all the attention that novels give to girls with "blooming skin," she is impatient only insofar as novelistic narratives had limited themselves to Linnaeus's public blooms rather than taking up all the narrative possibilities of second blooms and sexualized courtship outside a marital trajectory. The increasing self-consciousness about "bloom" and the formal innovations in this central plot set up a critical trajectory that I trace by foregrounding Austen, Eliot, and James. But as Eliot's metanovelistic prose registers—"I protest against all our interest . . . being given to the blooming skins"—bloom became such an often-used trope and narrative that in some forms it began to lose its vividness and potential for narrative interest. The sense of wearying repetition that is caught in Eliot's protest points to the way bloom became so legible in the first half of the nineteenth century as to make it able to be mined for novelistic cliché. As I will show, the tropological history of bloom is partly one of *ossification*, for only in the revivification of the bloom narrative by Eliot at midcentury does it retain its power to organize a narrative. Henceforth the history of bloom is in part an exercise in tracing the way some of the century's most celebrated novelists continue to explore and rework the representation of the sexual potential in courtship, and in part a story of how the courtship novel of the nineteenth century produced the very clichés of youthful blossoming that the twentieth and early twenty-first centuries unwittingly perpetuate.

The rendering of the blooming girl into a literary type is not, therefore, the only story to be told of its midcentury appearances, though it will precede my investigation into Eliot's transformation of the Linnaean bloom narrative. Subsequently I will detail the particular ways Eliot revises the received novelistic narrative of bloom, especially her attention to "second blooms," as well as "clandestine bloom" as a category of courtship. I will give particular attention to the ways that references to a Linnaean clandestine courtship between Hetty and Donnithorne might revise our critical understanding of the novel's pastoral qualities, for the pastoral in *Adam Bede* is a metanovelistic device in an essentially realist novel. In the third and longest section of this chapter, I turn to the ways Eliot's novels depend on a more general scientific vernacular coming from natural history. By excavating Eliot's practical experience as a naturalist just prior to the composition of her first fictions, I explore the ways a taxonomical nature accounts for a broader social milieu in *Adam Bede*. If in Austen bloom had primarily accounted for marital dispositions, in Eliot the expansion of the systematics of bloom to a more generally categorized nature corresponds to the way Eliot expanded her novels from linear marriage plots to multistrand narratives. Eliot's description of the social world through organizing principles derived from natural history, rather than the Linnaean system exclusively, is more typical of the mid-nineteenth century, where the influence of botanical practice was diffused into a wider range of natural objects and observational practices. Eliot's principles of realism both draw on and trouble the epistemologies of natural history, and from this perspective I determine the ways that Hetty may seem an experiment in a character-as-natural-object.

In devoting a significant portion of this study to the "scientizing" of bloom at midcentury, I privilege Eliot's contribution in what may have been an anomaly in bloom and narrative fiction at midcentury; nevertheless, Eliot's innovations not only best speak to the literary trajectory established by Austen's novels but also provide the inspiration for James's metanarratives of blooming girls at century's end. What Eliot presents us with, finally, is an anatomization of marriage as a "natural" fact—however we categorize it, clandestine or public—analogous to those more patently natural facts that rest behind the composition of *Adam Bede*.

Ossification: Midcentury Bloom in Dickens

The vernacularization of botany, and the shaping force it had over the novel, influenced the representation of nascent female sexuality deep into the nineteenth century. Perhaps nothing makes this clearer than the "tribute" that its metamorphosis into cliché suggests. The use of the term *bloom*, as well as the use of floral or botanical references as a shorthand for young female subjectivity, is culturally pervasive in the fiction of the first half of the nineteenth century: still available for novelistic use, bloom and its figurative cognates began to veer into cliché. As the meaning of bloom becomes increasingly transparent, it also hardens into a trope that is less vivid and less able to organize a narrative; that is, bloom's ossification renders it, paradoxically, both more legible and less able to represent the nuances of courtship in a marriage plot. The first half of the nineteenth century in part saw the beginning of the very clichés of bloom or youthful blossoming that we today inherit.

Yet the process of ossification is neither as simple nor as linear as this might imply, for insofar as the botanical vernacular of the late eighteenth century vivified a set of meanings around the floral and youthful femininity, bloom was not a word that originated in or emanated directly out of a scientific vocabulary; as I have shown, even the first appearances of bloom in the novel occurred prior to when the sexualist system was translated and reached its greatest currency. The association between flowers and youthful female beauty had a long history, and bloom, as I have suggested, would necessarily have invoked those other systems of signification: even prior to the later history of ossification, certain associations would have come from a range of reference that was prenovelistic. In particular, the long history of the pastoral, as well as various metaphorical associations from religious texts and literature, formed part of the literary history that Linnaean bloom both inherited and transformed. Thus the process of gradual ossification that occurs sometime in the early to mid-nineteenth century is not a linear one of flourishing followed by decay; far from following the natural life cycle of a flower, the trope undergoes a metamorphosis. In this sense it is important to differentiate the tropological history from tropological meaning, for in narrating this process as a literary history it is all too easy to impose a misleading linearity to what is, more accurately, an accretion of meaning. Bloom and its cognates became so pervasive as to veer back into the very semantic patterns that the vernacularization of botany had, in some sense, overwhelmed. So when Eliot writes that "Hetty's was a springtide beauty" and describes her as having "eyelids delicate as petals . . . long lashes curled like the stamen of a flower," the traces of both a botanical vernacular and the earlier range of reference are in play (*AB*, 85, 151). In becoming culturally pervasive, bloom and its cognates become as legible as its literary antecedents.

By the middle decades of the nineteenth century a change occurred in the meanings encoded in "bloom," and nowhere is that change more clear than in the fiction of Charles Dickens. With the creations of Rose Fleming, Dora Spenlow, Ada Clare, and Flora Finching, Dickens brings into being (and in the last case satirizes) the very cliché of the perfect, blooming girl that we own today. From *Oliver Twist* (1837–38) at the beginning of his career, to *David Copperfield* (1849–50) and *Bleak House* (1852–53) at the midpoint, through *Little Dorrit* (1855–57), Dickens uses the shorthand of bloom to capture the perfect mix of youthful female beauty and "marriageability" for which these characters are justifiably famous. Dickens did not simply repeat himself, however, for there is considerable variation among these blooming girls. If Rose Fleming and Ada Clare alike marry extraordinary female beauty with unusual moral rectitude, his narrative confidence in Ada is considerably less than in the reformative powers of Rose's blooming self (and rural garden). Likewise, the agonized critique of Dora—David's "Little Blossom" or "child-wife"—is on an entirely different plane from the untroubled comic satire of Miss Flora. After *Oliver Twist* Dickens becomes uncomfortable with the marital promise of the blooming girl and seeks alternatives to her sexual promise in heroines who embody perfect domesticity. If this is an innovation, it is an innovation with a cost: with bloom now weakened in its ability to represent that which is otherwise unrepresented (the promise of marital sexual fulfillment), it can only represent a quality (domestic happiness) that is equally well represented by a host of other figural systems. As a result, the unique force of bloom disappears, and what remains hardens into a caricature.

While *Middlemarch* on the one hand refuses the generic contours of the bloom plot, *Oliver Twist* on the other hand takes up the blooming girl to the extent that it is rendered a stereotype. It falls to Thackeray to employ what he understands as a cliché for the pleasures of parody. In *Memoirs of Barry Lyndon* (1844), Thackeray parodies the conflation of women, courtship, and the floral, in a scene set in the mid-eighteenth century:

> "No, Norelia," said the Captain (for it was the fashion of those times for lovers to call themselves by the most romantic names out of novels), "except for you and four others, I vow before all the gods, my heart has never felt the soft flame!" "Ah! you men, you men, Eugenio!" said she (the beast's name was John), "your passion is not equal to ours. We are like—like some plant I've read of—we bear but one flower, and then we die!"[2]

Here we see the clichéd usage of the botanical vernacular, which was available by Thackeray's time for rather easy satire. Unlike Dickens, whose novels demonstrate that a kind of ossified bloom was still viable through the middle of the century, Thackeray's nod to bloom reflects his satirical rejection of it as if it were a register not only too clichéd but, more pointedly, too novelistic to be employed anymore.

And yet the examples of Dickens and, as I will show, Eliot suggest that Thackeray's assessment perhaps made him too coolly percipient for his own good. Bloom had become a more general novelistic lexicon, and it certainly seemed to have temporarily lost its capacity for shaping an entire narrative of courtship—yet it had continuing viability as novelistic language. Certain of Eliot's uses of the word *bloom* suggest the degree to which it had entered the vernacular; in *Adam Bede*, for instance, Reverend Irwin panders to his elderly mother by saying "'you see how blooming my mother looks. She beats us young people hollow,'" and in toasting Donnithorne at his birthday feast refers to the "'tall, fine-looking young men here, as well as some blooming women'"(*AB*, 59, 267–8). In *Middlemarch*, bloom is used at the highest moments of moral seriousness but is also, tellingly, part of Casaubon's musty rhetoric in his proposal to Dorothea: "but I have discerned in you an elevation of thought and a capability of devotedness, which I had hitherto not conceived to be compatible either with the early bloom of youth or with those graces of sex" (*M*, 66). The obsolescence of bloom signaled by Thackeray's usage is not yet a fact; despite the ways its familiarity opened it to satire, bloom remained *viable*.

We might say in fact that an uneasy tonal mixture, one that yoked a satirical or even weary acknowledgment of bloom's cultural pervasiveness with a continued dependence on its representational viability, is the most salient aspect of bloom's midcentury appearances. George Meredith's *Ordeal of Richard*

Feverel (1859) is particularly notable in this regard. The novel's central romance plot, an adolescent infatuation between the eponymous hero and the young Lucy Desborough, is narrated through a heightened language of botanical and natural efflorescence—one that maintains a certain regard for the instinctual wonder of blooming, while (perhaps through the very excess of the language) registering the way *les premières amours* are so continually stereotypical. Richard meets Lucy by a riverside:

> Meadow-sweet hung from the banks thick with weed and trailing bramble, and there also hung a daughter of Earth. Her face was shaded by a broad straw-hat with a flexible brim that left her lips and chin in the sun, and sometimes nodding, sent forth a light of promising eyes. Across her shoulders, and behind, flowed large loose curls, brown in shadow, almost golden where the ray touched them. She was simply dressed, befitting decency and the season. On a closer inspection you might see that her lips were stained. This blooming young person was regaling on dewberries.[3]

Bloom has become so ossified as to become a theory within the novel— Richard's father Sir Austin's theory of development labels puberty "the Blossoming Season"—but it is not a theory with which Meredith can dispense. Meredith, that is, might understand Lucy Desborough as a cliché, an Ada Clare or a Rose Maylie, but that knowledge does not prevent him from producing yet another version. Lucy's bloom, both overtly sexualized and too decent to permit anything but the most licit sexuality, is narrated in a tone that verges, but only verges, on parody; Meredith needs, as counterpoise to the cynical languages elsewhere in his novel, the secure legibility of bloom but in using it is forced to recognize its all-too-familiar contours.

Rose Maylie of *Oliver Twist* epitomizes, and perhaps even inaugurated, the cliché of bloom that still has currency: if today one was to say, in referring to an adolescent girl, "she is in her bloom," one would want to wink in an effort to register our ironic self-consciousness. Although our urge to wink cannot be entirely attributed to Dickens, creations such as Rose Maylie at very least provide an inspiration for the kind of embarrassment we now feel in the marriage of moral perfection and virginal beauty intended for domestic life:

> The younger lady was in the lovely bloom and spring-tide of womanhood; at that age, when, if ever angels be for God's good purposes enthroned inmortal forms, they may be, without impiety, supposed to abide in such as hers. She was not past seventeen. Cast in so slight and exquisite a mould; so mild and gentle; so pure and beautiful; that earth seemed not her element, nor its rough creatures her fit companions. The very intelligence that shone in her deep blue eye, and was stamped upon her noble head, seemed scarcely of her age or of the world . . . the cheerful, happy smile; were made for Home; for fireside peace and happiness.[4]

It is Rose, of course, who saves Oliver when he is most imperiled; shot while participating in a burglary of the very home Rose resides in, Oliver is not only forgiven the criminal act but is taken in to be nursed and, eventually, made a protégé of young Rose. Mrs. Maylie and Rose in turn take Oliver to their countryside house where Rose's love and the pastoral landscape combine to transform Oliver from budding thief to a little scholar who not only studies botany and ornithology but rises joyfully at dawn to gather wildflowers for the women. Unlike Dickens's other novels, *Oliver Twist* is confident that the blooming girl is the route to an ideal marriage; the narrative's wistful close regretfully turns away from her in her married state:

> I would shew Rose Maylie in all the bloom and grace of early womanhood. . . . I would paint her the life and joy of the fireside circle and lively summer group; I would follow her through the sultry fields at noon, and hear the low tones of her sweet voice in the moonlit evening walk; I would watch her in all her goodness and charity abroad, and the smiling untiring discharge of domestic duties at home. . . . I would summon before me, once again, those joyous little faces that clustered round her knee. (*OT*, 350)

For unlike the goodhearted but fallen Nancy, who in the moral compass of the novel has to die at the hands of Sykes, Rose is a rose who thrives—her bloom is as transparent a marker for the pleasures of marriage as the prostitute's painted cheek is an advertisement for her trade.[5]

The reformative powers of a Rose's bloom are less confidently expressed in Dickens's later novel *Bleak House*. As in *Oliver Twist*, the blooming girl remains a perfect conflation of breathtaking virginal beauty, moral rectitude, and the sexual promise of marriage, but in *Bleak House* that promise is not enough to save her intended, not enough to ensure the proper culmination of the forecasted marriage plot. Instead the lure of Chancery for Richard Carstone leaves Ada widowed, frozen in a kind of black-garmented bloom: "I think my darling girl is more beautiful than ever. The sorrow that has been in her face—for it is not there now—seems to have purified even its innocent expression, and to have given it a diviner quality . . . in the black dress that she still wears" (*BH*, 988). She had of course epitomized the subjectivity of the blooming girl in being seventeen years old, and stereotypically attractive and innocent; on seeing her for the first time, Esther admires her as a "beautiful girl! With such rich golden hair, such soft blue eyes, and such a bright, innocent, trusting face!" (*BH*, 44) Skimpole, the childish romantic who veers toward a cruel selfishness, calls Ada blooming: "She is like the morning . . . with that golden hair, those blue eyes, and that fresh bloom on her cheek, she is like the summer morning. The birds here will mistake her for it . . . she is a child of the universe." Dickens's growing disquietude with the trope's easy association of marital sexuality with marital happiness is suggested in John Jardyce's reply to Skimpole's too-overblown appraisal: "the universe . . . makes rather an indifferent parent, I am afraid" (*BH*, 92–3). Here, practical guardianship trumps a romantic conception of nature that is entwined with an appreciation for feminine beauty; no wonder that it is Esther's lost beauty and premature matronliness, rather than Ada's bloom, that leads to the arc of successful courtship and marriage.

Dickens's later fiction actually becomes admonitory about bloom's promise of sex as a basis for courtship. In linking a woman's bloom with silliness and domestic ineptitude, he deprecates sexual attractiveness as an inadequate basis for courtship—a critique of the usual bloom narrative that disables its effectiveness. In *Bleak House*, Volumnia Dedlock, the unmarried silly cousin of Sir Leicester, is satirized as a "young lady (of sixty)" who wears an "indiscreet profusion in the article of rouge" and who marvels at the beauty of young girls: "'I felt sure that some uncommon eye must have picked that girl out. She really is a marvel. A dolly sort of beauty . . . but in its own way, perfect; such bloom I never saw!' Sir Leicester with his magnificent glance of displeasure at the rouge, appears to say so too" (*BH*, 449). The satiric portrait of a rouge-wearing spinster is matched, though more genially, in the Flora of *Little Dorrit*. Flora, or Mrs. Finching as she hates to be called—"oh not that nasty ugly name, say Flora!"—is the incarnation of Dickens's admonitory prose about bloom as a basis for marital choice (*LD*, 128). Disappointed in not being allowed to marry Flora in very early adulthood, Arthur Clennam returns twenty-five years later to find his youthful love far from either his physical or mental ideal; it is not the daughter but the by now elderly father Mr. Casby, as he twice repeats, who has a "blooming face," a face with a "bloom on it, like ripe wall-fruit" (*LD*, 123). The comedic misattribution of bloom that Dickens knowingly employs requires the reader to surmise that Flora has lost her own bloom:

> The return of Mr. Casby, with his daughter Flora, put an end to these meditations. Clennam's eyes no sooner fell upon the object of his old passion, than it shivered and broke to pieces. 'This is Flora.' Flora, always tall, had grown to be very broad too, and short of breath; but that was not much. Flora, whom he had left a lily, had become a peony; but that was not much. Flora, who had seemed enchanting in all she said and thought, was diffuse and silly. That was much. (*LD*, 125)

Dickens's unchecked pleasure in the significant name is at its height here; flowers ("Flora") eventually lose their bloom, the character teaches us, and when they do they become wives who are silly, eat too much, and hence are "overgrown," and, in Flora's logorrhea, are "less slim than formerly and dreadfully red on the slightest exertion particularly after eating I well know when it takes the form of a rash it might have been and was not through the interruption of parents" (*LD*, 132, 682). Only the "interruption of parents" saves Clennam from a bloom that was destined to turn into a florid dermatitis—what in the more polite earlier version was called the change from the white, graceful "lily" to the large, presumably red "peony." Clennam is saved from this fate so that he might marry the morally admirable, if dwarfish, Little Dorrit, which he does from the old Marshalsea prison. It is autumn when this marriage plot quickens, a time when the trees were "free from the bloom of drowsy summer weather, which had rested on it as the bloom lies on the plum." For Dickens, the promise of domestic happiness is signaled by the *absence* of bloom, which the selflessness of Little Dorrit—oddly both metonymic of and opposed to the prison's seasonlessness ("blossom what would, its bricks and bars bore uniformly the same dead crop")—ensures (*LD*, 679).

Dora of *David Copperfield* most troubles Dickens's seeming determination to distrust bloom's signals. The novel (among other things) is an extended meditation on the causes of marital felicity, and the characters of Dora Spenlow and Agnes Wickfield, Copperfield's two wives, are models of blooming on the one hand and sympathetic domesticity on the other. The self-consciousness of Dickens's conflation of immature love and floral signification goes beyond the diminutives that Dora is known by: "Little Blossom" and "child-wife." Each of Copperfield's early crushes involve some sort of floral exchange; Miss Larkins admires the flower in his suit ("pink camellia japonica, price half-crown"), and he gives it to her only to have to be consoled by her "sacred pledge, the perished flower" when she marries an older man; Steerforth, the object of young Copperfield's intense devotion, calls him "Daisy" and says the "sight of you, Daisy, in full bloom" makes him happy (*DC*, 265, 413). But it is Dora, of course, who captivates him, Dora who inspires an attraction that not inconsequentially is born in a garden, where she has her little dog sniff the flowers (*DC*, 379). His later accounts of his attraction are equally conversant with the cognates of bloom: "he stood up sometimes, and asked me what I thought of the prospect. I said it was delightful . . . but it was all Dora to me. The sun shone Dora, and the birds sang Dora. The south wind blew Dora, and the wild flowers in the hedges were all Doras, to a bud" (*DC*, 470). He must wait to marry until he is twenty-one; when that time arrives, he walks with Dora on the "Common . . . all in bloom"; the little house he outfits is decorated with carpets adorned with flowers, rose-colored furniture, and wallpaper that looks like the "green leaves . . . had just come out" (*DC*, 610, 613). His later impatience with Dora's domestic incompetence signals the narrative's warning that to choose a wife based on her blooming qualities is to risk marital unhappiness; only his aunt, who steps in to admonish him, can remind him of her attractions: "Little Blossom is a very tender blossom, and the wind must be gentle with her" (*DC*, 621). While the linkage here between bloom and domestic ineptitude is a Dickensian innovation, that innovation nonetheless operates within the standard field of bloom as a marker of marital sexuality; by now, however, the implied sexuality simply has lost its force as a narrative endpoint. The illness that Dora comes to suffer from is repeatedly linked to the death of a flower—"my aunt left her with a parting cry of 'Good night, Little Blossom,' . . . and [I] cried to think, O what a fatal name it was, and how the blossom withered in its bloom upon the tree"—and so it is not a surprise that her death is represented as a blossom that "flutters to the ground" (*DC*, 681, 745).

Despite the self-consciousness with which the text invokes a certain ossified bloom type, the narrative cannot think of Dora's premature death with
the lightness it might accord a flower's wilting. Although Dora is as incapable a
creature as *Little Dorrit*'s Flora, she is treated with the same degree of earnest-
ness that Rose Maylie enjoyed. And even though Dora's death is, in a crass
sense, a convenience to the narrator of this *Bildung*, the narrative implies it
only to refuse to recognize it as such. The novel resolves the problem of self-
presentation by enacting a trade between the "Little Blossom" and the wife of
David's maturity: Agnes reveals that Dora's final wish was that she be the one to
take her place (*DC*, 844). Despite the representational insistence that Dora is
all bloom and Agnes is all sympathetic domesticity, at the moment that Dora's
wish is enacted (when David asks Agnes to marry him), the suggestion is made
that Dora must lend Agnes her bloom: "And O Agnes, even out of thy true
eyes, in that same time, the spirit of my child-wife looked upon me, saying it
was well; and winning me, through thee, to tenderest recollections of the
Blossom that had withered in its bloom!" (*DC*, 842) If Dora, as she says, was
not fit to be a wife, she nevertheless possessed the thing that Agnes, up to this
point, had seemed to lack: the bloom that a sister (as David thinks of her) does
not have.

As if to reassure the doubting reader that this kind of union could produce
not only domestic but sexual happiness, Mr. Peggotty returns to England from
Australia to verify Agnes' bloom: "And it's allus been on my mind, as I must
come and see Mas'r Davy and your own sweet blooming self, in your wedded
happiness, afore I got to be too old" (*DC*, 846). The sexual promise of Agnes is
established retroactively in the pack of children she is said to have. For Dickens, bloom is best wedded to the kind of domestic rationality that is his preferred alternative to the blooming girl. Through Agnes Dickens transforms
what he receives—and perhaps, in a moment of sentimental attachment to
marital sexuality, to ring in the age of the woman who can do it all. Dickens
creates a literary type, but he also renders with remarkable variety a cliché that
is still viable, still compelling, today.

Revivification: Midcentury Bloom in *Middlemarch* and *Adam Bede*

Eliot's major fiction, *Adam Bede* and *Middlemarch* in particular, suggests a
concentrated impatience with both the genre of the public courtship plot
and the ossifying trope of bloom. The broadest critique of the courtship plot
comes with the refusal in *Middlemarch* to make courtship the organizing narrative principle; Casaubon is accepted by Dorothea early in the novel's first
book. Like Dorothea herself, Eliot seems impatient to get over the narratively
predictable topic of courtship in order to get to a variety of narrative strands,
including the less-explored arena of marriage itself. *Adam Bede* registers the
potential ossifying effect of bloom's figurative language, as well as the narrative

dangers of presuming that nature has a legible language; the novel is suffused with ambivalence about employing language that figuratively conflates females and flowers. Nevertheless, both *Adam Bede* and *Middlemarch* expand on and experiment with the Linnaean bloom narrative. Eliot uses a broader realist lens, one that expands the courtship plot to "second blooming" and "clandestine marriage": in the first instance to the possibility that bloom, or sexual response, is not limited to the unmarried female—that Dorothea, for instance, can bloom as an attraction for someone other than her husband; in the second instance to the possibility that courtship can be extended from the traditional "public marriages" of Linnaeus's taxonomy to his second primary category of blooming, what Linnaeus called "clandestine marriage." The premarital nature of Hetty and Donnithorne's sexual relation is narrated through botanical references to clandestine blooming, distinguishing the novel for its insistence on understanding their relationship as a courtship, their sexual experience as a "marriage" of the clandestine sort, rather than as the more traditional narrative of seduction and fall. In expanding the narrative of bloom beyond its previous novelistic manifestations, the novels return the scientific background to bloom and reinvigorate the botanical vernacular by invoking another of Linnaeus's possible narrative threads.

The narrative thread of public courtship had been amply performed by Austen, who unproblematically joined the physical description of bloom with the narrative destiny of marriage. Potential variations on marriage, suggested both by Linnaeus's nature and social reality alike, are scrupulously kept at the margins of Austen's narratives—the most famous being Lydia's elopement with Wickham, an act that the Bennets initially misapprehend as the pair seeking a clandestine marriage in Scotland. That version of courtship is not told but only inferred through letters before being rectified by Darcy's magnanimous coercion; it is only after Lydia is properly married from her uncle's London parish that she returns to the novel's present tense. Austen, one might say, refuses a narrative opportunity out of propriety or moral disgust, while Eliot takes up these alternative social realities. Linnaeus's taxonomical system, at even its broadest discriminations, suggests an alternative way of narrating courtship, a different version on which to base the projected erotic possibility of marriage. The vegetable blooms of this second category of "clandestine marriage" are not visible, of course, in much the same way that clandestine sexuality had not found a place in the courtship plot (but only in the plot of seduction familiar from the eighteenth century). For Eliot to extend the courtship plot to clandestine marriages was to make the very category of courtship markedly more capacious. Even if, as it should be noted, courtship remains restricted to a heterosexual domain, it is still a domain made more tolerant and broadly reflective of social reality than the one Eliot had found. What we find in Eliot's midcentury fiction, in other words, is bloom's realist, or nonallegorical, proliferation, where the corporeality of the blooming girl becomes more evident under the demands of nineteenth-century realist practice. The increased visibility of bloom as a physical sign, however, obviates its social-sexual fluidity; increasingly, bloom means physical ripeness and health and less, as it had so clearly in Austen, a quality of "marriageability," which implied both social and sexual meanings.

Eliot's novels, like their mid-nineteenth-century counterparts, employ the word *bloom* less restrictively than Austen's novels: Dinah Morris might refer to Bessy Cranage's "blooming youth, given up to folly and vanity," while in *Middlemarch* Mrs. Vincy can be said to have a "bloom of complexion" (*AB*, 93; *M*, 358). The fertile agricultural district of Loamshire, the setting of *Adam Bede*, is described in relation to stark Stonyshire "as a pretty blooming sister may sometimes be seen linked in the arm of a rugged, tall, swarthy brother" (*AB*, 19). Bloom is more generally a potential modifier of youthful physicality, as in *Middlemarch* when "Celia entered, blooming from a walk in the garden" (*M*, 79). Casaubon, who is repeatedly described as "faded," is also not blooming: "the house too had an air of autumnal decline, and Mr. Casaubon, when he presented himself, had no bloom that could be thrown into relief by that background" (*M*, 99). The Vincys' governess is also spoken of as not blooming, a look that makes her, as "Mrs. Vincy often said, just the sort of person for a governess" (*M*, 191). And yet bloom is not merely a surface look or rosy glow; even amid this promiscuous usage, it continues to draw on its Linnaean associations of sexual promise. Adam Bede, for instance, postpones marriage in his knowledge that a blooming girl corresponds with a growing family: "he had made up his mind that it would be wrong as well as foolish for him to marry a blooming young girl, so long as he had no other prospect than that of growing poverty with a growing family" (*AB*, 210–1). Eliot's novels reflect bloom's more generalized usage at midcentury, but they do so with a persistent sense of both the Linnaean meanings that originally informed bloom and the representational possibilities of a revised bloom narrative.

Scenes of Clerical Life

The force of contrast between bloom as a literary type at midcentury and Eliot's transformation of bloom into a revived and newly central narrative possibility is hinted at in Eliot's initial fictional foray, *Scenes of Clerical Life* (1858). In particular, the second of the three sketches that make up *Scenes of Clerical Life* self-consciously hearkens back to a time when the language of bloom was not a clichéd figure. "Mr. Gilfil's Love Story" uses bloom and its floral cognates without any sense of cliché, but nonetheless the narrative context suggests that the language and story of bloom are self-consciously late in time. In particular, the narrator of "Mr. Gilfil's Love Story" frames the story of "the Vicar's courtship and marriage" through the visage and manner of the now elderly Rev. Gilfil; thirty years have past since that time in 1788, thirty years in which his housekeeper "Martha had dusted and let the air upon, four times a-year, ever since she was a blooming lass of twenty; and she was now, in this last decade of Mr. Gilfil's life, unquestionably on the wrong side of fifty" (*SCL*,

130). Like Martha's now faded bloom, the narrative that contains the story of Mr. Gilfil's courtship of his wife is now an old one—an old story not only for Mr. Gilfil himself but *generically* as well.

Containing the bloom narrative within a historical frame distances the telling from the story itself; in that temporal cocoon Eliot chose to write a story of tragic bloom, one that, as late as 1858, seems to rely on a botanical vernacular and a received familiarity with bloom's meanings. As is not the case in Austen's novels, bloom does not signal the pace of the marriage plot, and more than the central female character is said to bloom; *Scenes of Clerical Life*, despite setting its stories late in the previous century, is markedly a mid-nineteenth-century fiction, in that bloom's Linnaean inflections have lost some of their ability to organize and drive an entire narrative. From the beginning of "Mr. Gilfil's Love Story" the reader is privy to the fact that Gilfil's bride has been long dead, so bloom is not an indicator of the erotic potential of a projected marriage (as it was in Austen) but rather a marker of promise long lost. Although the difference can in part be attributed simply to the choice of the past tense, the effect is more significant: bloom, no longer available to represent the intricacies of courtship, becomes subject to nostalgia. Before the "revisionary" bloom of *Adam Bede*, "Mr. Gilfil's Love Story" captures the wistfulness of a girl's bloom now long past and perhaps in turn asserts bloom's passing.

"Mr. Gilfil's Love Story" links blooming with courtship, but not the courtship plot that the title implies. That is, Caterina, Gilfil's wife, does not bloom because she enters into a marriage plot with her eventual husband but rather suffers a loss of bloom almost immediately from the effect of a treacherous lover. Unlike *Persuasion*, which tracks the reblooming of Anne Elliot with the return of the man she loves (and the return of the marriage plot), "Mr. Gilfil's Love Story" forecloses that possibility through the story's frame; as Mr. Gilfil's young bride, Caterina is remembered as pale and sickly, with eyes that looked "blank-like" before she died less than half a year after her marriage. Within the frame, the story begins with a reference to absent bloom: "you are at once arrested by her large dark eyes . . . it is only by an effort of attention that you notice the absence of bloom on her young cheek" (*SCL*, 131, 133). That early indication of bloom's absence—despite at seventeen embodying the quintessential age of bloom—is explained soon after in a scene falsely evocative of traditional courtship; an intense description of a flower garden contains the figures of Gilfil and Caterina, the first clearly in love and the second weeping at the loss of another man (*SCL*, 141).

The absent bloom is soon further understood as an arrested bloom, for Captain Wybrow, Caterina's love, had taken his courtship quite far, only to give it up for mercenary reasons. Although clearly they did not have a literal sexual relationship, the implication that their relationship augurs forward to sexuality is figured in the sketch through a repeated floral reference: he smells like roses. Whenever Wybrow comes near her, the scent of roses is in the air: "but when she heard him come in, and the scent of roses floated toward her, her heart gave one great leap." The scent of roses combines with what can only be described as Caterina's erotic response to him: "suddenly, a breath of warmth and roses seemed to float toward her, and an arm stole gently round her waist, while a soft hand took up her tiny fingers. Caterina felt an electric thrill, and was motionless for one long moment; then she pushed away the arm and hand" (*SCL*, 168–9, 144). Wybrow, who is described as a man of "calm passions" who does not have the capacity for love, seems unaffected by their close proximity, while Caterina is represented as a bundle of affect and feeling; her extraordinary singing, in particular, makes her sensuality paramount. When Wybrow returns to the family estate, now engaged to the woman their uncle wished him to marry, he can speak to her with perfect blitheness: "Well, Caterina, how do you do? You look quite blooming." Caterina's response contains all the passion that his lacks; her cheeks redden with anger at what she recognizes as his "perfect nonchalance" (*SCL*, 169).

The narrative seems to imply that a telos of sexual promise has been set in motion only to be prematurely stopped by an unfeeling lover, the effect being Caterina's loss of bloom and feverish wasting into near-death. Mr. Gates, the gardener, captures the particular kind of floral wasting that she is undergoing: "I shouldn't wonder if she fades away laike the cyclaemens as I transplanted. She puts me imaind on 'em somehow, hangin' on their little think stalks, so whaite an' tinder" (*SCL*, 184). The various unfoldings of the plot chart Caterina's physical decline in the presence of a rival whom we are to believe is also passionate about Wybrow; that this is a sexual rivalry becomes most clear on the fiancé's return to a room just after Wybrow had tried to placate Caterina with a caress: "as she stood nearly in the middle of the room, her little body trembling under the shock of passions too strong for it, her very lips pale, and her eyes gleaming, the door opened, and Miss Assher appeared, tall, blooming, and splendid, in her walking costume" (*SCL*, 199). Here, Miss Assher's bloom signals the forwarding of her marriage plot at the expense of Caterina, for this scene doubles an earlier one in which Wybrow kisses and caresses his jilted lover while stating that he will continue his engagement.

"Mr. Gilfil's Love Story," then, is not a love story in the way that bloom had come to organize that plot. Rather, his love story is one of salvation, for he nurses her back from near death in order to marry her. Although her initial consciousness occurs at the prompting of his voice, it is music's sensual potential that brings her more fully back to life; the sound prompts some form of re-birth, for she is compared to the "water-plant that lies withered and shrunken on the ground [which] expands into freedom and beauty when once more bathed in its native flood" (*SCL*, 240). As the frame narrative had earlier revealed, however, that projected reblooming is confined to that epiphanic moment, when the proximity of Gilfil and the music combine in one final gesture of physical possibility: "She nestled to him, and put up her little mouth to be kissed. The delicate-tendrilled plant must have something to cling to. The soul that was born anew to music was born anew to love" (*SCL*, 241). Represented as a vinous plant, she marries Gilfil even if she does not blossom, or bloom, again. The absence of the sexual connotations of bloom is further evident in the way the story narrates her death, for the plant metaphors suggest that pregnancy kills her: "but the delicate plant had been too deeply bruised, and in the struggle to put forth a blossom it died. Tina died, and Maynard Gilfil's love went with her into deep silence for evermore" (*SCL*, 243).

Thus one of Eliot's first pieces of fiction employs bloom as a narrative device about which it seems self-conscious—a girl's bloom seems only possible within a narrative frame that distances that kind of story from the telling of it. The second sketch in *Scenes from Clerical Life* may concentrate on a traditional public courtship, but its interest is in that narrative's failure and the embodied effect of sexual potential's frustration on the female heroine. In framing Mr. Gilfil's anticourtship, Eliot registers her discomfort with bloom's ossification; in producing a story within that frame that relies heavily on a received familiarity with bloom's meanings, the narrative registers an uneasy dependence on it. Ultimately "Mr. Gilfil's Love Story" is a muted experiment in the revision of a received narrative that gestures forward to the revisionary bloom narratives of *Adam Bede* and *Middlemarch*.

Adam Bede: Clandestine Bloom

The ambivalence of employing language that is workable but veering toward overfamiliarity is evident in particular in *Adam Bede*, which uses figurative associations between the floral and the feminine as novelistic language that is both viable and in need of qualification. Betraying an embarrassment about the comparison, as well as asserting a claim about the need for empirical experience of beauty in nature, the narrator says that "it is of little use for me to tell you that Hetty's cheek was like a rose-petal . . . of little use, unless you have seen a woman who affected you as Hetty affected her beholders" (*AB*, 85). Adam's courtship of Hetty, dismissed at one point as trying to produce a "marriage such as they made in the golden age," uses the clichéd language of flowers that elsewhere Eliot so sedulously avoids; he picks for her the pink bud of a rose rather than a scentless pink and white striped hybrid, which is the symbol of love rather than a scentless symbol of the "union of the houses of York and Lancaster" (*AB*, 219). Explicit botanical figures seem less subject to authorial qualification; for instance, Hetty's hair has "dark hyacinthine curves that fell on her neck," while her eyelashes, practically a fetish in the text, are described as "curled like the stamen of a flower" (*AB*, 141, 151). A botanical fact is used in describing Hetty's lack of response to Adam: "he could no more stir in her the emotions that make the sweet intoxication of young love, than the mere pictures of a sun can stir the spring sap in the subtle fibres of the plant" (*AB*, 100). *Adam Bede* manages an oscillating technique: employing and yet retracting plant analogies, at times palpably discomfited with the conventionality of comparing a woman to a flower, and at times insistent, as I will later show, that the reader see Hetty as a natural fact—that she is a flower, or something between a flower, an animal, and a "distractingly pretty girl of seventeen" (*AB*, 84).

The novel is particularly anxious that conventional novelistic language about flowers, or even more precise botanical associations, not substitute for a scientific understanding of nature. It is around the apprehension of Hetty, the novel's blooming girl, that the dangers of presuming that nature has a legible language are brought out:

> Nature, he knows, has a language of her own, which she uses with strict veracity, and he considers himself adept in the language. Nature has written out his bride's character for him in those exquisite lines of cheek and chin. . . . How she will dote on her children! She is almost a child herself, and the little pink round things will hang about her like florets round the central flower. (*AB*, 152)

The admonitory response—"Nature has her own language, and she is not unveracious; but we don't know all the intricacies of her syntax just yet"—suggests that Eliot believes that floral comparisons (even knowing botanical ones) can sometimes *novelize* what should be understood as natural facts. The example that Eliot uses is "long dark eyelashes," suggesting that nothing could be more "exquisite" but saying that they are not predictive of character but rather "express the disposition of the fair one's grandmother" (*AB*, 152–3). The urge to empty natural facts of their traditional narrative components corresponds with Eliot's commitment to a more total realism, one that not only refuses to conflate nature with human emotion—"what wonder that Nature's mood is often in harsh contrast with the great crisis of our lives?"—but that also insists on seeing what novels previously had obscured (*AB*, 294). This insistence on observation rather than novelization is made a requirement of the reader at one point in regard to Hetty, where we are instructed to "try rather to divest yourself of all your rational prejudices, as much as if you were studying the psychology of a canary bird, and only watch the movements of this pretty round creature" (*AB*, 250). As I will show, that Hetty is meant to be studied is key to understanding Eliot's realism—not only its methods but how it represents subjects previously outside novelistic purview such as clandestine blooms. In instructing us to study rather than to novelize Hetty, *Adam Bede* uses an empiricist eye to represent that which had previously been out of bounds: clandestine, as well as public, marriage.

Eliot's empiricist eye enables her to explore what the Linnaean focus on marriage as reproduction can sometimes obscure: that is, sexual attraction. Hetty's clandestine blooming allows Eliot to explore the specifically sexual aspects of the blooming girl and her effect on the world. Eliot's attention to the sexual aspects of blooming not only ennobles sexual attraction as a subject but links pleasure in a woman's beauty with aesthetic appreciation. The philosophical argument is grounded in Adam's pleasure in Hetty, which is likened to the appreciation of music:

> I think the deep love he had for that sweet, rounded, blossom-like, dark-eyed Hetty, of whose inward self he was really very ignorant,

> came out of the very strength of his nature, and not out of any in-
> consistent weakness. Is it any weakness, pray, to be wrought on by ex-
> quisite music—to feel its wondrous harmonies searching the subtlest
> windings of your soul, the delicate fibres of life where no memory
> can penetrate, and binding together your whole being past and pres-
> ent in one unspeakable vibration: melting you in one moment . . .
> (*AB*, 353)

In comparing the effect of music with the physical facts of female beauty—
"exquisite curves of a woman's cheek and neck and arms"—sexual response
turns into aesthetic response, both of which (the passage claims) cause one to
"vibrate" and "melt." Being moved by beauty (Eliot's seeming euphemism for
sexual attraction) is to get back to a biological place before memory, "the delicate fibres of life where no memory can penetrate."[6] Individual beauty—here,
the "blossom-like" Hetty—promotes a higher appreciation for beauty itself
(what she calls "this *impersonal* expression in beauty"). Moreover, the argument
suggests that the appreciation of individual beauty brings one closer to a "far-
off mighty love":

> it is more than a woman's love that moves us in a woman's eyes—it
> seems to be a far-off mighty love that has come near to us, and made
> speech for itself there; the rounded neck, the dimpled arm, move us
> by something more than their prettiness—by their close kinship with
> all we have known of tenderness and peace. (*AB*, 354)

The narrative does not explicitly assert that sexual attraction brings one closer
to God, but it does suggest that the language of the body brings one closer to
a love akin to the religious, just as religious awe sanctions, and is felt to suffuse,
the observational enterprise of naturalists.[7] This spiritualizing of visual pleasure may help account for the novel's persistent appreciation for Hetty's sexual
attractiveness, despite her faults of personality.

The sexual meaning behind bloom had never been as clearly articulated as
it is in *Adam Bede*. The physical manifestation of bloom on the body is disassociated from the marriage plot; unlike Austen's novels, where blooming or reblooming was the sign of the marriage plot quickening, *Adam Bede* insists that
the sexual attractions of bloom go on whether marriage ensues or not. Hetty
and Donnithorne's "marriage" is a marriage in the Linnaean sense of clandestine marriage: a euphemism for the act of sexual reproduction. That their
coupling actually results in reproduction—Hetty's illicit pregnancy—is the
spur to the novel's tragedy, but it does not cause a loss of bloom. The novel is
insistent actually that bloom's physical manifestation on the body not be dictated by the telos of the narrative: "on Hetty's blooming health, it would take
a great deal of such mental suffering as hers to leave any deep impress . . . an indifferent observer would have been more struck with the young roundness of
her cheek and neck, and the darkness of her eyes and eye-lashes, than with any
signs of sadness" (*AB*, 336). Hetty does not lose her bloom because she has

been jilted, nor does she lose it because she is pregnant, a fact that *Adam Bede* weds to its repeated claim that human reality is not reflected in nature:

> He would not know that hidden behind the apple-blossoms, or among the golden corn, or under the shrouding boughs of the wood, there might be a human heart beating heavily with anguish: perhaps a young blooming girl, not knowing where to turn for refuge from swift-advancing shame. . . . Such things are sometimes hidden among the sunny fields and behind the blossoming orchards. (*AB*, 363–4)

Hetty's swift-advancing shame is rendered explicit through her bloom and the surrounding references in the natural world to blossoming. "Blooming" has such a clear sexual reference that here it can be used as a euphemism for her pregnancy.

Eliot's empiricist eye, however, requires that we look specifically, rather than euphemistically, at the physical effects of Hetty and Donnithorne's courtship:

> The landlady sat opposite to her as she ate, and looked at her earnestly. No wonder: Hetty had thrown off her bonnet, and her curls had fallen down: her face was all the more touching in its youth and beauty because of its weary look; and the good woman's eyes presently wandered to her figure; which in her hurried dressing on her journey she had taken no pains to conceal; moreover, the stranger's eye detects what the familiar unsuspecting eye leaves unnoticed. "Why, you're not very fit for traveling," she said, glancing while she spoke at Hetty's ringless hand. "Have you come far?" (*AB*, 377–8)

The narrative lens persists in noting Hetty's attractiveness, the very curls—earlier particularized as "hyacinthine"—that perhaps set in motion her plot of bloom. The ringless hand, combined with the lines of Hetty's now visibly pregnant body, fix the nature of Donnithorne and Hetty's courtship as "clandestine," for as the landlady is quick to intuit, the sexual promise of Hetty's youthful, beautiful face has been fulfilled. The temporal structure of *Adam Bede* is not a courtship but a pregnancy; just over eight months passes between the time when Adam sees Hetty and Donnithorne embracing among the beech trees and the day Hetty's reprieve is issued (*AB*, 466). The fact that the hanging was to occur on the day that Adam had intended for his marriage seems a melodramatic touch in comparison to this other structure, one that seems deliberately to rewrite the time period of the public courtship plot of Austen in the alternative guise of the clandestine marriage plot.

The courtship between Hetty and Donnithorne is clandestine for reasons other than its illicitness, although like its botanical counterpart their "marriage" remains hidden, invisible to the naked eye. The novel also sets their coupling amid a forest that appears to be entirely pastoral and unreal but that we will see is particularized to the knowing reader as an environment of clandestine-flowering plants. The Fir-tree Grove is the novel's primary symbolic use of nature, for it is in the woods—as it is in Shakespeare's comedies—where that which cannot occur in normal social life (an affair between a dairymaid and a squire, a combat between a squire and an artisan) occurs. All the more fascinating, then, that the novel invokes pastoral conventions but that it indicates to its readers that it is doing so; that is, the narrative is self-conscious about its switch into a different narrative mode, and as such the pastoral is a metanarrative device. The tonal and figurative switch to this more conventional representation of nature is so distinctive as to be jarring with the rest of the novel. Why did Eliot do this? In knowingly employing a pastoral idiom, the narrative constructs the woods for the reader as Donnithorne and Hetty experienced it: as the idle gentleman who has read too much Ovid and too many romances, and the silly "shepherdess" who has imbibed the vernacularization of those conventions.

Donnithorne experiences those woods through narrative insofar as, being prohibited the actual maintenance of the estate's woods that his coming-of-age and inheritance would eventually bring, he goes to them to read and be idle: "it was the sort of day for lolling in the Hermitage, and he would go and finish Dr. Moore's *Zeluco* there before dinner. The Hermitage stood in the Fir-Grove" (*AB*, 128).[8] In the flush of his first awareness that "he was getting in love with Hetty," he "pitched *Zeluco*" into the corner of the Hermitage and vowed "*he must not* see her alone again" (*AB*, 132). The romance he is reading is the counterpoint to Hetty's nonliterate imaginings: "the baker's daughter goes home and dreams of the handsome young emperor, and perhaps weights the flour amiss while she is thinking" (*AB*, 100). Hetty, who "had never read a novel," still experiences the world of the Wood through a romance narrative. In fact, Hetty is described in the terms of a reader who has been immersed in the fantasy literature Eliot disliked: "a new influence had come over Hetty— vague, atmospheric . . . but producing a pleasant narcotic effect, making her tread the ground and go about her work in a sort of dream . . . showing her all things through a soft, liquid veil, as if she were living not in this solid world of brick and stone, but in a beatified world" (*AB*, 135, 100). That beatified fantasy, we are to understand, is Hetty's reality, despite the signs to the knowing reader that another, altogether different, reality is in store for her:

> She thought nothing of the evening light that lay gently in the grassy alleys between the fern, and made the beauty of their living green more visible than it had been in the overpowering flood of noon; she thought of nothing that was present. She only saw something that was possible: Mr. Arthur Donnithorne coming to meet her again along the Fir-tree Grove. That was the foreground of Hetty's picture. (*AB*, 135)

This is a reality, Hetty's "foreground": the term that Eliot uses to describe her own realism in the chapter "In Which the Story Pauses a Little." Her foreground, her reality, is oblivious to the details of nature; the reader suffused in the botanical vernacular would recognize that the "beauty of . . . living green" that surrounds her is composed of ferns, the most common example of a plant that blooms clandestinely. Hetty could not see what surrounded her ("nothing of what was present"), for she sees only Donnithorne—a perspective that, in contrast to the present living green of the fern, is not only myopic but also dangerously unreal.

In the chapters "In the Wood" and "Evening in the Wood," the narrative self-consciously takes on the tone and representational style of an idealized nature—the one of Hetty's hazy imaginings and Donnithorne's reading. This accounts, in part, for what Philip Fisher has acutely described as the novel's "willfulness in symbolically equating a furtive relationship with a natural setting."[9] The sense of unreality that pervades these chapters is deliberate, a self-conscious literary reference to Arcadian pastoral: "he may be a shepherd in Arcadia for aught he knows, he may be the first youth kissing the first maiden, he may be Eros himself, sipping the lips of Psyche—it is all one" (AB, 136). Even Donnithorne's trip designed to distract him from Hetty and the woods is to his friend "Gawaine's," a friend so archaic in his nomenclature that he is doomed to lose to Hetty's not-at-all archaic charms. The tone and representational style in these passages about the woods are palpably different from other moments in the novel; the natural scene is suddenly full of nymphs, as if it were an Ovidian landscape:

> It was a wood of beeches and limes, with here and there a light, silver-stemmed birch—just the sort of wood most haunted by the nymphs; you see their white sunlit limbs gleaming athwart the boughs, or peeping from behind the sweeping outline of a tall lime; you hear their soft liquid laughter—but if you look with a too curious sacrilegious eye, they vanish behind the silvery beeches, they make you believe that their voice was only a running brooklet, perhaps they metamorphose themselves into a tawny squirrel that scampers away . . . [and] paths which look as if they were made by the freewill of the trees and underwood, moving reverently aside to look at the tall queen of the white-footed nymphs. (AB, 129)

Arthur, with "a book under his arm," meets Hetty among these trees, transformed from what Adam will later admire as "grand beeches" to the playground of nymphs (AB, 297).[10] Their otherworldly relationship is matched by otherworldly prose. Here, the classical education that we can presume Donnithorne had at Oxford rules the prose; the key word in the passage is the Ovidian "metamorphose," which is in keeping with the passage's fantastic images of the natural world. The mythicized prose of these chapters seems deliberately anachronistic in relation to the rest of the novel, which positions itself as an empirical recorder of the world of Hayslope. In a short parable about natural history, the mode that dominates the other representations of the natural world in Adam Bede, the reader is warned that a "too curious sacrilegious eye" will make the nymphs vanish. As they do, when Hetty returns to the world outside the Fir-tree Grove.

Hetty's blooming in the Fir-tree Grove is inevitably a clandestine one, but clandestine in a specifically Linnaean sense. That is, the narrative insists that their "marriage" is a natural fact, even if it is not socially sanctioned. The narrative is sympathetic to Donnithorne and understanding about the inevitability of the attraction:

> Love is such a simple thing when we have only one-and-twenty summers and a sweet girl of seventeen trembles under our glance, as if she were a bud first opening her heart with wondering rapture to the morning. Such young unfurrowed souls roll to meet each other like two velvet peaches that touch softly and are at rest; they mingle as easily as two brooklets that ask for nothing but to entwine themselves and ripple with ever-increasing curves in the leafiest hiding-places.
> (*AB*, 131)

The seventeen-year-old girl and the suitor whose attention initiates her bloom "as if she were a bud" comprise the quintessential bloom narrative—despite the fact that this courtship quickens far from the confines of the drawing room. Here, desire is as natural and as common as two peaches touching or two brooks merging into one. Donnithorne and Hetty's desire to touch is overwhelmingly implied in the erotic analogues of nature: the soft touch of the peaches, and the brooks' desire to "entwine themselves" in the "leafiest hiding-places" with "ever-increasing" motion, have clear sexual implications. Their relationship is not part of public life, which is perhaps why their coupling is so relentlessly associated with the natural world.

The representation of Hetty and Donnithorne's sexual relationship is not, however, beyond the purview of social representation. Their sexual relationship has a counterpart in Linnaeus's broadest discrimination between public and clandestine marriage, for their clandestine relationship is marital in the Linnaean sense because it *is* sexual. Like Hetty's sexual relationship, which is not able to be publicly seen or acknowledged, clandestine marriage describes the kind of inflorescence that cannot be seen and is not often acknowledged: the flowers, invisible to the naked eye, of mosses, ferns, and fungi. Significantly, these are the plants that are invoked repeatedly in the description of the woods in which Hetty and Donnithorne meet. Donnithorne's first appointment with Hetty, for instance, takes place on a path edged with mosses, a fact that is repeated twice: "[they were] narrow, hollow-shaped, earthy paths, edged with faint dashes of delicate moss"; "it was along the broadest of these paths that Arthur Donnithorne passed . . . the purple pathway and its edge of faintly-sprinkled moss" (*AB*, 129). Hetty's preference for the clandestine marriage of the woods over a public marriage is constructed through her studied avoidance of the pleasuregrounds that Mr. Craig, the gardener and suitor who "made unmistakable avowals in luscious strawberries and hyperbolical peas," tended: "how relieved she was when she had got safely under the oaks and among the fern of the Chase!" (*AB* 97, 134–5).

The clandestine-blooming fern is the dominant image in the lovers' second meeting as well, where the evening light enlivens "the grassy alleys between the fern and made their living green more visible." Here, one is reminded of Eliot's detailed memorializing of what she called the "ferny wilderness" of the Queen's Farm Valley on Jersey (*J*, 280). Feverishly pondering his kissing of Hetty, Donnithorne wanders the woods, where he "lost himself among the narrow openings in the fern" (*AB*, 135, 137). When Adam comes on Hetty and Donnithorne in the Fir-tree Grove, he has been hurrying "on across the Chase, stalking along the narrow paths between the fern"; a moment later, he comes upon their clandestine embrace, upon which a fight ensues and Donnithorne is felled; are we surprised that the plant that he lands on is a fern? The detail is telling: "the blow soon came, and Arthur fell, his head lying concealed in a tuft of fern" (*AB*, 302). The ferns and mosses of the Fir-tree Grove evoke their clandestine, yet natural, marriage—a blooming that literally cannot be seen, in that Hetty and Donnithorne's relationship is socially prohibited, but like the fern's hidden inflorescence is a blooming nonetheless.

Eliot's use of mosses and ferns invokes an aspect of bloom that had been suppressed in the novel since Austen, whose commitment to the structure of the marriage plot had prohibited the representation of a clandestine sexuality. Eliot does not turn from that narrative, and in doing so revivifies a plot that, as in Dickens, had ossified under the weight of its repetition. A clandestine bloom could organize the details of courtship in the same way that public bloom once organized the details of a marriage plot. This is perhaps most clear in those very details, which include, for instance, the notation that as Hetty prepared for her second meeting in the wood, Mrs. Poyser noticed a "new flush of beauty in the little thing" (*AB*, 134). The trace of the bloom on Hetty's face does not mark the initiation of the marriage plot, as it would have in Austen, but rather the quickening of the clandestine marriage plot. This is a narrative, like Hetty's expectations as she goes to meet Donnithorne, that is formless, in that there has been no precedence for the representation of a natural, if still clandestine, plot of sexual courtship. *Adam Bede* initiates the representation of the clandestine bloom, a flowering that cannot be seen between the most blooming of women and the most attractive of suitors. What must be stressed here is that the clandestine bloom of Hetty is the taxonomical alternative to the public bloom of Elizabeth Bennett; Eliot follows Austen but in an altered fashion, in some sense picking up where Austen leaves off: Lydia gives way to Hetty, clandestine marriage now at the novel's center instead of beyond its sphere of representation.

Middlemarch: Second Blooming

In *Middlemarch*, bloom undergoes an alteration of sequence, in which the age of the heroine, the fact of marriage, and the fact of bloom are reordered from their traditional positions. *Middlemarch* is a formal innovation of the bloom plot that considers the possibility that bloom, the novelistic sign of sexual promise, can occur outside the boundaries of marriage, and even a second time, thereby making the associations of bloom with virginity or youth less hard. *Middlemarch* of course is a much broader novel than this focus implies: it attempts everything that its subtitle, "A Study of Provincial Life," implies. Indeed, *Middlemarch* seems impatient with the marriage plot, for Dorothea's initial courtship concluded within the first number of the novel's serial publication; Eliot's interest, we are meant to understand, is in the state of marriage rather than the promise of courtship. But as I will show, Eliot returns to the topic of bloom once she is securely outside that narrative's traditional temporal and social structure. In charting a marriage's failure, the novel takes up the subject of sexual potential and promise; it considers, first, the fact of an individual's sexual promise, despite the absence of a motivating force, and second, the fact that blooming is not limited to virgins. A married woman can "rebloom" under the influence of renewed courtship's promise.

Bloom does have a telos in *Middlemarch*, despite the fact that botanical references, as well as the word itself, are not used exclusively to chart Dorothea's reblooming. For example, Celia's happiness with Sir James Chettham's paternalistic love for her is signaled botanically: "her little hands were clasped, and enclosed by Sir James's as a bud is enfolded by a liberal calyx" (*M*, 318). As I have shown, these references are more generally applied to a broad spectrum of the novel's characters, including Dorothea's sister Celia, as well as Rosamond, whose perfect bloom is a spider's web in which the talents of Lydgate are captured and killed. What we might call the "departicularization" of bloom in *Middlemarch* is in the service of a new realist taxonomization—one that studies the various types of female bloom, in an almost spatialized, rather than sequential, series—in order that it might show their varying manifestations. This departicularization is productive of various "types," of course, in that bloom's multiplication presents the reader with the sense that sexual promise is a general fact rather than the effect of a singular romantic encounter. The reader's sympathy for Lydgate's response to Rosamond is delimited, for instance, as a result of her bloom's not being unique to the novel, and as such she is more likely to be seen as a novelistic type. This departicularization, as I will show in chapter 5, on Henry James, creates a novelistic type that James, in reviewing the mid-nineteenth-century novel, will name the "English girl" "of the blooming season."[11]

Dorothea's reblooming is part of a more general liberalization of courtship that occurs in Eliot's novels, including the representation of second love. This narrative, which is a prominent thread in *Middlemarch*, is first explored in *Adam Bede*; the narrator asks: "how is it that the poets have said so many fine things about our first love, so few about our later love?" (*AB*, 504). Despite the fact that his love for Hetty endures "so deep that the roots of it would never be torn away," Adam falls in love with Dinah Morris and marries her (*AB*, 530). Dinah, who is described conventionally as having a "face like a lily" or a "snowdrop," colors repeatedly while in Adam's presence, her whiteness giving way to the signs of what Ruth Yeazell has named "modest blushing" (M, 120–2).[12] It might now seem to us quaint that second love be considered such an aberrant narrative course, but it is worth reflecting on the relative absence of that social reality as a celebrated fact in the English novel. In *Adam Bede*, the second courtship is venerated as a natural and inevitable fact:

> This is a simple scene, reader. But it is almost certain that you, too, have been in love—perhaps, even, more than once, though you may not choose to say so to all your lady friends. If so, you will no more think the slight words, timid looks, the tremulous touches, by which two human souls approach each other gradually, like two little quivering rain-streams, before they mingle into one—you will no more think these things trivial, than you will think the first detected signs of coming spring trivial, though they be but a faint indescribable something in the air and in the song of the birds, and in the tiniest perceptible budding on the hedgerow branches. (*AB*, 493–4)

That Eliot's realism refuses the uniqueness demanded by the traditional bloom narrative is evident from the extended plea to the reader ("you, too, have been in love"); the experience of "budding" is commonplace, as common as spring itself, and repeatable as well—we may have been in love "perhaps, even, more than once." Eliot's claim here makes the bloom narrative a potentially iterative one, both for the individual who may "fall in love" more than once and for the culture for whom the figure of the blooming girl is no longer a strange or singular one.

Despite the fact that *Middlemarch* uses the trope of "reblooming" to chart the contours of Dorothea's romantic and sexual cleaving toward Will Ladislaw, it nevertheless is cognizant of the potential cliché in the conflation of courtship and flowers. Casaubon's language in courting Dorothea, for instance, is chillingly conventional in its rhetoric: "I have been little disposed to gather flowers that would wither in my hand, but now I shall pluck them with eagerness, to place them in your bosom." The narrative comment that follows, however, does not disparage Casaubon's sincerity but points to the fact to which the novel continually returns—that the language of courtship may be commonplace, but it is experienced as realistic: "no speech could have been more thoroughly honest in its intention: that frigid rhetoric at the end was as sincere as the bark of a dog, or the cawing of an amorous rook" (M, 73). The allowance that Eliot makes for Casaubon is not merely sympathy, not merely understanding for the faded scholar's unpracticed conceits, but rather the allowance that courtship is often mediated through cliché. As in *Adam Bede*, the realism of *Middlemarch* incorporates the conventional narratives through which its characters experience their own stories.

Like Donnithorne and Hetty, who come together in the haze of Arcadian myths, Lydgate and Rosamond have a courtship that is driven by the stuff of convention. Lydgate's eventual realization that Rosamond's bloom has been fatal to any other narratives his life may have followed is supported by the narrative's account of his experience of her—"Lydgate hovered about the flower of Middlemarch"—and his expectations for marriage: "Lydgate felt sure that if he ever married, his wife would have that feminine radiance, that distinctive womanhood which must be classed with flowers and music, that sort of beauty which by its very nature was virtuous, being moulded only for pure and delicate joys" (*M*, 328, 193). A less partisan analysis might fault Lydgate as well for allowing his conventional reading of Rosamond to interfere with his ambitions; indeed, the narrator accuses him of just that: "He went home and read far into the smallest hour, bringing a much more testing vision of details and relations into this pathological study than he had ever thought it necessary to apply to the complexities of love and marriage, these being subjects to which he felt himself amply informed by literature" (*M*, 193). In desiring Rosamond, Lydgate desired a cliché, and one that *Middlemarch* insists blurs the vision of its otherwise clear-sighted scientist.

Lydgate's perception of her as the height of blooming "marriageability" is recorded in the narrative through indirect discourse, which teaches us to understand the degree to which he experiences her through the clichés of bloom: "She blushed and looked at him as the garden flowers look at us when we walk forth among them in the transcendent evening light: is there not a soul beyond utterance, half-nymph, half-child, in those delicate petals which glow and breathe about the centres of deep colour?" (*M*, 386). Lydgate's first sight of Rosamond infuses the narrative with his perception of her conventional perfection, her "rising to reach for her hat, which she had laid aside before singing, so that her flower-like head on its white stem was seen in perfection above her riding-habit" (*M*, 144). Here he sees her as a flower, one that, to his ultimate peril, he admiringly substitutes for her head.

Lydgate's misperception is accounted for in part by a narrator who vehemently echoes the more nuanced censure of the accomplished girl in *Mansfield Park*; the narrator of *Middlemarch* asserts that accomplishments are artful entrapments for men: Rosamond "was always that combination of correct sentiments, music, dancing, drawing, elegant note-writing, private album for extracted verse, and perfect blond loveliness, which made the irresistible woman for the doomed man of that date" (*M*, 301). Lydgate's increasing susceptibility to Rosamond is marked by an increasingly heightened recourse to the bloom narrative. In his first private conversation with her, for example, his quickened awareness of her is represented as wonder at the opening of a flower: "Lydgate was almost forgetting that he must carry on the conversation, in thinking how lovely this creature was, her garment seeming to be made out of the faintest blue sky, herself so immaculately blond, as if the petals of some gigantic flower had just opened and disclosed her" (*M*, 188). In his perception of her *as* a bloom, Lydgate of course quickly imagines marriage, only to check that narrative in light of his poor income. Yet when he speaks to her to make clear his inability to marry, he instead proposes marriage—a turn of events that is accounted for through the image of blue flowers:

At this moment she was as natural as she had ever been when she was five years old: she felt the tears had risen, and it was no use to try to do anything than let them stay like water on a blue flower or let them fall over her cheeks, even as they would. That moment of naturalness was the crystallizing feather-touch: it shook flirtation into love. Remember that the ambitious man who was looking at those Forget-me-nots under the water was very warm-hearted and rash. (M, 335)

Rosamond's moment of naturalness "shook flirtation into love," and hers is a nature that has two equally picturesque choices: to let her tears "stay like water on a blue flower," or "to let them fall over her cheeks," an option that reminds us of Hetty's equally picturesque tears in the wood, and Donnithorne's parallel easing of good intent. Lydgate's thwarted intention is attributed as if to a more sensitive perception of her natural beauty: her eyes become "forget-me-nots," those pale blue fragile flowers of spring whose common name is a cliché of courtship.

The "gossamer web" or fantasy that Lydgate spins as an accepted lover is matched by Rosamond, who is deceived also in her affection; she "was in the water-lily's expanding wonderment at its own fuller life" (M, 380). As the relationship deteriorates, Lydgate increasingly is unable to see the conventional narrative that had won him over, even though her physical beauty remains intact. When Captain Lydgate's fateful visit occurs, Lydgate's perception of her bloom has diminished to the extent that the narrative invokes it to show her poor judgment; despite Lydgate's warning, she admires in his cousin that which is "doated on by some flower-like blond heads as 'style'" and agrees to horseback-riding while pregnant (M, 627). Rosamond's bloom is so powerfully tied to the perception of men that she only blooms again when she learns that Mr. Ladislaw, who she believes admires her, is returning: "while Lydgate was reading the letter to Rosamond, her face looked like a reviving flower—it grew prettier and more blooming. There was nothing unendurable now: the debts were paid, Mr. Ladislaw was coming, and Lydgate would be persuaded to leave Middlemarch" (M, 811). Here, her physical revivification tells the story of her selfishness rather than the cliché of domestic perfection that earlier he had read in her face: she revives at the moment when Lydgate is most troubled, blooming in part in response to the attention of another man.

The obvious disapprobation accorded Rosamond's bloom narrative is in line with the novel's critique of the compulsion to marriage and the forms that it requires of individuals. Casaubon's decision to marry a "blooming young lady" because "it had occurred to him that he must not any longer defer his intention of matrimony" is criticized through its devastating failure: Casaubon's principle that "a man of good position should expect and carefully choose a blooming young lady" is not validated, first by Dorothea's refusal of Chettham and more powerfully by Eliot's refusal to endow that narrative with success (M, 312). It is Sir James who is twice described as a blooming man, as if the novel is knowingly gesturing to the fact that he is the conventional narrative choice to which it refuses to capitulate (*M*, 38, 81). Although Dorothea is misguided in her reasons for choosing Casaubon ("she read his pamphlet as if it had been a bouquet" and "the reasons that might induce her to accept him were already planted in her mind, and by the evening of the next day the reasons had budded and bloomed"), her principles, with one notable exception, are never reversed (*M*, 61, 46). Even after her marriage Dorothea asserts values at odds with the conventional expectations of her family, but the reversal that Dorothea must allow is a reversal in her expectations of marriage: early in book 1 we learn that Dorothea's enthusiasms "included neither the niceties of trousseau, the patterns of the plate, nor even the honours and sweet joys of the blooming matron" (*M*, 50). The single reversal that Dorothea accepts in her philosophy is the importance of the "sweet joys of the blooming matron," a reference that can be read in part as the sexual pleasures of marriage. What one might say, in regard to the tradition of aggrieved commentary that the conclusion to Dorothea's plot has elicited, is that even if her life ends in a conventionality that she had not foreseen, the narrative path by which she arrives there is anything but conventional.[13] Far from being a capitulation to the traditional plotting of women's lives, the telos of Dorothea's life is a persistent self-selection; conventional, but also, in Eliot's eyes, haloed. Hers is a destiny that is all too easy from a contemporary stance to dismiss as Eliot's conservatism, especially considering it in light of *Middlemarch*'s persistence in narrating alternative realities for women.

Dorothea is, in the terms of a novel, a "blooming young lady"; Casaubon does not mistake her; nor does the narrative when it refers to her as "a marriageable girl" (*M*, 312, 30). Dorothea is described repeatedly as blooming; she is "hardly more than a budding woman," with a "youthful bloom" that attracts Lydgate's bemused notice (*M*, 50, 119). He believes he is entering into a traditional plot of courtship—he imagines "that matrimonial garden-scene, where, as all experience showed, the path was to be bordered with flowers"—just as Dorothea mistakenly believes that she has made a good decision (*M*, 111). The novel describes that choice as "passion . . . transfused" into the "first object that came within its level"; what is neglected in that choice is her "transfigured girlhood," as she comes to learn, or those dimensions of self that include the body and mind of an adult woman (*M*, 68). In choosing to martyr herself to Casaubon's wasting talents, Dorothea neglects her body so that her mind would be taken seriously; only with Casaubon's moral failure to treat her as an intellectual equal does Dorothea fully realize the extent of her mistake. On the couple's return from Rome, the landscape at Lowick has shrunk in proportion to her expectations. This landscape of disappointment reflects the fact of physicality that Dorothea had neglected about herself: "Her blooming full-pulsed youth stood there in a moral imprisonment which made itself one with the chill, colourless, narrowed landscape, with the shrunken furniture, the never-read books, and the ghostly stag in a pale fantastic world that seemed to be vanishing from the daylight" (*M*, 307–8).

Despite the absence of a motivating force—a husband that she respects or loves—Dorothea has "blooming full-pulsed youth." That is, there is the fact of her sexual promise, despite the fact that it is currently imprisoned by the moral requirements of marriage. This imprisoning force finds its affinity in the landscape, described in terms of colorless, cold sterility.[14] In not having Dorothea's bloom fade in proportion to her diminished expectations for marriage, the narrative suggests that her bloom is an inherent fact, not dependent on the vicissitudes of her relation to a man. Not until Casaubon requires her pledge that she blindly carry out his authorial and personal intentions after death does Dorothea suffer a loss in bloom; it is the effect of what is characterized as a "bruised heart." Her maid Tantripp worries about her new pallor, for she says that Dorothea was "not to say high-coloured, but with a bloom like a Chiny rose" (*M*, 521). Never "high-coloured," Dorothea always had her bloom, a fact that suggests that sexual promise is inherent to the individual and not so strictly tied to the vicissitudes of the marriage plot as previously described.

Dorothea does eventually find a worthy object for that bloom in Will Ladislaw. The disruption to the conventional plot of marriage is one of sequence, not of content: the sequence of bloom may be altered, but the fact of bloom has not. Dorothea marries before she blooms—an alteration of the bloom narrative that transforms the principles behind the marriage plot. The courtship of Ladislaw and Dorothea is a protracted courtship because of its initial impossibility due to her being married, followed by its undesirability because of Casaubon's will; nevertheless, it has a distinct erotic telos. In fact, the erotic valence is more pronounced when Casaubon is still alive, despite the seeming prohibition against their sexual quickening toward each other:

> Dorothea . . . looking in her plain dress of some thin woolen-white material, without a single ornament on her besides her wedding ring, as if she were under a vow to be different from all other women; and Will sat down opposite her at two yards' distance. . . . Each looked at the other as if they had been two flowers which had opened then and there. (*M*, 398)

Two flowers that had opened then and there: Ladislaw and Dorothea seem to bloom in each other's presence, as a result of each other's presence, despite the signs (wedding ring and dress of a light color) that Dorothea is far from the widow that she will soon become. The sign of sexual promise is separated here from marital promise; this is an alternative way of narrating courtship, one that until this point had not been celebrated in the English novel and that even here is markedly different from the novel of adultery, with which it may have had affinity. That is, their attraction is "clandestine" rather than illicit, invisible and yet not actually adulterous.

That Dorothea might, on a first glance, be classified as "blooming"—a category that is valid despite the wealth of social and psychological information about her that we possess, and despite her marital status—is the lesson of

Ladislaw's appreciation of her at the Vatican Museums. His visual study combines a heightened aesthetic appreciation with sexual awareness:

> the two figures passed lightly along the Meleager toward the hall where the reclining Ariadne, then called Cleopatra, lies in the marble voluptuousness of her beauty, the drapery folding around her with a petal-like ease and tenderness. They were just in time to see another figure standing against a pedestal near the reclining marble: a breathing blooming girl, whose form, not shamed by the Ariadne, was clad in Quakerish grey drapery; her long cloak, fastened at the neck, was thrown backward from her arms, and one beautiful ungloved hand pillowed her cheek. (*M*, 219–20)

The study in contrast between the voluptuous but insentient marble and the "breathing blooming girl" in the "Quakerish" clothing does not find Dorothea the loser. The two figures inform each other as the men's eyes travel between Dorothea's drapery and that which enfolds the statue with "petal-like ease and tenderness." The statue and Dorothea, as Ladislaw's German friend suggests, make "a fine bit of antithesis," but it is an antithesis that Ladislaw fails to affirm and that is undermined by the subtle attentions paid to the figure that both breathes and blooms. The cloak, though fastened at the neck, reveals bare arms; the single ungloved hand, and the use of "pillow" as a verb, subtly implies an intimate nakedness. In this context, Dorothea's "blooming" feels palpably erotic, inaugural of a bloom narrative based not on the stale rhetoric that Casaubon recycled but on the physical mechanisms of attraction.

Mutual attraction, despite the institutional forms that prohibit it, defines this altered bloom narrative; Dorothea's attraction is less apparent, in part because of the mandate that the narrative not imply her infidelity. Nevertheless, in the tête-à-tête that proves to be so deflating of Dorothea's opinion of Casaubon, Ladislaw is described as having "hair [that] seemed to shake out light," while Casaubon "on the contrary, stood rayless" (*M*, 241). Dorothea fulfills her marital vow to its exact imprisoning specifications but does not conform to it beyond what the vow required; that is, Casaubon required that she work on his "Key" after his death and not marry Ladislaw, two requirements that she abjures. The bloom narrative between Ladislaw and Dorothea, however, does not wait for Casaubon's death, for it persists without consideration to marital forms.

This socially illicit bloom, one without the prospect of marriage, corresponds with Dorothea's resignation to her life with Casaubon. Sitting in her boudoir, she sees the miniature of Aunt Julia, Ladislaw's grandmother, and experiences his attraction for her through the incipiently erotic gaze of the portrait, whose "hair and eyes seemed to be sending out light"; in an interesting gender transposition, "the face was masculine and beamed on her with that full gaze that tells her on whom it falls that she is too interesting for the slightest movement of her eyelid to pass unnoticed and uninterpreted" (*M*, 308). With

Dorothea looking as if on Ladislaw, and despite the imprisoning state of marriage, Dorothea's bloom quickens in this scene in the boudoir:

> She was glowing from her morning toilette as only healthful youth can glow; there was gem-like brightness on her coiled hair and in her hazel eyes; there was warm red life in her lips; her throat had a breathing whiteness above the differing white of the fur which itself seemed to wind about her neck and cling to her blue-grey pelisse with a tenderness gathered from her own, a sentient commingled innocence which kept its loveliness against the crystalline purity of the out-door snow. (*M*, 306)

Dorothea blooms: a quality described as a "sentient commingled innocence" that seems to invoke, in conjunction with the "warm red life in her lips" and "breathing whiteness," a *vital* innocence. This oddly sentient innocence is the blending of the fact of sexual promise with its very impossibility.

After Casaubon's death, the alternative bloom narrative progresses in terms we recognize from Austen's bloom narratives, although in *Middlemarch* there is an increased attempt to represent the male as well as the female figure as blooming under the influence of courtship. In a meeting that follows soon after, they both bloom for each other: "Will sat down opposite her at two yards' distance, the light falling on his bright curls and delicate but rather petulant profile, with its defiant curves of lip and chin. Each looked at the other as if they had been two flowers which had opened then and there" (*M*, 398). Casaubon's death, although it would seem to free the way for these established lovers, binds them further; nevertheless, Dorothea's face, despite her "heavy solemnity of clothing," looks "all the younger with its recovered bloom" (*M*, 585). Yet not until Ladislaw returns from his self-imposed exile do the full dimensions of this alternative bloom narrative become clear. Dorothea, openly avowing her approval of his actions in leaving her, is rendered a flower: " 'you acted as I should have expected you to act,' said Dorothea, her face brightening and her head becoming a little more erect on its beautiful stem" (*M* 866). The analogy reminds us of Rosamond, but unlike her floral self, Dorothea's bloom is noble in intention: this is a bloom perpetuated by Ladislaw's proposal to stay away from her, not to marry her. The parting amid the storm functions as a marriage proposal, but one altogether different from Rosamond's tear-filled forget-me-nots; Dorothea offers a partnership rather than dependence. Their coming together, a physical culmination of the sexual promise of her bloom, occurs with a storm outside raging. The only issue remaining is financial; when Dorothea pledges to support Ladislaw with her reduced fortune the traditional marital arrangement is emptied of its financial basis.

In this, Eliot's altered articulation of the bloom narrative, the possibility of a second blooming restores the original narrative's freshness and the original narrative's capacity for an eroticized, as well as infinitely extendable, closure. This new bloom narrative ends in a concord as firm as its progenitor's. Dorothea, for whom "no life would have possible . . . which was not filled with emotion," has happiness, "a little boy," and ultimately a "small row of cousins" to bring back to Middlemarch (*M*, 894–5). That this alternative bloom narrative is a bloom under the positive pressure of realism is clear from one of the novel's final lines, where Dorothea's late bloom is situated among the limiting, "mixed" conditions that, for midcentury fiction, constituted the field of the "real," as in Eliot's well-known description of "the mixed result of a young and noble impulse struggling amidst the conditions of an imperfect social state" (*M*, 896). In Dorothea's second marriage we should nonetheless recognize Hetty's clandestine bloom and Adam's second chance, a legacy of the clandestine that *Middlemarch*'s ending makes tentatively public.

Organic Realism: Eliot and Natural History

O rganic realism"—does not the term itself strike an oxymoronic tone, a combination of ideas that seems at odds with our very idea of realism in the literature of the nineteenth century? The whirl of social life, and the precise description of place and time, might seem more at home in urban settings, places that seem inevitably hostile to nature and thus inhospitably coupled with the term "organic." Taken up with the narratives and details of country life, fictions such as *Adam Bede* might seem at best as irrelevant, even hostile, to the realist imagination—as pastoral narratives that, like vestigial survivals in a new evolutionary era, have persisted well beyond the social conditions that initially determined their usefulness. A realism based in rural nature, it would seem, is scarcely a realism at all: a realism in retreat, perhaps, from the complex organizations of urbanized existence that provide its impetus. What I would suggest instead is a deep and hitherto unexplored connection between an impulse toward realist representation and the practical studying of the natural world, particularly the taxonomic version of that study carried out by early to mid-nineteenth-century naturalists. Situating realist practice within pre-Darwinian, largely amateur, taxonomic sciences may teach us much about the tensions within the classical novel's realism: tensions between singularity and commonness, between attraction and repulsion, between the object and its categorization—tensions that are endemic to the epistemology of naturalist science.

Eliot might provide us with the best example for this inquiry, since although her serious engagement with evolutionary science and its forebears has been thoroughly explored, the importance of natural history to her early novels has been underemphasized—as if the eventual decline of natural history, compared to the fame of evolution in its twentieth-century assimilation, justifies natural history's status as a topic of only antiquarian interest.[15] Eliot and Lewes spent the summers of 1856 and 1857 "naturalizing"—observing, studying, and identifying nature's incarnations—and it is through that particular lens that we can begin to understand a brand of nineteenth-century realism that is indebted less to the social mappings of the city than the taxonomic orderings possible in natural settings.

Eliot's naturalist pleasures, palpable in her earliest prose, coincided with her incipient turn to fiction writing and precipitated her commitment to realism. Embedded within, yet set off from, the rest of Eliot's journal are several expository essays, including "Recollections of Ilfracombe 1856," "Recollections of the Scilly Isles, 1857," and "Recollections of Jersey 1857." In "Recollections of Ilfracombe" one can trace Eliot's growing principle of realism that is inextricably connected to the experience of nature and wishing to name it:

> I have talked of the Ilfracombe lanes without describing them, for to describe them one ought to know the names of all the lovely wild flowers that cluster on their banks. . . . I never before longed so much to know the names of things as during this visit to Ilfracombe. The desire is part of the tendency that is now constantly growing in me to escape from all vagueness and inaccuracy into the daylight of distinct, vivid ideas. The mere fact of naming an object tends to give definitiveness to our conception of it—we have then a sign that at once calls up in our minds the distinctive qualities which mark out for us that particular object from all others. (*I*, 272)

Eliot links the desire to "know the names of things" with a "tendency" that is "now constantly growing" in her—a clear link between a scientific urge to know nature through taxonomic study and her turn to realism: "into the day-light of distinct, vivid ideas."[16] To describe a place, Eliot writes, one "ought to know the names" of flowers; to "give definitiveness to our conception" of an object, it is necessary to take up the task of "the mere fact of naming." As I will show, natural history and, more specifically, taxonomization—the "mere fact of naming" objects in nature—are central to the growth of Eliot's realism. The observation and naming of natural objects is epistemologically the central fact of natural history; taxonomy is key to my understanding of Eliot's "organic realism," a realism owing its force to eighteenth-century developments in the taxonomization of nature. Although Eliot's realism has most often been understood in relation to Riehl's sociology, which she was then reviewing, what has been neglected is the fact that Eliot wrote that review at the sea; this is a fact that returns us to Eliot's contemporaneous immersion in natural history research and suggests a relation between her fiction's realism and an aesthetic and scientific vision of the world that natural history provided. Eliot's realism is as indebted to the natural history that she and Lewes practiced as it is to Riehl's sociology of common life, which Eliot's essay so strongly praised.[17]

The pleasures of taxonomic science, despite Darwin's storm on such a near-horizon, endured in the 1850s, even for such engaged intellectuals as Eliot and Lewes. This period, which we might call Eliot's naturalist phase, has not received much attention in recent critical work. The two research trips—to the Pembrokeshire coast in 1856 and to the Scilly Isles and Jersey in the spring of 1857—correspond with Eliot's first turn to fiction writing ("The Sad Fortune of the Reverend Amos Barton" in 1856; *Adam Bede* was begun on her return in 1857). Lewes, as a result of those trips, wrote *Sea-Side Studies* (parts of which can be traced to Eliot's hand), a text that epitomizes a kind of descriptive and experimental natural history that was still possible in the years leading up to Darwin's pivotal thesis. As Gillian Beer has so aptly demonstrated, evolutionary theory, from the publication of Charles Lyell's *Principles of Geology* between 1830 and 1833, caused an "imaginative turmoil" in England that was "concentrated in 1859" by the publication of Darwin's thesis.[18] But, as Lewes's own earnest efforts suggest, the work of the naturalist is viable well into the 1850s, coexisting with science informed by and engaged with the developmental hypothesis. This is a coexistence that increasingly creates two separate domains of scientific inquiry, one dominated for the most part by amateurs and the other increasingly by professional scientists. The growing professionalization of science meant increasing specialization, with naturalists occupying what was increasingly thought of as a secondary, even antiquarian, position within science. As the very idea of fixed categories came under suspicion, taxonomization suffered but did not cease; the naturalist, rather than working against the developmental hypothesis, worked apart from it, in a space characterized by fieldwork and practical taxonomization. Eliot's journals, as well as her first major novel, make palpable the persistence of observation and categorization as a scientific model.

Eliot's naturalist vision is lent most powerfully to her depiction of Hetty Sorrel, whose beauty is repeatedly conjoined with references to observation—that is, the *practice* of looking at, or observing, her. The sustained and voiced discomfort of the narrator in privileging Hetty's beauty locates the implicit problem Eliot grapples with in developing her realism: the need to study the individual object—whether that be a sea anemone, a flower, or a Hetty Sorrel—troubles the ethical claim of "representativeness" that is her realism's stated goal. The structural demand, both for the author and the naturalist, to study the individual object interferes with the ethical and epistemological impetus behind the cognate projects of natural history and realism. This, as I will show, is precisely the problem with Hetty Sorrel, and the source of the narrator's oft-noted hostility toward her.

Our own relative distance from a popular culture suffused with naturalist knowledge makes the effort to recover the centrality of Eliot's naturalist vision more difficult and speculative. And yet Eliot herself seemed to imagine the difficulty of understanding her descriptions without the benefit of naturalist knowledge. In fact, at one point in *Adam Bede* she ties understanding itself to empirical observation. The narrator, in attempting to articulate Hetty's beauty, emphasizes the pointlessness of description in the absence of firsthand knowledge: "it is of little use for me to tell you . . . of little use, unless you have seen a woman who affected you as Hetty affected her beholders" (*AB*, 85). The reader's comprehension of Hetty's beauty—"for otherwise, though you may conjure up the image of a lovely woman, she would not in the least resemble that distracting kitten-like maiden"—is tied specifically to whether the reader has been an observer of nature:

I might mention all the divine charms of a bright spring day, but if you had never in your life utterly forgotten yourself in straining your eyes after the mounting lark, or in wandering through the still lanes when the fresh-opened blossoms fill them with a sacred, silent beauty like that of fretted aisles, where would be the use of my descriptive catalogue? I could never make you know what I meant by a bright spring day. (*AB*, 85)

The narrator pleads for a reader whose experience will lend meaning to its "descriptive catalogue," as if his narrative without the experience of nature would be like reading a bird manual without ever having seen a bird. The ideal reader is one who in "straining your eyes after the mounting lark" has enjoyed the pleasures of precise observation and practical experience. The kind of perception that is imagined here is not, as it is in Shelley's "To a Sky-Lark," perception without sight, or of a nature almost beyond the possibility of empirical knowledge.[19] In being compared to ecclesiastical architecture, the beauty of these blossom-strewn lanes invokes a sacredness that is nevertheless coupled with the precise description of the narrator's "catalogue." Together, these directions to the reader require what we might call a kind of sacred straining, a model of perception that is reminiscent of eighteenth-century natural history, whose "revelation" of the natural world as divinely received had staying power deep into the nineteenth century. This model of sacred straining also echoes the language of the pastoral tradition, specifically the topos of inexpressibility, the key difference being the way that natural history seems to step in, or substitute, for inexpressibility and thus recode the aesthetic tradition of pastoral vision within a system that records the particularities of observation. Eliot's ideal reader is at least partially a naturalist: one who both appreciates the truthfulness of her catalogue and is spiritually awed at the beauty being described.

The sacred straining that Eliot posits is present in her own observations of the natural world, written glimpses that capture the transition, one that is not at all unidirectional, between taxonomic science and evolutionary theory. In a letter of June 1857 describing a school of jellyfish, we get an account of her inclination toward the sensual reality of natural history over the more abstract work of biology:

I really give the preference to the wonderful Cydippes that we found yesterday floating on the sunny sea—tiny crystal globes with delicate meridians of cilia, and long streams spreading behind them as they float. I feel every day a greater disinclination for theories and arguments about the origins of things in the presence of all this mystery and beauty and pain and ugliness, that floods one with conflicting emotions. (*L*, 341)

The Cydippes' "delicate meridians of cilia," the sense of wonder in the face of "all this mystery," and the growing "disinclination" for theories about the "origins of things" are the statements of a naturalist, one who, at least at the moment of writing the letter, preferred observation over theory, description and beauty over abstract argument about origin. As an enthusiastic naturalist, Eliot did not have to chasten her wonder at the natural world but, rather rapturously, could associatively spin a string of impressionistic terms—"all this mystery and beauty and pain and ugliness"—for what she is disinclined to theorize about. The wonder Eliot expresses in watching this natural object is not the wonder of uniqueness, for various species of the Cydippes are very common to the British seas; rather the wonder is motivated by a beautiful but not unique natural object whose display of beauty is nevertheless undiminished by that lack of singularity: a *classificatory beauty*. This is Eliot's naturalist vision, a perspective that she most powerfully lends to her depiction of Hetty as a beauty that both conforms to and troubles categories of natural history and organic realism.

Eliot's Natural Histories

The January 1857 edition of *Blackwood's Edinburgh Magazine* has a telling parallel—it contains Eliot's first installment of *Scenes from Clerical Life* and Lewes's first essay on natural history, "New Facts and Old Fancies about Sea Anemones." Lewes opens his essay with an allusion to the popularity of natural history, citing the "zoological fervour" of the "British mind" excited by the "appearance of the hippopotamus in Regent's Park." Yet the sea anemone was the current fascination: "no animal has touched it to such fine issues and such exuberant enthusiasm as the lovely sea anemone, now the ornament of countless drawing-rooms, studies, and back parlors, and the delight of unnumbered amateurs."[20] The peculiar significance of the sea anemone for *Adam Bede* will be explored later, but for now it is important to recognize how Lewes's reference to the "delight of unnumbered amateurs" points us to one of the central facts about nineteenth-century natural history: its amateurness. Natural history, as Lynn Merrill has suggested, is a term that signs the amateur study of nature: "for centuries, natural history and science had meant pretty much the same thing: knowledge about the natural world. But gradually, in the nineteenth century, the two disciplines divided. . . . Natural history remained accessible to amateurs, while biology, like the other sciences, became the province of professionals."[21]

The professionalization of science meant specialization: geology, botany, biology, and physiology were in some sense newly constituted in opposition to the generalism of natural history. Explorations of the kind Darwin made famous with the HMS *Beagle*, as well as the spread of railroads in the 1840s in England itself, were factors that contributed to the popularization of natural history and expanded the imaginative world of the general public.[22] In 1830, a cheap version of the microscope made one of the primary tools of natural history accessible. A marker of the popularity of natural history into the nineteenth century is the 1827 reissue of *The Natural History of Selborne* (1798), by Gilbert White, which became a runaway best-seller. Natural histories became one of the preferred genres of "railroad fiction," inexpensive editions of popular texts sold at stations; one such work, Rev. J. G. Wood's *Common Objects of the Country*, sold an astronomical one hundred thousand copies in a single week.[23] Inexpensive railway travel, even to the remote coasts of Wales and Cornwall, made natural history a possible pastime for people of differing classes; if the momentum for natural history began among the leisured classes in the eighteenth century, the nineteenth century brought natural history to the middle and even the working classes.[24] Northern industrial workers were, as one nineteenth-century botanical writer observed, "some of the most zealous botanical collectors in the kingdom."[25] One of the more famous of these working-class botanists, Richard Buxton, published a flora of the environs of Manchester.[26] It might be interesting to think in this connection of Elizabeth Gaskell's novel *Mary Barton*, insofar as the novel has traditionally been considered a paradigm of industrial fiction. One of the primary characters in the novel is a naturalist and another an herbalist, which suggests the degree to which natural history permeated even those fictions whose industrial focus would seem to limit them to a particularly urban, reformist brand of realism.[27]

The popularity of natural history in the first half of the nineteenth century reached what Lynn Barber has characterized as "a national obsession."[28] Newspapers ran natural history sections, and drawing rooms were festooned with ferns, insect collections, Wardian cases, and aquariums. The "language of flowers" sentimentalized the study of botany, while more prosaic books literally included mounted specimens of plants; shore collecting—of shells, seaweeds, and marine animals—had a large surge in popularity in the 1850s. Lewes and Eliot's scientific forays to the seashore in 1856 and 1857 seem to reflect more a temperament of the time, and one perhaps that they wished to capitalize on through their professional writing, than an idiosyncratic personal interest.

Unlike Lewes, Eliot did not formalize her relation to natural history by publishing original work on the subject; her enthusiasm for the specifics of the natural world finds its way into her correspondence and into long expository journal pieces, but not formally into print until we see its traces in the early novels. As Eliot's biographer Gordon Haight points out, however, Lewes "lifted bodily" portions of Eliot's journal for *Sea-Side Studies*, effectively making Eliot an anonymous collaborator in this natural history.[29] Eliot's letters and the prose pieces embedded within her journals—"Recollections of Ilfracombe 1856," "Recollections of the Scilly Isles 1857," and "Recollections of Jersey 1857"—best reveal the development of a naturalist's approach to nature: an orientation described by Merrill as "visual, tactile, and aesthetic," and a set of activities that included "collecting, describing, [and] taking pleasure in nature's multiplicity and complexity."[30] The language and structures of these

Recollections, which I consider to be early prose experiments, help elucidate the strategies of a natural history realism that, as I will show, saturate *Adam Bede*.

"Recollections of Ilfracombe 1856" discusses Eliot and Lewes's five-week visit to Ilfracombe, a small seaside town on the North Devonshire coast; even their lodgings are initially guided by the recommendation of Philip Henry Gosse, the great Victorian naturalist who had stayed in this town during the some thirty years he spent naturalizing and writing on the English coasts.[31] From the very first moment, Eliot's orientation is that of the naturalist, for she likens the seaside houses to "barnacles" and notices that some building near Ilfracombe "looks as if it were the habitation of some mollusk that had secreted its shell from the material of the rock" (*I*, 264–5). They would soon meet the Reverend George Tugwell, a "zoological curate" who had written the guidebook *Manual of Sea Anemones Commonly Found on the English Coast*; it was with Tugwell that they received their first practical lessons, exchanged specimens, spoke about tools, and took naturalist walks.[32] Of course, neither Lewes nor Eliot arrived at Ilfracombe ignorant of the "developmental hypothesis," and yet, in preparation for Ilfracombe, they also obtained Gosse's *Rambles on the Devonshire Coast*, a volume written in a taxonomic rather than a theoretical vein (*I*, 269). Certainly, for Eliot and Lewes natural history coexisted with the evolutionary hypothesis, just as it did more generally in Victorian culture through the early 1860s.

Nor was Eliot just a coincident presence in the naturalist project essentially performed by her romantic partner; she learned natural history alongside Lewes, peppering her letters and journal pieces with specific knowledge; for instance, she speaks concretely of "exquisite little Eolides" and a variety of sea anemones, such as: Mesembryanehemum, Anthea Cereus, Actiniae, Actinia Crassicornis, Eolis pellucida, Aplysia, A. Gemmacea, Tublurain, etc. (*I*, 265–6). When they move to Tenby, a surprisingly witty Eliot emerges, as she writes to a friend that "we intend to migrate to Tenby, for the sake of making acquaintance with its mollusks and medusae" (*L*, 253). There, they reread another popular natural history text, Gosse's *Tenby, a Seaside Holiday*, a book that Eliot would review for the July 1856 edition of the *Leader*. At Tenby they ventured out to the tide pools in the dark, in order to better see the phosphorous quality of certain mollusks, the Actinae; Eliot writes: "we have a project of going into St. Catherine's caverns with lanterns some night when the tide is low about 11, for the sake of seeing the zoophytes preparing for their midnight levels. The Actinae, like other belles, put on their best faces on such occasions" (*L*, 256).

During their three months on the coast in the spring of 1856, Eliot and Lewes had few other social engagements other than the midnight revels with the mollusks.[33] From her journals we know that half of each day was spent near the sea, the other half devoted to inland walks with Lewes. Eliot's particular natural history interests seemed to lean toward the botanical, for after completing "The Natural History of German Life" in the spring of 1856, she set herself the task of learning seaweeds. Hers is an aesthetic and a taxonomic orientation, for she calls the seaweeds "lovely," saying that "these tide pools made one quite in love with sea-weeds," and yet consults David Landsborough's *Popular History of British Seaweeds* and learns their proper names: *Ulva, Enteromorpha, Mesogloia vermicularis, M. virescens (I, 266).*[34] Landsborough's text introduces its reader to the workings of the Linnaean system as well as the newer, "natural" system.[35] The fact that Eliot used botanical handbooks on her walks speaks to her naturalist orientation; the density of detail and her use of proper taxonomic terms for various plants in the *Recollections* suggest that Eliot brings a naturalist orientation to these early writing exercises. For instance, during an inland walk on the Isle of Jersey, recorded in her *Recollections*, she employs a term that gardeners and botanists alike employ—"the curious fresh green *Euphorbia*"; she comments on the ubiquity of the "broad blades" of the yellow iris in "moist ground" (*J*, 280–1). At Ilfracombe, her descriptions are both aesthetic and taxonomic, for she writes of "recesses glossy with liverwort, and feathery with fern" and of springs "gushing in shady recesses covered with liverwort, with here and there wafting tufts of fern and other broadleafed plants that love obscurity and moisture" (*I*, 272, 268). The *Recollections* combine a specific knowledge of the empirical objects of nature with an aesthetic manner, a mode that tonally earmarks them as precursors to *Adam Bede*.

In the *Recollections* Eliot practices what, in reviewing Ruskin's *Modern Painters* for the *Westminster Review* in the spring of the same year, she pinpoints as the source of realism: "the truth of infinite value that he teaches is realism— the doctrine that all truth and beauty are to be attained by a humble and faithful study of nature, and not by substituting vague forms, bred by imagination on the mists of feeling, in place of definite, substantial reality."[36] In the chapter in *Adam Bede* entitled "In Which the Story Pauses a Little," natural history lingers behind Eliot's evocation of a realist mandate: "Certainly I could, my fair critic, if I were a clever novelist, not be obliged to creep servilely after nature and fact, be able to represent things as they never have been and never will be" (*AB*, 177). Although Eliot's praise for Ruskin anticipates her declaration of appreciation for Dutch genre painting in *Adam Bede*, her own first sketches of "definite, substantial reality" tellingly are faithful studies of nature. What Eliot calls servile creeping in the name of truth ("nature and fact")—among the first and strongest claims in the polemical chapter—is a model that might with equal justice suggest the labor of natural history as Dutch painting. Dutch painting, as Eliot points out, provides "faithful pictures of monotonous homely existence," while natural history, unnamed in the chapter, might be said to provide the analogue for the novel's considerable attention to the natural world, as well as life lived in the country, in and in relation to the natural world. Even if the human referents of Dutch painting seem more congenial to novelistic prose than the nonhuman referents of naturalist practice, we would do well to remember the continual surround of natural objects in which *Adam Bede*'s characters find themselves placed. Their immersion in the organic world produces a realism that is as indebted to schemes of nonhuman observation as to the strictly human.

That Eliot's descriptions of nature emanate out of the perspective of the natural historian is visible in the evidence that suggests her frustration with abstract accounts of nature not based on local observation.[37] In a letter to Charles Bray of March 1858, Eliot writes that for the past two years she has been consulting "Calendars of Natural History," but found it "quite futile" to be able to translate the blooming times from different parts of England (*L*, 381).[38] Her frustration at the attempts of almanacs or calendars to precisely predict how nature will generally manifest itself leads to her reliance on local detail. This is a discussion she actually embeds within *Adam Bede*; Mr. Poyser and Mr. Craig, the Hall's gardener, discuss the worth of "almanecks" and "met'orological almanecks," with Mr. Craig weighing his own experience higher: "the met'orological almanecks can learn me nothing, but there's a pretty sight o' things I could let *them* up to, if they'd just come to me" (*AB*, 205). Like Mr. Craig, Eliot garners her authority not from theoretical accounts of nature but from firsthand observation. To the extent that she uses research as she did calendars of natural history in *Adam Bede*, her evocation of place is local, but not so exacting that it pretends to an empirical precision that she herself calls futile.

In fact, Eliot transcribes her inland naturalist rambles at Ilfracombe to the fictional Hayslope, a county imagined to be far from the sea. *Recollections* is often anticipatory of *Adam Bede*—"what a picture this farmyard remains in my memory," she writes, going on to detail the various cows, gates, lanes, flower-strewn hedgerows, wild verdure, orchards, and grass:

> The long grass was waving in all the glory of June before the mower has come to make it suffer a "love-change" from beauties into sweet odours; and the slopes on each side of us were crowned or clothed with fine trees. Little Gyp, Mrs. Webster's dog, whom we had made our pet, was our companion on this walk. (*I*, 270–1)

That Gyp, Mrs. Webster's dog and their adopted pet, is the name of Adam's dog in *Adam Bede* is but a small coincidence, but we recognize the state of the grass as one of the novel's primary motifs. The time of year in *Adam Bede* is evoked repeatedly in terms of the state of the grass: "it was at that moment in summer when the sound of the scythe being whetted makes us cast more lingering looks at the flower-sprinkled tresses of the meadow" (*AB*, 20). Likewise, our first introduction to the Hall Farm is at "the drowsiest time of the year, just before the hay-harvest." Even the famous scene of Dinah's religious contemplation from her bedroom window insists on noting the length of the grass before she "closed her eyes" in order to better feel a "Divine Presence": Dinah "look[s] out on the peaceful fields beyond which the large moon was rising, just about the hedgerow elms. She liked the pasture best, where the milch cows were lying, and next to that the meadow where the grass was half mown, and lay in silvered sweeping lines" (*AB*, 155–6). The state of the grass not only indicates the time of the year but also requires the reader to register nature as a central fact of the world the narrative is evoking.

Most dramatically, perhaps, certain naturalist passages in *Adam Bede* seem to have been adapted directly from these early natural histories. From July 1857—three months before the composition of *Adam Bede* would begin—we find this in "Recollections of Jersey": "When the blossoms fell away from the orchards my next delight was to look at the grasses mingled with the red sorrel; then came the white umbelliferous plants making a border or inner frame for them along the hedgerows and streams" (*J,* 281). If we turn to the first chapter of *Adam Bede,* we find its striking adaptation: "He saw instead a foreground which was just as lovely—the level sunlight lying like transparent gold among the gently-curving stems of the feathered grass and the tall red sorrel, and the white umbels of the hemlocks lining the bushy hedgerows" (*AB,* 20). There is a persistent verbal similarity: the syntax, rhythm, and vocabulary of the naturalist passages in *Adam Bede* seem to have been adapted directly from Eliot's natural history writing. Furthermore, the content and form of her natural history method, with its intent gaze on the natural world in the interests of a taxonomical analysis of that world, dictate the presentation of this early moment in Eliot's first successful novel. An "umbelliferous plant" and "umbels" are botanical terms; first named in the seventeenth century by the British botanist John Ray, plants of the *Umbelliferoe* order bear flowers arranged in "umbels," a mass of many flowers borne on stems of equal length and coming from a common center. Description here draws on a taxonomical syntax borrowed from the observational sciences, notably botany, of the eighteenth and early nineteenth century. A further surprise lurks in these passages: the passage from *Adam Bede* is the first time in the novel that we hear of "sorrel." As Gillian Beer has noted, our first introduction to Hetty's surname is as a plant name.[39] Although Hetty herself will not be described for some time, she has already been prefigured as a plant in a scene that transmutes actual natural history writing into novelistic discourse. Eliot's realism is one of perspective, emanating in part from Ruskin's painterly values but shaped as well by her natural history concerns: a "foreground" of "grasses" and "sorrel." That is, here the observational position eschews the more typical aristocratic landscape ("doubtless there was a large sweep of park and a broad glassy pool in front of that mansion") for the foreground of commonplace grasses, red sorrel, hedgerows, and hemlock umbels. The traveler cannot see the grounds of the Hall; what Eliot *does* have her traveler see is the foreground of sorrel, and by extension Hetty, the dairymaid. When we see "tall, red sorrel" and a flower made known to us by its taxonomical category, we see a Hetty made known to us via the methods of organic realism.

In a more famous passage from *Adam Bede*—chapter 17, "In Which the Story Pauses a Little," Eliot's embedded realist manifesto—the narrative speaks directly about the relation between the concept of foreground and the representation of "commonplace things." Here Eliot stakes out for herself a realist project that will represent both the commonplace and the few in the foreground—a foreground that we might remember from the implied introduction of Hetty as the plant sorrel:

> Let us always have men ready to give the loving pains of life to the faithful representing of commonplace things—men who see beauty in these commonplace things, and delight in showing how kindly the light of heaven falls on them. There are few prophets in the world; few sublimely beautiful women; few heroes. I can't afford to give all my love and reverence to such rarities: I want a greater deal of those feelings for my everyday fellow-men, especially for the few in the foreground of the great multitude. (*AB*, 180)

The tension in the passage arises from a conflict between rarity and commonness; the passage explicitly sides with the commonplace as opposed to the "few" prophets, beautiful women, and heroes of stock narrative but then turns to a "multitude" that is in turn best characterized by the "few in the foreground." What is apparent here is a tension between the categorical ("the great multitude") and the singular that is a persistent structure of natural history's methodology, one that was never successfully resolved. The site of Eliot's realism is the foreground, and the foreground is a natural scene full of commonplace things: sorrel and Sorrel.

Why, then, sorrel? Eliot surely had any number of plants from which to choose, so the fact that she chooses sorrel suggests that the eponymous heroine is being subtly evoked, and perhaps even introduced. Sorrel, plant and Hetty alike, are thus surrounded by other botanically specific ones and among a "great multitude" of nature: sorrel is a single object, in the foreground of a crowd of other possible subjects, whose importance is nevertheless undiminished, despite its, or her, lack of singularity. The invocation of Hetty as a natural entity here is firm, as if insisting on the fact that she, like the natural objects that surround her and with which she is initially conflated, must be understood within the broad categories that organize the natural world. To choose one object over another from that "great multitude" is to conform nonetheless to the representative aims of natural history and realism alike. In being situated as an object to be studied within natural history, Hetty is at the center of the natural history of Hayslope that the novel performs, and through her we can best detect the embedded tensions between commonness and singularity that Eliot's realism continually negotiates.

Educating the Eye: Structures of Natural History

In certain moments in *Adam Bede* one hears tonal registers familiar from natural history—an intensity or particularity of description that derives from the amateur practice of natural history. But beyond these tonal or lexical similarities, I want to suggest three key structural homologies between the practice of taxonomic natural history and the organic realism of *Adam Bede*: a practice of *naming*; coming from this, a practice of *categorizing* that produces a continual dialectic between the general and the particular; and an ideal of *specificity* that is directed against the vagaries of nostalgic idyll. Eliot's description of the Hall Farm in early summer embodies the detailed intensity and epistemological task of natural history:

> Adam walked round by the Rick yard, at present empty of ricks, to the little wooden gate leading into the garden . . . a true farmhouse garden, with hardy perennial flowers, unpruned fruit-trees, and kitchen vegetables growing together in careless, half-neglected abundance. In that leafy, flowery, bushy time, to look for any one in this garden was like playing at "hide-and-seek." There were the tall hollyhocks beginning to flower, and dazzle the eye with their pink, white, and yellow; there were the syringas and gueldre roses, all large and disorderly for want of trimming; there were leafy walls of scarlet beans and late peas; there was a row of bushy filberts in one direction, and in another a huge apple-tree. (*AB* 218–9)

The narrative perspective is not just observant but naturalist: a series of general categories ("a true farmhouse garden," "that leafy, flowery, bushy time") that are then divided into a series of named particulars ("hollyhocks," "syringas," "gueldre roses"). The repeated structure of "there was" creates a list, one that contains common and botanical names for plants. The passage begins with the general outline of the natural setting—perennial flowers, fruit trees, kitchen vegetables—then matter-of-factly breaks down those categories into their particulars: hollyhocks and syringas are perennials, as is the gueldre rose, the common name for viburnum; the "fruit trees" are specified as filberts and an apple tree; "kitchen vegetables" are particularized as beans and peas.

In light of a structure that describes a natural scene through a logic of general categories and specific species, it is not surprising that the novel also contains literal references to natural history. Bartle Massey taught natural history as well as reading and writing in his simple schoolroom, for hanging from its walls was a bunch of seaweed; Adam, we learn, had "long exhausted the resources of his imagination in trying to think how the bunch of leathery seaweed had looked and grown in its native element" (*AB*, 232). A secondary interest of Adam's, albeit one that runs a far second to his passion for work, is the observation of the natural world; he once asks Hetty whether she had ever observed an ant carrying a caterpillar: "have you ever seen those tiny fellows carrying things four times as big as themselves?" Her indifferent reply—"not caring to know the difficulties of ant-life"—is typical of Hetty, who, as well as not liking children, is repeatedly said not to like living things (*AB*, 222). Natural history is one of Adam's leisure-time pleasures; one of the few places he has traveled to is Eagledale, primarily to "see about some work" but also to study the area's unique geology: "It's a wonderful sight—rocks and caves such as you never saw in your life. I never had a right notion o'rocks till I went there" (*AB*, 222–3). The chapter entitled "Church" is primarily given over to the events prior to arriving at that institution, especially the Poysers' walk, punctuated by a series of natural history observations: the Poyser boys, Marty and Tommy, are young naturalists who found the "Sunday walk through the fields . . . fraught with great excitement . . . [and] saw a perpetual drama going on in the hedgerows." First, Marty sees what he believes to be a "yellowhammer on the boughs of the great ash," which, "while he was peeping, he missed the sight of a white-throated stoat." While Tommy sees the stoat, as well as a "little greenfinch, just fledged," Hetty, unsurprisingly, did not "give any heed to these things," and Marty finds the prize, "the speckled turkey's nest"; both look wistfully at a "small pond full of tadpoles" (*AB*, 192–3). These instances of a kind of vernacularized natural history in the novel are important to Eliot's realism only insofar as they point to natural history as a structuring logic behind her observational practices.

Natural history conditions the narrative; the forward momentum virtually comes to a halt in these natural history–inspired scenes, for the stillness of the person looking at nature is registered in the prose style, which emulates that stillness in a lingering and particularizing description. Eliot's prose manifests the naturalist's pleasure in looking at the natural world and determining correct categories and precise particularities—a *taxonomic* pleasure:

> The thirtieth of July was come, and it was one of those half-dozen warm days which sometimes occur in the middle of a rainy English summer. No rain had fallen for the last three or four days, and the weather was perfect for that time of the year; there was less dust than usual on the dark green hedge-rows, and on the wild camomile that starred the roadside, yet the grass was dry enough for the little children to roll on it, and there was no cloud but a long dash of light, downy ripple, high, high up in the far-off blue sky. Perfect weather for an out-door July merry-making, yet surely not the best time of year to be born in. Nature seems to make a hot pause just then—all the loveliest flowers are gone; the sweet time of early growth and vague hopes is past; and yet the time of harvest and in-gathering is not come, and we tremble at possible storms that may ruin the precious fruit in the moment of its ripeness. The woods are all one dark monotonous green; the wagon-loads of hay no longer creep along the lanes, scattering their sweet-smelling fragments on the blackberry branches; the pastures are often a little tanned, yet the corn has not got its last splendour of red and gold. (*AB*, 249)

The particularity and duration of the lingering description go far beyond a symbolic analogy between nature and its human inhabitants. The season is a particular one, not merely "summer" but that time of year that, in the parlance of an agricultural community, is "that pause between hay and corn-harvest"— the end of July, which brought, as she notes in "Recollections of Jersey" as well as here, a "monotonous" green (*AB*, 249; *J*, 281). The lingering on the scene is both aesthetic and empirical; no rain has fallen in several days, so the dust from the roads has not coated the hedgerows and camomile, even as the grass is "dry enough" for romping children. The aesthetic eye turns on the passing of the "loveliest flowers," the monotonous dark green of the wood, the color of the pastures; the empirical eye sees crops not yet gathered, stratospheric clouds, the possibility of rain. The confluence of the aesthetic and the empirical is the position of an author influenced by the tonal and methodological aspects of natural history. Here, Eliot's prose, lingering both out of pleasure and a desire to record the specifics, suggests a perspective that Eliot learned as a naturalist, just prior to her composition of *Adam Bede*.

What we also learn from this passage—and that is the third key lesson of Eliot's use of taxonomical structures—is that the nostalgic tones of *Adam Bede* are not the idealizing memories traditional to a pastoral vision of nature but rather the specific effects of a natural historian recording the natural moment and anticipating its demise.[40] In the chapter "Adam Visits the Hall Farm" the reader might attribute nostalgia to this direct address: "Ah! I think I taste that whey now—with a flavour so delicate that one can hardly distinguish it from an odor. . . . And the light music of the dropping whey is in my ears, mingling with the twittering of a bird outside the wire network window—the window overlooking the garden, and shaded by tall gueldre roses" (*AB*, 218). However, the narrator's appreciation for this moment is unlike nostalgia in its specificity; aware that time has passed, organic realism returns the specificity of the everyday to a past that when it was present was itself insistently mutable.[41] The commonplace moment of Adam drinking a glass of Mrs. Poyser's whey inspires the narrator to interrupt and *extend* the moment by recording the taste, smell, and sound of the whey, as well as other sensory details. Although it has been common to attribute a nostalgia typical of pastoral to this scene, Eliot's prose here is indebted more to natural history—a genre that attempts to record and fix nature daily, not in order to freeze it in vague, unspecific memory as the nostalgia of pastoral does but in order to remember empirically, a empiricism that might remind us more of the detailed recollection later to be known as hypermnesia. Eliot's realism records both the immediacy of the specific moment and the incessant mutability of nature. Leaves may lose their spring transparency and furze blossoms will die off, just as a glass of whey is drained, and both leave behind a changed aspect to record. That fact may inspire the reader's lament, but it does not produce the vagueness of nostalgia—in fact, the detail proliferates in the recording.

Eliot's choice to set *Adam Bede* in the near past of 1799 has been misleading in this way. Here again Eliot's experience with natural history is instructive, for the natural history expositions that she wrote just prior to her composition of *Adam Bede* were written explicitly as "recollections," months after the experiences recorded in them occurred. Eliot's first major novel develops that mode first practiced in the journal essays, where recording the specific detail of the natural world takes place within a historical structure of "recollection." Eliot made her own "humble and faithful study of nature" in anticipation of writing *Adam Bede*. Haight establishes that Eliot consulted the *Gentleman's*

Magazine for 1799, a publication that contains precise meteorological diaries for each month, a prose summary of precise changes in the natural world, average prices of corn and other agricultural products by county, as well as a bill of mortality.[42] One example from the *Gentleman's Magazine* will suffice. When Eliot writes that "the harvest was likely still to be retarded by the heavy rains, which were causing inundations and much damage throughout the country, that the rains continued even though it was "beyond the middle of August," and that there had been a "rapid rise in the price of bread," one need only consult the August number of the *Gentleman's Magazine* to see the precision of Eliot's research (*AB*, 293). From the meteorological diary in the August issue, Eliot would have known that the summer of 1799 was rainy, that the hay crop was in constant jeopardy (as in the novel), that there were only five days in July of 1799 that were fine, and that one of those five days was July 30.[43] It turns out that the natural world described in the chapters about Donnithorne's coming-of-age feast on the thirtieth of July does not arise out of the haze of nostalgia, for it is empirically verified: the "thirtieth of July" *was* one of those "half-dozen warm days which sometimes occur in the middle of a rainy English summer" (*AB*, 249).

Even at the novel's most recognizable moments of heightened affect, the novel encodes pastoral figures in a scientized mode. The moment, previously cited, when Hetty, a "lost lamb" hiding among blossoms and fields of corn, contemplates drowning herself because of her "swift advancing shame" contains a number of seeming pastoral topoi. These objects, however, at first familiar as objects with pastoral connotations, are subject to the kind of realistic observation that natural history foregrounds.[44] If Hetty is a lost lamb, she is also a visibly pregnant one; this is not just a fallen Arcadia but a vivified one, a natural place where the detailed evocations of blossoms, corn, and brooks do not insist on their pastoral legacy but become part of a complex material catalogue of nature, including the biological reality of Hetty's pregnancy. Just before the passage, we learn that "if there came a traveler to this world who knew nothing of the story of man's life upon it, this image of agony would seem to him strangely out of place in the midst of this joyous nature" (*AB*, 363). Eliot's project is to show that joyous nature and realism are not at odds with each other but coexist—only the traveler, a term we can understand as a euphemism for reader, who "knew nothing of the story of man's life" would think that a beautiful representation of nature was at odds with Hetty's agony. This complex material catalogue of nature is a catalogue that includes for the first time the effects of a clandestine marriage.

One last way in which natural history infiltrates the novel's procedures calls for comment: the prevalence of the natural proverb— the moralization of nature into socially prevalent adages—in which naturalizing becomes an actual lexicon for the novel's characters. These proverbs draw on noted natural facts that help categorize social reality. Categorization and stability are, in fact, what natural history gives its speakers in Eliot's text. The proverb transforms the dispersed facts of social existence, such as ownership, courtship, and loss, into systems of order. Not simply systems of order, however: a fascination with natural objects, a sense of wonder, permeates natural history as well, and if natural proverbs stabilize observed reality, they often do so to enable a fascinated gaze. Less an embedded "structure of natural history" than natural history's way of structuring human order, the proverb is natural history at the most vernacular level possible.

The representation of social community through an ordered nature in *Adam Bede* covers a broad array of issues intrinsic to community: farming practices, views on religion, sense of family, gender relations, values, mourning practices, an individual's rights, maturation, tenancy, local politics, and the definition of "home." The proverbs address the broad array of social issues constitutive of the community of Hayslope that are adjudicated through a vernacular natural history. The salience of these proverbs is most commonly associated with Hetty's aunt, Mrs. Poyser, and what Henry James referred to as her "epigrammatic sallies."[45] These natural proverbs bring together a social issue with a natural fact; they mediate social forms through the terms of an ordered nature. Nature that is understood through natural history is an organized nature, a nature that has been seen and contained, and a nature that can become proverbial. The use of these speech patterns is realistic in the context of the agricultural community of Hayslope, for the novel's natural proverbs embody the very kind of vernacular knowledge of the natural world that would be probable among the farming class of the novel, if perhaps almost invisible to the modern reader. Even Adam Bede—who, the narrative points out, understood "mechanics and figures" and knew how to "write a plain hand," spell, and read music—seems to have had a more proverbial than strictly literate understanding of the natural world: "this rough man . . . for whom the motion and shape of the earth, the course of the sun, and the changes of the seasons, lay in the region of mystery made visible by fragmentary knowledge" (*AB*, 212–3).[46]

Mrs. Poyser's untutored field of knowledge should not be confused with ignorance, which she openly derides: "and as for her cheese, I know well enough it rose like a tin last year. An' then she talks o' the weather bein' i' fault, as there's folks 'ud stand on their heads and then say the fault was i' their boots" (*AB*, 189).[47] What must be stressed about these "natural proverbs" is their *social efficacy*, the manner in which they are continually engaged in making judgments and forming categories about social existence. For example, Mrs. Poyser establishes the proper age for marrying by invoking the difference between a crabapple and an eating apple: "for it isn't to be counted on as Adam and Seth 'ull keep bachelors for the next year to please their mother. . . . I'm no friend to young fellows a'marr'ing afore they know the difference atween a crab an' a apple; but they may wait o'er long" (*AB*, 145). Mr. Poyser contributes the following representation of the immaturity of young girls by discussing the physical qualities of unripe grain: "them young gells are like th' unripe grain; they'll make good meal by-and-by, but they're squashy as yit" (*AB*, 155). The proverb (or a proverb extended into a parable) is the primary mode of speech for his wife, whose discussion of the social community—of which she is certainly at the center—is one of the novel's most common means in which the social world adjudicates and represents itself. These proverbs are an often overlooked aspect of Eliot's novel, often dismissed as the "genial, merry, broad-grinning" sort of pastoralism that Eliot had so decidedly disavowed in favor of "real breathing men and women" (*AB*, 518, 178). Why, if this is true, would she so repeatedly thwart her stated narrative goals? By looking closely at a number of Mrs. Poyser's proverbs we can better see how the social world is represented through a vernacularized natural history.

The persistence of a hierarchical Anglicanism, as opposed to Methodism, for instance, is represented through a natural parable about agricultural plenty: "it's summat-like to see such a man as that o'the desk of a Sunday! as I say to Poyser, it's like looking a full crop o'wheat, or a pasture with a fine dairy o'cows in it; it makes you think the world's comfortable-like" (*AB*, 95). Elsewhere, Dinah had remarked on the "deadness to the Word" in villages in which people lived "among green pastures," a comment that had been seconded by Reverend Irwin's comment that farm laborers took life "as slowly as the sheeps and cows" (*AB*, 93). Through an analogy about a plentiful crop and a stocked pasture, Mrs. Poyser effectively explains the phenomenon of the religious and class complacency of their community. Turning to the inscrutable flight pattern of bats, she invokes Loamshire's incomprehension of Methodism: "but I suppose you must *be* a Methodist to know what a Methodist 'ull do. It's ill guessing what the bats are flying after"(*AB*, 480). One might even say that the social values expressed within the text can only be expressed through the proverbial. For instance, Adam establishes what men feel like toward family obligations by invoking the patterns of birds: "if we're men, and have men's feelings, I reckon we must have men's troubles. We can't be like the birds, as fly from their nest as soon as they're got their wings, and never know their kin when they see 'em, and get a fresh lot every year" (*AB*, 165). Here, a vernacularized commentary on the habits of birds effectively represents a reality of Hayslope; children, such as Adam, do not disown their family.

Other social issues are represented through these vernacularized natural histories. Gender relations, for example, inspire a number of proverbs; Mrs. Poyser, for instance, suggests that "for the men are mostly so slow, their thoughts overrun 'em, an' they can only catch 'em by the tail . . . it's the dead chicks take the longest hatchin'" (*AB*, 524). Bartle replies through a small parable about horseflies, in order to illustrate what elsewhere is a diatribe against women and their effect on social life: "she's such a match as the horsefly is to th' horse: she's got the right venom to sting him with" (*AB*, 525). Perhaps most compelling are the ways natural images are used to represent what we might think of as the community's central social forms: mourning, the experience of tenancy, and how home is defined. Tributes to the dead are represented as useless activities, in the order of irrigating an already-gathered crop:

"an' it's poor work allays settin' the dead above the livin'. . . . It's but little good you'll do a-watering the last year's crop" (*AB*, 203). In refusing old Donnithorne's attempt to divide the Hall Farm, Mrs. Poyser likens the poor tenancy he is offering to the worry that churning butter brings; her knowledge of dairy work is knowledge about the natural world that stands in for her lack of knowledge about tenancy and landlords, and enables her to articulate her refusal of his proposal (*AB*, 346). These natural proverbs create a vernacular form of knowledge in which natural facts are employed to articulate and make coherent the broadest aspects of social reality in the novel. They are representative, we might say, of natural history's structuring powers, of the social applicability of attention to the natural world.

Crises of Categorization: Sorrel to Sea Anemone

Who then, or what then, is sorrel? Spencer Thomson, the author of one of the botany manuals Eliot consulted, describes the wood-sorrel as "truly . . . one of our prettiest natives."[48] Agnes Catlow in *Popular Field Botany*, Eliot's other botanical guide, details a variety of sorrels; *Rumex Acetosella*, "Sheep's Sorrel," is red and frequent in pastures; *Rumex Acetosa*, "Common Sorrel," is also frequent in pastures; *Oxalis Acetosella*, "Common Wood-Sorrel," is found in woods and shady places. Hetty Sorrel, dairymaid and lover, is like these English sorrels in being found in either the pasture or the wood; she is found almost exclusively either among cows or in the woods of the Chase, despite her desire to "sit in a carpeted parlour and always wear white stockings" (*AB*, 100). Catlow writes that these common plants have distinctive leaf shapes: sheep's sorrel has an "axe-shaped" leaf, common sorrel has an "arrow-shaped" leaf, wood-sorrel is distinctive for having "three perfect heart-shaped" leaves.[49] In light of Hetty's amorous activities in the wood, should we be surprised that the sorrel of the pasture visually suggests the infliction of wounds—Cupid's or otherwise—while the sorrel of the woods is "heart-shaped"? Like Hetty, the flowers of the wood sorrel "fade almost as soon as gathered."[50] These common plants are among the "commonplace things" to which Eliot had dedicated her art, while the fact that Hetty shares a surname with a common plant suggests that Eliot merges the representations of the putatively social and natural worlds.

So Hetty is placed at least partially in a stable category that comes from natural history and taxonomic botany, that of the plant "sorrel." Such a finding would be consistent with the linkage between *Adam Bede* and the epistemologies of natural history. But here I want to diverge slightly, to read Hetty as in fact the novel's central way of troubling the very efficacy and certainty of the naming and categorizing that elsewhere obtains so strongly. Hetty presents us with a crisis of naturalist categorization, one that engages the problems of beauty and wonder for naturalists and by extension Eliot's realism. Organic realism, a form of realism that derives from natural history, works by looking at a particular object and considering it as an instance of a general category. A problem emerges, however, when one of two things occurs: when the particular object's beauty, or capacity to evoke wonder, continues to overwhelm us despite our capacity to place it into a category, and thus disables our capacity to make general judgments; or when the object itself resists the available categorizations. These are precisely the problems with Hetty Sorrel. The need to study the individual object—whether that is the jellyfish Cydippes that so enraptured Eliot, or Hetty Sorrel—is the crisis of Eliot's realism, for to focus on a single object, while knowing it is only one of many in its category, troubles the representativeness that is her realism's stated goal, "the faithful representing of commonplace things" that stood as an ideal. Eliot's rhetoric about realist practice stressed, as I have shown, both a categorical "multitude" and the individual particularity of the "few"; but these dual responsibilities do not coalesce without friction. Organic realism perhaps is a way of naming this central difficulty: the novel's difficulty in balancing the claims of category and individual object, a problem most visible in the presentation of Hetty.

The fact that the novel combines wonder at Hetty's beauty with reluctance, even resentment, about it may seem unaccountable, unless one considers that as a naturalist one repeatedly encounters two specific challenges to the importance of individual beauty: *overabundance* and the *commonness of the ugly*. Overabundance is precisely the source of the narrator's irritation with the collective delight in what characters in the novel see as Hetty's special beauty; repeatedly, the narrator wants to point out that she is just one instance of an order of beauty that includes many individual instances: "there are various orders of beauty . . . but there is one order of beauty which seems made to turn the heads not only of men, but of all intelligent mammals. . . . It is a beauty like that of kittens, or very small downy ducks . . . or babies just beginning to toddle" (*AB*, 84). Eliot locates Hetty's beauty first within an "order," a term that resonates at least in part as a term of taxonomy, and then in a series of similes—her beauty is "like" these other kinds. The simile challenges the singularity of beauty, for it suggests the comparative logic of taxonomy, which sees individual beauty as less significant than similarities. The commonness of ugliness is a second challenge to the importance of individual beauty. In her record of her observation of the Cydippes, Eliot sees nature as a mixture of both beauty and ugliness and is "flood[ed] . . . with conflicting emotions." Instances of ugliness in nature are as frequent as instances of beauty, which requires the naturalist to reconsider the privileging of individual instances of beauty; in a taxonomical system, the aesthetic appeal of the natural object holds no sway, even as that consideration has long influenced which objects get studied.

This is analogous to the narrator's position in *Adam Bede*, which vacillates between resisting the privileging of the beautiful at the expense of everything else and yet not being able to help itself from focusing on—the narrative equivalent of *staring at*—Hetty. In this the narrator is aligned with Hetty's aunt: "Mrs. Poyser, who professed to despise all personal attractions and intended to be the severest of mentors, continually gazed at Hetty's charms by the sly, fascinated in spite of herself" (*AB*, 85). Eliot, like Mrs. Poyser, is fascinated in spite of herself. Eliot makes the ethical claim that these individual, and perhaps rare, instances should not hold her attention: "I can't afford to give all my love and reverence to such rarities" (*AB*, 178). Eliot's ambivalence toward Hetty bespeaks a larger ambivalence of the naturalist and the trouble she faces as a realist: how to faithfully represent, or make real, the commonplace thing without succumbing to the lure of the individual and rare thing. Hetty is the troubled substantiation of her realist model; her beautiful particularity makes us, and perhaps her creator, forget that there are others like her, and in forgetting that fact Eliot seems to lose control of what she had articulated in "In Which the Story Pauses a Little" as the ethical claims of her realism. Having claimed that she would not look at the "few" sublimely beautiful women, prophets, or heroes, Eliot focuses on Hetty's particular beauty to the extent that she is made one of those rare few. This fact fuels what I would term the narratorial ambivalence toward Hetty in *Adam Bede*. Behind her ambivalence about Hetty is Eliot's ambivalence as a naturalist: staring hard at the individual object, even as one component of the realist's desire is to get to the larger category of which that object is a part.

The narrative repeatedly lingers on the curves of Hetty's flesh, admiring beauty itself in its persistent attention to Hetty's person. The following is a partial list: "they are the prettiest attitudes and movements into which a pretty girl is thrown in making up butter—tossing movements that give a charming curve to the arm, and a sideward inclination of the round white neck"; "that beautiful bit of neck where the roundness of her cheek melted into another roundness shadowed by dark delicate curves"; "the dark hyacinth curves fell on her neck. It was not heavy, massive, merely rippling hair, but soft and silken, running at every opportunity into delicate rings (*AB*, 85–6, 250, 149). Ultimately, even Adam's persistent passion for Hetty is applauded in terms of beauty:

> [It] came out of the very strength of his nature, and not out of any inconsistent weakness. Is it any weakness, pray, to be wrought on by exquisite music . . . ? If not, then, neither is it a weakness to be so wrought upon by the exquisite curves of a woman's cheek and neck and arms, by the liquid depths of her beseeching eyes, or the sweet childish pout of her lips. For the beauty of a lovely woman is like music: what can one say more? Beauty has an expression beyond and far above the one woman's soul that it clothes . . . the rounded neck, the dimpled arm, move us by something more than their prettiness— by their close kinship with all we have known of tenderness and peace. The noblest nature sees the most of this *impersonal* expression in beauty. (*AB*, 354–4)

The curves of "cheek and neck and arms" begin a list about beauty that always returns to the beauty of the body: beseeching eyes, pouting lips, rounded neck, and dimpled arms. Although there is a hostility to vanity in the novel, this is not synonymous with the beauty that inspired the condemned vanity.[51] The separation of the physical fact of beauty from a moral reaction to it seems deliberate; in the preceding passage the reader is encouraged to greedily take up the chance to take pleasure in Hetty's beauty. We are told that we cannot help but be entranced by Hetty's beauty; Hetty, like nature, seems meant to be observed, studied, and celebrated solely for her materiality, this "*impersonal* expression in beauty" (*AB*, 354).

There is a second troubling of the epistemologies of natural history, and organic realism, with which Hetty presents us: the possible failure of categories as such, the possible inability to locate her in any one category securely. Eighteenth-century taxonomical projects, from Linnaeus on, sought a revealed perfection in nature that would only be guaranteed by perfectly delimited categories; what this taxonomical scheme implied is that every object has a secure, and singular, place within a harmonious order—a claim that developmental theories of biology would of course eventually disturb. Let us return to the sea anemone, the natural object that Lewes and Eliot studied, in order to be precise about the function and meaning of natural history in *Adam Bede*. The sea anemone is the vernacular for various Actinoid Zoophytes, distinctive for being an animal that resembles a flower. Philip Henry Gosse defines the sea anemone in his 1855 *Marine Zoology* as "the extensive group known popularly as Sea anemones or Animal flowers, from the blossom-like appearance of their expanded disks and tentacles, and their gorgeous flowers" (see fig. 9).[52]

Blackwood, Lewes and Eliot's publisher, refers to them as "these living sea weeds," while Eliot herself remarks in *Recollections of the Scilly Isles* on the sea anemone looking like a fern: "It was here that we found our first Comatula, which looked small and insignificant when we first set eyes on it clutching the root of the laminaria, but expanded like a red and white fern when we put it into the bottle red and white fern" (*J*, 356).[53] *Anemone*, of course, is also the name of a wildflower found commonly in England, so the common name strongly invokes a flower. Lewes, in his article for *Blackwood's* magazine entitled "New Facts and Old Fancies about Sea anemones," speaks of going to the tide pools at midnight to see "the anemones in full blossom," and of certain "Ascidians" who root themselves to a rock or shell as "firmly as the plant is rooted in the earth." He closes his article with a sense of melancholy for the fact that he has just one remaining sea anemone on his desk, which he calls "the last rose of summer, all its blooming companions having been dissected long ago." All the more stunning, then, when in reading Lewes's article one finds that this is more than mere metaphor—that, at the time, there was no scientific basis for distinguishing the sea anemone as "exclusively animal." Lewes poses the question to his reader: "How do I know that it is an animal, and not a flower, which it so much resembles? Well, to be perfectly candid, I do not know it. Nobody does."[54]

Eliot observed, collected, and described these creatures that Lewes, and surely Eliot too, believed were animals but nevertheless could not distinguish from flowers. We might think of that animal-flower informing the representa-

FIGURE 9 "Actinia Mesembryanthemum." Plate 6 from Philip Henry Gosse, *Actinologia Britannica* (London, 1860). Originally in color; representation of the sea anemone *Actinia mesembryanthemum*. Courtesy of the General Research Division, The New York Public Library, Astor, Lenox and Tilden Foundations.

tion of Hetty, who, we are repeatedly told, "if ever a girl looked as if she had been made of roses, that girl was Hetty" (*AB*, 186). As has often been noted, Hetty is linked persistently to both plants and animals. The narrative repeatedly describes Hetty in terms of animals: "kitten," "small downy ducks," "star-browed calf," "butterfly," "spaniel," "tropic bird" (*AB*, 84, 134, 136, 129). Donnithorne, using the conventional language of the lover, also calls Hetty "you little frightened bird! little tearful rose! silly pet!" (*AB* 136). Plant analogies, and scenes in which Hetty appears surrounded by flowers, abound. In employing and retracting plant analogies, Eliot suggests a discomfort with the conventionality of comparing a woman to a flower—not unlike the classificatory confusion that permeates the entire representation of Hetty. In one example, Hetty's cheek is likened to the petals of a rose, but the narrator is somehow dissatisfied with that analogy—"it is of little use for me to tell you that her cheek was like a rose-petal" (*AB*, 85). The conventionality of the comparison is followed by more precise botanical references: Hetty's eyelashes "curled like the stamen of a flower"; children cluster around Hetty "like florets round the central flower" (*AB*, 151–2). Although after the infanticide the narrative shifts to the issue of Hetty's morality, this is a late development in the characterization of Hetty, who is something between a flower, an animal, and a "distractingly pretty girl of seventeen" (84). Hetty is never compared to a sea anemone, although Gwendolen Harleth of *Daniel Deronda* is.[55] The absence of a simplifying analogy, however, is insignificant in light of Eliot's actual sustained study of and appreciation for that creature just prior to the composition of *Adam Bede*. The sea anemone's liminality—that is, the scientific indeterminacy over whether the sea anemone is a plant or an animal—governs the representation of Hetty.

The sea anemone, flower-like and beautiful, is most like Hetty in being compelling despite detracting qualities. Compelling enough, in fact, to be a "pet" and "subject of dissection" and an "ornament of countless drawing-rooms," despite having to be fed raw beef. Lewes writes: "it is difficult to say what occasioned this sudden enthusiasm for anemones; lovely, indeed, but by no means the most lovely, and certainly not the most interesting wonders of the deep."[56] Hetty of course perhaps *is* the "most lovely" creature, but like the sea anemone she is both distasteful in her acts and uninteresting in manner. One of the most persistent facts about Hetty is that her beauty is the object of wonder despite her original venality and later commission of infanticide, a fact that the narrative warns us not to distance ourselves from: "before you despise Adam as deficient in penetration, pray ask yourself if you were ever predisposed to believe evil of any pretty woman" (*AB*, 152). In the courtroom, when Adam looks on Hetty, his wonder, and ours, at her beauty remains: "there they were—the sweet face and neck, with the dark tendrils of hair, the long dark lashes, the rounded cheek and pouting lips: pale and thin—yes—but like Hetty, and only Hetty" (*AB*, 433). Our fascination with Hetty's beauty, and the narrative's encouragement to keep looking at her, corresponds with the way natural history instructs its practitioners to look at, wonder about, and delight in nature. That Hetty has no redeeming qualities—not even the simple love of children, who had been "the very nuisance of her life—as bad as buzzing insects"—is a fact that in its absoluteness insists on her status as a material object (*AB*, 153). Like the intrusion of raw beef into the drawing room, Hetty's venality is not an obstacle to physical admiration. And so it is with many natural objects: despite the reality of their physical existence, parts of which may not always conform to the "beautiful," wonder persists.

Thus the classificatory crisis that Hetty inspires: is she animalistic or floral? Is she rare and haloed, or utterly common? Hetty Sorrel is Eliot's experiment in seeing a person primarily as a natural object. The narrative's fascination in looking at Hetty is redolent of nothing so much as a natural object to be studied: beautiful, the subject of intense admiration, but nevertheless still or fixed. The sea anemone, which seemed to both blossom like a flower and live like a marine animal, is a natural object that operates, in the natural history researches carried out by Eliot and Lewes, much as Hetty operates within *Adam Bede*: an object of intense wonder and an entity that is more material object than sentient creature. She is, in short, the equivalent in the novel to the natural object in natural history.

If Eliot renders Hetty through a natural history lens, Lewes anthropomorphizes the sea anemone. As Lewes describes it, the sea anemone had "little more than beauty to recommend it"; it was a "monotonous" creature as well as "an indifferent parent"; we are reminded in Lewes's description of the sea anemone that Hetty is accused of the same monotony of beauty and a marked indifference to children. Although what is most often emphasized about Hetty is her vanity, vanity too speaks to her representational status as natural object, for that human foible is a trait in service of her material being. And yet Lewes's fascination with the sea anemone could as easily apply to the narrative's fascination with Hetty; he writes: "is beauty nothing? Is it not the subtle charm which draws us?"[57] And indeed beauty is not nothing in *Adam Bede*; Eliot's narrative lingers long and often over Hetty's personal charms, attending to them with a particularity that both derives from and in turn troubles natural history epistemology. Thus the particular, and often violently stated, hostility to beauty in this text; Hetty's attractiveness is, after all, "a beauty with which you can never be angry, but that you feel ready to crush for inability to comprehend the state of mind into which it throws you, Hetty Sorrel's was that sort of beauty" (*AB*, 84).

The crisis of categorization that Hetty produces as the beautiful object issues finally not only in a palpable resentment but also even in a kind of narratorial murderousness. The only possible revenge on the object that entrances and distracts the naturalist, or naturalist-author, from her larger purpose—her realism, her "faithful representing of commonplace things"—is to cage it. The sea anemone, we know from Eliot and Lewes's writings, would tend to die after several days in the sort of captivity required for its study, if it had not already succumbed to the dissector's knife; likewise, Hetty's final captivity in Australia gives way to her reported death, as if the quality of immobility we most would like in order to finally *fix* her can only lead to her demise. Escaping categories, one might say, is a risky enterprise, and one finally that Eliot's realism cannot leave either undissected or unpunished.

FIVE

Inside and Outside the Plot
Rewriting the Bloom Script in James

Why is it that in George Eliot the sun sinks forever to the west, and

the shadows are long, and the afternoon wanes, and the trees vaguely

rustle, and the color of the day is much inclined to yellow? . . . Why

is it that in Jane Austen we sit quite resigned in an arrested spring?

—Henry James, "The Lesson of Balzac"

Why is it that when James refers to Austen and Eliot he does so in the context of the natural, and even horticultural, world—rustling trees and arrested springs—and why is it that he does so in the form of a question, of a remark designed to point out the generic qualities of Austen's and Eliot's naturalized worlds, the way those rustling trees and arrested springs are *literary conventions*?[1] The answer is largely to be found in James's unique, pivotal, and continually renewed attention to the bloom narrative of the late eighteenth and nineteenth centuries—an attention that was self-consciously aware of bloom as a concept with a history of usage in the classical novel. By the late nineteenth century this history had become all determining: bloom, as a figural system, had become detached from a scientific surround and exclusively associated with the literary. This is not to return James wholesale to a strictly formalist mode but rather to suggest that in relation to James's representation of the marriageable girl it is important not to abjure the formal. For James was self-consciously responding to the novelistic genre of the blooming girl that he identifies in his literary critical essays rather than to any still-vibrant botanical vernacular.[2] The fate of the bloom narrative takes the following path: something that had been outside either authorial or readerly control—something, that is, formed outside of a strictly literary discursive field—becomes a self-conscious topic for this novelist and novel-theorist.[3]

In James's novels the formal meanings of bloom persist—including the accretions of both innovation and cliché that we see at midcentury—despite the fact that the kind of pervasive botanical vernacular of the first half of the nineteenth century does not remain in place. Bloom's initial explosion of meaning set the stage for the endurance of its general significations, even as the vernacularization of botanical science from which it drew its original complexity increasingly disappeared from view. The residual proof of bloom's narrative energies and meanings is to be found in James's novels, for what persists there is a fascination with the figure of the girl at the point of bloom and a formal, literary-historical understanding that this entails a plot of the classical novel. This is an understanding that James's novels and literary criticism alike suggest he uses self-consciously to reanimate the cultural subjects of girlhood and innocence.

James's clear self-consciousness about bloom as a concept with a history works backward, in a sense, to affirm bloom's pervasiveness in the novel before James. James's literary criticism establishes his authorial awareness of bloom's meanings in the classical novel, and his novels (about what Eliot called) the "marriageable girl" confirm that self-consciousness. In particular, James's fictions suggest an authorial self-consciousness about female maturation as a *scripted* fact: that is, the classical novel's telos of maturation and marriage created a standard story for the social fact of maturation. Certain of James's novels explore the effect on the girl of that intense self-consciousness about maturation's proper story, especially the question of whether it is possible to *be* marriageable—whether, for instance, the appearance of feminine innocence was so rigorous as to make it impossible to be innocent, to be the "real thing."

The discussion of whether a girl can ever be what the representation of girlhood in James's world demands, or whether the appearance of innocence demands a consciousness that belies the category of unconscious innocence, is part, of course, of James's broader aesthetic concern about the intersection between mimesis and a reality outside representation. And yet the consistency with which he returns to the subject of the girl's innocence and whether it is possible to bloom—to embody a feminine perfection at the very moment when courtship solidifies into a marital offer—suggests that this version of the more general aesthetic question is an animating concern for James. *The Portrait of a Lady* (1882), *The Awkward Age* (1899), and *The Wings of the Dove* (1902) in varying ways take up this subject. In addition, *Portrait* and *Wings* take up alternative narrative scenarios for the girl in bloom—in the first, resistance to conventionality, and in the second, terminal illness—and as such are at the center of this inquiry. As will become evident, the persistence of the bloom narrative is persistence in altered form: a bloom narrative in which the formal legacy of the novelistic genre is far more present than the botanical science from which its meanings originally came. James's formal innovations away from the inherited type of the blooming girl reflect not a wholesale rejection of the plot but rather a narrative that explores the cultural effect of the nineteenth-century novel's representation of this female type. As much as recent readings of James have deepened our sense of other typed groupings in his fiction—especially those of the racial and the national—the blooming "type," unlike these others, is openly considered by James a fictional effect, and openly evaluated for its determining role in female maturation.[4]

James's contribution to the bloom plot takes two dominant forms: its interiorization and its increasing decadence. *Portrait of a Lady* takes as its subject a marriageable girl who twice refuses not only traditional life choices but traditional novelistic narratives. Isabel Archer's attempt to live differently results in a tragic mistake, one made most vivid by the fact that her husband tries to control what the novel represents as an *interior blooming*: a bloom that signals a heightening of the individual's intellect and capacity for pleasure, rather than a readiness for marriage. The increasing decadence of bloom is, in part, a secondary effect of James's self-consciousness about bloom's cultural significations and novelistic history. But the decadence of the bloom narrative was also the effect of its separation in late nineteenth-century fiction from its traditional mooring in the healthy, marriageable girl. For this reason I will consider here the analogous case of Oscar Wilde's *Picture of Dorian Gray* (1891) and its (altered) use of bloom discourse; in Wilde's novel, the homosexual male, in perhaps the most dramatic extension of the province of the Linnaean narrative, blooms in response to a quickening of sensual awareness. As I will show, when bloom does not circulate around a girl in the marriage plot it is capable of suggesting the very facts of sexual diversity that Linnaeus's classification system, in being structured around potential reproduction, obscures.

This development in bloom's novelistic usage can perhaps be called decadent: a self-conscious usage that draws on cultural significations that are now acknowledged as being superannuated. In this, Wilde's *Dorian Gray* is similar to James's late novel *Wings of the Dove*, for like Milly Theale, who blooms in death, Dorian blooms only to see that peak aesthetic perfection immediately fall off—a decline that he can only stop through the transfer of his experience onto the painting. In both *Dorian Gray* and *Wings of the Dove* the decadence of bloom is marked by bloom's dissociation from transience, which is an essential component of what makes flowers compelling and which, in being suspended in these two novels, informs the dramatic tension around these ever-blooming characters.

James is, in many ways, an illuminating ending, and a figure whose literary criticism and fictions make transparent the meanings of bloom in the nineteenth-century novel.[5] In turning first to James's literary criticism, we see that he was distinctly aware of the history of bloom in the novel. James's fiction is where the contemporary reader finds her own skepticism about the "naturalness" of blooming matched, where our current tendency to read everything as a socially constructed fiction finds a sympathetic home in James's account of female maturation—even if James, in his awareness of bloom's literary history, is less indebted than we are to the persistence of the idiomatic meanings of bloom. If today we know what is implied when someone is said to look "blooming," we do so with little awareness that it was the classical novel that spawned those cultural meanings. *The Portrait of a Lady*, *The Awkward Age*, and *The Wings of the Dove* reanimate this narrative of female maturation and courtship by recognizing that the novel had helped shape the very ways that James's culture understood and acted on those processes. In turning to James I show the force of what G. S. Rousseau has called the "linguistic ripples" of Linnaean taxonomy, even though those ripples were, by James's moment, more clearly emanating from their novelistic precedent than from their original taxonomic center.[6]

The Critic and Bloom

In her advice manual entitled *What a Young Girl Ought to Know* (1905), Mrs. Mary Wood-Allen, M.D., drew heavily on a liberal understanding of the cultural meanings of "flowerings" in order to discuss sexual topics. Mothers are warned about the "deformity" of "forced fruits" and "premature bloom," and the ways of the natural world are cited as proof of the need for caution in raising girls: "you know how it is with flower-buds. You can sometimes pull them apart and make them look like a full-blown flower, but they fade very soon, and the beauty of the bud is lost altogether."[7] Mrs. Mary Wood-Allen's admonitory discourse was not a mode that James found congenial, yet these two significantly different authors shared a cultural language for writing about the clichés of girlhood and maturation. Wood-Allen may have embraced the clichés as a means of writing openly about sexuality, while James distances himself from those very clichés of bloom by showing the degree to which they had become "type."

It is James who puts a name to what he had come to understand as the literary type of the blooming girl. In an article on the fiction of Anthony Trollope that he wrote for *Century* magazine in July 1883, James refers to the "English girl" who was "in her flower," girls who belong to the "blooming season" (*EW*, 1349–50). James in a sense invents the term "blooming" for literary history in recognizing the blooming girl's stereotypical status. In reviewing Trollope's *Miss Mackenzie* for the *Nation* (July 13, 1865), he commends Trollope's choice in choosing a maiden outside her "teens" or "twenties" but ultimately pans the book, asking "why should we follow the fortunes of such people . . . why should we stoop to gather nettles when there are roses blooming under our hands?" (*EW*, 1312, 1316). And so one might expect that James would have preferred the relative youthfulness of Alice Vavasor in *Can You Forgive Her?* for Trollope's courtship plot in this novel is more conventional in centering on, as James writes, "the settlement in life . . . of a beautiful young lady" (*EW*, 1317). But, as James insists, Trollope's treatment of this (by now) familiar narrative makes the reader indifferent to Alice's fate—a failure, James asserts, because Trollope conceptualizes the title's promise not as a "moral question" but as a "sin against convention":

> We trust to novels to maintain us in the practice of great indignations and great generosities. Miss Vavasor's dilemma is doubtless consider-

able enough in itself, but by the time it is completely unfolded by Mr. Trollope it has become so trivial, it is associated with so much that is of a merely accidental interest, it is so deflowered of the bloom of a serious experience, that when we are asked to enter into it judicially, we feel almost tempted to say that really it is Miss Vavasor's own exclusive business. (*EW*, 1318)

It is not the subject matter (marriage) with which James takes issue but rather Trollope's unwillingness to explore the tragic possibilities of "jilting" (*EW*, 1317, 1319). For James, the "bloom of a serious experience" was the *promise* evident in Trollope's courtship plot, while Trollope's decision to emphasize the breaching of convention—to remain, that is, within the limits of the conventional—"deflowered" what was a potentially interesting moral dilemma around marriage. That James employs the language of bloom to discuss both the narrative's promise and its failure suggests the stirrings of his interest in the genre and the subject, as well as a clear indication that he would take a different tack:

when it is proposed to represent a young girl as jilting her lover in such a way as that the moral of the tale resolves itself into the question of the venality of her offence, it evinces in the novelist a deep insensibility to his opportunities that he should succeed, after all, in making of the tragedy but a simple postponement of the wedding-day. (*EW*, 1319–20)

That James considered himself to be one of the most theoretically aware voices writing on the novel needs no further elaboration.[8] More specifically, the female protagonist is of particular interest to James in his literary critical essays, as well as his fiction, as has often been remarked on in his own modeling, for instance, of Isabel Archer on Dorothea Brooke.[9] For example, he defends what he sees as the incipient banalization of "type" in a review of a reprint of a series of London *Saturday Review* articles—*Modern Women, and What Is Said of Them*—calling the articles "trivial, commonplace, and vulgar" (*EW*, 19). He rejects the papers' proposed typing of "The Girl of the Period" on behalf of the American audience of the reprint, suggesting that the strangeness of the articles to the American reader owes as much to the exaggeration of the English girl's failings as to the degree of difference between society in New York or Boston and London. James, in searching for the origin of this critique of the modern woman, suggests that these journalistic pieces find their source in the classical English novel:

The relation of the Girl of the Period to marriage forms, under one aspect or another, the subject of the greater number of the ensuing articles. We find it reiterated, of course, with emphasis, that to marry, and to marry well, is the one great object of young girls' energies and desires. According as a girl marries or not, life is a prize or a blank. . . .

> It is all a very old story, and English novels have long since made us
> acquainted with it: how a matchmaking matron fixes her cold, mag-
> netic eye upon the unsuspecting possessor of a comfortable income.
> (*EW,* 21)

James could be describing the machinations of Mrs. Bennet at the opening of
Pride and Prejudice. Yet he goes further, asserting that the situation for women at
"the present moment" is so dismal as to make the vagaries of marriage and
spinsterhood an unsuitable subject for the comic novel: "but to our minds
there is nothing comical in the situation, and as a field for satirical novelists it
has ceased to be actively worked" (*EW,* 22). A character such as Austen's Miss
Bates, for instance, is a character of the past and not one to be "actively
worked" in the contemporary novel, and certainly not in sensational pieces
masquerading as journalism.

James's thoughts on the tradition of the young female protagonist in the
nineteenth-century novel are as varied as they are copious.[10] James admires
Turgenev, for example, for his characterization of the Russian girl, a type he
suggests is like her American counterpart: "Russian young girls, as represented
by Lisa, Tatiana, Aria Alexandrovna, have to our sense a touch of the faintly
acrid perfume of the New England temperament—a hint of Puritan angular-
ity" (*FW/P,* 982). The "American girl" is James's particular fascination, in part
because of her well-known affinity with the issue of American innocence encountering a European social world that he dramatizes as intricately dangerous.[11] For James, American femininity is a condition to which his heroines are
subject, a condition that, as Lynn Wardley has shown in relation to *Daisy Miller,*
reflects popular nineteenth-century accounts of adolescence as well as nativist
anxiety about immigration.[12] As much as the American girl has a historically
specific context, being an American girl is also in part about epitomizing the
fictional ideal of the blooming girl. Arriving full-blown on European shores,
the American girl, as his fictions and his literary criticism emphasize, is ripe for
cutting. To the European, or the American who had been too long in Europe
(Winterbourne, Gilbert Osmond), bloom had become a self-conscious, even
literary, system in which it was hard to believe: "it was impossible," Winterbourne believes of Daisy, "to regard her as a wholly unspotted flower" (*DM,*
59). The inability to recognize innocence, and its correlative bloom, goes hand
in hand with what James sees as the European fictionalizing of the status of the
blooming girl. European society, in other words, does not mark the blooming
girl's extinction, but it effectively compromises the blooming girl by the con-
tamination of adult society, with its efforts at cultivating the appearance of innocence at the expense of actual or "real" innocence. On the one hand we
have Daisy Miller, whom James characterizes in the preface to the New York
edition of the novel as the child "of nature and freedom"; on the other hand
we have the girls, as described in the preface to *The Awkward Age,* that he encounters in the drawing rooms of England: "one could count them on one's

fingers (an abundant allowance), the liberal firesides beyond the glow which, in a comparative dimness, female adolescence hovered and waited" (*FW/P*, 1269, 1123). Daisy Miller is "the real thing," but like the aristocrats in James's story of the same name, she does not approach the fictional ideal or appearance of innocence.

In a sense, James claims America as the next outpost of the novel's tradition of bloom and his own novels as the place where that long but now almost defunct, novelistic inheritance would be continued. Perhaps only in James would the blooming girl flourish; only in America, his fictions seem to suggest, do they actually exist. In looking back to Eliot and Trollope in his retrospective essays on their work, James locates the subject (of bloom, and the narrative destinies of female heroines) with which his own fiction will be consumed. As I have suggested, James identifies the bloom figure most clearly in Trollope, an author who after *Barchester Towers* "settled down steadily to the English girl" (*EW*, 1349–50). The competence (for James, never more than competence) of Trollope's novels in finding their way to the marriage altar seems oddly to have provided a locus, if a negative one, for James's unique and renewed attention to the bloom narrative: an attention newly critical of the dominance of the marriage plot, an attention committed to the reanimation of the subject of girlhood.

The positive locus for James's new attention to the subject of the girl was in the literary trajectory of bloom that I have traced. It is in fact in Eliot's words that James seems to have found his own aesthetic manifesto about the girl as literary subject: "George Eliot has admirably noted it—'in these frail vessels is borne onward through the ages the treasure of human affection'"(*FW/P*, 1077). In Eliot's concession to the heroine James finds a subject for his own work:

> The frail vessel, that charged with George Eliot's "treasure," and thereby of such importance to those who curiously approach it, has likewise possibilities of importance to itself, possibilities which permit of treatment and in fact peculiarly require it from the moment they are considered at all. (*FW/P*, 1079)

"Peculiarly required" to take up the subject that he identifies as George Eliot's legacy, James finds his own literary path by curiously approaching the long-established novelistic subject of the girl. In evoking the midcentury stereotype of the Trollopian girl in bloom, in his touchstone evocations of Austen, and in discussing the girl in Eliot, James finds his subject in a lineage that I have called the bloom narrative. To James the girl is his inevitable subject, for "the girl hovers, inextinguishable." As James goes on to say, his job is not to repudiate completely what he receives through the literary type of bloom in Trollope, as well as the more nuanced girls from Eliot, but rather to "translate her into the highest terms of that formula": a formula that has by now become entirely formulaic (*FW/P*, 1079–80).

The Girl as Topic: *Watch and Ward* and *The Awkward Age*

Daisy Miller:A Study (1878) appeared just two years after Louisa Mae Alcott published *Rose in Bloom* (1876), the sequel to her popular novel *Eight Cousins*. In *Rose in Bloom*, young Rose returns from Europe to be surrounded by her cousins who "clustered around the girls, like butterflies round two attractive flowers." As if sequels to novels followed some natural trajectory of maturation, Rose metamorphoses across the two novels from a child in *Eight Cousins* to the eponymous Rose "in bloom": "the little girl, whom they had all loved and petted, had bloomed into a woman."[13] In chapter 4 I suggested that bloom by the 1840s and 1850s began to veer into cliché, becoming a culturally pervasive shorthand in the English novel for young female subjectivity, even as it remained available for novelistic use as a generic feature. Eliot's innovations with regard to "clandestine bloom" aside, the overall arc of the trope was toward increased transparency. The degree to which bloom's ossification rendered it more legible, and less able to represent the nuances of courtship, is especially obvious in relation to *Rose in Bloom*: Alcott could presume on the transparency of bloom's associations to such an extent that it would form a cogent title rather than organize the narrative.

Layers of generic familiarity had by Alcott's time overwhelmed the botanical vernacular, which had originally shaped bloom's meanings. In the process, bloom became increasingly conventional and separate from its botanical underpinnings—hence the blooming heroine is named "Rose" in *Rose in Bloom*, echoing Dickens's Rose in *Oliver Twist* rather than the more botanically particularized "Sorrel" of *Adam Bede*. James neither returns to Eliot's range of botanical signification nor replays Alcott's conventional association between flowers and feminine virtues. In both *Daisy Miller* and *Portrait of a Lady*, James gestures to the typologization of the girl by giving flower names (Daisy, Pansy) to his characters with the most exaggerated stake in feminine innocence. For James the blooming girl had become a figure, a self-conscious topic rather than the person around which his narratives hinged: although there is a Daisy and a Pansy in his novels, there are no Roses (in bloom).

James's innovation on the inherited type of bloom is not simply a rejection of it; nor is his innovation based on a particularizing or scientizing of bloom in the manner of Eliot. Rather, James explores in his narratives the cultural effect of the nineteenth-century novel's representation of this female type. That is, James does not write bloom narratives in the way we have come to understand them from Austen, for girls do not bloom in James's novels as a function of a marriage plot's representation of sexual promise. Rather, in his work given over to the marriageable girl, James writes about female maturation and courtship as social processes that are in part understood through their novelistic representation. In James's fictions, the girl—and the myriad issues that surround her maturation into a socially recognized adult—is not just a character but also a way of thinking about the novel.

James seems self-consciously to take as his subject the very narrative the novel had long transparently played out in its fascination with the girl's maturation in the "plot" of marriage—although in James, this self-consciousness produced doubt about the simultaneity of social and physical maturation. The trend can be seen across the span of James's career: from his first novel *Watch and Ward* (1871) and his early novellas *Daisy Miller* (1878) and *Washington Square* (1880) through his midcareer success in *The Portrait of a Lady* (1882) and *The Awkward Age* (1899) and finally in the late novel *The Wings of the Dove* (1902), James's use of bloom as a trope evolves to become increasingly self-conscious, self-referential, and decadent. *Portrait of a Lady* is the first of James's novels fully to realize the switch from bloom as a quality of the girl at the center of the narrative to bloom as the subject of the narrative's inquiry. In *Portrait of a Lady*, as I will show, Isabel's bloom is an interiorized one, a flowering of consciousness that leads her directly to a man who is not only a fortune-hunter but someone who responds to this interior bloom as an objective value. Although Isabel experiences herself as different from Pansy—conscious of a destiny she experiences herself as choosing in a way that the younger woman does not—Osmond defeats Isabel's alternative flowering by letting her understand that she had chosen a destiny that objectified her. In *Wings of the Dove*, as I will show, James takes the bloom narrative to its decadent extreme in separating bloom from its reproductive telos; Milly's bloom, because of her terminal illness, is one that does not refer to a marriage plot but instead is understood as the personal "satisfaction" of having experienced passion.

In *The Awkward Age*, and in his earlier novella *Washington Square*, James is less taken up with self-consciously innovating new narrative scenarios and destinies for his marriageable girls and more consumed by defining girlhood as a social as well as temporal stage. In *Washington Square*, it is Catherine Sloper's married aunt who voices the reasons behind Catherine's difficulty in attracting suitors and in doing so defines girlhood as a matter of representation: "the reason Catherine has received so little attention, is that she seems to all the young men to be older than themselves. She is so large, and she dresses so richly. They are rather afraid of her, I think; she looks as if she had been married already, and you know they don't like married women" (*WS*, 60–1). Catherine Sloper is not courted because she does not seem to be what she is; that is, even though she is young and virginal, she is unsuccessful in the self-representation of a girl. Unable or unwilling to maintain a look that signs her actual subjectivity as an innocent girl, Catherine is mistaken for something she is not: "older . . . as if she had been married already." Unlike Lily Bart in *The House of Mirth*, who at the age of twenty-nine is actually old in relation to the marriage market, Catherine Sloper is young, even though she seems unconscious that she must appear in the guise of the *jeune fille à marier*. While Lily Bart knowingly puts aside her cigarettes and red crepe-de-Chine in the presence of Percy Bryce, Catherine Sloper buys herself red satin: "our heroine was twenty years old before she treated herself, for evening wear, to a red satin gown trimmed with gold fringe . . . it made her look, when she sported it, like a woman of thirty" (*WS*, 38).

Catherine Sloper is slow in coming to the kind of self-consciousness for which Lily Bart is famous, for Catherine fails to experience herself as a character in a plot—a plot whose successful resolution depends on the efficacy of the appearance of her "bloom." Though Catherine is slow to intuit her role in this scripted process, her father is not. Dr. Sloper, for instance, sees it as a ploy of Morris Townsend to set up the situation as a conventional fiction—the traditional father and the barred romantic figure—and refuses the role: "She is past the age at which people are forbidden, and I am not a father in an old-fashioned novel" (*WS*, 92–3). The consequences of refusing roles, however, are different according to gender, since Dr. Sloper's refusal to engage in the part of the admonitory father only concentrates his power, while Catherine's naïve choice to stray from her appropriate costume brings her very identity into question. The narrative by which Catherine is being judged comes from the very "old-fashioned novel[s]" to which Dr. Sloper alludes, for they provide a fictional model for female maturation that dictates the events contained in her story, especially the fact that she seems older than the men who would otherwise court her.

To be, then, what Lily Bart knowingly called the "*jeune fille à marier*" is to hone the appearance of the young unmarried girl: to perform the role but to perform it in the knowledge of its antiquated shape.[14] No simple condemnation of a social system that makes men innocent victims of worldly girls, James's fictions suggest that the men actively collude in the established fiction: they are conscious consumers, even collectors, of the conventional image of the blooming girl. In *The Awkward Age*, Vanderbank initially prefers "little Nanda" (who is nineteen) to "little Aggie" because she is considerably more intelligent but ultimately rejects Nanda because of her "knowingness": as Mrs. Brookenham intuits, "he'd like her if he could, but he can't" (*AA*, 263). Likewise, the men in Catherine Sloper's set reject her because of her "married" looks. The *jeune fille à marier* is less an actual person than a character, a concept created by literary consensus.

James's consciousness that blooming is a plot is never more apparent than in his own plots. Catherine Sloper, for instance, is not only, as her father seems to believe, an unmarriageable girl but a character drawn around a consciousness about the bloom trope: "at the age of twenty-two, Catherine Sloper is regarded as a rather mature blossom, such as could be plucked from the stem only with a vigorous jerk" (*WS*, 62). The fact of Catherine's reception is what is emphasized here—she is regarded as being full-blown—rather than some actual state of bloom. That is, *Washington Square* is not a narrative that traces Catherine's blooming in response to courtship but rather a narrative whose very subject is the inability to conform to the fictional expectations of what it means to be a young girl. The refusal to adhere to the narrative expectations around the young girl is in the service of James's realism, for in representing Catherine's failure in gaining a husband he employs the unconventional ending from which he felt George Eliot shied away: he writes of "her [George Eliot's] inclination to compromise with the old tradition—and here I use the word 'old' *without* respect—which exacts that a serious story of manners shall close with the factitious happiness of a fairytale" (*EW*, 933).

For James, the idea that bloom is a natural phenomenon (and marriage its inevitable consequence) is contrary to the realist imperative. In a sense he unmoors bloom from its traditional conflation of a putatively bodily fact and a social position. That conflation previously had been underwritten by Linnaeus's classification system and the way his system naturalized marriage by turning the horticultural fact of reproduction into a marriage. What James's plots represent is a historicizing of the bloom narrative: an inquiry into the moments of its construction and consensual maintenance by various, always multiple social forces.

Watch and Ward borrows a tale familiar from such late eighteenth-century novels as *A Simple Story* (1791) by Elizabeth Inchbald and *Belinda* (1801) by Maria Edgeworth: a man adopts a girl just before she becomes an adolescent, raising her with the intention that she will become his wife.[15] In *Watch and Ward* we watch Nora grow up, go to Europe to be "finished" by the woman who had refused to marry the guardian, and return a blooming woman. *Watch and Ward* holds the germ of James's more sophisticated efforts at working against the constraints imposed on the novel by the bloom narrative, for even in the early James there is a displayed consciousness about the bloom narrative.[16] When Nora is still a girl, a challenge to Roger's deferred marital intentions comes in the form of an already blooming young woman he has met: "it was in Lima that his poor little potential Nora suffered temporary eclipse. He made here the acquaintance of a young Spanish lady whose plum and full-blown innocence seemed to him divinely amiable. . . . Her charm was the charm of absolute *naïveté* and a certain tame, unseasoned sweetness" (*WW*, 29). The threat to his potential marriage is articulated through the attraction of another's "full-blown innocence," as if the eclipse of the intended bloom plot could only occur under the narrative pressure of another bloom. The self-consciousness about bloom is evident here in the way that all potential courtship is routed through the language of bloom—a point made all the more emphatic by a later introduction of a "Miss Sandys" whom Roger admires but who only earns a silent gift of a single violet, "a mere pin's head of bloom," as an indication of his attraction in light of his continued devotion to Nora (*WW*, 125).

Nora's maturation is an event that is described in a way that invokes a familiar set of conflations, including botany, flowers, and sexual promise:

> Roger had no wish to cultivate in his young companion any expression of formal gratitude; for it was the very keystone of his plan that their relation should ripen into a perfect matter of course; but he watched patiently, like a wandering botanist for the first woodland violets of the year, for the shy field-flower of spontaneous affection.

He aimed at nothing more or less than to inspire the child with a passion. Until he had detected in her glance and tone the note of passionate tenderness, his experiment must have failed. It would have
succeeded on the day when she should break out into cries and tears
and tell him with a clinging embrace that she loved him. (*WW*, 22)

James constructs this odd bloom narrative around this image of the guardian as
a botanist, waiting for a first spring flower, which is a less than subtle euphemism for the blossoming of the child who "seemed to him to exhale the very
genius of girlhood" (WW, 27). The botanist-cum-lover, that is, waits for her
physical maturation and the feelings of an adult: "the note of passionate tenderness" which would inspire a "clinging embrace." Because the botanical leit-
motif is so sexually explicit that it passed as socially acceptable prose is hard to
believe; Leon Edel, for one, wonders, "in a city as addicted to banning books,
this should have passed unnoticed in Boston."[17] In fact, it seems as if botany's
long-established licitness, despite its sexual content, persisted, providing a
camouflage of sorts for the sexual implications of the prose. In contemplating
a flirtation that Nora enters into as a young woman, Roger considers its effect
on his charge:

He caught himself wondering whether, at the worst, a little precursory love-making would do any harm. The ground might be gently
tickled to receive his own sowing; the petals of the young girl's nature, playfully forced apart, would leave the golden heart of the
flower but the more accessible to his own vertical rays. (*WW*, 46)

Roger's consideration of "a little precursory love-making" invokes the older
sense of "court," but the passage as a whole is more sexually suggestive than this
might indicate. The passage's sexual imagery does not demand a particularly
complex understanding of botany, but it presumes a vernacular understanding
of botany that is so thoroughly assimilated that, without prejudice, it can suggest the act of sexual penetration: all one needs to know about botany is the
fact that petals surround the reproductive parts of the plant. When he imagines
"playfully forc[ing] apart" the "petals of her nature" to make way for "his own
vertical rays," he is imagining through a botanical metaphor sexual penetration. This more elaborate botanical image is coupled with a cliché for male
sexuality—"sowing"—that is clearly referring to himself ("his own sowing").
Although the passage begins with a consideration of another man's relation to
Nora, the erotic fantasy clearly involves himself, not some other man.

When Nora returns from Europe the reader is not surprised to learn that
two things have bloomed: Nora's person and Roger's passion. "It happened as
naturally as he had never allowed for it. The flower of her beauty had bloomed
in a night, that of his passion in a day" (*WW*, 117). Nora, now seventeen, is perceived by another suitor as not only a beautiful but a blooming girl: "she had
left home a simple maiden of common gifts, with no greater burden of loveliness than the slender, angular, neutral grace of youth and freshness; yet here

she stood, a woman turned, perfect, mature, superb! It was as if she had bloomed into golden ripeness in the potent sunshine" (*WW*, 92). Here, the somewhat clichéd terms through which Hubert experiences Nora's transformation—she is a woman "turned," a flower having "bloomed" into ripeness under the influence of the "potent" sun—suggest that his passion for her is mediated through the very narrative terms that had lent the courtship plot its sexual connotations. The competition between Hubert's and Roger's apprehension of her bloom marks the competition between the two for Nora's affection. Nora does not at first share Roger's perspective but is rather repulsed by the idea of marrying the person who had served as a father. That James's first novel transplants a vocabulary of sexual courtship into a pairing between a guardian and a ward is a telling oddity; even though Nora eventually comes around to Roger's intention, it is only, in the spirit of James's later failed marriage plots, after the desired suitor is revealed as a scoundrel in having been already engaged. Bloom in *Watch and Ward* is a language for sexual promise, one that, in its discomfiting conflation of father and lover, sets the stage for the various complicated innovations of bloom in James's later fiction.

In *The Awkward Age*, some thirty years after the publication of *Watch and Ward*, that initial innovation of the bloom narrative fully develops.[18] Perversely, bloom becomes the weapon of a mother against her daughter in an unstated competition over a man. In the preface to the New York edition of the novel James characterizes the conflict that propels the novel as one of competition between mother and daughter, a "crisis" that he had witnessed in certain drawing rooms in London: he characterizes it as "the difference made in certain friendly houses and for certain flourishing mothers by the sometimes dreaded, often delayed, but never fully arrested coming to the forefront of some vague slip of a daughter . . . the 'sitting downstairs,' from a given date, of the merciless maiden" (*FW/P*, 1121). The friendliness of "flourishing" women who are also mothers drives the plot of *The Awkward Age*—Mrs. Brookenham vies for the attention of the man who is alternately courting her daughter and being intimate with her—as does the complication over what constitutes girlhood.[19] Unlike Nanda, who does not seem childlike, her counterpart Aggie is preternaturally innocent, brought up in a way that the novel characterizes as French and that her aunt the Duchess describes as "under an anxious eye . . . privately, carefully, tenderly, and with what she was not to learn—till the proper time—looked after quite as much as the rest" (*AA*, 47). In contrast, she scolds Mrs. Brookenham for "planting" her unmarried daughter in the drawing room, the pollution of which comes from what the Duchess admiringly calls her "impossible house" (*AA*, 50).

The Duchess articulates a model of "growing" a girl that had been more elaborately developed in *The Portrait of a Lady* (1882). In that novel, Pansy is secreted in a convent, away from the dangers of adult conversation. As in *Portrait*, the method is thought to produce the perfect blooming girl, one whose biological age is less important than experiential age.[20] Maturation, according to this method, is something to be scripted, even by the most extreme of hothouse conditions; that James is eager to reveal its status as a fiction suggests the degree to which in his novels blooming is not a natural fact to be recorded but rather a decadent effect of a society ruled by second-order representations derived from an antiquated first-order representation (the Linnaean bloom plot). Aggie, we are meant to understand, is a *trained* flower, "as slight and white, as delicately lovely as a gathered garden lily, her admirable training appeared to hold her out to them all as with precautionary finger-tips" (*AA*, 68). And yet unlike Pansy in *Portrait of a Lady*, Aggie is essentially corrupt: she proves that it is not possible to *be* innocently blooming if the requirement is that she *appears* so. Aggie—until her marriage called, treated like, and with the modest affectations of, "a little girl"—comes out with a vengeance, for just after she is married she takes a lover.[21]

The Duchess defends Aggie's sudden libertinism by defending the system of raising young girls as flowers:

> "When did it ever, in any society that could call itself decently 'good,' *not* make a difference that an innocent young creature, a flower tended and guarded, should find from one day to the other her whole consciousness changed? People pull long faces and look wonderful looks . . . and say to each other that my poor darling has 'come out.' *Je crois bien*, she has come out! I married her—I don't mind saying it now—exactly that she should." (*AA*, 248)

Before marriage Aggie looked the part of absolute innocence and was dressed "exactly in the key of her age, her complexion, her emphasized virginity" (*AA*, 68). What the Duchess characterizes as a "flower, tended and guarded" is clearly Aggie's virginal subjectivity, which is meant, under the pressure of the wedding night, to bloom. The language that the Duchess uses to describe the quick process of social maturation that Aggie undergoes conflates social usages with botanical sexuality. That is, to "come out" is understood conventionally as a process of beginning to participate in a social world beyond the family, and yet here that process is almost exactly coincidental with the loss of virginity. In order to articulate what happens when sexual promise is fulfilled the Duchess equates the loss of virginity with the unfolding of Aggie's flower.

The conflation of sexual imagery and social process is remarkably clear, so clear that one could characterize it as intentionally *deflationary* of the conflation of bloom and the marriage plot. The gain in clarity from Austen and Eliot is also a loss of what can only be called "naturalness." In a sense, the novel dramatizes the hypocrisy of a perverted bloom—a marriage system in which the traffic is in images of proffered virginity, of flowers waiting to be plucked, and where the highest value is the mimicked presentation of innocence.[22] James's fiercest vilification is for a moral system that conflates ignorance with virtue under the term "innocence." Nanda's appearance of innocence, already compromised in her being nineteen and allowed her own drawing room, is deliberately undermined by a mother who in the guise of concern reveals that Nanda has read a scandalous French novel; it is in fact a public challenge. *The*

Awkward Age suggests that the appearance of innocence demands a consciousness that belies the very category of the unconscious innocent, and yet if
Nanda's consciousness is the mark of her lack of complicity in that system, it is
also the engineer of what Peter Brooks has called "both her superiority and
her worldly failure."[23]

James takes the marriage plot and brings it to one of many logical ex-
tremes; here, the mother deliberately sabotages the representation of innocence that will make her daughter marriageable; in *Portrait of a Lady* and *Wings
of the Dove*, the plotting of marriage turns sinister in that the girl is deliberately
plotted against. The marriage plot gone awry is perhaps the singularly most
important structure of this set of James novels; in skewing the convention of
bloom as the promise of marital sexuality, these novels take apart what had
been established as a natural association between blooming and marriage. In
not feeling compelled to "close with the factitious happiness of a fairytale,"
these novels can explore the aesthetic question of "realness": whether it is
possible to "be" a girl, in the novelistic sense of the confluence of physical and
social maturation (*EW*, 933). James's exploration of that issue is not a reac-
tionary policing of female behavior like the *Saturday Review* articles ("Modern Women, and What Is Said of Them") he reviewed but is rather a moral
and aesthetic critique of the plots that determined girlhood in the society he
represented.

A Blooming Consciousness: *The Portait of a Lady*

That Isabel Archer's story demonstrates for us the new possibility of the interiorization of bloom—its status as a fact of consciousness, and as an individual's way of narrating the growth of consciousness—is quite possibly a
paradoxical fact, given that so much of her novel is devoted to the ways she is
objectified, ways that depend in no small measure on the very botanical vernacular that is otherwise so thoroughly psychologized. Take the following
evaluation of Isabel by Rosier, that collector of fine porcelain and young
women, as paradigmatic:

> like his appreciation for her dear little stepdaughter it was based partly
> on his eye for decorative character, his instinct for authenticity; but
> also on a sense for uncatalogued values, for that secret of "luster" be-
> yond any recorded losing or rediscovering. . . . Mrs. Osmond, at
> present, might well have gratified such tastes. The years had touched
> her only to enrich her; the flower of her youth had not faded, it only
> hung more quietly on its stem. (*PL*, 418)

Although the aesthetic terms here are the terms of a collector of porcelain, we
are meant to understand that Gilbert Osmond shares in the terms of evaluation; Osmond had valued the uniqueness of Isabel's bloom, as well as her
money, for he had recognized it, in Rosier's terms, as being new, as yet "un-

catalogued"—a bloom that, as I will show, was constituted by an intellectual flowering as well as its more typical physical manifestations. That Osmond values, in the economic and aesthetic senses of the word, a woman's promise is the horror that Isabel is fated to discover: ultimately she learns that she too had "gratified such tastes" for the very authentic decorativeness that "the flower of her youth" personified. The tragedy that *Portrait of a Lady* records concerns Isabel's realization that she had not escaped the traditional story of a marriageable girl but had been subject to what the reader eventually understands as a particularly malicious author-figure within the novel.[24] The "tragedy" of bloom is generated by the way James sets up consciousness, the pivot on which Isabel's bloom turns, alongside the already scripted path of a novelistic, public bloom.

The energy that James gave to the interiority of his characters needs no further elaboration, except perhaps to add a corollary about bloom. *Portrait of a Lady* extends the physical and sexual promise implied in an onlooker's perception of bloom to the character herself; that is, bloom is no longer an outward social fact but a psychological state that Isabel self-consciously experiences. This development, what I have called the *interiorization* of bloom, is an innovation that depends crucially on the commonness of the subject: only when a given figural system has become so culturally pervasive as to be vernacularized can it then take up a life within consciousness. Put another way, the prior ground of James's making of bloom a fact about consciousness is the all-too-common status the bloom narrative had achieved. That James thought bloom common is best captured in his deliberately simple claim about the novel in his preface to the New York edition: "this single small cornerstone, the conception of a certain young woman affronting her destiny, had begun with being all my outfit for the large building of 'The Portrait of a Lady.'" As James goes on to insist, "millions" of girls "daily" affront their destiny"—so why should we "make an ado about it?"—why should this "presumptuous girl . . . find itself endowed with the high attributes of a Subject?" (*FW/P*, 1076–7). Indeed, as James practically begs us to consider, what makes Isabel Archer's marital choices—after all, one of the most conventional plots of the novel—different, and worthy of further novelistic consideration?

For James the difference would lie in the formal properties of the telling of what was this conventional story, the structure out of which the "interiorization" of bloom occurs. He traces that conventional story back to Eliot, whom he praises for the "deep difficulty" of her work on the girl, even as he asserts that there was formally a superior way to tell the story: "the really addicted artist . . . feel[s] almost even as a pang the beautiful incentive. . . . So I remember feeling here . . . that there would be one way better than another— oh, ever so much better than any other!" (*FW/P*, 1079). His subject of "the mere young thing" is one that he shares, as he points out, with both George Eliot and Shakespeare, their "Juliets and Cleopatras and Portias . . . their Hettys and Maggies and Rosamonds and Gwendolens." Yet as I have shown, James understands himself as innovating on rather than following in a longstanding narrative tradition: "What better field could there be for a due ingenuity? The girl hovers, inextinguishable, as a charming creature, and the job will be to translate her into the highest terms of that formula, and as nearly as possible moreover into *all* of them" (*FW/P*, 1078–80).[25]

The formal change to the bloom narrative that James imagined was one that affected the weighting—he uses a set of scales as his metaphor—of the narrator's interest. Typically, James explains, the weight is placed on the scale that stands for the reactions of others *to* the young heroine, what he describes as a narrative that revolves around either "the view of her relation to those surrounding her" or "predominantly a view of *their* relation." That is, he suggests that the traditional narrative is about the relationship of others to the girl rather than the interiority of the girl. This is the narrative mode that the marriage plot in the nineteenth century took for granted; in *Pride and Prejudice*, for example, Elizabeth Bennet's bloom reflects her relation to her male suitor, as it is witnessed by the narrative. James saw himself as changing that balance: "place meanwhile in the other scale the lighter weight (which is usually the one that tips the balance of interest): place least hard, in short, on the consciousness of your heroine's satellites, especially the male" (*FW/P*, 1079).

The innovation that James proposes is one that switches the narrative weight away from representing relations between the heroine and her male suitors and toward the heroine herself: "'Place the center of the subject in the young woman's own consciousness,' I said to myself, 'and you get as interesting and as beautiful a difficulty as you could wish. Stick to that—for the center; put the heaviest weight into that scale, which will be so largely the scale of her relation to herself" (*FW/P*, 1079). The center of his subject, that "much ado" about a young girl's destiny, takes place away from social mediation: within the young woman's own consciousness. The outward social facts being represented have not changed, for like many novelists before him James is writing a story about a young woman's destiny, where destiny is defined almost univocally through marital destiny. What has changed is the formal switch in where the narrative's interest lies; it is a change that alters the nature of the story.[26] This formal switch leads to a change in the way that bloom itself is encoded by the novel, for what (in the novel before James) we had understood as the result of a social relation between the girl and her suitor becomes in *Portrait of a Lady* a psychological state: an interior bloom.

That Isabel's consciousness is a blooming place is established in the following key passage about Isabel's thought processes; we learn that, far from thinking of herself as being at the center of some plot of maturation, she conceives of herself as plotting her own life:

> She was always planning out her development, desiring her perfection, observing her progress. Her nature had, in her conceit, a certain garden-like quality, a suggestion of perfume and murmuring boughs, of shady bowers and lengthening vistas, which made her feel that introspection was, after all, an exercise in the open air, and that a visit to

the recesses of one's spirit was harmless when one returned from it with a lapful of roses. But she was often reminded that there were other gardens in the world than those of her remarkable soul, and that there were moreover a great many places which were not gardens at all—only dusty pestiferous tracts, planted thick with ugliness and misery. (*PL,* 107)

That the language of bloom is here used to describe a purely meditative quality is perhaps the most striking part of this passage and the others like it; no longer simply a social sign, bloom has become the figural register in which a young woman narrativizes her own life. What has traditionally been the province of the blooming girl's mother is here made a function of interior agency: the "planning" of a girl's "development," the "desire" for her "perfection," and the "observation" of that process. Development is also defined as intellectual and emotional progress; the more conventional notion of female development is restricted to Isabel's sister, who conflates development with adult socialization: "Isabel had developed less, however, than Lily had thought likely—development, to Lily's understanding, being somehow mysteriously connected with morning calls and evening-parties" (*PL,* 372). For Isabel, self-evaluation and introspection leads to blooming places: her nature has a "garden-like quality," as if the scent of flowers (the "suggestion of perfume") and the sound of trees moving ("murmuring bows") are metonymic of her own self. The likening of that self to "shady bowers" and "lengthening vistas" invokes the secrets of secluded thoughts and the profundity of a perspective not limited or blocked. Both images are spatial principles of the garden, concretely making analogies between physical space and mental facts. Like the shady bower, the "recess" to which Isabel retreats in her mind is clearly a rich site, for to go there is to return with a "lapful of roses"; here James conflates cognition or introspection with the garden, suggesting that for Isabel to think deeply is to gather a plethora of healthy blooms.

The passage not only celebrates Isabel's blooming consciousness but also foreshadows that which threatens it—others whose own so-called gardens are more like "dusty pestiferous tracts, planted thick with ugliness and misery" (*PL,* 107).[27] Both the promise and the threat, that is, are expressed within the botanical (here also a novelistic) vernacular; it should come as no surprise that even Ralph Touchett's retrospective assessment of Isabel's career employs this language: "You seemed to me to be soaring far up in the blue—to be sailing in the bright light, over the heads of men. Suddenly some one tosses up a faded rosebud—a missile that should never have reached you—and straight you drop to the ground" (*PL,* 395). The coalescence of interiorized figuration and interpersonal figuration is precisely the problem: no matter how thoroughly Isabel meditates on her own blooming consciousness, she is vulnerable to a traditional plot of marriage (what Touchett calls Osmond's "faded rosebud"). A revitalized, interior blooming is matched with a conventional, plotted "rosebud"—and the doubled discourse, one as workable in the exterior world of social dispositions as in the interior world of imaginative possibility, is precisely the novel's problem, its engine for generating tragedy.

What results from this doubled use of bloom's figurations is a uniquely perverse, and sinister, possibility: that a blooming consciousness, despite its interiorized privacy, can be nonetheless treated as a social fact; that within this figural garden there may be real (socially empowered) toads, who can recognize the value of the blooming mind and arrogate to themselves the right to tend it. The doubled discourse of bloom is in fact a danger: even an interiorized bloom is still susceptible to manipulation, and is nonetheless socially visible.[28] The struggle for Isabel's mind is a struggle over the place that we know to be a blooming place, the place Isabel could return from "with a lapful of roses":

> The real offense, as she ultimately perceived, was her having a mind of her own at all. Her mind was to be his—attached to his own like a small garden-plot to a deer-park. He would rake the soil gently and water the flowers; he would weed the beds and gather an occasional nosegay. It would be a pretty piece of property for a proprietor already far-reaching. (*PL*, 481)

The fact that Isabel's bloom is psychological, a fact of her "remarkable soul," makes Osmond's effort to appropriate it all the more remarkable: the male role in the bloom plot, which had hitherto been limited to a desire for social-sexual possession, has now been extended to the kind of inner dominion that bloom's prior status as "exterior" sign had always precluded. A mind that we remember as having a "garden-like quality" is condemned to being "attached," as if a "small garden-plot to a deer-park," in marriage to Osmond. His acts as a gardener turn her into so much physical stuff to be domesticated: "rake the soil," "water the flowers," "weed the beds," "gather an occasional nosegay." Far from what James called one of Eliot's "fairy-tale endings," *Portrait of a Lady* shows a darker side to bloom's promise.

There is, of course, a representation within *Portrait* of the blooming girl as exterior sign only: Pansy. In a conventional bloom narrative she would have been at its center, but here the fact of Pansy's training at the hands of Osmond is the most salient fact about her. Her bloom is aestheticized as well: Pansy "in the bloom of her juvenility had a hint of the rococo" (*PL,* 409). James, like Eliot before him, fashions a female pair who are supposed to represent opposing versions of female bloom; Isabel and Pansy function as opposites in the way that Dorothea and Rosamond, or Dinah and Hetty, functioned in *Middlemarch* and *Adam Bede*. In the Isabel and Pansy pairing, however, Isabel fancies herself Pansy's opposite, but having thought herself free in choosing Osmond, she finds that "Madame Merle had married her," in effect as if she were, as Pansy is, Madame Merle's child (*PL*, 564).

That is, James initially sets up Pansy and Isabel as seeming opposites, one raised as a "little convent flower" and the other as a free American young woman, only to have Isabel's tragedy revolve around her realization that she has been manipulated as if she were a "pansy," a too typical bud, ordinary even within the common discourse of bloom. Ironically, Isabel initially colludes in the pleasing idea of Pansy as the conventional girl, thinking that Pansy attending her "had the effect of one carrying a nosegay composed all of the same flower" (*PL*, 456). Osmond, who continually sends Pansy into the garden to pluck flowers and who calls her his *mignonne*—French for "sweetheart" and the name of a flower popular in America—tries to cultivate a conventionally perfect blooming girl in the style of the old world (*PL*, 289). The choice to raise Pansy in a continental manner is also a choice, as Isabel thinks, to raise her according to the standards of a novel: "Isabel had never seen a little person of this pattern; American girls were very different—different too were the maidens of England. Pansy was so formed and finished for her place in the world. . . . She was like a sheet of blank paper—the ideal *jeune fille* of foreign fiction" (*PL*, 328). Pansy's bloom is a literary narrative, which for James is a literary figure and a fact of representation rather than a quality of the real. As long as Isabel remains unaware that she too was "married" as Pansy will be some day, she is charmed rather than disquieted that Pansy is more like a character—a "*jeune fille* of foreign fiction"—than a person: "Isabel wondered at her; she had never had so directly presented to her nose the white flower of cultivated sweetness. How well the child had been taught, said our admiring young woman; how prettily she had been directed and fashioned; and yet how simple, how natural, how innocent she had been kept!" (*PL*, 366). Pansy has been raised to embody the promise of the "white flower"; both "natural" and "simple," hers is a floral presentation of innocent sexual promise. Isabel's admiration for her at first alternates with skepticism about the reality of her persona—"was the extremity of her candour but the perfection of self-consciousness?"—but those questions fade under the pressure of realizing that she had been as manipulated as the *jeune fille* in front of her (*PL*, 366). Innocent efflorescence can here only suggest a sinister, even corrupt, arrangement of surfaces.

Isabel's tragedy is in realizing that she has willingly revoked the freedom that James associates with America, a freedom to bloom that Isabel had attributed to Henrietta Stackpole: "I like the great country stretching away beyond the rivers and across the prairies, blooming and smiling and spreading till it stops at the green Pacific! A strong, sweet, fresh odour seems to rise from it, and Henrietta—pardon my simile—has something of that odour in her garments" (*PL*, 147). Isabel fails to maintain that distinctly American smell, a scent of a blooming prairie that echoes the "lengthening vistas" of her own mind. Instead, she enters a world in which a Henrietta Stackpole is someone who can only be appreciated, as Madame Merle does here, as an aberration: "she mightn't be inhaled as a rose, but she might be grasped as a nettle" (*PL*, 331). Merle, of course, is far from the novel's moral compass, having sacrificed Isabel and given up her child and lover in the name of propriety, but nevertheless Henrietta's destiny is never set up as a real alternative for Isabel. Madame Merle's obsession with propriety is that which the novel would have us believe perverts female development and bloom's promise: "her [Madame Merle's] great idea has been to be tremendously irreproachable—a kind of full-blown lily—the incarnation of propriety" (*PL*, 592). Isabel's return to Rome does not echo Madame Merle's guiding obsession, for Isabel returns not out of propriety but for Pansy—if not to save her from the bloom that she had become, at least to provide some kind of buffer from the bloom narrative that Osmond will try to enforce. Pansy, having been forcefully returned to the convent, expresses her fear of Osmond and Merle, which prompts Isabel to offer the following promise: "'I won't desert you,' she said at last. 'Good-bye, my child'" (*PL*, 603). Isabel seeks to redeem her own freedom by returning to Rome to mother Pansy: in a sense, by not abandoning Pansy to her bloom.

Bloom's Decadence: *The Wings of the Dove* and *The Picture of Dorian Gray*

The decadence of the bloom narrative in James's *The Wings of the Dove* and in Oscar Wilde's *The Picture of Dorian Gray* is reflected in bloom's displacement away from the marriageable girl onto new character types. The separation of bloom from its female subject denaturalizes the plot's expectation that blooming signifies the healthy sexual promise of a marriageable girl. In *Wings of the Dove* James works off the traditional plot in two ways: first, his heroine has a terminal illness, and second, bloom does not circulate around successful marriage plots. In the first case, Milly Theale's illness clashes with bloom's traditional meanings, for the illness makes impossible the promise of sexual reproduction on which bloom is predicated; as such, her desire to achieve "the sense of having lived" marks the narrative's decadence, for bloom is separated from its reproductive telos while the promise of individual sexual pleasure is made primary. In Milly Theale's choice to pursue "as many of the finer vibrations as possible" there are echoes of Isabel Archer's resistance to conventional marital choices—but in *Wings*, as I will show, Milly scripts her bloom so successfully that, despite the central tragedy of her premature death, she has achieved the satisfaction of passion (*FW/P*, 1287). For Merton Densher, Milly blooms in death, achieving in his memory a kind of eternal bloom that is not unlike the eternal bloom that Dorian Gray achieves through his Faustian bargain with his portrait.

Dorian's physical perfection is represented as a "bloom," but like Milly Theale's bloom it is a perfection made possible by its very decadence: Dorian's peak aesthetic perfection is possible only when he freezes it, thereby separating its connotations from the natural world out of which those connotations were born. Wilde's use of bloom as a way of representing the sexual promise of male homosexuality depends on the inherited (dominantly hetero-) sexual meanings of bloom. The ascription of bloom to Dorian suggests the facts of sexual diversity that Linnaeus's system had previously obscured. But as I will show, if bloom in *The Picture of Dorian Gray* enables certain of the fiction's representational goals, it also signals its decadence and even death. Dorian's bloom, like

Milly's, depends on its dissociation from transience, perhaps the flower's defining aesthetic: in making a flower ever-blooming, Wilde and James drain the figure of its capacity to capture a specific temporal moment in narrative.[29] The separation of bloom from its reproductive telos makes possible the representation of pleasures obscured by Linnaeus's system, but the narrative price is steep: ever-blooming, Dorian and Milly can only die.

James and Wilde reanimate the bloom narrative by returning to maturation, a subject that was far from new in the history of the novel. Wilde's reanimation is in some sense more obvious in that he extends what had been a narrative restricted to the heterosexual marriage plot to the dynamics of a young blooming male on the cusp of diverse experience. In that narrative extension the absence of homosexual plots in Linnaeus's system, as well as in the classical novel, becomes more vivid. James's reanimation is one that begins by recognizing that the novel had shaped the very ways his culture understood and acted on the processes of maturation and courtship. What I might call James's *intensified consciousness* is the effect of a self-awareness about the effect of prior novelistic representation on the very realities his novels seek to imagine. In Wilde's confounding of the gendered expectations about blooming, and in James's upending of the presumptions about health that had been subsumed in bloom, the bloom narrative is reanimated in its decadence.

Milly Theale is represented as a specimen of the American girl. The American quality of Milly is represented several times through a botanical lens, including the moment when Milly intuits Lord Mark's perception of her as not only a "mere little American" but a "cheap exotic, imported almost wholesale," from a "habitat" known for its "conditions of climate, growth . . . immense profusion but its few varieties" (*WD*, 161). Lord Mark can think he knows her as an American, a type that for him, with his nurtured self-consciousness about class, has as sure a taxonomical status as the plant to which she is compared. Milly's Americanness helps fix the taxonomical order in which she is to be grouped, but the broader category out of which she comes is the class known as the marriageable girl; this, and the specifics of her almost unique social status as an orphan, make her nationality perhaps less pressing than in other late-phase James novels. As Mrs. Stringham sees her, she is a member of a "luxuriant tribe" from New York, but what is more important is the fact that she is the *last one*: "the rare creature was the final flower . . . [of an] immense extravagant unregulated cluster" (*WD*, 126). As James writes about Milly in his preface to the New York edition, "she should be the last fine flower—blooming alone, for the fullest attestation of her freedom—of an 'old' New York stem" (*FW/P* 1290). The claim works, as it were, two ways: she is the last member of her New York family to be alive, and she is also, we might intuit, the final blooming girl familiar to us from Austen, and revivified through James's decadent bloom.

The Wings of the Dove is a decadent bloom narrative in its very self-awareness: it works against a traditional conception of the marriage plot's goals and closural processes.[30] In this version, the blooming girl's value is not in her sexual promise but in the precariousness of her health: "wouldn't her value, for the man who should marry her, be precisely in the ravage of her disease?" (*WD*, 346). Densher recognizes the telos as odd, for it means that he must back away from consummation at the very moment the conventional narrative moves toward closure with its implied promise of sex: "the actual grand queerness was that to be faithful to Kate he had positively to take his eyes, his arms, his lips straight off her—he had to let her alone. He had to remember it was time to go to the palace" (*WD*, 401). Ultimately, of course, in performing this unusual faithfulness the marriage that Densher and Kate had envisioned is irrevocably poisoned.

What makes Milly distinctive from the other American girls in James's repertoire is that she is both an orphan and terminally ill; the two facts turn her potential bloom into a sort of melodrama, while the second seems to make her blooming definitionally impossible. That is, the promise of ill health and death is not the promise bloom had traditionally signed; the sexual promise of marriage, as well as the sexual reproduction that Linnaeus's blooms always implied, seems impossible under the regime of death. As Densher remarks, "one has to try a little hard to propose to a dying girl" (*WD*, 396). And yet, as James asks in his preface, "why should a figure be disqualified for a central position by the particular circumstance that might most quicken, that might crown with a fine intensity, its liability to many accidents, its consciousness of all relations?" (*FW/P*, 1288). In using a sick heroine, a heroine whose health necessarily impedes the traditional sequence of courtship and marriage, James finds his way back to caring about the destiny of the blooming girl. Only in Milly Theale, dying yet capable of blooming, and Kate Croy, whose excess of life does not guarantee her bloom, does James become the paternal lover that he accused Trollope of being. In that process he guarantees Milly a pleasure that her dying and bloom's teleological focus had seemed to put out of her reach.

Milly can bloom, despite her terminal illness, because as a marker of sexual pleasure bloom is separated from its traditional marital trajectory. Milly's passion for Densher is never predicated on a fantasy that she will become well and marry him but rather on a sustained fiction that in "living" she will be able to live; that is, not die right away. "Living" is a vocabulary established between Milly and her doctor, for when Milly takes life to mean "mainly, gentlemen," her doctor replies by converting that bit of frankness back into the code of the bloom narrative itself: "when I talk of life I mean more than anything else the beautiful show of it, in its freshness, made by young persons of your age" (*WD*, 307). The difficulty of fixing a referent in this discussion, and more generally in James's late fiction, is evident, and yet as much as Milly works to keep the reference of illness at bay through her intense subtlety, the referent to "life" is fairly clearly implied: live to love, and hence to bloom.[31] What we might say, in fact, is that the famous obscurity of James's late-phase prose is buttressed—partially made possible, in fact—by the too overt, excessively legible, botanical vernacular that provides the referents James refuses to name in any other register.

That Milly does in fact bloom is evident in the following passage from the sixth book, where what blooms is not her body (as some sort of marital sexual promise) but *pleasure* itself:

> That she now believed as she did made her sure at last that she might act; so that what Densher therefore would have struck at would be the root, in her soul, of a pure pleasure. It positively lifted its head and flowered, this pure pleasure, while the young man now sat with her. (*WD*, 300)

Here a pleasure "lifted its head and flowered": pleasure blooms under the influence of Densher's presence and her certainty in his collusion with her. That bloom, as we have understood it in the classical novel's past as indicative of the sexual promise of marriage, is here converted to a "pure pleasure" is crucial, for it seems to separate bloom's telos of sexual promise from what was in Linnaeus its stated reproductive function. Milly's individual pleasure is female sexual pleasure distinct from social convention or the reproductive drive. As Kate would explain later to an unhearing Densher, "she wanted you . . . for that was your strength, my dear man—that she loves you with passion" (*WD*, 458).

A parallel locution in the novel suggests that this flowering of pleasure functions for Milly as if it were an actual physical consummation. When Kate Croy agrees to a sexual consummation with Merton Densher, the text uses a euphemism that is echoed in a later conversation between Densher and Milly: "Kate had come to him; it was only once . . . yet she had come, that once, to stay, as people called it" (*WD*, 399). In the increased intimacy afforded by their being alone in Venice, Milly and Densher have a conversation that, in light of the phrase used to suggest Kate's sexual choice, implies Milly's satisfaction with the intimacy they have had. The conversation quickens when she asserts that she is not only "capable of life" but that she wants to thrive in some unnamed way: "I mean,' she went on, 'that I want so to live—!'" (*WD*, 406). The euphemistic quality of her conversation is matched by James's refusal, in his late phase, to have an omniscient narrator gain access to a character's named desires; here Milly's desires are perhaps opaque to herself, which James formally matches with (as he calls it) "the author's instinct everywhere for the indirect presentation of his main image" (*FW/P*, 1303). Her conversation at this moment is characterized by indirection, as well as what is called "the intensity of it," a suggestion whose meaning becomes known soon afterward when the two discuss a floated plan for her visiting his rented rooms.

His hesitation about the plan is a product of his desire that he not "sweeten Milly's hopes. He didn't want to be rude to them, but he still less wanted them to flower again in the particular connexion" (*WD*, 405–6). That her hopes could "flower" in contemplating a visit to his rooms—rooms that now resound with his and Kate's night of intimacy—is not only a painful irony but a reminder that Milly's bloom is about her pleasure alone. As long as she believes in her passion it does not really matter whether he actually reciprocates. Hence Milly's response to his hesitation about the visit is a telling refusal on her part to let the fiction fail, as well as an assertion that she is satisfied:

> "You can come," he said, "when you like." What had taken place for him, however—the drop, almost with violence, of everything but a sense of her own reality—apparently showed in his face or his manner. . . . "I see how you feel—that I'm an awful bore about it . . . it drives you away to escape us. We want you not to go." It was beautiful how she spoke for Mrs Stringham. Whatever it was, at any rate, he shook his head. "I won't go." "Then *I* won't go!" she brightly declared. "You mean you won't come to me?" "No—never now. It's over. But it's all right." (*WD*, 407)

This exchange, cloaked in an obfuscation that even Densher falls prey to, is meant to be understood unambiguously: unlike Kate, she will never "come" to him, or any man, for with Densher's hesitation about her visit she realizes that this was her only chance: "no—never now. It's over." This is not of course a literal sexual proposition, for all along Mrs. Stringham was to have been her chaperone; it is, rather, one of the versions of (what James called) "however briefly and brokenly, the sense of having lived" (*FW/P*, 1287). Having lived her romance to the limits of Densher's endurance, Milly will neither come to his rooms nor feel that she has failed in her desire to "wrest from her shrinking hour still as much of the fruit of life as possible" (*FW/P*, 1289). And yet for Milly, "it's all right" (*WD*, 407).

If "it's all right" is not exactly a ringing expression of *jouissance*, in the context of Milly's story it is a veritable willing of pleasure.[32] Having been, as Mrs. Lowder expresses it, practically prescribed ("at the doctor's direction") the cure of falling in love, Milly's response is to will that possibility (*WD*, 322). The promise of love and marriage that she might have hoped for if she was well is not a possibility:

> She had been treated—hadn't she?—as if it were in her power to live; and yet one wasn't treated so—was one?—unless it had come up, quite as much, that one might die. The beauty of the bloom had gone from the small old sense of safety—that was distinct: she had left it behind her there for ever. But the beauty of the idea of a great adventure, a big dim experiment or struggle in which she might more responsibly than ever take a hand, had been offered her instead. (*WD*, 214)

Bloom as a narrative possibility is no longer possible; what is possible is this new "adventure" or "experiment" for which she is responsible.[33] Densher and Croy of course orchestrate their own part in this experiment, but it would be misleading to suggest that Milly was duped in the way that Isabel had been by Madame Merle.[34] Until Lord Mark forces a semipublic acknowledgement of Densher's duplicity, Milly wills the very fiction that she sees herself as having entered in coming to London and meeting Kate (whom she recognizes from fiction as the "London girl" from "old porings over Punch and liberal acquaintance with the fiction of the day") (*WD*, 164–5). In coming to England Milly had conceived of herself as entering into a fiction—"a mixed wandering echo of Trollope, of Thackeray, perhaps mostly of Dickens"—so it is not surprising that when she enters the novel's classic plot she insists on its verisimilitude remaining unbroken (*WD*, 178). What has usually gone unremarked in critical accounts of the novel is precisely the agency implied in Milly's playacting: she scripts her story as surely as Kate and Densher plot out their own. This is perhaps a surprising claim, but one entirely warranted by James's careful, and well-known, use of screens between the reader and Milly's own consciousness.

We can detect Milly's agency most clearly in her sighting of a look on Kate's face that signaled that she was "the peculiar property of someone else's vision . . . it struck our young woman as absurd to say that a girl's looking so to a man could possibly be without connexions." This occurs in the fifth book: "Kate had lost, on the way upstairs, the look—the look—that made her young hostess so subtly think . . . yet she stood there none the less, so in her bloom and in her strength so completely again the handsome girl beyond all others . . . that to meet her now with the note of the plaintive would amount somehow to a surrender" (*WD*, 220). Milly helps write a script, a plot of romantic pleasure, knowing that Kate blooms, even if clandestinely, for Densher. We never *see* Milly's impression from the fifth book reversed—what James in the preface calls "Milly's now almost full-blown consciousness"—but rather are meant to *believe* that Milly has been deceived. James is careful that this impression is conveyed through Densher and Kate's focalization, not Milly's, so that the concept of deception becomes an indeterminate one. James may want us to believe in their conspiracy, but he also would have us understand that she participates in it. Her refusal to "surrender" to Kate in the preceding passage is a refusal to acknowledge Kate and Densher's connection; instead she enters into what she had imagined after her doctor's visit as the "great adventure, a big dim experiment," which required an exchange of the "familiar" flower on her lapel for "some queer defensive weapon, a musket, a spear, a battle-axe" (*WD*, 214). Milly does not surrender her fiction until Lord Mark, as it were, breaks the fourth wall of the play they are acting out: the effect is a state of nonparticipation, what Mrs. Stringham describes as her having "turned her face to the wall" (*WD*, 424).

Her life, in a sense, depends on her being able to perpetuate the fiction, but it would be a mistake to think, as Densher does, that her life depends on her not knowing what he experiences as his confidence game. We need not understand Milly through moral oppositions—as either cunning manipulator or innocent dupe—if we recognize the extent to which she earnestly (not maliciously) maintains a plot of her own devising. The letter timed to arrive Christmas Eve elaborately scripts her forgiveness, and like the rest of the plot she has participated in, the story is so legible that it does not even have to be read.[35] Kate, despite the self-serving nature of her understanding of Milly, is correct in explaining to Densher that Milly had been satisfied: "'the great thing . . . is that she's satisfied.' Which, she continued, looking across at him, 'is what I've worked for.'" Densher's disbelief is signaled in a retort that draws on the conventional bloom narrative: "satisfied to die in the flower of her youth?" Densher, who has by now fallen in love with Milly's promise, cannot believe that this flower could have died "satisfied," for he had not performed the act that her flowering promised. Kate intuits that Milly had achieved everything that she wanted: "the peace of having loved . . . of having *been* loved . . . of having,' she wound up, 'realised her passion. She wanted nothing more. She has had *all* she wanted" (*WD*, 462). Satisfaction here is explained as the act of having "realized her passion"—a strong claim, alongside Milly's desire to "live," that what had been at stake is a kind of abridged sexual pleasure. Milly's pleasure had flowered, and here, if we believe Kate, she has consummated those passions.[36] Milly's blooming is a blooming of pleasure: a decadent blooming, one that needs neither marriage nor literal consummation (let alone reproduction) to satisfy its heroine.

For Densher, however, Milly blooms in death. In life, she had only been "the little American girl who had been kind to him in New York," while to him Kate had "pure talent for life"; with the novel's sexual connotations around that word, Kate was the incarnation of sexuality to Densher, while Milly does not even register. Kate's talent for life is entwined with one of the novel's primary facts: their mutual passion, what the novel calls their "essential wealth of life," the "love and desire of the other" (*WD*, 361–2, 290, 285). However, Densher, having fallen in love with Milly's memory (as Kate intuits), fixes Milly in a kind of ever-blooming state: she is promise, frozen in the white dress that she adopts just once for the Venetian party, looking "different, younger, fairer" (*WD*, 388). The "accepted effacement" that Kate had adopted that evening for Milly's benefit continues beyond what she had intended. From Densher's perspective, Milly is ever blooming, while Kate has changed when he returns from Venice:

> He wondered if he were as different for her as she herself had imme-
> diately appeared. . . . she had never been so handsome. That fact
> bloomed for him, in the firelight and lamplight that glowed their
> welcome through the London fog, as the flower of her difference;
> just as her difference herself—part of which was her striking him as
> older in a degree for which no mere couple of months could ac-
> count—was the fruit of their intimate relation. (*WD*, 449)

The difference that Densher appreciates is, as he says, "the fruit of their intimate relation"; in a vulgar sense, he is intimating that her attractiveness had
been realized in sexual consummation, her flower had become fruit. What is
blooming here is not Kate but his realization of her difference: "the flower of
her difference" being the fact that she seems much older than she had seemed
before their sexual encounter. Before Venice he had admired Kate for her
modernity—she "didn't pretend to be a sheltered flower . . . but the contem-

porary London female, highly modern, inevitably battered, honourably free"—but here he punishes her for her unconventionality (*WD*, 91). The beauty of Kate's bloom is more acutely evident after its fading, in its now palpable transience, to which Milly's blooming (if dead) promise will never be subject.

In their life before Milly, Densher and Kate's pleasure in each other had been articulated through garden metaphors; for instance, their emotional connection is described as their mutual propping of ladders against a garden wall to "see over in to the probable garden on the other side," where they had found themselves face to face (*WD*, 89). Their relationship is rendered in the spatial terms of the garden, locating them at the moment of their engagement in the very picturesque grounds that the classical novel had claimed for public courtship: "they were in the open air, in an alley of the Gardens; the great space . . . seemed to arch just higher and spread wider for them. . . . They moved by a common instinct to a spot, within sight, that struck them as fairly sequestered, and there, before their time together was spent . . . they had exchanged vows and tokens . . . their agreement to belong only, and to belong tremendously, to each other" (*WD*, 117). James's self-consciousness about the marriage plot is here at its most palpable, for the secrecy of their marital intentions is established in a public garden. In establishing a clandestine relation in a public garden, James gestures to that which his own aberrant plot depends on—this is a marriage-plot going awry as surely as Kate Croy's family has veered off its traditional path.

The particular dynamics of Kate's family make it impossible for her to bloom in the traditional manner, for her father's abandonment of the family requires her to marry wealth. She keeps her engagement to Densher a clandestine one and acquiesces to her aunt's attachment of "value" to her on the London marriage market. In doing so she enters into a fiction very different from the one that her courtship in the city's gardens had promised: "this estimate ruled on each occasion at Lancaster Gate the social scene; so that he now recognised in it something like the artistic ideal, the plastic subject, imposed by tradition . . . so all this was what Kate was to do for the character she had undertaken under her aunt's roof, to represent" (*WD*, 271). Even though Densher thinks of her as unlike these marriageable girls of fiction ("the women one meets—what are they but books one has already read? You're a whole library of the unknown, the uncut") Kate still plays the fictional part (*WD*, 290). Kate feels forced into the role because of what James calls a "so compromised and compromising father [who] was all effectively to have pervaded her life, was in a certain particular way to have tampered with her spring" (*FW/P*, 1295). Kate's "spring" had been tampered with by a father who not only abandoned the family but who, at the novel's start, in refusing to take her in, forces her back onto her aunt's intentions. Kate meets his frivolous plea of poverty with the truth that his actions are stealing her bloom: she replies: "You live. You flourish. You bloom" (*WD*, 61, 63). The decadence of bloom is evident here, where its superannuated meaning is so available as to be a meaningful retort to a father's refusal to protect her innocence and happiness. For Kate to accuse her father of blooming in the novel's opening scene is to cover up the ugly fact of what he is saying to her; the father's rejection is the key act that jeopardizes Kate's bloom, the key fact that sends her back to her Aunt Maud to inhabit the now-decadent character of the marriageable girl.

The failure of Kate's bloom is evident in the novel's final pages; Milly's now dead but ever-blooming promise effectively wrecks the bond between the two lovers. The physical world reflects the change in the trajectory of their courtship, made evident in their return to the public gardens where they had become engaged; they return on "the shortest day of the year," which, "by a whim of weather," was almost as warm "as the days of sunny afternoons when they had taken their first trysts" (*WD*, 470). Densher, now cognizant of the fact that he has had to play a part in a script written alternately by two women, tries to wrest control back; the condition he places on their marriage is that Kate reject their conspiracy and return to a conventional plot of marriage: "it's as I am that you must have me" (*WD*, 472). But as Kate is now aware, Densher's affections are divided; in what Densher bitingly calls "an act of splendid generosity," Kate had made a prodigious mistake in offering to share him with the "angel with a thumping bank account," for she will now be forced to extend that generosity: she will share Densher's love with the memory of Milly (*WD*, 496, 283). The effect on their marital plans of his having fallen in love with the memory (in Milly) of permanent promise is left ambiguous, though Kate Croy's famous final line is a fair approximation not only of their fate but of the bloom narrative in the wake of its decadence: "we shall never be again as we were!" (*WD*, 509). In this, *Wings of the Dove* almost resigns itself to melodrama, almost adopts the superannuated plot implied by Mrs. Stringham: "she doesn't *want* to die. Think of her age. Think of her goodness. Think of her beauty. Think of all she is. Think of all she *has*" (WD, 425). Milly's melodramatic death empties her bloom of its transience as surely, as I will show, as the bargain that Dorian Gray strikes with his portrait makes possible a bloom lacking in ephemerality.

The transience that marks Kate's bloom and made Milly's bloom only possible in her death is a key aesthetic feature in the late nineteenth-century decadence of bloom. This is what *The Wings of the Dove* presents us with: the spectacle of the bloom narrative's sickness, its shift from a posited physical "health" to various forms of dysfunction, lack, decline. And yet in that seeming illness the bloom trope is recuperated, made viable again in its transformation from the plotting of the sexual promise of marriage to a register of sexual pleasure outside the regime of marriage. That recuperation is best matched by Oscar Wilde's 1891 novel *The Picture of Dorian Gray*, which extends a narrative previously restricted by sexual affinity in the classical novel to the dynamics of a young blooming male on the cusp of homosexual experience. Unlike, for instance, Edith Wharton's tragic plotting of Lily Bart's almost preternatural bloom, Wilde celebrates the instantiation in Dorian of his ongoing bloom even as the narrative teleology born of this structure ultimately requires a violent closure.[37] The transience that defines the marriageable girl's bloom is thwarted by the portrait. The thwarting of transience creates a kind of perpetual bloom for Dorian and a problem for the narrative: what defines closure when the representation of sexual promise is extended indefinitely? In making a flower ever blooming, the figure is drained of its capacity to capture a specific temporal moment in narrative, and so the very peak aesthetic perfection that the novel celebrates is that which complicates its ending. In his bloom, Dorian embodies male homosexual promise; in its permanence his bloom becomes unnatural and, like Milly Theale's bloom, closer in its decadence to death than budding life.

Dorian Gray's physical perfection is celebrated in the novel's first chapter as the epitome of youthful beauty; he is described as "wonderfully handsome," with "finely-curved scarlet lips . . . frank blue eyes . . . crisp gold hair," all of which contribute to a beauty defined by youthfulness and sexual innocence: "there was something in his face that made one trust him at once. All the candour of youth was there, as well as all youth's passionate purity. One felt that he had kept himself unspotted from the world."[38] Sexual promise is evident from the novel's opening line, which describes the scent of the studio given over to the task of capturing what the artist imagines as a subject as transient as the flowers perfuming the air: "the studio was filled with the rich odour of roses, and when the light summer wind stirred amidst the trees of the garden there came through the open door the heavy scent of lilac, or the more delicate perfume of the pink-flowering thorn" (*DG*, 23). The odor of blossoms sets the stage for Dorian's blooming, for in Wilde's novel blooming is not just a state that one enters into, as it were, naturally but is the effect of the young man's exposure to the proper stimulant. Specifically, Dorian blooms in Basil Hallward's garden under the influence of Lord Henry's stimulating conversation.

In vocalizing Dorian's desires—"you, Mr. Gray, you yourself, with your rose-red youth and your rose-white boyhood, you had had passions that have made you afraid"—Lord Henry seems to bring them to life; the narrative describes this process in terms of a physical awakening, for "these few words . . . had touched some secret chord . . . that was now vibrating and throbbing to curious pulses." Sexual passion here seems opposed to the literary conceits that Lord Henry uses to describe his boyhood, and indeed, under the influence of these "fresh influences" Dorian's boyhood, with its "rose-red" and "rose-white" coloring, metamorphoses into a more passionate state of red: "life suddenly became fiery-coloured to him" (*DG*, 42). The scene takes place in a garden suffused with flowers, which lend their sexual connotations to the discussion of maturation between Dorian and Lord Henry. However, Dorian's sudden experience of the knowledge of pleasure—life suddenly "fiery-coloured"—corresponds almost immediately with the suggestion of physical decline. At the moment Dorian first experiences sexual promise, that "fiery-coloured" state that takes over from his rose-red youth, Lord Henry instructs him not to frown, and to avoid sun lest he become sunburnt. The scene confuses his experience of pleasure with the ephemerality of physical beauty, which sets in motion the conflict between experience and beauty that Dorian then plays out through the portrait.

That conflict is represented in the antithesis between Lord Henry's stale rhetoric (he discusses time's "wars against your lilies and your roses") and an extraordinary description of a flower being pollinated:

> Dorian Gray listened, open-eyed and wondering. The spray of lilac fell from his hand upon the gravel. A furry bee came and buzzed round it for a moment. Then it began to scramble all over the oval stellated globe of the tiny blossoms. He watched it with that strange interest in trivial things that we try to develop when things of high import make us afraid, or when we are stirred by some new emotion . . . after a time the bee flew away. He saw it creeping into the stained trumpet of a Tyrian convolvulus. The flower seemed to quiver, and then swayed gently to and fro. (*DG*, 46–7)

The passage is striking in the way it marries precise botanical terms with a lyrical description of a bee in the act of spreading pollen. "Stellated" is a term often used in botanical writing and here is employed usefully as a descriptor of the lilac's structure (a mass of miniature flowers that seem to comprise, as it were, a single large bloom), while "Tyrian convolvulus" is a highly specialized way of referring to the trumpet-flower of that vinous family of plants. The added detail that the blossom is "stained" contributes to the sexual implications, for what stains the corolla of a plant is pollen, or what Linnaeus called "dust" and the "male sperm." The self-consciousness of the writing, with its careful paralleling of Dorian's emotions and the bee's spreading of the flower's male effluence, suggests an attempt to revive a botanical vernacular in the service of representing a masculine bloom. In a use of Linnaean language whose legibility is plain, Wilde makes a "licit" reading of the Linnaean tropes impossible: how to read this except as a young man on the cusp of his first (homoerotic) sexual experience?

In *The Picture of Dorian Gray*, the male bloom is, like the female bloom that came before it in the history of the novel, at its height only at the moment in which physical perfection and quickened courtship coalesce: Lord Henry prepares Dorian for his falling off, and discusses transience in an aesthetic debate with Basil Hallward, who conceives of his portrait as a gesture of fidelity to, as well as a record of, the ideal that Dorian represents. Lord Henry's response—"what a fuss people make about fidelity"—gives an indication of the nature of the courtship he intends for Dorian; indeed, in response to Dorian's infatuation, he decries women's fondness for the word "always," claiming that "they spoil every romance by trying to make it last forever" (*DG*, 53, 47). The relationship between the two men is initially presented as a courtship, in which the sudden awakening that Dorian experiences in Lord Henry's presence is particular to the older man; Dorian blushes in his presence, much like the girls in Austen's novels, so that Lord Henry believes that "he would seek to dominate him." At this moment, with his awareness that his physical perfection will fade, Dorian cries out against that which will record his fading—"I am jealous of everything whose beauty does not die. I am jealous of the portrait you have painted of me. Why should it keep what I must lose?"—and sets in motion the bargain with the portrait. But it is important to note that Dorian does this in a passion induced by Lord Henry, who believes in the transience of romantic relationships as well as beauty; thinking of Dorian, he muses, untroubled, "what a pity it was that such beauty was destined to fade!" (DG, 60). In a sense, the bargain Dorian strikes between the portrait and himself is his effort at extending the implied courtship between the two men.

This courtship is projected into a more socially acceptable relation: Dorian's aestheticization of an actress on stage, Sibyl Vane. Wilde's ironic self-consciousness about the courtship plot is signaled by her name for Dorian, Prince Charming, as well as the multiple descriptions of Sibyl through a series of floral clichés. Elsewhere in the novel Wilde is exquisitely careful about avoiding floral clichés, so here they are striking; Sibyl has "flower-like lips," while Dorian experiences himself as "a common gardener walking with a rose" (DG, 91). In explaining to Lord Henry how attractive she was on stage in boy's clothing, Dorian describes her dress in rich detail but resorts to cliché ("her hair clustered round her face like dark leaves round a pale rose") when describing her face (DG, 103). Dorian's inability to understand his feelings for Sibyl in a way other than in the terms of the narratives she performs on stage perhaps leads to this hardening of language; however, it is also the case that Dorian employs cliché in substituting the actress for the "exquisite poison in the air . . . [his] passion for sensations" that he tells Lord Henry he experienced for "days after I met you" (DG, 73). In a sense, Dorian's first act of cruelty—abandoning Sibyl Vane—is the result of his substitution of one set of desires for a more conventional one.

This act of cruelty is the precipitating factor in the painting's first alteration and that which prompts Dorian's remembrance that he had wished for this very thing. Dorian, remembering the scene in the studio, expresses the terms of his Faustian bargain through an intransient bloom:

> The whole expression had altered. It was not a mere fancy of his own. . . . he began to think. Suddenly there flashed across his mind what he had said in Basil Hallward's studio the day the picture had been finished. Yes, he remembered it perfectly. He had uttered a mad wish that he himself might remain young, and the portrait grow old; that his own beauty might be untarnished, and the face on the canvas bear the burden of his passions and his sins; that the painted image might be seared with the lines of suffering and thought, and that he might keep all the delicate bloom and loveliness of his then just conscious boyhood. (DG, 119)

In the same way that Milly Theale's terminal illness prevented her ever maturing past the age of pure promise, Dorian's portrait enables him to keep "all the delicate bloom." Dorian, in remembering that moment of physical perfection, links it with "his then just conscious boyhood"; the two modifiers of conscious ("then" and "just") are temporal details that precisely pinpoint that coming to consciousness. The coalescence of the consciousness of sexual feelings and bloom suggests the bloom narrative's reanimation through a male homosexual courtship narrative—the very terms of sexual diversity that Linnaeus's taxonomical spectrum of floral sexuality left out.

The failure of Dorian's passion for Sibyl and her subsequent suicide is meant to be understood as a failed bloom narrative, the result of which leads to the portrait's first loss of bloom and Dorian's subsequent forays into other sexual alternatives. The "wilder joy and wilder sins" that leave their traces on the portrait, rather than on his face, might suggest that the narrative is equating sexual experience outside marriage with moral degradation (DG, 135). Although the narrative may imply this, the narrative in imagining the possibility of eternal bloom is enthralled with the idea; despite the ugliness of the portrait, the idea that one could maintain "all the delicate bloom . . . [of] just conscious boyhood" is so captivating as to be one of the organizing principles of this reanimated bloom narrative. Dorian understands that pleasure in watching the painting change as he maintains his as-if-frozen bloom, standing as he does "where spring trembles on the verge of summer." Despite Dorian's death, the narrative seems transfixed with the idea that it is possible to "keep the glamour of boyhood"—an ideal that Wilde articulates through the bloom trope: "not one blossom of his loveliness would ever fade" (DG, 136).

There are narrative as well as thematic consequences in dissociating bloom from its transient state. This is apparent when one considers that bloom has traditionally been the mark of the marriage plot's quickening, the sign of the sexual promise of marriage outside the boundaries of the novel's close. Here, perpetual bloom is the sign of perpetual promise: it is a structure oddly resistant to closure, as both the plots (and endings) of *The Wings of the Dove* and *The Picture of Dorian Gray* suggest. In making a flower (or a person) ever-blooming, the figure loses its capacity to chart change over time; Milly's promise will never fade in Densher's memory—hence the firmness of Kate's declaration that "we shall never be again as we were"—just as Dorian's face would never have faded. Indeed, in the novel's *fabula* almost twenty years pass before an event occurs to interrupt this (potentially) never-ending story:

> he was almost saddened by the reflection of the ruin that Time brought on beautiful and wonderful things. He, at any rate, had escaped that. Summer followed summer, and the yellow jonquils bloomed and died many times, and the nights of horror repeated the story of their shame, but he was unchanged. No winter marred his face or stained his flower-like bloom. (DG, 169)

The potential infinity of Dorian's life (and the narrative) is apparent; interestingly, by alluding to repetition as a potential problem for narrative Wilde returns to the language of "flower-like bloom." The flowers referred to in the passage, jonquils, are also a sign of potential endlessness, for in being a species of *narcissus* (or daffodil) the jonquil, unless its bulb is dug up and destroyed, will return every spring.

The destruction of the (perennial) flower is the only narrative solution to the decadent bloom narrative; although James's psychologized idiom demanded that the idea of perpetuity be an emotional state, Wilde's magical portrait could have produced a literal perpetuity at odds with narrative closure. Indeed, Dorian first escapes from James Vane's vengeful hand because "the face of the man he had sought to kill had all the bloom of boyhood, all the unstained purity of youth" (*DG*, 227). The solution comes eighteen years—tellingly, the conventional temporal span of maturation—after the fateful day in the studio's garden; the best lilacs since the year Dorian met Lord Henry are in bloom, which is perhaps a reference to the first flower that the bee alights on in that early vital scene. In the lead-up to the climactic moment when he destroys the painting, Dorian "felt a wild longing for the unstained purity of his boyhood"—language which precisely echoes James Vane's description of his face (*DG*, 258–9). In that echo one hears a common longing for unconscious innocence, an innocence, as it were, prior to a fall—as well, perhaps, as a cry for it all to be over, for the teleology of a decadent bloom is backward. In asking to bloom, to return to his boyhood, Dorian is in effect pointing in the direction of traditional closure. The consequences of bloom's decadence is that the bloom narrative, in this late instantiation, points less toward promise and more in the direction of death. In both *The Wings of the Dove* and *The Portrait of Dorian Gray*, the bloom narrative—courtship's sexual promise, ending in implied reproduction—gives way to the idea of eternal bloom, to a state of being that neither Linnaeus nor Austen imagined but bloom's decadent practitioners realize.

CODA

Later Bloomings
Molly's Bloom

"I never thought that would be my name Bloom . . . "

—James Joyce, *Ulysses*

Beyond the nineteenth century the force and meaning of the bloom narrative persists: altered, diverted perhaps from its previous tonal registers, but nonetheless still useful, still part of a novelistic apparatus, not yet so archaized as to be illegible.[1] The pervasive botanical vernacular has, by the twentieth century's earliest decades, largely disappeared from culture, but the idiomatic meaning of "bloom," as well as its literary meanings, persists. Bloom remains in force today, from its use in popular journalistic language to even smaller and more thoroughly disseminated levels of cultural production, even as its origins in a very real science have disappeared from view. That strange persistence ranges from the parodic to the naïvely mimetic, in either contemporary idioms of adolescence or the idioms of pornography—but its most striking modern appearance occurred early in the twentieth century, in a literary text that has for many defined the hegemonic, all-encompassing impulses of modernist cultural production: James Joyce's *Ulysses* (1922).[2] In Joyce's encyclopedic work, which is a history of the novel in miniature, we see the unapologetic reentry of the bloom narrative in Molly Bloom's soliloquy.

The return to bloom as a sign of sexual promise in *Ulysses* is in part the consequence of Henry James's metanarratives of bloom, his transformation of the marriageable girl from the site of mimesis to his aesthetic subject and topic. What we might call Joyce's resumption of the language of bloom subjects it to the ironies of parody and extends this figure of the classical novel into the realm of the overtly sexual. What Joyce reasserts and reclaims is the eroticism of the courtship plot, an eroticism figured through various "bloomings"—especially the bloom of Marion Bloom, whose nickname "Molly" and married surname "Bloom" directs us back to the literary narrative we have been tracing. Molly, or "moll," that familiar and departicularizing euphemism for both girl and prostitute, reminds us that Molly Bloom's name points to a primary subject of the nineteenth-century classical novel, as well as the subject of this book: the (sexualized) girl in bloom. Her famous soliloquy is the narrative of female bloom: this is the transcription of Molly's (and not Leopold's) blooming because as a woman Molly inherits that novelistic tradition, just as it is Molly who acquires the name "Bloom" in the act that defines her. As Suzette Henke has written, "a flower of Gibraltar and Howth, Molly says 'yes' to Leopold and herself becomes a Bloom. She knows that sexual and marital consent are in this case identical."[3]

The botanical sex that was only an implied vernacular behind Austen's early nineteenth-century novels emerges in the early twentieth-century *Ulysses* into an explicit depiction of botanical sex. The girl in bloom is a received trope that gets transmuted into Molly Bloom; the narrative becomes a person, the bloom a Bloom. In a sense, Molly Bloom's soliloquy reads like poststructuralist reading of the nineteenth-century bloom narrative, where the conventions of mimesis are replaced by the disunifying play of various signifiers—but, crucially, where the suddenly liberated, and wildly proliferated, signifier of "bloom" opens up what had only been an implicit prior content. In the soliloquy's self-conscious recapitulation of the bloom narrative the sexual content of the figure of bloom races to the surface of the text. As a result, the various blooms of Austen, Eliot, and James are enlivened under the new representational possibilities of the modern novel, although "enlivened" is perhaps too weak a word to describe this achievement of the final monologue. The final pages of Molly's soliloquy have been celebrated by French feminists in particular as an example of erotic *jouissance*, and, most famously, Hélène Cixous has cited Molly's soliloquy as a model of writing independent of male discursive practices, an example par excellence of *écriture feminine*.[4] Certainly one of the great achievements of the soliloquy, whether or not one subscribes to the particular theoretical implications of *écriture feminine*, is the joyous transcendence by the individual female voice of the archetypes of femininity (the virgin-as-Gerty McDowell, the mother-as-Mina Purefoy, and the whore-as-Circe prostitutes) deployed in the main body of the novel. But as I have implied, this transcendence goes beyond the destruction of archetype; the soliloquy's form enables the articulation of what had previously remained only implied in the classical novel: the experience of blooming, the experience of sexual promise. Moreover, it locates the literary expression of that experience in the female type who had been the object of literary expression. In this way Molly Bloom's sexual *jouissance* is the speaking of that which novelistic bloom had gestured at but had left unspoken: an implied trace, hinting at that which remained far beyond the boundaries of conventional mimesis. One could say that in Molly's blooming the representational goals of the figure at the periphery of the late eighteenth-century botanical vernacular, Erasmus Darwin, are finally realized.

In other words, the soliloquy brings the overt representation of sex to the courtship narrative, for in the novel prior to James the botanical vernacular implicitly informed the representation of erotic courtship without literally representing sex; with the exaggerations of parody, however, Joyce makes the physicality of bloom more evident than in any of its earlier avatars. As I have shown, references to the act of sex, and its particular relation to the bloom of the heroines, appear in Eliot's *Adam Bede* and James's *Wings of the Dove*. These representations of illicit sexuality, or "clandestine flowerings," are but extensions of the marriage plot—public or clandestine—that Linnaeus's taxonomic system had enabled. In *Portrait of a Lady* Isabel's "bloom" becomes an interior fact, a reference to her budding consciousness. In *Ulysses*, Joyce extends the representational limits of sex as they had been established in such novels as *Adam Bede* and *Wings of the Dove* and combines it, crucially, with the interiorized bloom that James had established in *The Portrait of a Lady*. That is, *Ulysses* represents actual sexual acts as well as the interiority of Molly Bloom as she remembers herself blooming.

Molly, famously, reaches orgasm as she blooms, the result of what is, as Joyce's wider parameters enable us to see, Molly Bloom's first sexual encounter:

> I remember shall I wear a white rose and I wanted to put on the old stupid clock to near the time he was the first man that kissed me under the Moorish wall my sweetheart when a boy it never entered my head what kissing meant till he put his tongue in my mouth his mouth was sweetlike young I put my knee up to him a few times to learn the way what did I tell him I was engaged for for fun to the son of a Spanish nobleman named Don Miguel de la Flora and he believed me that I was to be married to him in 3 years time theres many a true word spoken in jest there is a flower that bloometh a few things I told him true about myself just for him to be imagining the Spanish girls he didnt like I suppose one of them wouldnt have him I got him excited he crushed all the flowers on my bosom he brought me. (743)

Molly remembers her first sensation of sexual excitement, the indecision over what she should wear, and the joke she tells her mate: "I was engaged for fun to the son of a Spanish nobleman named Don Miguel de la Flora." The joke was that she was to have been married to a man of flowers in three years time, but as she realizes, "theres many a true word spoken in jest." That is, she marries a man of flowers—Bloom, aka Henry Flowers—a fact which goes along with the enigmatic phrase that follows: "there is a flower that bloometh." Molly is the flower that bloometh, or at the very least one of them, and like that literary narrative that she epitomizes, she blooms because the "first man," her "sweetheart," kisses her. The extended representational parameters allow us to see farther than we have ever seen ("I got him excited he crushed all the flowers on my bosom he brought me"), but what we see is still along the same trajectory that Linnaeus's botanical system had always projected. The "jest" of the soliloquy, its overproduction of Linnaean terms and images, is still a "true word," still capable of representing sexual maturation.

It would be impossible to think that bloom is only a detail in a rich bed of details, given that Joyce has bestowed the word on his characters themselves, and that the primacy of bloom is visible in the explicit unfolding it receives in the novel's final words. Those words are Molly Bloom's description of her loss of virginity in Gibraltar:

> In the Alameda gardens yes . . . the rosegardens and the jessamine and geraniums and cactuses and Gibraltar as a girl where I was a Flower of the mountain yes when I put the rose in my hair like the Andalusian girls used or shall I wear a red yes and how he kissed me under the Moorish wall and I thought well as well him as another and then I asked him with my eyes to ask again yes and then he asked me would I yes to say yes my mountain flower and first I put my arms around him yes and drew him down to me so he could feel my breasts all perfume yes and his heart was going like mad and yes I said yes I will Yes. (768)

The reiteration of yes—"yes I will Yes"—and the assertion "I thought well as well him as another" have famously composed Molly Bloom's stated desire for and consummation of sex. The references are precise floral memories, of "jessamine," "geraniums," and "cactuses," which in turn inspire the memory of the rose in her hair when she is "kissed under the Moorish wall." The memories of this first sexual experience and her acceptance of a marriage proposal are conflated, so that the ambivalence of her choice "I thought well as well him as another" could refer either to her first choice of a sex partner or husband. Marriages, clandestine or public, collapse in Molly's memory, as if the plants that surround her earliest memory of sex, and the pet-name "mountain flower" that accompanies this and her later licit courtship can no longer be used to distinguish between clandestine or public marriages: "16 years ago my God after that long kiss I near lost my breath yes he said I was a flower of the mountain" (767). Unlike the nineteenth-century marriage plot, the bloom of a sexualized courtship in *Ulysses* need not end in marriage; Molly's bloom takes us back to her girlhood in Gibraltar, a place her thoughts soon lead to in remembering the day that she "got him [Leopold] to propose to me" as they were "lying among the rhododendrons on Howth head" (767). But much like the nineteenth-century version, marriage is at least implicated in the use of bloom language (which is here always a Bloom language), entwined with if not identical to the fact of bloom. She is a mountain flower at Howth as well as Gibraltar, and at least at the climax of the traditional bloom narrative, the moment of proposal, Molly's sexual promise is for Leopold: "yes so we are flowers all a woman's body yes that was one true thing he said in his life and the sun shines for you today yes that was why I liked him because I saw he understood or felt what a woman is and I knew I could always get round him and I gave him all the pleasure I could leading him on till he asked me to say yes" (767). Here, of course, sexual promise cuts in two directions: her flowering body, at least for today, is destined for Leopold. Her flowering body refers to the sexual promise that was (in the classical novel) marriage's implied reward, a reward the prose suggests she shrewdly exacts from him by "leading him on till he asked me to say yes."

Thus the fate of the bloom narrative is, tonally at least, *parody*: a Joycean parody so affectionate and thorough as to seem almost a repetition (if an outsized repetition) of nineteenth-century narrative modes. And yet the parody in Molly's soliloquy is crossed by a series of delicate ironies. That Molly should gain the name "Bloom" when she marries is perhaps the largest of these parodic Linnaean ironies, rather than an unself-conscious association of marriage and sexual bloom:

> that old Bishop that spoke off the altar his long preach about womans higher functions about girls now riding the bicycle and wearing peak caps and the new woman bloomers God send him sense and me more money I suppose theyre called after him I never thought that would be my name Bloom when I used to write it in print to see how it looked on a visiting card or practicing for the butcher and oblige M Bloom youre looking blooming Josie used to say after I married him well its better than Breen or Briggs does brig or those awful names with bottom in them Mrs Ramsbottom or some other kind of bottom. (761)

"Blooming" here refers to a friend's punning at her married name (a name that is still preferable to names that invoke the buttocks), while "bloomers" are the subject for a bishop's prudish sermon about girls riding bicycles and wearing the new underclothing of that name. If later in Molly's soliloquy the equation between bloom and marriage is blurred, with blooming a fact of a woman's body rather than a social state—"we are all flowers all yes a womans body"— here blooming is a subject of satire.

Joyce seems to have viewed the novelistic narrative of bloom as one worthy of generous parody; an invented suitor is named "Don Miguel de la Flora," while Leopold's adulterous pseudonym is "Henry Flower." Joyce, like James before him, both considers and departs from the narrative of bloom, even as he reinvigorates the implicit sexuality of the botanical vernacular in his miniature retelling of this history of the novel. It is the closing of a representational circle that we are offered by Joyce's text: the sexual connotations of "bloom," as an analogical system and a narrative, which had been culturally available since the late eighteenth century, are excavated by a writer whose awareness of previous novelistic tropes and plots was nothing short of encyclopedic. Joyce, that is, strives to end the novel of courtship where it began: in Bloom.

NOTES

Introduction. The Girl and the Water Lily

1. The epigraph to the Introduction is from Jean-Jacques Rousseau, *Reveries of a Solitary Walker*, trans. Peter France (Harmondsworth: Penguin Books, 1979), 120.

2. The Royal Botanical Garden at Kew was the first to successfully germinate *Victoria regia* in Britain, although it had its first European flowering at Chatsworth, where Joseph Paxton had constructed a special hothouse for it.

3. Recent historical work on Linnaeus, and work on the cultural diffusion of botany and natural history, and what that diffusion produced for histories of literary work and gender, has been of immeasurable value to my work. A partial list would include: Lisbet Koerner, *Linnaeus: Nation and Narration* (Cambridge: Harvard University Press, 2001); Ann Shteir, *Cultivating Women, Cultivating Science: Flora's Daughters and Botany in England 1760–1860* (Baltimore: Johns Hopkins University Press, 1996); *Cultures of Natural History*, ed. N. Jardine, J. A. Secord, and E. C. Spary (Cambridge, England: Cambridge University Press, 1996); *Visions of Empire: Voyages, Botany, and Representations of Nature*, ed. David Philip Miller and Peter Hans Reill (New York: Cambridge University Press, 1996); Barbara Gates, *Kindred Nature: Victorian and Edwardian Women Embrace the Living World* (Chicago: University of Chicago Press, 1998); Peter Raby, *Bright Paradise: Victorian Scientific Travelers* (Princeton: Princeton University Press, 1997); Londa Schiebinger, *The Mind Has No Sex: Women in the Origins of Modern Science* (Cambridge: Harvard University Press, 1989); Lynn Merrill, *The Romance of Victorian Natural History* (Oxford: Oxford University Press, 1989).

4. Jane Austen, *Persuasion*, ed. R. W. Chapman (Oxford: Oxford University Press, 1982), 6.

5. Ibid., 31.

6. Although other methods are needed to uncover bloom's novelistic workings, the interdisciplinary efforts of a history of audiences or reading have influenced my

thinking about the dissemination of early botanical practice. The following have been of particular value: Roger Darnton, "First Steps toward a History of Reading," in *The Kiss of Lamourette: Reflections in Cultural History* (New York: Norton, 1990), 154–87; Janice Radway, *Reading the Romance: Women, Patriarchy, and Popular Literature* (Chapel Hill: University of North Carolina Press, 1984); Jacqueline Pearson, *Women's Reading in Britain, 1750–1835: A Dangerous Recreation* (Cambridge, England: Cambridge University Press, 1999); Kate Flint, *The Woman Reader: 1837–1914* (New York: Oxford University Press, 1993); Cathy Davidson, "Toward a History of Books and Readers," in *Reading in America: Literature and Social History*, ed. Cathy Davidson (Baltimore: Johns Hopkins University Press, 1989), 1–26; Hans-Robert Jauss, *Toward an Aesthetic of Reception*, trans. Timothy Bahti (Minneapolis: University of Minnesota Press, 1982).

7. My use of "reading formation" is borrowed from Tony Bennett's definition of "a set of discursive and intertextual determinations that organize and animate the practice of reading, connecting texts and readers in specific relations to one another by constituting readers and reading subjects of particular types and texts as objects-to-be read in particular ways." See "Texts in History: The Determinations of Reading and Their Texts," in *Reception Study: From Literary Theory to Cultural Studies*, ed. James Machor and Philip Goldstein (London: Routledge, 2001), 66.

Chapter 1. Linnaeus's Blooms: The Birth of the Botanical Vernacular

1. The epigraph to this chapter is from Dorothy Wordsworth, *The Grasmere Journal*, in *Journals of Dorothy Wordsworth*, vol. 1, ed. E. de Selincourt (New York: Macmillan, 1941), 38.

2. George Eliot, *Adam Bede*, ed. Stephen Gill (New York: Penguin Books, 1980), 128, 198.

3. Jane Austen, *Persuasion*, ed. R. W. Chapman (New York: Oxford University Press, 1982), 104.

4. "Botany," in *Encyclopedia Britannica, or, a Dictionary of Arts and Sciences, Compiled upon a new Plan, in which the different sciences and Arts are digested into distinct Treatises or systems*, vol. 1 (Edinburgh, 1771), 653.

5. Rudolph Jakob Camerarius (1665–1721) published his researches on the sexuality of plants in *De Sexu Plantarium epistola* (1694). His work followed on the researches of Nehemiah Grew (*The Anatomy of Plants*, 1676), who first suggested the true nature of pollen and ovules. Although the sexuality of plants was not demonstrated until 1694, there is evidence that the system of pollination had been at least intuited as early as Hammurabi's code, which mentions the practice of hand pollinating date palms. Nevertheless, even in classical botanical works as Theophrastus's *Historia Plantarum* and *De Causis Plantarum* (ca. 300 BCE), both of which pursued the classification and physiology of plants, plant reproduction is not yet clearly understood. See Johann Georg Gmelin, *Sermo academicus novorum vegetabilium post creationem divinam exortu . . . et propter materiae nexum D. Rud. Jac. Cameraris . . . De sexu plantarum epistola* (Tubingae: Literis Erhardtianis, 1749); Nehemiah Grew, *The Anatomy of Plants* (London, 1682); Theophrastus, *Historia plantarum*, ed. Friderics Wimmer (Wvarislaviae, 1842); Theophrastus, *De Causis Plantarum*, trans. Robert E. Dengler (Philadelphia: Westbrook, 1927).

6. *The Gardener's Dictionary* was the standard textbook on gardening in England during the eighteenth century. It is not until the eighth edition of 1768 that Miller,

the secretary to the Royal Horticultural Society, adopted the Linnaean system for plant nomenclature.

7. For a history of botany from classical to modern times, see Robert Down, *Landmarks in Science: Hippocrates to Carson* (Denver: Libraries Unlimited, 1982).

8. Thornton's project was to create a book that was both beautiful to look at and instructive of Linnaean botany. The project set technical botanical illustrations against a pastoral painted background; both the technical drawing of the plant and the painting—not necessarily that of the plant's natural environment—that surrounded it were in color. The intent was to illustrate all of the Linnaean classes and orders at an unparalleled aesthetic level. The great expense of Thornton's project contributed to it never being completed. Robert John Thornton, *A New Illustration of the Sexual System of Linnaeus* (London, 1799–1810).

9. Biology, as distinct from natural history, was founded as a discipline in the first years of the nineteenth century, during what has become known as the second scientific revolution of 1780–1850. This was a time in which new scientific disciplines (biology, physiology, geology) came into being and existing ones, such as chemistry and physics, were reconfigured. Jan Golinski has described this vital period as one in which "entirely new domains of knowledge (unrecognized, for example, in Enlightenment encyclopedias) were being carved out." Jan Golinski, *Making Natural Knowledge: Constructivism and the History of Science* (Cambridge, England: Cambridge University Press, 1998), 67.

10. Linnaeus did not create what was then known as a "natural" system, a classification system theoretically based on an observed set of multiple affinities and differences among plants, but rather a self-consciously "artificial" classification system: a system based on a single chosen principle from which affinities and differences would be observed as the basis for classification. Linnaeus limited the basis of his classification to a single comparison, that being the reproductive system of the plant, rather than making what was known as a "total comparison" (as Buffon and Jussieu would do). In turning to this artificial stratagem, Linnaeus made it considerably easier to describe and identify a plant.

11. Linnaeus's system was so popular as to be the source of satire—Julien Offray de la Mettrie satirized Linnaeus's sexual system in his pornographic *L'homme plante* (1748), which he dedicated to the Swedish botanist. Julien Offray de la Mettrie, *L'homme-plante*, ed. Francis L. Rougier (New York: Columbia University Press, 1936).

12. Linnaeus, though based at a provincial Swedish university, enjoyed an international reputation, and certainly educated people in Britain read his work in the original Latin before its translation in the 1760s into English. By the late eighteenth century the nationality of a scientist was of little import, for as Norman Hamson writes, "by the end of the century, in the days of Lavoisier and Priestley, the network of scientific societies was so close, and the contacts so frequent, that science might truly be described as international." Norman Hamson, *A Cultural History of the Enlightenment* (New York: Pantheon, 1968), 125.

13. See Ray Desmond, *A Celebration of Flowers: Two Hundred Years of Curtis's Botanical Magazine* (Kew: Royal Botanic Gardens, 1987).

14. John Brewer draws a distinction between the old cabinet of curiosities and the new collections of natural objects by way of understanding the intellectual changes afoot in the eighteenth century: "whereas natural objects had earlier been collected for their singularity, curiosity and strangeness and included in cabinets of

curiosities along with remarkable manmade things, they were now arranged in types or series, ordered to reveal patterns, or laws, of nature. Though there was much debate about the source of such order—was it God-given, from nature itself, or imposed by the human mind?—there came to be broad agreement that laws of nature existed and could be discovered and revealed. The project of ordering knowledge of man and his creations—of writing histories, dictionaries and great synthetic works like the *Encyclopédie*—was extended to the natural world, which ceased to be a cabinet of curiosities and became an ordered collection." John Brewer, *The Pleasures of the Imagination: English Culture in the Eighteenth Century* (Chicago: University of Chicago Press, 1997), 622–3.

15. See Peter Raby, *Bright Paradise: Victorian Scientific Travelers* (Princeton: Princeton University Press, 1997). His book is an invaluable source for understanding the late eighteenth-century and Victorian history of plant-collecting, and scientific travel more generally, in its social and economic contexts.

16. G. S. Rousseau, "Science Books and their Readers in the Eighteenth Century," in *Books and their Readers in Eighteenth-Century England*, ed. Isobel Rivers (New York: St. Martin's Press, 1982), 197–225.

17. See Lisbet Koerner, "Linnaeus's Floral Transplants," *Representations* 47 (1994), 144–69.

18. See Ann B. Shteir, *Cultivating Women, Cultivating Science: Flora's Daughters and Botany in England 1760–1860* (Baltimore: Johns Hopkins University Press, 1996).

19. Much of late eighteenth-century "elegant botany" was still invested in the scientific aspect of the art, and the botanical culture spawned by these related pursuits is an important aspect of the vernacularization of botany. Even though the domain was feminine, it was conceived of not in opposition to the science but rather as precise artistic responses to botanical science.

20. Nicolette Scourse, *The Victorians and Their Flowers* (Portland, OR: Timber Press, 1983), 3–5.

21. Plant collecting was not the only way that botany left its mark on fashion. Hannah More memorably ridiculed a fad in hair fashions in the 1770s, making it seem that to be *au courant* one not only had to have a florist for accessories but maybe even a gardener on hand: "I hardly do them justice when I pronounce that they had, amongst them, on their heads, an acre and a half of shrubbery, besides slopes, grass plots, tulip beds, clumps of peonies, kitchen gardens, and greenhouses." As cited in Shteir, *Cultivating Women, Cultivating Science*, 246.

22. Peter Raby shows that the career of the naturalist-academic was tenuous even through the 1850s; the chair of natural history at King's College London was discontinued in 1834 for lack of interest. Raby, *Bright Paradise*, 8.

23. "Artisanal botany," for example, took place in the pub and had formal organizational structures for disseminating newly acquired botanical knowledge. See Anne Secord, "Artisan Botany," in *Cultures of Natural History*, ed. N. Jardine, J. A. Secord, and E. C. Spary (Cambridge, England: Cambridge University Press, 1996), 378–93; Secord, "Corresponding Interests: Artisans and Gentlemen in Natural History Exchange Networks," *British Journal for the History of Science* 27 (1994), 383–408.

24. Linnaeus in *Deliciae Naturae* (1770) thought that men and women alike could study botany. See Lisbet Koerner, "Women and Utility in Enlightenment Science," *Configurations* 3 (1995), 155.

25. Lisbet Koerner, "Carl Linnaeus in His Time and Place," in Jardine, Secord, and Spary, *Cultures of Natural History*, 145.

26. Hooker is said to have believed in the superiority of the natural classification system of Jussieu, but he acknowledged the accessibility of Linnaean botany. The natural or Jussieuan system eventually eclipsed the Linnaean system in professional scientific circles, but Linnaeus's classifications continued to be widely used among amateurs throughout the nineteenth century. William Withering's *Botanical Arrangement of all the Vegetables Growing in Great Britain* was the most popular classification of British plant life, and it is not until the seventh edition of 1830 that Withering abandons Linnaeus for Jussieu's natural system. The continued popularity and use of Linnaeus, even after the system has been eclipsed, is clear. For a complete discussion of the professional rise of Jussieuan botany, see Peter F. Stevens, *The Development of Biological Systematics: Antoine-Laurent de Jussieu, Nature, and the Natural System* (New York: Columbia University Press, 1994).

27. Rousseau, "Science Books," 206–10.

28. W. T. Stearn, "Linnaeus's Sexual System of Classification," in *Species Plantarum*, facsimile ed. (London: Ray Society, 1957).

29. "Botany," in *Encyclopedia Britannica*, 652–3.

30. Rev. John Bennett, *Letters to a Young Lady, on a Variety of Useful & Interesting Subjects* (Philadelphia, 1818), 130.

31. Priscilla Wakefield, *An Introduction to Botany, in a Series of Familiar Letters* (London, 1811), iv.

32. See the most notable recent scholarship on Linnaeus, Lisbet Koerner, *Linnaeus: Nature and Nation* (Cambridge: Harvard University Press, 2001).

33. See the following excellent work for a more complete treatment of the subject: *Visions of Empire: Voyages, Botany, and Representations of Nature*, ed. David Philip Miller and Peter Hans Reill (New York: Cambridge University Press, 1996); Shteir, *Cultivating Women, Cultivating Science*.

34. Carl Linnaeus, *Lachesis Lapponica, or a Tour in Lapland*, ed. James Edward Smith (London: White and Cochrane, 1811), 188–9, hereafter abbreviated as *LL*. Quotations from Linnaeus's texts will be cited parenthetically with the following abbreviations. *PB*: "Philosophia Botanica," in *Elements of Botany*, trans. Hugh Rose (London: T. Cadell, 1775); *SN*: *Systema Naturae*, 12th ed., vol. 1 (London: Lackington, Akens, 1806).

35. The secondary title of the first English translation of Linnaeus's Lapland diary advertised itself as a translation from the original manuscript journal. J. E. Smith, then president of the Linnaean Society, selected sixty sketches from the diary to illustrate the translation. Although the Andromeda episode is included in the text, Smith chose to censor the accompanying erotic sketch for the English edition, even though the drawing is quite significant, as well as elaborately drawn, in that it accompanies the discovery of a plant that forms a new genus. J. E. Smith, M.D., F.R.S., *Lachesis Lapponica, or a tour of Lapland, now first published from the Original Manuscript Journal of the celebrated Linnaeus* (London, 1811).

36. In the seventeenth and eighteenth centuries, as Londa Schiebinger has shown, plant sexuality became an important fact whose attribution many people competed over, including Sébastian Vaillant and Claude Geoffrey; Nehemiah Grew (*The Anatomy of Plants*, 1682) was the first to identify the stamen as the male part of plants. Londa Schiebinger, "Gender and Natural History," in Jardine, Secord, and Spary, *Cultures of Natural History*, 165.

37. As Lisbet Koerner establishes, Linnaeus became enamored of the idea that sexual reproduction could organize plant classification by reading a review of Sébas-

tian Vaillant's (1669–1722) work on plant sexuality. Koerner, "Carl Linnaeus in His Time and Place," 146.

38. Lawrence Rothfield, *Vital Signs: Medical Realism in Nineteenth-Century Fiction* (Princeton: Princeton University Press, 1992), 11.

39. See Koerner, "Carl Linnaeus in His Time and Place," 155. However, that Linnaeus explicitly advocated a classification system free from metaphor or other figurative styles is not proof that the system is without figurative meaning—style without literary figures is itself a rhetoric. On the contrary, the logic behind Linnaeus's system is itself a figure, for the system conflates sexuality and marriage; moreover, some of the plants that Linnaeus names, such as the previously cited *Andromeda*, directly contradict his own statements about classification free of literary allusion or figuration.

40. Linnaeus's system of classification was presented in the 1735 *Systema Naturae* and developed in the 1753 *Species Plantarum*. The following is a selective publication history of Linnaeus's major works: *Systema Naturae* (1735), *Fundamenta botanica* (1736), *Genera Plantarum* (1737), *Flora Lapponica* (1737), *Critica Botanica* (1737), *Philosophia Botanica* (1751), *Species Plantarum* (1753; the starting point of modern botanical nomenclature), *Systema Naturae*, 12th ed. (1758–59). A modern translation of *Philosophia Botanica* has recently become available as *Linneaus's Philosophia Botanica*, trans. Stephen Freer (Oxford: Oxford University Press, 2002).

41. The eighteenth-century English translation of the Linnaean system was made by a botanical society that included Erasmus Darwin and that sought the advice of Samuel Johnson in its translation. The Latin (in which Linnaeus originally wrote and which appears side by side with the English version) employs the same social-sexual vocabulary as the translation; in other words, the radical social-sexual analogies between humans and plants are not playful and liberal metaphorizations by his eighteenth-century English translators but are fairly literal renderings of Linnaeus's system.

42. See Linnaeus, *Philosophia Botanica*, 86.

43. Claims most famously associated with Ian P. Watt, *The Rise of the Novel: Studies in Defoe, Richardson, and Fielding* (Berkeley: University of California Press, 1957), and Erich Auerbach, *Mimesis: The Representation of Reality in Western Literature*, trans. Willard Trask (Princeton: Princeton University Press, 1953).

44. Michel Foucault, *The Order of Things: An Archeology of the Human Sciences* (New York: Random House, 1970), 132–3.

45. I am indebted here to Michel Foucault's lucid and evocative discussion of botanical character. Although *The Order of Things* does not discuss any connections between the novel and natural history classification, his thinking here about the broader implications of these systems of knowledge has influenced the direction of my thought here in ways that are difficult to pinpoint but necessary to acknowledge. Foucault, *The Order of Things*, 138–45.

46. *Persuasion* may be an exception to this claim. Admiral and Mrs. Croft provide a model for a seafaring marital life that Anne and Wentworth will not doubt later imitate. Mrs. Croft's spirited, almost Wollstonecraftian, defense of the rationality and strength of women takes place at the Musgrove's dinner party, at which she scoffs at the notion that "women were all like fine ladies, instead of rational creatures. We none of us expect to be in smooth waters all our days." The representation of the Crofts' marriage throughout the novel is one of partnership; the only threat to their marriage is defined as separation proscribed by traditional gender roles. Although

NOTES TO PAGES 33-40

Persuasion is still a courtship plot, the seafaring marriage that the novel explores suggests that perhaps Austen's narrative interest (at the end of her career) may have been taking a turn toward the long-term state of marriage. I am indebted here to Abby Wolf and her thoughts about this aspect of the novel. Austen, *Persuasion*, 70.

47. William Withering, *A Botanical Arrangement of all the Vegetables Growing in Great Britain* (London: Cadel and Elmsley, 1776), vii.

48. W. T. Stearn has suggested that Linnaeus's reintroduction of binomials—which was standard to the vernacular names used by early modern herbalists—reflected not only a scientific need but a linguistic desire for synthesis into groups and particularization into individual kinds. Stearn, "Linnaeus's Sexual System of Classification," i.

49. Exceptions to this rule occur late in the history of the bloom narrative. As I will show in chapter 5, in James's novels bloom becomes his subject, rather than the narrative for the novels to play out; it is an increasing self-consciousness about bloom that is part of the bloom narrative's movement toward decadence in the late nineteenth century. In Oscar Wilde's *Picture of Dorian Gray*, bloom is applied to a man so that the sexual potential of bloom serves the narrative of homosexuality.

50. I have been influenced in my thinking about bloom's logic of substitution by Kenneth Burke's book *A Grammar of Motives*. Bloom's substitutive logic renders a description tangible by reducing an abstract state or quality ("blooming") to an equivalent rooted in scientific attention to detail. This is what Burke calls "reduction," pointing out that it is a common device of scientific realism. The scientific reductions of bloom are precisely the point here: the abstract state of sexual potential is rendered corporeal, and more vividly expressible, through its scientized linkage to the flower's own mechanics. See Kenneth Burke, *A Grammar of Motives* (New York: Prentice-Hall, 1952), 506.

51. Withering, *A Botanical Arrangement*, v.

52. For a more complete understanding of the relation of women and botanical culture in England, see Shteir, *Cultivating Women, Cultivating Science*. Shteir's deep range of scholarship demonstrates the degree to which botany suffused the culture, and the degree to which it remained a vexed and yet important subject for young female students—both as science in and of itself and as an endeavor to teach moral and religious lessons.

53. Samuel Richardson, *Clarissa: Or the History of a Young Lady*, ed. George Sherburn (Boston: Houghton Mifflin, 1962), 450.

54. Ibid., 451.

55. Ibid., 451.

56. Ibid., 209.

57. See for instance Beverly Seaton, "Toward a Historical Semiotics of Literary Flower Personification," *Poetics Today* 10 (1989), 679–701.

58. Henry Fielding, *The History of Tom Jones, A Foundling*, ed. Sheridan Baker (New York: Norton, 1973), 118.

59. Henry Fielding, *Joseph Andrews*, ed. R. F. Brissenden (Harmondsworth: Penguin Books, 1977), 56–7.

60. Ibid., 321–2.

61. Samuel Richardson, *Pamela, or Virtue Rewarded* (New York: Norton, 1958), 195–6.

62. John Cleland, *Memoirs of a Woman of Pleasure*, ed. Peter Sabor (New York: Oxford University Press, 1985), 20.

63. Ibid., 122.

64. Ibid., 122.

65. Ibid., 122.

66. Ibid., 40.

67. Fanny Burney, *Evelina, or the History of a Young Lady's Entrance into the World*, ed. Edward Bloom and Lillian Bloom (New York: Oxford University Press, 1968), 44.

68. Ibid., 97–8.

69. See Mary Ann O'Farrell's brilliant account of Jane Austen's adaptation of the blush in the novel of manners; although she does not explicitly address *Evelina*, O'-Farrell's argument about the "erotics of embarrassment" in which the blush (a sign of good manners) is turned into a sign of desire is nevertheless pertinent here. Mary Ann O'Farrell, *Telling Complexions: The Nineteenth-Century English Novel and the Blush* (Durham, N.C.: Duke University Press, 1997), 28.

70. Burney, *Evelina*, 79.

71. *Henry James: Literary Criticism: Essays on Literature; American Writers; English Writers* (New York: Library of America, 1984), 1350, hereafter abbreviated as *EW*. Quotations from James's other literary criticism are cited parenthetically as *FW/P: Henry James: Literary Criticism: French Writers; Other European Writers; The Prefaces to the New York Edition* (New York: Library of America, 1984).

Chapter 2. Imaginative Literature and the Politics of Botany

1. The epigraph to this chapter is from Jean-Jacques Rousseau, *The Collected Writings of Rousseau*, vol. 8, ed. Christopher Kelly and trans. Charles E. Butterworth, Alexandra Cook, and Terence E. Marshall (Durham, N.H.: University Press of New England, 2000), 244.

2. Jean-Jacques Rousseau, *Reveries of a Solitary Walker*, ed. Peter France (New York: Penguin Books, 1979), 84.

3. Ibid., 120–1.

4. Ibid., 115.

5. Rousseau, *Collected Writings*, 133.

6. See G. D. R. Bridson, *The History of Natural History: An Annotated Bibliography* (New York: Garland, 1994).

7. Rousseau, *Collected Writings*, 136.

8. In *Émile*, Rousseau writes that "the quest for abstract and speculative truths, principles, and axioms in the sciences, for everything that tends to generalize ideas, is not within the competence of women. . . . Nor do women have sufficient precision and attention to succeed at the exact sciences." Jean-Jacques Rousseau, *Émile, or On Education*, ed. Harold Bloom (New York: Basic Books, 1979), 386–7.

9. See Erasmus Darwin, *A Plan for the Conduct of Female Education in Boarding Schools* (London, 1797).

10. Joseph Gascoigne, *Joseph Banks and the English Enlightenment: Useful Knowledge and Polite Culture* (Cambridge, England: Cambridge University Press, 1994), 77.

11. Alan Bewell's work on the revolutionary politics associated with Erasmus Darwin's botanical poetics convincingly demonstrates those valences. See Alan Bewell, "Jacobin Plants: Botany as Social Theory in the 1790s," *Wordsworth Circle* 3 (1989), 132–9.

12. Claudia Johnson, *Equivocal Beings: Politics, Gender, and Sentimentality in the 1790s* (Chicago: University of Chicago Press, 1995), 10.

13. Richard Polwhele, *The Unsex'd Females; A Poem* (orig. 1798; New York, 1800), 29.

14. Mary Wollstonecraft, *A Vindication of the Rights of Woman*, ed. Miriam Brody (New York: Penguin Books, 1992), 293.

15. Ibid., 233.

16. More, for instance, approves of Oliver Goldsmith's *Animated Nature*, while disapproving of Buffon's, even though Goldsmith's natural history was widely understood to be derivative of Buffon's both in content and style. More credits Goldsmith for his "many references to a Divine Author," which seems to compensate for the potential salaciousness of the content. Nevertheless, even though it is the content that bothers her—"the indelicate and offensive part"—she articulates it as a stylistic concern: "it is to be wished that some judicious person would publish a rendition of this work." Hannah More, *Strictures on the Modern System of Female Education* (London: Cadell and Davies, 1801), 213.

17. Ibid., 205.

18. As Wollstonecraft's skillful argument invokes, in the age of enlightened thought it would be impossible to simply say that the pursuit of knowledge was contrary to modesty. In particular the long rhetorical tradition of the study of nature as conducive to knowing the perfection of God's creation made any direct attack on botany difficult.

19. More, *Strictures*, 226.

20. Ibid., 154.

21. Ibid., 156.

22. One figure in the dialogue is Augusta, a motherless twelve-year-old girl who, despite being educated by a governess, lacks the ennobling morality that the natural history conversations give the Harcourt children. By the conclusion of the narrative, Augusta has been transformed by the conversations and declares her intention to become a botanist.

23. Ann Shteir, "Botany in the Breakfast Room: Women and Early Nineteenth-Century British Plant Study," in *Uneasy Careers and Intimate Lives: Women in Science, 1789–1979*, ed. Pnina G. Abir-am and Dorinda Outram (New Brunswick, N.J.: Rutgers University Press, 1987), 31–43.

24. Emanuel Rudolph, "Almira Hart Lincoln Phelps (1793–1884) and the Spread of Botany in Nineteenth-Century America," *American Journal of Botany* 71 (1984), 1161–7.

25. The "fern craze" of the 1840s threatened to endanger certain indigenous species. See D. E. Allen, *The Victorian Fern Craze: A History of Pteridomania* (London: Hutchinson, 1969); for an abbreviated account, see David Allen, "Tastes and Crazes," in *Cultures of Natural History*, ed. N. Jardine, J. A. Secord, and E. C. Spary (Cambridge, England: Cambridge University Press, 1996), 394–407.

26. See Bridson, *History of Natural History*.

27. John Lindley, *An Introduction to Botany* (London, 1832), vi–vii.

28. Samuel Taylor Coleridge, *The Friend: A Series of Essays to Aid in the Formation of Fixed Principles in Politics, Morals, and Religion*, vol. 3 (London: William Pickering, 1837), 138–9.

29. Lindley, *Introduction*, vi–vii.

30. Ann B. Shteir, *Cultivating Women, Cultivating Science: Flora's Daughters and Botany in England 1760 to 1860* (Baltimore: Johns Hopkins University Press, 1996), 153.

31. Robert John Thornton, *A New Illustration of the Sexual System of Linnaeus: comprehending an elucidation of the several parts of the fructification; a prize dissertation on the sexes of plants; a full explanation of the classes and orders of the sexual system; and The Temple of Flora, or Garden of nature, being picturesque, botanical, coloured plates of select plants, illustrative of the same, with descriptions* (London, 1799–1810).

32. See P. Phillips, *The Scientific Lady: A Social History of Women's Scientific Interests 1520–1918* (New York: St. Martin's Press, 1990); Londa Schiebinger, *The Mind Has No Sex: Women in the Origins of Modern Science* (Cambridge: Harvard University Press, 1989).

33. Maria Edgeworth, *Letters for Literary Ladies, to which is added An Essay on the Noble Science of Self-Justification* (Vermont: Tuttle, 1993), 21.

34. Ibid., 20.

35. The novel interrogates what it means to embody innocence. Belinda's innocence is questioned because of her body's refusal to conform to an increasingly complex signage of innocence; she blushes, which the Delacours' dissolute society sees as an act of probable artifice, a dissimulation of innocence inasmuch as rouge, what Lady Delacour uses, simulates health and youth. The question whether Belinda is "truly" innocent or in possession of the skills to appear innocent is a primary concern of *Belinda* and many late eighteenth-century novels.

36. See especially the standard authority on the subject: Ruth Bernard Yeazell, *Fictions of Modesty: Women and Courtship in the English Novel* (Chicago: University of Chicago Press, 1991).

37. Ibid., 4, 74.

38. Ibid., 54, 59.

39. Maria Edgeworth, *Belinda*, ed. Eva Figes (New York: Routledge and Kegan Paul, 1986), 9. Subsequent references will be cited parenthetically as *B*.

40. The novel also signals moral difference by discriminating between the science of botany and horticultural fashion. In much the same way that *Letters for Literary Ladies* hopes that botany will become less connected with frivolous female accomplishment, *Belinda* condemns the fashionable employment of the cult of the horticultural. For instance, repeatedly Lady Delacour is said to surround herself with the scent of "ottar of roses," a perfume that her husband cannot stand, while accessorizing her birthday dress in gilded "laburnums"—both fashionable employs of the horticultural meant for her lover rather than her husband (*B*, 27). The most significant condemnation of Lady Delacour's character is related through an anecdote about a plant; in pursuit of horticultural fashion, Lady Delacour swindles an old gardener out of a rare aloe that was "just going to blossom" and that he intended to exhibit to the public for money (*B*, 92). The aloe is a foreign and rare plant; in an age that invented the greenhouse, and that made plant collecting a fashionable and expensive hobby, Lady Delacour's actions epitomize the confluence of fashion and botany that the novel deplores. After the scene of reformation inspired by the duckweed, Lady Delacour makes amends for the aloe by settling an annuity on the gardener. We understand the extent of her reformation by the botanical signs; to compensate for the aloe plant, Lady Delacour sets up the old gardener in a house where "a morello cherry-tree in the garden . . . had succeeded the aloe in his affection" (*B*, 283). That plants as a category can do the work of ethical signification is evident from this episode, for the two plants stand in for two competing ways of being: Lady Delacour is an aloe, a useless hothouse exotic, who is reformed into an indigenous fruit-bearing tree. The ease with which the novel employs a botanical register for a

complex ethical transformation suggests that plants are more than conventional tropes in the age of the botanical vernacular.

41. Virginia's name is a play on Bernardin de Saint-Pierre's famous *Paul et Virginie*, thus situating Virginia within a more stereotyped plot of romance.

42. Wordsworth's poem "The Small Celandine," a poem that would at first seem indebted to observational botany—"There is a flower, the lesser Celandine, / That shrinks, like many more, from cold and rain; / And, the first moment the sun may shine, / Bright as the sun himself, 'tis out again!"—becomes instead an excuse for poetic reflection, in which the decaying flower offers up an opportunity for a regretful, if splenetic, meditation on age. William Wordsworth, "The Small Celandine," in *English Romantic Writers*, ed. David Perkins (New York: Harcourt Brace, 1967), 293.

43. Stuart Curran, editor's introduction to *The Poems of Charlotte Smith* (New York: Oxford University Press, 1993), xviii.

44. Charlotte Smith, *The Poems of Charlotte Smith*, 242. Further references are cited within the text parenthetically.

45. Erasmus Darwin, *The Botanic Garden, A Poem, in Two Parts; Including The Loves of Plants* (London, 1825), 117. Subsequent references will be cited parenthetically.

46. Darwin cites the studies of a Dr. Hales, and Mr. Walker, as well as Linnaeus. The structure of the note is like a short analytical abstract or précis of what could be a longer paper. In later editions, Darwin updates the science to conform to standard vocabulary; he writes: "since the above was first printed, I have thought that these sap-vessels . . . ought rather to be called umbilical than placental vessels. As they supply the young bud with nutrition; whereas the placenta of the animal is a respiratory organ" (117).

47. Between each canto in *Loves of Plants* is a prose interlude in which a "Bookseller" and the "Poet" converse about literature and philosophy. In interlude 2 the bookseller asks: "Then a simile should not very accurately resemble the subject?" The Poet's answer suggests the relationship Darwin saw between the "botanical real" and poetry: "No; it would then become a philosophical analogy, it would be ratiocination instead of poetry: it need only so far resemble the subject, as poetry ought to resemble nature" (162). Darwin seems to be suggesting that poetical verisimilitude is key to representing the scientific real—that it is the improbable simile that makes the real seem like an analogy. In the context of his poem, one in which the internal parts of flowers are represented as damsels and suitors, such a claim is striking. Darwin clearly does not see that poetic move as an improbable simile, or merely an analogy, but that which represents the scientific "real."

48. Londa Schiebinger, "The Private Lives of Plants: Sexual Politics in Carl Linnaeus and Erasmus Darwin," in *Science and Sensibility: Gender and Scientific Inquiry 1780–1945*, ed. Marina Benjamin (Oxford: Blackwell, 1991), 123.

49. My point is not to suggest that botanical literature is emptied of metaphor. Despite Erasmus Darwin's insistence that the relationship between humans and plants is not mere simile, he also exploits previous metaphorical meanings of the flowers as he is describing what botanists, including himself, consider a physiological reality. And yet if Darwin's *Loves of Plants* presumes the reader's reference will include some traditional poetical associations between flowers and persons, it also confirms scientific botany's rejection of the idea that the vegetable and the human are linked only in a metaphorical sense.

50. See Maureen McNeil, *Under the Banner of Science: Erasmus Darwin and His Age* (Manchester: Manchester University Press, 1987).

51. James Lee, *An Introduction to Botany: Containing an explanation of the theory of that science, extracted from the works of Linnaeus* (Edinburgh, 1806).

52. Rousseau, *Collected Writings,* 133-4.

53. Darwin is describing a known society, called the Areoi, a people who have a single promiscuous marriage of one hundred males and one hundred females. Darwin, *Loves of Plants,* 188.

54. For additional discussion about the political import of botany in the 1790s, see Bewell, "Jacobin Plants," 132-9.

55. Schiebinger, *The Mind Has No Sex,* 242.

56. Janet Browne has shown that *The Loves of the Plants* received surprisingly little censure when it appeared in 1789; she suggests that Darwin's unorthodoxy was tolerated in part because his liberal representation of sexuality emanated from a class position (aristocratic and professional) where such discussions were common and permissible. Janet Browne, "Botany for Gentlemen: Erasmus Darwin and *The Loves of Plants*," *Isis* 80 (1989), 593-621.

Chapter 3. Austen's Physicalized Mimesis: Garden, Landscape, Marriageable Girl

1. The epigraph to this chapter is from *Jane Austen's Letters*, ed. Deirdre Le Faye, 3rd ed. (Oxford: Oxford University Press, 1995), 214.

2. In this letter dated February 9, 1807, Austen writes of the improvement of their garden in terms not only of perspective but plant variety; she asks for lilacs and laburnum. Austen's more famous reference in *Mansfield Park* to Cowper—Fanny's quotation "O ye fallen avenues!"—refers more specifically to the architecture of the picturesque, but here in Austen's letters we see that Austen's personal supervision of the improvement of the garden at Southampton focused on the botanical, including the desire for better varieties of roses than the "indifferent sort" that are there. *Jane Austen's Letters,* 51.

3. Ibid., 188. Austen's note about the peony is from a letter written on May 29, 1811; in the same letter she writes of other plants in bloom, including pinks, columbine, and sweet william. She also writes about the state of the hedges and fruit trees. A repeated topic of the letters is blooming times; writing from London on April 25, 1811, Austen notes that in London "ours are in bloom" while "your Lilacs are in leaf"; she then goes on to write about the horse chestnuts, elms, and flower paths of Kensington Gardens. Letters between Austen and Cassandra suggest that Austen enjoyed flowers and garden issues, even if sometimes she wittily makes fun of Cassandra's perhaps more consuming interest. In a letter dated May 31, 1811, Austen charmingly writes to Cassandra: "I will not say that your Mulberry trees are dead, but I am afraid they are not alive." *Jane Austen's Letters,* 188, 192, 184, 190.

4. The nineteenth-century history of Kew is illustrative. Kew Gardens was made a public botanical garden in 1841 under the control of the Commissioner of Woods and Forests. It was to the Commissioner that the curator W. J. Hooker, and later his son Joseph, would apply for financial support, and it is from those reports that we learn a suggestive fact: that Kew Gardens by 1848 was a more popular destination than either Windsor Castle or the Tower of London, and only Hampton Court drew more visitors. Kew had 91,708 visitors, while the Tower reported 49,366, Windsor 26,897, and Hampton Court 150,321. In 1850, 179,627 people vis-

ited Kew, and by 1851—the year of the Great Exhibition—327,900 people were drawn to the botanical gardens. Attendance dropped some in 1852, but in 1853 the enormous crowds matched and then exceeded the unusual numbers of the Crystal Palace year: Hooker notes that the Gardens for the first time offered a public summer lecture series for "botanical instruction," which in part accounts for the interest of some 331,210 people who made their way to Kew that year. From 1853 into the late 1870s, the Hookers report continued growth in gate numbers and the public's fascination with the botanical gardens. The gate figures give us an evocative, if partial, picture of the nineteenth-century fascination with the botanical, for they are misleading in one aspect. Their sudden rise in the 1850s does not speak to an equally sudden rise of interest in the botanical in the century's middle decades because that high level of botanical interest was by midcentury securely in place. We might account for the rise in gate receipts by noting the cultural interest in botany combined with the revitalization of Kew by William Hooker when he took over as curator in 1841. The gardens had fallen into a two-decade-long disrepair following the death in 1820 of the famous horticulturist and champion of Kew, Joseph Banks. William and Joseph Hooker, *Reports to the House of Lords from 1784–1884*, manuscript, Royal Botanical Gardens at Kew.

5. John Harvey, *The Nursery Garden*, catalogue to the Museum of London's permanent living history of London's nursery trade (Mansfield, Notts: Linneys ESL Ltd., 1990).

6. James Lee was famous for his introduction of the fuchsia plant to England in 1788, but he was first known as the nurseryman who introduced Linnaeus to a popular audience with *An Introduction to Botany* (1760), a redaction of Linnaeus's *Philosophia Botanica*. Other famous nurseries of this period included Loddiges's Nursery in Hackney, which was in business for a hundred years (1760–1860), and Malcolm's Nursery, Kennington and Stockwell (1757–1815). By the late eighteenth century Loddiges issued catalogues organized around a deep and scientifically classified collection of plants. Loddiges and Malcolm were nurserymen who were important collectors, sponsoring plant collectors who were going to the tropics. See *The Nursery Garden*.

7. Jane Austen, *Pride and Prejudice*, ed. R. W. Chapman (Oxford: Oxford University Press, 1982), 165, hereafter abbreviated as *PP*. Other citations from Austen's works will be parenthetically cited throughout with the following abbreviations. *E*: *Emma*, ed. R. W. Chapman (Oxford: Oxford University Press, 1982); *MP*: *Mansfield Park*, ed. R. W. Chapman (Oxford: Oxford University Press, 1980); *P*: *Persuasion*, ed. R. W. Chapman (Oxford: Oxford University Press, 1982).

8. Raymond Williams, *The Country and the City* (New York: Oxford University Press, 1973).

9. Frances Burney, *Evelina, or the History of a Young Lady's Entrance into the World*, ed. Edward Bloom and Lillian Bloom (New York: Oxford University Press, 1968), 117. Subsequent references will be cited within the text as *EV*.

10. Vauxhall opened in 1661, and did not close until the mid-nineteenth century but, according to nineteenth-century accounts, was most fashionable between 1732 and approximately 1790. Ranelagh, a resort in what was then the village of Chelsea, opened in 1741, quickly becoming known as a more aristocratic, and staid, Vauxhall. Marylebone Gardens, like Vauxhall and Ranelagh, was an exceptionally popular entertainment spot but was by no means unique; other green spots for public entertainment in London included the Cumberland Gardens, St. Helena Gardens, China

Hall, Cuper's Gardens, Royal Beulah Spa, and the Apollo Gardens. See Warwick W. Wroth, *The London Pleasure Gardens* (London, 1896), 21.

11. Evelina's visit to Marylebone Gardens, for instance, includes seeing an illumination of the Orpheus and Eurydice myth in fireworks. In a letter to her sister on June 19, 1799, Austen indicates that she has been to Sydney Garden, a pleasure garden east of Bath, and enjoyed the fireworks and illuminations. *Jane Austen's Letters*, 47.

12. Horace Walpole visits the pleasure garden in 1750, and references to these places occur often in the *Spectator* and James Boswell's *Life of Johnson*. In Henry Fielding's *Amelia* (1751) the pleasure gardens are depicted as elegant spots, if also places of potential sexual intrigue.

13. David Philip Miller, introduction to *Visions of Empire: Voyages, Botany, and Representations of Nature*, ed. David Philip Miller and Peter Hans Reill (New York: Cambridge University Press, 1996), 4.

14. Janet Browne finds that the horticultural fascination of the late eighteenth century manifested itself in the objects and interests of the upper classes; she points to the diversity of plants, both inside and out, as well as "books, printed catalogues, garden designs, color plate illustrations, hothouses, flower gardens, woodland parks and shrubberies, even furniture, paintings, and wallpapers." Janet Browne, "Botany in the Boudoir and Garden: The Banksian Context," in Miller and Reill, *Visions of Empire*, 154.

15. I use the term "garden" in the eighteenth-century sense, as denoting the landscape and environs extending far from the house, and not just a flower garden, as we would perhaps understand *garden* to mean today.

16. Placing Evelina in a private arbor at the end of a garden walk is to firmly situate her within a horticultural space suggestive of courtship. The arbor is a space in the garden with more specifically horticultural than literary connotations. An arbor and a bower are alike in form, but the associated connotations mitigate any formal qualities that they share. *Bower* is a term whose connotations, from Spenser's *Faerie Queene*, are allegorical; in contrast, *arbor* comes from the old French *herviér*, a place covered with grass or a garden of herbs. For Evelina to be situated within an arbor rather than a bower is to invoke a horticultural rather than the more familiarly allegorical register.

17. In *Sense and Sensibility*, for example, Marianne meets Willoughby during a walk on which she injures her ankle; in his carrying her home in his arms, the ardency and rashness of their physical attraction and subsequent courtship is signed through the particularly physical quality of their walk.

18. William Hogarth, *The Analysis of Beauty, Written with a View of fixing the Fluctuating Ideas of Taste* (London, 1810), 57. Further references appear within the text as *A*.

19. Hogarth writes: "nature, in shells and flowers, &c. affords an infinite choice" (*A*, 39). In analyzing a line, Hogarth most often turns to objects of natural history; he admires the variety of lines in the Calcidonian iris, for example, and suggests that the lack of curving lines is the basis of the torch-thistle's lack of beauty.

20. Hogarth writes: "this love of pursuit, merely as pursuit, is implanted in our natures, and designed, no doubt, for necessary and useful purposes. Animals have it evidently by instinct . . . cats will risk the losing of their prey to chase it all over again" (*A*, 24).

21. Edmund Burke, *A Philosophical Enquiry into the Origin of our Ideas of the Sublime and Beautiful*, ed. J. T. Boulton (New York: Columbia University Press, 1958), 115.

22. If one transposes this into narrative terms, the picturesque is more able to be narrated than the beautiful, for it is more irregular and therefore more capable of having stories attached to it; in *Pride and Prejudice*, think of the difference in narrative interest between mild, amiable, *beautiful* Jane and the irregular, playful, or what we might think of as *picturesque* Elizabeth.

23. Alan Liu, *Wordsworth: The Sense of History* (Stanford: Stanford University Press, 1989), 63.

24. Ibid.

25. Uvedale Price, "An Essay on the Picturesque," in *Genius of the Place: The English Landscape Garden 1620–1820*, ed. John Dixon Hunt and Peter Willis (Cambridge: MIT Press, 1988), 356.

26. It is this descriptive convention—the comparison of the female form with the landscape—that suggests that the blooming girl, rather than her male escort, is sexualized by the picturesque landscape in Austen's novels.

27. See Ronald Paulson, *The Beautiful, Novel, and Strange: Aesthetics and Heterodoxy* (Baltimore: Johns Hopkins University Press, 1996).

28. Mary's ambivalence about and lack of sensibility toward landscape is an early cue that her courtship with Edmund will fail; this is because it not only signals a disjunction of interests between them but foreshadows what will later be revealed as her moral bankruptcy. The fact that Mary would prefer to have the process of landscape improvement hidden from her is meant to shed light on an aspect of her character; as Edmund eventually finds out, Mary dislikes self-consciously improving herself, relying instead on the appearance of morality. Unlike his sister, Henry Crawford is more actively interested in the details of landscape improvement, and so it is not surprising that his attempt at self-improvement for Fanny's sake is performed in detail. Via the figure of landscape improvement, the text implies the question of whether the Crawfords themselves can be improved, and whether real and abiding change is possible or if "improvement" by definition is only superficial change. Edmund's hope that Mary's character will improve on knowing Fanny and Henry Crawford's ostentatious project of self-improvement both, of course, fail—a failure that the novel asks us to read as an affirmation of Fanny's assessment of the Crawfords but might as easily be attributed to Fanny's refusal to recognize, or *see*, Henry Crawford's improvement (hence setting in motion the events that suggest his improvement was superficial simulation). The Crawfords' attitude toward landscape improvement in the first quarter of the novel foreshadows the late events of the novel; closer attention to that figural system might alert readers much earlier to what has sometimes been read as Austen's sudden and brutal ending. In this way, landscape improvement informs the novel at its deepest levels, for it informs the structure of personality that is so crucial to the way that the novel's plot is resolved.

29. Richard Payne Knight, *An Analytical Inquiry into the Principles of Taste* (London: T. Payne, 1808), 9.

30. The interest in landscape in the eighteenth century stemmed from interconnected sources, including the popularization of the Grand Tour in Italy, the importation of landscape as the most important genre of painting, the reinvigoration of the garden, and the subsequent formation of taste around landscape. Many historians of landscape suggest that the pictorial quality that rural scenery begins to take on might be more complexly understood as coming from sixteenth-century Dutch landscape painting. The body of scholarship on the history and analysis of English landscape is large; see especially Christopher Hussey, *The Picturesque: Studies in a Point of View*

(Hamden, CT: Archon Books, 1967), and *English Gardens and Landscapes, 1700–1750* (New York: Funk and Wagnalls, 1967). I am indebted in particular to John Barrell, *The Idea of Landscape and the Sense of Place 1730–1840: An Approach to the Poetry of John Clare* (Cambridge, England: Cambridge University Press, 1972); John Dixon Hunt, *Gardens and the Picturesque: Studies in the History of Landscape Architecture* (Cambridge: MIT Press, 1992); and Liu, *Wordsworth*.

31. Mark Laird's recent book *The Flowering of the Landscape Garden: English Pleasure Grounds 1720–1800* (Philadelphia: University of Pennsylvania Press, 1999) functions as a corrective to conventional histories of the picturesque that have tended to flatten the connections between design and plant material.

32. Browne, "Botany in the Boudoir," 154.

33. Horace Walpole's influential *History of the Modern Taste in Gardening* (1771) explicitly connects the explosion in available varieties of plants with the composition of the picturesque: "the introduction of foreign trees and plants, which we owe principally to Archibald duke of Argyll, contributed essentially to the richness of colouring so peculiar to our modern landscape. . . . The weeping-willow and every florid shrub, each tree of delicate or bold leaf, are new tints in the composition of our gardens." Horace Walpole, *History of the Modern Taste in Gardening* (New York: Ursus Press, 1995), 46.

34. Exceptions include Jill Heydt-Stevenson, "Unbecoming Conjunctions: Mourning the Loss of Landscape and Love in *Persuasion*," *Eighteenth-Century Fiction* 8.1 (1995), 51–71; Christina Marsen Gillis, "Garden, Sermon, and Novel in *Mansfield Park*: Exercises in Legibility," *Novel* 18.2 (1985), 117–25.

35. Alistair Duckworth, *The Improvement of the Estate: A Study of Jane Austen's Novels* (Baltimore: Johns Hopkins University Press, 1971); Rosemarie Bodenheimer, "Looking at Landscape in Jane Austen," *Studies in English Literature, 1500–1900* 20.4 (1981), 605–23.

36. Duckworth, *The Improvement of the Estate*; Martin Price, "The Picturesque Moment," in *Sensibility to Romanticism*, ed. Frederick Hilles and Harold Bloom (New York: Oxford University Press, 1965); W. A. Craik, *Jane Austen: The Six Novels* (London: Methuen, 1966).

37. See especially Marilyn Butler, *Jane Austen and the War of Ideas* (Oxford: Oxford University Press, 1975); Claudia Johnson, *Jane Austen: Women, Politics, and the Novel* (Chicago: University of Chicago Press, 1988); Ann Bermingham, *Landscape and Ideology: The English Rustic Tradition 1740–1860* (Berkeley: University of California Press, 1986); Isobel Armstrong, *Jane Austen, Mansfield Park* (London: Penguin Books, 1988); W. G. Hoskins, *The Making of the English Landscape* (Harmondsworth: Penguin Books, 1970).

38. Barrell, *Idea of Landscape*, 29–30.

39. Liu, *Wordsworth*, 63.

40. Thomas Whately acknowledges that the success of a picturesque landscape often depends on "adding many changes" to a preexisting reality; the business of a gardener is to select and to apply whatever "is great, elegant, or characteristic in any of them; to discover to show all the advantages of the place upon which he is employed; to supply its defects, to correct its faults, and to improve its beauties. For all these operations, the objects of nature are still his only materials." Whately's emphasis on the correction and improvement of faults and beauties constructs the landscape as in process: a preformed, even immature state that awaits the sage hand of the

gardener. Thomas Whately, *Observations of Modern Gardening, Illustrated by Descriptions* (London: T. Payne, 1770), 1–2.

41. In *Pride and Prejudice* this issue is discussed between Charlotte Lucas and Elizabeth; Charlotte presciently warns Elizabeth that Jane's manners do not betray enough, that they are so naturally innocent as to perhaps be misinterpreted as lack of feeling. Of course, Charlotte Lucas—whose choice of a husband clearly disqualifies her from being Austen's model for marriage—is right about Jane's manners, for Bingley is easily convinced by his friends of her ambivalence toward him. Darcy will later justify his actions toward Bingley by suggesting that Jane did not appear to be in love. That Jane's happiness is almost lost because of lack of art suggests that Austen's preference for the natural will occasionally yield to the necessities of art.

42. Austen's novels suggest that a certain degree of improvement is deemed reasonable. For instance, both Fanny in *Mansfield Park* and Elizabeth in *Pride and Prejudice* walk every day for reasons of health and to improve their complexions. Estate improvement, like personal improvement, follows a similar logic of degree. The line is difficult to fix but seems to conform to the distinction Thomas Whately so famously made between the "expressive" and the "emblematical" in the garden; the emblematical is those elements that are unnatural contrivances (including statues, columns, and shrubs used for their mythological resonances), while the expressive consists of those that belong naturally in a garden and hence do not produce allegorical connotations. Austen's aesthetic about the marriageable girl is remarkably similar, for she is distrustful of the emblematical qualities of virtue (think of Mary's much-made-of harp playing) and prefers the quieter, more suggestive figuration of Fanny's unaided bloom. Whately, *Observations of Modern Gardening*, 150–1.

43. Ibid., 151–2.

44. Joseph Litvak has convincingly read Fanny's début as an example of Sir Thomas's deployment of the very theatrical techniques he ostentatiously disapproves of in ending his children's amateur theatricals; Litvak suggests that the ball is "thoroughly a theatrical event." The clear merits of the analogy to the performing arts notwithstanding, the début is also represented through the aesthetic terms of the garden. Fanny's debut in *Mansfield Park* is a series of discrete moments in which she is seen, almost as if for the first time, from a specific perspective. The most telling scene occurs just prior to her entrance at the ball: "her uncle and both her aunts were in the drawing room when Fanny went down. To the former she was an interesting object, and he saw with pleasure the general elegance of her appearance and her being in remarkably good looks. . . . Fanny saw that she was approved, and the consciousness of looking well, made her look still better" (*MP*, 278). Even though Fanny is in a ballroom and not a garden, she is at the center of a setting; moreover, the text invokes the garden by using a horticultural metaphor ("transplantation") to describe Sir Thomas's visual perspective on Fanny: "without attributing all her personal beauty . . . to her transplantation to Mansfield, he was pleased with himself for having supplied everything else" (*MP*, 282). See Joseph Litvak, *Caught in the Act: Theatricality in the Nineteenth-Century English Novel* (Berkeley: University of California Press, 1992), 22–3.

45. One way of understanding this refusal to narrate sexual courtship beyond Trilling's (and others') point that Fanny's prudish morality controls the narrative is that the refusal gestures to the anxiety that Austen maintained around the issue of acquired naturalness, whether for landscapes or girls.

NOTES TO PAGES 102–114

46. The connotations suggested by the walk that Henry Crawford and Maria take, of course, suggest a more blatant sexuality, one not unlike the walks in Burney's *Evelina*; leaving Mr. Rushworth deliberately behind, the two quickly go as far as possible from the house and the marital trajectory implied by it.

47. *Jane Austen's Letters*, 184.

48. Ibid., 231.

49. Schiebinger points out that Linnaeus's dividing of the plant world into two major groups according to public or clandestine marriage mimics the two types of marriage customary in Europe during much of Linnaeus's life. It was only in 1753, as Schiebinger acutely reminds us, that "Lord Hardwicke's Marriage Act [did] away with clandestine marriages by requiring a public proclamation of the banns." Londa Schiebinger, "Gender and Natural History," in *Cultures of Natural History*, ed. N. Jardine, J. A. Secord, and E. C. Spary (Cambridge, England: Cambridge University Press, 1996), 167.

50. Austen's self-consciousness that girls of a certain age function as a social category is evident from her letters. She often registers a sarcastic awareness that age predicts one's narrative destiny, in the real world as well as the fictional one. For instance, in a letter from 1811, when Austen would have been in her mid-thirties, she describes a "Miss H" as "elegant, pleasing, pretty looking girl, about 19 I suppose, or 19_ or 19_, with flowers in her head, and Music at her finger-ends." *Jane Austen's Letters*, 189.

51. Uvedale Price, "An Essay on the Picturesque," in *Genius of the Place*, 357.

52. Richard Payne Knight, "Principles of Taste," in *Genius of the Place*, 86, 87.

53. One of Elizabeth's first questions for Jane on returning to Longbourne after Lydia's elopement was "had they no apprehension of any thing before the elopement took place?" (*PP*, 290). Upon reading Lydia's thoughtless elopement letter to Mrs. Brandon, Elizabeth is certain that Lydia's intentions had been good—that is, "that *she* was serious in the object of her journey" (*PP*, 292). Lydia's thoughtlessness, as Elizabeth terms it, is evident from the letter, where she calls her elopement a "laugh," a "good joke," and (twice) a "surprise." Although elsewhere Austen promotes the idea of a woman's imagination as that which structures courtship, here the ascription of thoughtlessness to Lydia's marital intentions, in combination with the inability of others to see (or apprehend) their affection, suggests that imagination is only a principle for licit courtship. The sequence that Lydia proposes—a sequence of surprise—is one that devalues publicity and the proper working out of the sequence of a "lady's imagination." Fancy and imagination are Austen's values for courtship, but they are strictly prescribed for licit courtship. In a sense, a "lady's imagination" or "fancy" is the opposite of Lydia's fanciful thoughtlessness, for it is imagination in the service of a strict marital sequence.

54. When Fanny is first asked to dine at the Parsonage, for example, Lady Bertram does not wonder if it is proper for her to go, as Edmund insists the question be considered, but wonders whether she herself can "do without" Fanny for the evening—a question she asks four times in the course of the conversation (*MP*, 218–20).

55. This is a spatial position that is played out repeatedly in the novel; she is asked to read the lines of the play for both Edmund and Mary and ends up facilitating their tête-à-tête; in another scene Fanny gives up her pony to Mary in hopes that Edmund will notice his failure to remember her. The most pervasive triangulation is not physical, however, but moral, for Edmund repeatedly asks and expects Fanny to function as a model of modesty and propriety for Mary's improvement.

56. Lionel Trilling, "Jane Austen and *Mansfield Park*," in *The Opposing Self* (New York: Viking Books, 1955), 212.

57. The blush is a descriptive sign of flourishing, but it is not a specific narrative of blooming in the way I mean that term to be understood here; that is, bloom is not a metaphor for the somatic function of blush. Ruth Bernard Yeazell and, more recently, Mary Ann O'Farrell discuss the import of the blush in the nineteenth-century English novel. Although the girl "in bloom" may often blush, a blush, as O'Farrell has shown, is a legible sign (or the fantasy of legibility) that has various functions both in and outside the novel. The hermeneutics of the blush in the novel is distinct from my analysis of the vocabulary of bloom, but considering that they both revolve around fictions of the marriageable girl, they will inevitably share some common ground. See Mary Ann O'Farrell, *Telling Complexions: The Nineteenth-Century English Novel and the Blush* (Durham, N.C.: Duke University Press, 1997); Ruth Bernard Yeazell, *Fictions of Modesty: Women and Courtship in the English Novel* (Chicago: University of Chicago Press, 1991); Pat Gill, *Interpreting Ladies: Women, Wit, and Morality in the Restoration Comedy of Manners* (Athens: University of Georgia Press, 1994).

58. I am here offering an alternative to a recent school of thought in Austen studies that posits Austen's closural processes as ones that foreground a combination of pedagogy and mortification. These readings have provided an important and influential interpretive framework. In *Emma*, however, that tendency to read closure only through the lens of mortification fails to take into account the fact that the narrative's climax also coalesces with the character's new awareness of sexual pleasure. That Emma blooms, I argue, signals that Emma's response to Knightley seems newly sexualized, not merely chastened, and that the sexual response, rather than correspondent to the chastening, has been narratively forecasted (and then realized) through her blooming. For influential accounts of Austen's closural processes, see: D. A. Miller, *Narrative and Its Discontents: Problems of Closure in the Traditional Novel* (Princeton: Princeton University Press, 1981); Claudia Johnson, *Jane Austen: Women, Politics, and the Novel* (Chicago: University of Chicago Press, 1988); Marilyn Butler, *Jane Austen and the War of Ideas* (Oxford: Oxford University Press, 1975). Other key accounts of mortification and modesty include Yeazell, *Fictions of Modesty*, and O'Farrell, *Telling Complexions*.

59. Certain lilies, for instance, found in the eastern hemisphere and introduced into England at the end of the eighteenth century, bloom in both the spring and fall.

60. Likewise, when Wentworth leaves off his resentment and becomes a suitor again, his evaluation of Anne's beauty is informed by something more than a coldly physical appraisal. Wentworth, his proposal having been accepted, says, "to my eye you could never alter." Anne remembers the earlier appraisal but does not remind him of it: "Anne smiled, and let it pass. It was too pleasing a blunder for a reproach. It is something for a woman to be assured, in her eight-and-twentieth year, that she has not lost one charm of earlier youth: but the value of such homage was inexpressibly increased to Anne, by comparing it with former words, and feeling it to be the result, not the cause of a revival of warm attachment" (*P*, 243). Whether Anne's bloom causes or is the effect of Wentworth's renewed attachment is unclear, and further indicative of its status as something other than a simple change in complexion.

61. The text does not of course give the reader access to Wentworth's feelings beyond his discomfiture on entering a room that Anne occupied alone except for a child. His own emotional reaction, though here somewhat obscure, is implied by what Anne perceives to be his studied attempt to avoid her thanks and conversation;

his resentment, coupled with his need to alleviate her distress, implies his lack of equanimity in her presence.

62. David Nokes points out that we know virtually nothing about Austen's emotional life during her years in Bath because so few of her letters survived; we do know, however, that prior to her father's death in January of 1805, she had taken a seaside tour with her family in the summer of 1804. She arrived in Lyme in the late summer, where she particularly enjoyed sea-bathing and walks by the sea. One particular walk, on which Austen saw a perilous set of steps between the Upper and Lower Cobbs, perhaps inspired the image for Louisa's fall in *Persuasion*. Nokes suggests that Austen's letter from Lyme on the September 14 is significant in being the first letter that survives after a three-year silence. As Nokes shrewdly points out, "it will hardly do to scrutinize her words for any signs of alteration or disillusionment in the attitudes of the twenty-eight-year-old Jane Austen from those of her twenty-five-year-old self. This letter survived Cassandra's censorship, we may surmise, precisely *because* it offers no tell-tale insights." There is no definitive proof that Austen was aware of the natural history doings in Lyme or that she bought any of the fossils commonly available for sale to the visitors at the resort—but in light of the broad swath that Cassandra's censorship cut, especially during these five years, it seems fair to say that it is not possible to say that Austen was unaware of Lyme's natural history connotations or activities. David Nokes, *Jane Austen: A Life* (New York: Farrar, Straus and Giroux, 1997), 267–71.

63. Lyme's reputation ensued in part because of the fossil-collecting career of Mary Anning (1799–1847), a young prospector and dealer in fossils, who provided the seaside bathers with curios to take home. See Michael Taylor and Hugh Torrens, "Fossils by the Sea," *Natural History* 104.10 (1995), 66–72.

Chapter 4. Eliot's Vernaculars: Natural Objects and Revisionary Blooms

1. The epigraph to this chapter is from George Eliot, *Middlemarch*, ed. W. J. Harvey (Harmondsworth: Penguin Books, 1965), 312, hereafter abbreviated as *M*. Citations from Eliot's works will be cited parenthetically throughout with the following abbreviations: *AB*: *Adam Bede*, ed. Stephen Gill (Harmondsworth: Penguin Books, 1985); *I*: "Recollections of Ilfracombe 1856," in *The Journals of George Eliot*, ed. Margaret Harris and Judith Johnston (Cambridge, England: Cambridge University Press, 1998); *J*: "Recollections of Jersey 1857," in *The Journals of George Eliot*, ed. Margaret Harris and Judith Johnston (Cambridge, England: Cambridge University Press, 1998); *L*: *The George Eliot Letters, vol. 2, 1852–1858*, ed. Gordon S. Haight (New Haven: Yale University Press, 1954); *S*: "Recollections of the Scilly Isles, 1857," in *The Journals of George Eliot*, ed. Margaret Harris and Judith Johnston (Cambridge, England: Cambridge University Press, 1998); *SCL*: *Scenes of Clerical Life*, ed. David Lodge (Harmondsworth: Penguin Books, 1973).

2. W. M. Thackeray, *The Memoirs of Barry Lyndon, Esq.*, ed. Andrew Sanders (New York: Oxford University Press, 1984), 31.

3. George Meredith, *The Ordeal of Richard Feverel: A History of Father and Son*, ed. Edward Mendelsohn (Harmondsworth: Penguin Books, 1998), 127.

4. Charles Dickens, *Oliver Twist*, ed. Kathleen Tillotson (New York: Oxford University Press, 1982), 180–1, hereafter abbreviated within the text as *OT*. Other citations from Dickens's novels will be cited paranthetically with the following ab-

breviations: *DC: David Copperfield*, ed. Nina Burgis and Andrew Sanders (New York: Oxford University Press, 1999); *LD: Little Dorrit*, ed. Harvey Suckersmith (New York: Oxford University Press, 1999); *BH: Bleak House*, ed. Nicola Bradbury (New York: Penguin Books, 1996).

5. When Oliver meets Nancy for the first time he innocently does not recognize that she is a prostitute, but the reader is meant to recognize the telltale signs immediately: "When this game had been played a great many times, a couple of young ladies called to see the young gentleman; one of whom was named Bet, and the other Nancy. They wore a good deal of hair: not very neatly turned up behind; and were rather untidy about the shoes and stockings. They were not exactly pretty, perhaps; but they had a great deal of colour in their faces; and looked quite stout and hearty. Being remarkably free and agreeable in their manners, Oliver thought them very nice girls indeed" (*OT*, 57).

6. See Peter Allan Dale, *In Pursuit of a Scientific Culture: Science, Art, and Society in the Victorian Age* (Madison: University of Wisconsin Press, 1989), 92. As Dale points out, Feuerbach as well as Comte influence Eliot's thinking; Feuerbach locates God within the love between humans, one that has "flesh and blood, which vibrates as an almighty force through all living things." One hears the echoes of Feuerbach, whom Eliot of course translated, within this passage from *Adam Bede*. See Ludwig Feuerbach, *The Essence of Christianity*, trans. George Eliot (New York: Harper and Row, 1957).

7. Dale argues that Eliot is influenced by Comte, and by Comte indirectly through Lewes, especially his conception that within the impulse for human sexuality lies the basis for a new conception of religious charity. The emotional origins of religious sentiment is an idea that Lewes, following Comte and, more radically, Feuerbach shared with Eliot: "she had clearly taken up Comte's (and Lewes') point that the 'germ' of ideal or altruistic love, what St. Paul calls charity, lies in the human sexual impulse." Ibid., 92–3.

8. The other book that we know Donnithorne is reading is the romance's opposite: a book on agricultural theory. Donnithorne reads "Arthur Young's books," contemporary books on agricultural improvement. Eliot clearly sets up the two types of literature in an oppositional relationship, each representing one of the two relationships, romantic or utilitarian, Donnithorne has toward nature.

9. Philip Fisher, *Making up Society: The Novels of George Eliot* (Pittsburgh: University of Pittsburgh Press, 1981), 46.

10. The two worlds—the idyllic world of Donnithorne and Hetty's imaginings and the farming community of Hayslope—are famously brought together in a scene in which Adam's confusion over a tree marks the intervention of a realistic nature into the fantastic one: "he could not help pausing to look at a curious large beech which he had seen standing before him at a turning in the road, and convince himself that it was not two trees welded together, but only one. For the rest of his life he remembered that moment when he was calmly examining the beech . . . the beech stood at the last turning before the Grove ended in an archway of boughs that let in the eastern light; and as Adam stepped away from the tree to continue his walk, his eyes fell on two figures" (*AB*, 297).

11. *Henry James: Literary Criticism: Essays on Literature; American Writers; English Writers* (New York: Library of America, 1984), 1349–50.

12. See Ruth Bernard Yeazell, *Fictions of Modesty: Women and Courtship in the English Novel* (Chicago: University of Chicago Press, 1991), 65–80.

13. See, e.g., Ellen Moers, *Literary Women* (London: Women's Press, 1978).

14. The fantastic stag wallpaper and the colorless landscape evokes its physical opposite, that being the environment of the studios in Rome to which Will had encouraged Dorothea to go and which he describes in an odd but telling natural history analogy: "Mrs. Casaubon should not go away without seeing a studio or two. . . . That sort of thing ought not to be missed; it was quite special: it was a form of life that grew like small fresh vegetation with its population of insects on huge fossils" (*M*, 245).

15. See, most prominently, Gillian Beer, *Darwin's Plots: Evolutionary Narrative in Darwin, George Eliot, and Nineteenth-Century Fiction* (Boston: Routledge and Kegan Paul, 1983); Sally Shuttleworth, *George Eliot and Nineteenth-Century Science: The Make-Believe of a Beginning* (Cambridge, England: Cambridge University Press, 1984); George Levine, *Darwin and the Novelists* (Cambridge: Harvard University Press, 1988).

16. Gordon Haight in his biography of Eliot offers the following surmise about Lewes's researches and contemporary realism; it is a useful, if brief, connection between Eliot's development as a writer and natural history: "sharing in Lewes's biological researches had intensified her desire to 'escape from all vagueness.' . . . In his close examination of marine animals Lewes was pursuing the 'humble and faithful study of nature' advocated by Ruskin just as Riehl was in his analysis of German peasants." See Gordon Haight, *George Eliot: A Biography* (Oxford: Oxford University Press, 1968), 199.

17. Eliot is completing "The Natural History of German Life" for the *Westminster Review*, but her attention is drawn to the naturalist pursuits that had drawn Lewes to the sea: "in spite of my preoccupation with my article," Eliot writes, "every day I gleaned some little bit of naturalistic experience, either through G's calling on me to look through the microscope or from hunting on the rocks" (*L*, 243–4). "The Natural History of German Life," a review of the first two volumes of Wilhelm Heinrich von Riehl's *Naturgeschichte des Volks*, was published in the *Westminster Review* in July 1856. The essay has been much remarked on by critics as an early example of Eliot's commitment to realism. In "Optic and Semiotic in Middlemarch," J. Hillis Miller writes that the subtitle to *Middlemarch* ("A Study of Provincial Life") is suggestive of art, but "the more powerful association of the word . . . is with scientific study"; Miller goes on to modulate the claim by invoking the Riehl essay and conflating scientific study with sociology. See J. Hillis Miller, "Optic and Semiotic in Middlemarch," in *The Worlds of Victorian Fiction*, ed. Jerome Buckley (Cambridge: Harvard University Press, 1975), 125–45. See also: Gillian Beer, *George Eliot* (Bloomington: Indiana University Press, 1986); Ian Adam, "The Structure of Realisms in *Adam Bede*," *Nineteenth-Century Fiction* 30:2 (1975), 127–49.

18. Beer, *Darwin's Plots*, 14.

19. Eliot actually invokes Shelley's lark in "Recollections of the Scilly Isles," where she emphasizes that the experience of observing the lark gave her a new appreciation for Shelley's poem: "Now and then however, we had a clear sky and a calm sea, and on such days it was delicious to look up after the larks that were singing above us, or to look out on the island and reef-studded sea. I never enjoyed the lark before, as I enjoyed it at Scilly—never felt the full beauty of Shelley's poem on it before" (*S*, 278).

20. George Henry Lewes, "New Facts and Old Fancies about Sea Anemones," *Blackwood's Edinburgh Magazine* 81.1 (1857), 58.

21. Lynn L. Merrill, *The Romance of Victorian Natural History* (Oxford: Oxford University Press, 1989), 12.

22. See Peter Raby, *Bright Paradise: Victorian Scientific Travelers* (Princeton: Princeton University Press, 1996).

23. Merrill, *Romance of Victorian Natural History*, 10.

24. See Anne Secord, "Artisan Botany," in *Cultures of Natural History*, ed. N. Jardine, J. A. Secord, and E. C. Spary (Cambridge, England: Cambridge University Press, 1996), 378–93; Secord, "Corresponding Interests: Artisans and Gentlemen in Natural History Exchange Networks," *British Journal for the History of Science* 27 (1994), 383–408.

25. Spencer Thomson, *Wild Flowers: How to See and How to Gather Them* (London: Routledge, 1853), 147.

26. Richard Buxton, *A Botanical Guide to the Flowering Plants, Ferns, Mosses, and Algae, Found Indigenous within Sixteen Miles of Manchester* (London, 1849).

27. Gaskell writes about these working-class naturalists: "there is a class of men in Manchester, unknown even to many of the inhabitants, and whose existence will probably be doubted by many, who yet may claim kindred with all the noble names that science recognizes. . . . In the neighbourhood of Oldham there are weavers, common hand-loom weavers, who throw the shuttle with unceasing sound, though Newton's 'Principia' lies open on the loom, to be snatched at in work hours, but revelled over in meal times, or at night. . . . There are botanists among them, equally familiar with either Linnaean or the Natural system, who know the name and habitat of every plant within a day's walk from their dwellings . . . there are entomologists, who may be seen with a rude looking net, ready to catch any winged insect . . . practical, shrewd, hard-working men, who pore over every new specimen with real scientific delight." Elizabeth Gaskell, *Mary Barton, A Tale of Manchester Life,* ed. Macdonald Daly (Harmondsworth: Penguin Books, 1996) 38–9.

28. Lynn Barber, *The Heyday of Natural History: 1820–1870* (Garden City, NY: Doubleday, 1980), 13–4.

29. Haight, *George Eliot*, 198.

30. Merrill, *Romance of Victorian Natural History*, 13.

31. It was Philip Henry Gosse whose bestselling books on tidal life started the shore-collecting fad in England. He also invented the aquarium, which became a drawing-room feature. His books were often best-sellers, the prose being enthusiastic and nonacademic; moreover, he encouraged participation, inviting his readers through his prose and direct invitations to do fieldwork—not for the benefit of science, or to better understand theory, but for the sheer pleasure in the objects themselves. Gosse's life work is a complex collection of biology and natural history, technical monographs, textbooks, and popular natural history; the last, for which Gosse is best remembered, are books of aesthetic natural history, in which the naturalist's approach is meditative, pleasure seeking, and above all, curious. They include but are not limited to: *The Ocean* (1845), *A Naturalist's Rambles on the Devonshire Coast* (1853), *The Aquarium* (1854), *Tenby: A Sea-Side Holiday* (1859), *Evenings at the Microscope* (1859), *The Romance of Natural History* (1860), *A Year at the Shore* (1865).

32. Haight, *George Eliot*, 198–9.

33. Lewes continues during this time to correspond with naturalists such as Pigott and Owen and visits two naturalists during the spring of 1857—Richard Couch, a specialist on marine animals, and Joe Cocks, author of *The Weed Collector's Guide* (1853).

34. It is important to distinguish Eliot's dedicated amateurism from other more serious naturalists of the period. On the subject of seaweeds, for example, Eliot's interest is far surpassed by the dedication of Anna Atkins (1799–1871). Atkins spent ten years collecting, cataloguing, and photographing seaweeds for her book *British Algae* (1843). For an excellent study of women's contribution to natural history in the nineteenth century, see Barbara Gates, *Kindred Nature: Victorian and Edwardian Women Embrace the Living World* (Chicago: University of Chicago Press, 1998).

35. Eliot's knowledge of botany is even more expansive than this suggests, for in a letter to Sara Hennell from the Isle of Jersey (May 22, 1857) she indicates that she has been taking inland walks with a botany book: the woods are full of "distracting wild flowers that Miss Catlow never says anything about, just because they are the very flowers you want to identify" (*L*, 329). In her journal essay *Recollections of Jersey 1857*, Eliot writes more in depth about her botanical education: "I have been getting a smattering of botany from Miss Catlow and from Dr. Thomson's little book on Wild Flowers, which have created at least a longing for something more complete on the subject" (*J*, 281). The "Miss Catlow" with whom Eliot is impatient is the author of *Popular Field Botany* (1848), a field guide that employed *both* the "Artificial"—the term used at this point for the Linnaean system—and the "Natural" systems; Thomson is the author of the aforementioned *Wild Flowers: How to See and How to Gather Them*. Both Catlow and Thomson recommend the older Linnaean system for beginners over the newer "natural" system, even though both acknowledge that the newer system provides more "true knowledge."

36. *Westminster Review*, April 1856; as cited in Haight, *George Eliot*, 251.

37. For an account of the literary features of Victorian natural history written by women, see Gates, *Kindred Nature*. For Victorian natural history as a social phenomenon, see: David Elliston Allen, *The Naturalist in Britain: A Social History* (London: A. Lane, 1976); Barber, *The Heyday of Natural History*; Nicolette Scourse, *The Victorians and their Flowers* (Portland, OR: Timber Press, 1983).

38. The calendars that she consults catalogue the precise times when natural phenomena occurred for that particular naturalist, including such phenomena as (in the case of Gilbert White's *Naturalist's Calendar*) the time when young partridges fly (June 28–July 31), the date wild cherries ripen (July 22), the period when snails copulate (May 4–June 17), and the time oats are cut (August 1–16). Gilbert White, *The Natural History and Antiquities of Selborne, with Observations on Various Parts of Nature, and The Naturalist's Calendar*, ed. William Jardine (London: Routledge, 1904).

39. Beer, *George Eliot*, 61. Beer also makes the point that the passage begins with the "swelling" slope of meadows and ends with the "tresses" of meadows—and that this is "a faint suggestion of a female body." Eliot seems to be perpetuating a common eighteenth-century landscape trope in seeing the female body in the curves of the natural landscape. In particular she, like Austen before her, is informed by the aesthetics of William Hogarth, who in his *Analysis of Beauty* studies the "tresses" or hair of women in depth in order to better understand the beautiful, swelling line in the landscape.

40. For discussions of the issue of pastoral in relation to *Adam Bede*, see: Fisher, *Making up Society: The Novels of George Eliot*; Dorothy Van Ghent, *The English Novel: Form and Function* (New York: Rinehart, 1953); Barbara Hardy, *The Novels of George Eliot: A Study in Form* (London: Athlone Press, 1963); U. C. Knoepflmacher, *George Eliot's Early Novels: The Limits of Realism* (Berkeley: University of California Press,

1968); Shuttleworth, *George Eliot and Nineteenth-Century Science:The Make Believe of a Beginning*; Alexander Welsh, *George Eliot and Blackmail* (Cambridge: Harvard University Press, 1985).

41. For an account of the necessary connection between nostalgia and vagueness, see Nicholas Dames's account of the nineteenth-century development of a "nostalgia" in which "the past in its particularity gradually vanishes." *Amnesiac Selves: Nostalgia, Forgetting, and British Fiction, 1810–1870* (New York: Oxford University Press, 2001), 14.

42. Haight, *George Eliot*, 250.

43. *Gentleman's Magazine*, 69:2 (July/August 1799). In August 1799, according to the meteorological table, it rained for fourteen out of the first nineteen days of the month; the note about the eighteenth of the month reads as follows: "the lowlands are laid under water with the rain of yesterday and the day before. Cattle have in some places been in danger of perishing; families have been obliged to remove; the hay has floated." In July, the agricultural commentary notes an unprecedented agricultural shortage: "a considerable importation of hay from London and other parts of this kingdom into Liverpool; a circumstance before unknown." In *Adam Bede*, there are repeated references to various anxieties about and stages of that year's endangered haymaking—one could say that the novel moves less by seasons, as would be more conventional in a pastoral, and more by agricultural commentary. Indeed, when the fall comes, it is marked in the novel by the calendric term *Michaelmas* but more profoundly by a shift in agricultural products—the coming of "purple damsons," "paler purple daisies," "apples and nuts"—and processes: "the scent of whey departed from the farmhouses, and the scent of brewing came in its stead" (*AB*, 350).

44. Alexander Welsh has noted that *Adam Bede* combines the formal distancing of pastoralism with scientific reflections, but only as a way of contributing to the novel's pastoral quality. Welsh, *George Eliot and Blackmail*, 139.

45. Henry James, "The Novels of George Eliot," in *Henry James: Literary Criticism: Essays on Literature, American Writers, English Writers* (New York: Library of America, 1984), 922.

46. Eliot details the educational attainments of Adam Bede by way of showing the degree to which even a clever man of his class would have been limited in the nature of his education: "It had cost Adam a great deal of trouble, and work in over-hours, to know what he knew over and above the secrets of his handicraft, and that acquaintance with mechanics and figures, and the nature of the materials he worked with, which was made easy to him by the inborn inherited faculty—to get the mastery of his pen, and write a plain hand . . . to learn his musical notes and part-singing. Besides all this, he had read his Bible, including the apocryphal books; 'Poor Richard's Almanac,' Taylor's 'Holy Living and Dying,' 'The Pilgrim's Progress,' with Bunyan's Life and 'Holy War,' a great deal of Bailey's Dictionary, 'Valentine and Orson,' and part of a 'History of Babylon' which Bartle Massey had lent him. He might have had many more books from Bartle Massey, but he had no time for reading 'the commin print,' as Lisbeth called it, so busy he was with figures in all the leisure moments which he did not fill up with carpentry" (*AB*, 213).

47. The precision but nevertheless parabolic quality of Eliot's writing is something Gillian Beer has briefly remarked on: "Eliot was bent on finding a proper scale for writing, a scale which . . . would pay so intense a respect to detail that detail could figure both as contingency and parable." Beer, *George Eliot*, 60.

48. Thomson, *Wild Flowers*, 190.

49. Catlow, *Popular Field-Botany*, 138, 215–6.

50. Ibid., 95–6.

51. A critical tradition that developed in the first half of the twentieth century argued that Eliot is deeply hostile to beauty in *Adam Bede*, which some speculated could be attributed to her reputed homeliness; see for instance, Walter Allen, *George Eliot* (New York: Macmillan, 1964); V. S. Pritchett, *The Living Novel* (London: Chatto and Windus, 1946). Although this overt misogyny has dropped out of criticism less interested in biographical connections, the assumption that Eliot is hostile to beauty has oddly persisted.

52. Philip Henry Gosse, *A Manual of Marine Zoology for the British Isles* (London: J. Van Voorst, 1855–56).

53. Haight, *George Eliot*, 251.

54. Lewes, "New Facts and Old Fancies," 60, 74, 59.

55. In *Daniel Deronda*, the sea-anemone's tendency to contract itself in an attempt to make itself impenetrable to attack serves as a metaphor for Gwendolen's sensitivity. In Gwendolen's case, the attack is the lover's declaration: "the perception that poor Rex wanted to be tender made her curl up and harden like a sea-anemone at the touch of a finger." George Eliot, *Daniel Deronda*, ed. Barbara Hardy (New York: Penguin Books, 1967), 113.

56. Lewes, "New Facts and Old Fancies," 58.

57. Ibid., 60.

Chapter 5. Inside and Outside the Plot:
Rewriting the Bloom Script in James

1. The epigraph to this chapter is from *Henry James: Literary Criticism: French Writers; Other European Writers; The Prefaces to the New York Edition* (New York: Library of America, 1984), 126, hereafter abbreviated within the text as *FW/P*. Other citations from James's works appear in the text with the following abbreviations: *AA*: *The Awkward Age*, ed. Ronald Blythe (Harmondsworth: Penguin Books, 1987); *EW*: *Henry James: Literary Criticism: Essays on Literature; American Writers; English Writers* (New York: Library of America, 1984); *DM*: *Daisy Miller*, ed. Geoffrey Moore (Harmondsworth: Penguin Books, 1986); *PL*: *The Portrait of a Lady*, ed. Geoffrey Moore (Harmondsworth: Penguin Books, 1984); *WS*: *Washington Square*, ed. Brian Lee (Harmondsworth: Penguin Books, 1987); *WW*: *Watch and Ward. Henry James: Novels 1871–1880* (New York: Library of America, 1983); *WD*: *The Wings of the Dove*, ed. John Bayley (Harmondsworth: Penguin Books, 1986).

2. It is not my intention to return James to the image of an isolated and aloof artist, to remystify James as somehow transcending the forces of his historical moment and culture. Rather I hope to show how James was self-conscious in his literary-critical essays about a formal property of the novel (bloom) and how in turn that generic self-consciousness helped produce innovations on the narrative of the blooming girl—how, in fact, James's formalist understanding of bloom in the classical novel is part of the historical specificity of his novels.

3. See the following for a lucid account of James's contribution to novel theory: Dorothy Hale, "Henry James and the Invention of Novel Theory," in *The Cambridge Companion to Henry James*, ed. Jonathan Freedman (Cambridge, England: Cambridge University Press, 1998), 79–101.

4. For key work centering on James's use of type, see Sara Blair, *Henry James and the Writing of Race and Nation* (Cambridge, England: Cambridge University Press, 1996).

5. On more than one occasion in his literary criticism James sees the connection between Austen and Eliot, even if he does so in the following instance (*Nation*, August 16, 1866) to differentiate his own ambitions from the "delightfully feminine" work of his predecessors: "They belong to a kind of writing in which the English tongue has the good fortune to abound—that clever, voluble, bright-colored novel of manners which began with the present century under the auspices of Miss Edgeworth and Miss Austen. George Eliot is stronger in degree than either of these writers, but she is not different in kind . . . she is eventually a feminine—a delightfully feminine—writer. She has the microscopic observation, not a myriad of whose keen notations are worth a single one of those great synthetic guesses with which a real master attacks the truth" (*EW*, 911).

6. G. S. Rousseau, "Science Books and their Readers in the Eighteenth Century," in *Books and Their Readers in Eighteenth-Century England*, ed. Isobel Rivers (New York: St. Martin's Press, 1982), 214.

7. Mrs. Mary Wood-Allen, M.D., *What a Young Girl Ought to Know*, new rev. ed. (Philadelphia: Vir, 1905), 65, 165.

8. I am indebted for much of my understanding of James's authorial self-construction to the anthology *Henry James's New York Edition: The Construction of Authorship*, ed. David McWhirter (Palo Alto, CA: Stanford University Press, 1995); see also Sarah Daugherty, *The Literary Criticism of Henry James* (Columbus: Ohio University Press, 1986); Hale, "Henry James and the Invention of Novel Theory."

9. See, e.g., George Levine, "Isabel, Gwendolen, and Dorothea," *English Literary History* 30:3, 1963.

10. In his prefaces to the New York edition, James's commentary on his own fictional heroines are copious and suggest almost a love affair with the genre of the marriageable girl. The affective relations implied within the prefaces, as Eve Kosofsky Sedgwick argues, are unmistakable, though Sedgwick suggests that the central erotic fixation of the prefaces is between the older author and his younger self—what Sedgwick calls an "intergenerational flirtation." *Henry James's New York Edition*, 236.

11. See, e.g., Virginia Fowler, *Henry James' American Girl: The Embroidery on the Canvas* (Madison: University of Wisconsin Press, 1984).

12. Lynn Wardley, "Reassembling Daisy Miller," *American Literary History* 3:2 (summer 1991), 232–54.

13. Louisa Mae Alcott, *Rose in Bloom* (Boston: Little, Brown, 1927), 7.

14. Edith Wharton, *The House of Mirth* (Harmondsworth: Penguin Books, 1986), 69.

15. Peter Brooks and Nancy Miller have written about the relationship between James and the eighteenth-century novel before Austen, what Brooks has called "the novel of worldliness." See Peter Brooks, *The Novel of Worldliness* (Princeton: Princeton University Press, 1969); Nancy K. Miller, "Novels of Innocence, Fictions of Loss," *Eighteenth-Century Studies* 11:3 (1979), 325–39.

16. *Watch and Ward* has traditionally been thought of as an intellectual embarrassment for James, but several recent articles have attempted to situate James's interest in the novel's themes and hence reconsider its place in James's literary canon. See, e.g., Richard Henke, "The Embarrassment of Melodrama: Masculinity in the Early

James," *Novel: A Forum on Fiction* 28:3 (Spring 1995), 257–83; Lindsey Traub, "'I Trust You Will Detect My Intention': The Strange Case of *Watch and Ward*," *Journal of American Studies* 29:3 (Fall 1995), 365–78.

17. Leon Edel, introduction to *Watch and Ward* (New York: Grove Press, 1959), 6.

18. The oddness of *The Awkward Age* has been brought out in fortunate ways by two recent articles by Susan Mizruchi and Michael Trask. Mizruchi's article on the novel is a compelling account of its relation to contemporary Anglo-American concerns in the social sciences; it situates James's portrait of a declining British upper class within late nineteenth-century cultural anxieties about the transmission of inherited values within a decadent modern society (and especially those values contained by the idea of the female adolescent's innocence). Susan L. Mizruchi, "Reproducing Women in *The Awkward Age*," *Representations* 38 (spring 1992), 101–30; Michael Trask, "Getting into It with James: Substitution and Erotic Reversal in *The Awkward Age*," *American Literature* 69:1 (1997), 105–38.

19. Julie Rivkin addresses the "awkward age" of adolescence as more than a metaphor for *fin-de-siècle* social transformation; she argues, among other things, that social meaning itself turns on the representation of female virginity in *The Awkward Age*. Julie Rivkin, *False Positions: The Representational Logics of Henry James's Fiction* (Stanford: Stanford University Press, 1996).

20. Mr. Longdon is surprised when he looks at Aggie's photograph that she is referred to as a little girl: "she is very beautiful—but she's not a little girl." Vanderbank's response reveals that biological maturity is overwhelmed by experiential age in a social milieu that prizes innocence, or its representation: "At Naples they develop early. She's only seventeen or eighteen, I suppose; but I never know how old—or at least how young—girls are" (*AA*, 26).

21. There is no middle term between "little girls" and married women in *The Awkward Age*; the novel consistently records the ascription of "little girl" to both Aggie and Nanda, until Aggie marries and it becomes all too clear that Nanda cannot be considered in that type. The Duchess draws the clear distinction between the young girl in bloom and the married woman, and the line enforced between the two: "I think little girls should live with little girls, and young *femmes du monde* so immensely initiated should—well . . . let them alone. What do they want of them at all, at all?" (*AA*, 48).

22. Although Vanderbank ultimately succumbs to the representation of innocence, at first it seems as if he sees through its machinations. In discussing the Duchess, he says that now her husband is dead "she lives in her precious little Aggie"—a role that suits her, having "bloomed in the hothouse of her widowhood—she's a Neapolitan hatched by an incubator" (*AA*, 26). The implication is that Aggie's value (on the English marriage market) corresponds to the degree to which the Duchess, freed by her widowhood, has tended her niece, another hothouse flower.

23. Peter Brooks, *The Melodramatic Imagination: Balzac, Henry James, Melodrama, and the Mode of Excess* (New York: Columbia University Press, 1985), 170.

24. Stephanie Smith has suggested that James is consciously revising the gothic generic formula as well. Stephanie Smith, "The Delicate Organisms and Theoretic Tricks of Henry James," *American Literature* 62:4 (December 1990), 583–605.

25. For an alternative version of Isabel Archer's uniqueness, see Kurt Hochenauer, "Sexual Realism in *The Portrait of a Lady*: The Divided Sexuality of Isabel Archer," *Studies in the Novel* 22:1 (spring 1990), 19–25.

26. In locating the narrative interest in his heroine's consciousness, James changes bloom from a reflection of the blooming girl's relation to her male suitor to an individual psychological state. In many ways this is an unacknowledged feminism on James's part. For one persuasive account of the presentation of consciousness in James's fiction, see Dorrit Cohn, *Transparent Minds: Narrative Modes for Presenting Consciousness in Fiction* (Princeton: Princeton University Press, 1978).

27. Peter Buitehuis articulates the more traditional understanding of the image of Isabel's consciousness as a garden by stressing the influence of Nathaniel Hawthorne's short story "Rappaccini's Daughter" on *The Portrait of a Lady*. Peter Buitenhuis, "Americans in European Gardens," *Henry James Review* 7:2–3 (1986), 124–30.

28. In this reading I emphasize the malevolence of Gilbert Osmond's aestheticism, but as Jonathan Freedman has convincingly demonstrated, James's representation of the aesthete is multidimensional, placing him squarely within the satirical, historically specific, popular response to British aestheticism in the early 1880s. Jonathan Freedman, *Professions of Taste: Henry James, British Aestheticism, and Commodity Culture* (Stanford: Stanford University Press, 1990).

29. On flowers and aesthetic theory, see Elaine Scarry, "Imagining Flowers: Perceptual Mimesis (Particularly Delphinium)," *Representations* 57 (winter 1997), 90–115.

30. My argument here owes a debt to Jonathan Freedman's reading of *The Wings of the Dove* as a novel in the tradition of decadent aestheticism, for my own impulse to see *Wings* as a decadent bloom narrative has been in some sense ratified by Freedman's appraisal of *Wings* as "the ultimate decadent text" as well as his extensive work on the text's self-conscious use of what he calls the "imaginative structures of British aestheticism." The bloom narrative in its decadent form is partly the effect of its self-conscious deployment but also the effect of authorial disillusionment and his effort at cultural criticism. As Freedman writes, James adopted the narrative of the aesthetic movement and the dream that he shared with "Ruskin, Pater, and Wilde . . . [that] heightened consciousness could provide a redemptive example for its degraded world"—only to eventually suggest through *Wings* that the idea is empty, and the people he represents as having this heightened consciousness are perpetrators of "acts of acquisition and exploitation." Freedman, *Professions of Taste*, 202–57.

31. The challenge of fixing sexual referents in James's novels, as well as in his life, is demonstrated by two recent books on James and sexuality. See *Henry James and Homoerotic Desire*, ed. John Bradley (New York: St. Martin's Press, 1999); Hugh Stevens, *Henry James and Sexuality* (Cambridge, England: Cambridge University Press, 1998).

32. Revisionary feminist readings of *The Wings of the Dove* have deemphasized Milly's victim status, seeing in Milly's story an active participation in her fate. See, e.g., Sharon Cameron, *Thinking in Henry James* (Chicago: University of Chicago Press, 1989); Susan Mizruchi, *The Power of Historical Knowledge* (Princeton: Princeton University Press, 1988); Michael Moon, "Sexuality and Visual Terrorism in *Wings of the Dove*," *Criticism* 28:4 (fall 1986), 427–43; Sallie Sears, *The Negative Imagination: Form and Perspective in the Novels of Henry James* (Ithaca, NY: Cornell University Press, 1986); Ruth Bernard Yeazell, *Language and Knowledge in the Late Novels of Henry James* (Chicago: University of Chicago Press, 1976).

33. Although Milly sees herself as responsible for orchestrating pleasure for herself before she dies, she does seem to gain strength from the doctor's ratification of her attractiveness. Tellingly, it is in the doctor's presence that Milly *imagines* herself

blooming; that she imagines that this response is for him suggests the almost erotic relation between the two: "what was he, in fact, but patient, what was she but physician. . . . She would leave the subtlety to him; he would enjoy his use of it; and she herself, no doubt, would in time enjoy his enjoyment. She went so far as to imagine that the inward success of these reflections flushed her for the minute, to his eyes, with a certain bloom, a comparative appearance of health; and what verily next occurred was that he gave colour to the presumption. . . . 'But, help or no help, you're looking, you know, remarkably well'" (*WD*, 330).

34. As Leo Bersani has suggested, however, it is difficult to discriminate between Kate and Densher's shared consciousness and that of the narrator's. See Leo Bersani, "The Narrator as Center in *The Wings of the Dove*," *Modern Fiction Studies* 6 (summer 1960), 131–44.

35. Millicent Bell has gone against a certain traditional reading of Milly as a Christlike figure in suggesting that the religious vocabulary that the novel's title suggests invokes a "powerful vocabulary . . . of the ethic of generous love" but that there is no textual demand to specifically equate Milly with Christ—there is "no need to see allegory in the novel." Millicent Bell, *Meaning in Henry James* (Cambridge: Harvard University Press, 1991), 294.

36. The reader here is meant to believe Kate, for otherwise the ending is merely an exercise in aligning oneself with what some see as moral growth, and others as moral self-righteousness, at the expense of the very character we have been encouraged to admire. Densher's refusal of Milly's money is a testimony to the memory that he loves, even as it masquerades as moral disaffection. The question of whether Kate is unknowable has been long debated and has an impact on whether one believes Kate in the novel's climactic moments; here I align myself with Yeazell and Mizruchi, both of whom suggest that the reader has access to, and can know, Kate. See Yeazell, *Language and Knowledge in the Late Novels of Henry James*; Mizruchi, *The Power of Historical Knowledge*.

37. Unlike Wilde's aestheticism and celebration of Dorian's perpetual beauty, the naturalism of *The House of Mirth* insists that Lily's quality of seeming ever-blooming is evidence of a decline. Like Dorian, her beauty was not some "mere ephemeral possession," for it had a "kind of permanence," but this is not celebrated by the text. Even though Lily's physical beauty continues to be celebrated in terms consistent with bloom, her ability to represent herself as blooming is challenged by the social surround that would punish her for not marrying sooner. The very cultivation that made the blooming girl's beauty possible is that which seems to make her unable to survive in the world that has created her: "she could not figure herself as anywhere but in a drawing room, diffusing elegance as a flower sheds perfume"; "she was like some rare flower grown for exhibition, a flower from which every bud had been nipped except the crowing blossom of her beauty." Wharton, *House of Mirth*, 100, 317.

38. Oscar Wilde, *The Picture of Dorian Gray*, ed. Peter Ackroyd (Harmondsworth: Penguin Books, 1985), 39. Subsequent references will be cited parenthetically as *DG*.

Coda: Later Bloomings: Molly's Bloom

1. The epigraph of this chapter is from James Joyce, *Ulysses* (New York: Vintage Books, 1990), 761. Subsequent references will appear in the text parenthetically.

2. See, for instance, Jacques Derrida's humorous dismay before not only the enormity of *Ulysses* itself but also the enormity of the scholarship it has spawned, in

"*Ulysses* Gramophone: Hear Say Yes in Joyce," trans. Tina Kendall, in *James Joyce: The Augmented Ninth*, ed. Bernard Benstock (Syracuse, NY: Syracuse University Press, 1988), 27–75.

3. Suzette Henke, *James Joyce and the Politics of Desire* (London: Routledge, 1990), 121.

4. Hélène Cixous, "The Laugh of the Medusa," trans. Keith and Paula Cohen, *Signs* 1 (1976), 875–93.

INDEX